Teaching History and the Changing Nation State

Also available from Bloomsbury

Teaching Controversial Issues in the Classroom, Paula Cowan
Teaching the Holocaust in School History, Lucy Russell
Education, Extremism and Terrorism, Dianne Gereluk
MasterClass in History Education, Christine Counsell, Katharine Burn and Arthur Chapman

Teaching History and the Changing Nation State

Transnational and Intranational Perspectives

Edited by
Robert Guyver

Bloomsbury Academic
An imprint of Bloomsbury Publishing Plc

BLOOMSBURY

LONDON • OXFORD • NEW YORK • NEW DELHI • SYDNEY

Bloomsbury Academic
An imprint of Bloomsbury Publishing Plc

50 Bedford Square
London
WC1B 3DP
UK

1385 Broadway
New York
NY 10018
USA

www.bloomsbury.com

BLOOMSBURY and the Diana logo are trademarks of Bloomsbury Publishing Plc

First published 2016

British Library Cataloguing-in-Publication Data
A catalogue record for this book is available from the British Library.

ISBN: HB: 978-1-4742-2587-8
ePDF: 978-1-4742-2586-1
ePub: 978-1-4742-2588-5

Library of Congress Cataloging-in-Publication Data
Names: Guyver, Robert, editor.
Title: Teaching history and the changing nation state : transnational and intranational perspectives / edited by Robert Guyver.
Description: New York : Bloomsbury Academic, 2016. | Includes bibliographical references and index.
Identifiers: LCCN 2015026958| ISBN 9781474225878 (hardback) | ISBN 9781474225861 (epdf) | ISBN 9781474225885 (epub)
Subjects: LCSH: History—Study and teaching. | Historiography—Philosophy. | History—Philosophy. | Transnationalism. | Globalization. | BISAC: EDUCATION / General. | EDUCATION / History. | EDUCATION / Secondary.
Classification: LCC D13 .T395 2016 | DDC 907.1—dc23 LC record available at http://lccn.loc.gov/2015026958

Typeset by RefineCatch Limited, Bungay, Suffolk

Contents

Contributors

Sedat Bulgu is a Turkish/English translator and interpreter in Australia. He translated the official Australian Government's Gallipoli website into Turkish and was the recipient of two Australian Military History Research Grants to enable him to research Turkish archives for the experiences of the Australian prisoners of war captured at Gallipoli.

Marlene Cainelli is Associate Professor at the State University of Londrina, Paraná, Brazil. Since completing her PhD thesis, at the Federal University of Paraná, Brazil (2003), entitled 'History of Brazil, histories of Brazilians: History, past and identity in popular memory', she has been coordinating history education studies applied to primary and secondary students and, ultimately, has been researching comparative enquiries concerning the historical consciousness of Brazilian and Portuguese students. Marlene has also examined the roles of history and memory in the construction of historical thought. She coordinates the Research Group 'History and History Teaching'.

Gülçin Dilek is Assistant Professor at Sinop University in Turkey. She researched the teaching of women's history and gender perspective for her PhD thesis (2012). Gülçin has also been researching international perspectives on history education, including historical thinking and learning, as well as women's history and gender and women's history teaching.

Tamara Eidelman was born in Moscow, where she graduated from the History department of Moscow University in 1981. Since then she has taught history and civics in Moscow schools. She has been involved in the activities of EUROCLIO (the European Association of History Educators) since its beginning. Tamara was coordinator of the EUROCLIO/Matra project *Mosaic of Cultures: Teaching the Multicultural Society in Russia* (2002–5) and she was editor of the publication *Fair and Balanced History* (2009) as part of the EUROCLIO/Matra Project in Bulgaria, *European Dialogues: A Cultural Rainbow for the Future* (2006–9). At the moment she is board president of the Moscow History Teachers' Association.

Jonathan Even-Zohar is Director of the EUROCLIO Secretariat in The Hague, the Netherlands. He has managed international civil society history education development projects, mainly in South-East Europe, and has a degree in History from the University of Leiden, the Netherlands. His fields of expertise include implementation of history education projects, cross-border peer learning and capacity building.

Eleni Filippidou is a Researcher at the Faculty of Primary Education at the National and Kapodistrian University of Athens, Greece. She is working on the fields of Turkish history education and history didactics. Eleni has researched the shared history of İstanbul from a Greek and Turkish point of view. She is a member of the Executive Board of the Hellenic Educational Society.

Robert Guyver is Adjunct Associate Professor in the Faculty of Education at the University of Tasmania, Australia. After working as a primary teacher then an advisory teacher for primary history, he was a lecturer in education for nineteen years. From 1989 to 1990, while still a primary school teacher, he was a member of the Department of Education and Science National Curriculum History Working Group for England. He is an editor of the *International Journal of Historical Learning Teaching and Research* and of *Agora* (the journal of the History Teachers' Association of Victoria, Australia). Robert is also a Fellow of the Royal Historical Society.

Jennifer Lawless is an Australian history educator and historian. She was formerly the History Inspector for the New South Wales Board of Studies, responsible for the history curriculum. She has held several positions in Australian universities lecturing in history method. Jennifer has been awarded a number of Australian teaching and writing awards, including the NSW Premier's History Prize, a Churchill Fellowship and an Endeavour Fellowship.

Ramón López Facal is Assistant Professor at the University of Santiago de Compostela (Spain) and coordinator of a research network on the teaching of social sciences (*Red 14* [14 Net]). He is on the board of directors of leading educational journals in history education in Spanish such as *Íber, Enseñanza de la Ciencias Sociales* (Teaching of Social Sciences), *Didáctica de las Ciencias Experimentales y Sociales* (Teaching Experimental and Social Sciences), *HER&MUS* (Heritage and Museography) and *Clio: History and History Teaching*; and has published in other education journals, e.g. *Revista de Educación, Educatio Siglo XXI* and *Revista Galega de Educación*. He and Jorge Sáiz Serrano are researching history education, especially the role of identities.

Alan McCully is Senior Lecturer in Education (History and Citizenship) at Ulster University, Northern Ireland. His career has spanned forty years as teacher, teacher educator and researcher during the period of conflict and post-conflict transformation in Northern Ireland. His areas of expertise are teaching history in divided societies, educational responses to conflict and peace-building, and the teaching of controversial and sensitive issues.

Cyndi Mottola Poole is an Adjunct Instructor of Education at the University of Pittsburgh and an (online) Adjunct Instructor of History at Valencia College, Orlando, Florida. She has earned a PhD (2014) in Social Science Education (Global Perspectives of Pre-service Teachers: A Comparative Study) from the University of Central Florida. Dr Mottola Poole also has multiple years of experience as a K-12 foreign language and social studies teacher and department chairperson.

Nadia Naser-Najjab is an Associate Research Fellow, European Centre for Palestine Studies, Institute of Arab and Islamic Studies, University of Exeter, UK. Prior to this she was an Assistant Professor in the Department of Philosophy and Cultural Studies at Birzeit University, Palestine, working on the MA programme in Arab Contemporary Studies. In 2010 she was a visiting scholar at The Center for Contemporary Arab Studies, Georgetown University, Washington DC, USA. The same year she was awarded the AMIDEAST 'Teaching Excellence Award', which recognizes teaching commitment to teaching and non-traditional class methods. Her fields of research include Palestine and the Palestine–Israel conflict and conflict resolution, intergroup reconciliation and identity.

Ilan Pappé is Professor of History and Director of the European Centre for Palestine Studies and a Fellow in the Institute for Arab and Islamic Studies at the University of Exeter. He has written fifteen books to date, among them *The Ethnic Cleansing of Palestine* (2007), *The Modern Middle East* (third edition 2014) and *The Idea of Israel* (2014). He is now engaged in exploring the applicability of the settler colonial paradigm for the Israel/Palestine case study as well as the one-state solution for the conflict there.

Helena Pinto is History Teacher at Agrupamento de Escolas do Vale de S. Torcato, Guimarães, Portugal, and a Researcher in Heritage Education and History Education. She is Integrated Researcher of CITCEM - Centre of Transdisciplinary Research 'Culture, Space and Memory'. She also teaches history and cultural heritage education for lifelong learning, and coordinates the production of education material at several local museums. Helena's PhD (2011) at University of Minho was on history and heritage education: how the past is read through present sites by students and teachers. She has been supported by the Foundation for Science and Technology – Portugal.

Jorge Sáiz Serrano is Associate Professor of Social Sciences Education in the University of Valencia and he is also a teacher in Social Sciences (Geography and History) in a public high school (IES Tirant lo Blanc, Torrent, Valencia) (secondary education). He has a PhD in Geography and History (Medieval History) (2003) from the University of Valencia, and is now finishing another PhD in Teaching History (2015). Jorge's current research interests are history education and national narratives, historical thinking, national identities and textbooks, and also medieval history. He is the author of over forty research contributions including articles, books, chapters, communications and presentations to national and international conferences.

Mark Sheehan is the Secondary Programme Director at Victoria University of Wellington and has been involved in history education matters in New Zealand for almost forty years as a teacher, lecturer, researcher, museum educator, advisor and textbook writer. He conducts research on historical thinking, assessment, memory/remembrance and the place of knowledge in twenty-first-century curricula. He is often called on by the Ministry of Education to provide advice on history curriculum matters. He is the co-editor of *History Matters: Teaching and learning History in New Zealand* *secondary schools in the 21st century* (2012). Mark's PhD (2009) was a study of the New Zealand debate about the transformation of the discipline of history into a senior secondary school subject.

Glória Solé (PhD) is Assistant Professor at the University of Minho, Braga, Portugal within the Department of Integrated Studies, Literacy, Didactics and Supervision, in the area of History and Social Studies Didactics. She is a member of the Centre for Research in Education (CIEd), and her research has been focusing on history education, especially among primary students, with an emphasis on historical time and historical consciousness. Glória's PhD (2009) was on children's conceptions of time and historical understanding in the first cycle of basic education, and the contexts for their development.

Tony Taylor is currently Adjunct Professor at the Australian Centre for Public History, University of Technology Sydney. He was director of the 1999–2000 Australian national inquiry into school history, director of the Australian National Centre for History Education from 2001 to 2007 and national curriculum consultant to the Australian government from 2008 to 2012. He is author of *Denial: History Betrayed* (2008) and the forthcoming *Class War: The Politicisation of Education in Australia.* With Robert Guyver he edited *History Wars and the Classroom: Global Perspectives* (2012).

Polina Verbytska is Professor and Chair of the History of Ukraine, Lviv Polytechnic National University, and Executive Director of Nova Doba, the All-Ukrainian History Teachers Association, of which she is a former president. Polina is an honorary Ambassador of EUROCLIO. Her fields of research include historical didactics, historical memory and cultural heritage.

Fionnuala Waldron is Head of Education in St Patrick's College, Dublin City University and Dean of the Faculty of Education. Fionnuala began her career in education as a primary teacher before becoming a teacher educator with a specialization in history education. She is Chair of the Centre for Human Rights and Citizenship Education which she established in 2005, in partnership with Amnesty International (Ireland). In 2014 she was awarded a Cregan Professorship in Teacher Education by Dublin City University.

Gail Weldon is an independent Education Consultant based in Cape Town, South Africa. She was formerly Senior Curriculum Planner for History in the Western Cape Education Department and a member of the writing team for the national history curriculum in South Africa from 2001 to 2010. She co-founded and facilitated a teacher professional development programme for history teachers in 2002, *Facing the Past – Transforming our Future*. This was run in partnership with *Facing History and Ourselves*, Boston, USA and *Shikaya*, a non-profit organization in Cape Town. From 2012 to 2014 she managed the *Facing History and Ourselves* programme in China. Her PhD (2009) was a comparative study of the construction of memory and identity in the curriculum in Rwanda and South Africa as societies emerging from conflict.

Acknowledgements

I would like to thank Richard Toye for suggesting Bloomsbury Academic, Arthur Chapman for supporting me during the planning process, and the publishers themselves, especially Alison Baker, for patiently helping me to see this project through to completion and making several creative suggestions, including the use of 'discussant' chapters.

The idea stemmed from a border-crossing article by Fionnuala Waldron and Alan McCully in the *International Journal of Historical Learning Teaching and Research* (IJHLTR), Volume 11 Number 2 (2013). I had edited that special number and had been glad also to work then with Gülçin Dilek, whom I knew was interested in how Turkish history was taught in Greece, and Greek history in Turkey. It was fortunate that Eleni Filippidou was able to work with Gülçin on this dimension. Similarly I had come across the work of Ramón López Facal in my role as an editor of IJHLTR, and was grateful that he was able to work intranationally with Jorge Sáiz Serrano, an academic from another part of Spain, Valencia. Within the organization History Educators' International Research Network (HEIRNET), and indeed EUROCLIO, the European Association of History Educators, I was aware of networks of history teachers and history teacher educators whose professionalism knew no national boundaries and who were experienced in transnational cooperation. I would like to thank Jon Nichol (supervisor for my MEd and PhD) and Hilary Cooper for their inspiration and encouragement over the years and for their efforts in extending HEIRNET to South Africa, Turkey, Brazil, the USA, Canada, Russia and Greece. I had already met Gail Weldon in South Africa and was glad that she could share her PhD research on her home country and Rwanda in this book.

My thanks go to Sylvia Semmet, Joke van der Leeuw-Roord and Jonathan Even-Zohar for their willingness to use the EUROCLIO network to secure the involvement of Polina Verbytska and Tamara Eidelman. The fact that Polina and Tamara were able to sustain a meaningful dialogue while conflict was actually raging in eastern Ukraine is remarkable. The work of EUROCLIO provided a living and very relevant background to the chapter, which Jonathan demonstrated in his effective communication by Skyping his co-authors. I would also like to thank Helena Pinto and Glória Solé, both based in Braga, Portugal, for bringing Marlene Cainelli, based in Paraná, Brazil, into this project.

For help with my own chapter I would like to give thanks to Jamie Byrom, who was able without giving away any confidences to talk me through the rationales behind the outcomes associated with the English history curriculum review in the first half of 2013. Linked with this I am also grateful to Robert Tombs, Jonathan Clark, David Abulafia, Christine Counsell, Michael Riley, Lord (Paul) Bew and Sir Richard J. Evans for answering my emails. Thanks must also go to Arthur Burns, Jeremy Black and Rebecca Sullivan for oral feedback given after meetings or seminars.

I was most fortunate to have the Institute for Arab and Islamic Studies on my doorstep in Exeter and although I decided to email all research staff in the Institute I had no idea what the result would be. I had already met Ilan Pappé in the summer of 2014 at the Dartington *Ways with Words* literary festival, but had not anticipated that he and his co-author Nadia Naser-Najjab would be able to meet me in person over coffee more than once to discuss their chapter within walking distance of my home.

I was very glad to be working again with Tony Taylor and Mark Sheehan, having co-edited with Tony *History Wars and the Classroom* (2012) – a book to which Mark had contributed a chapter. Mark had also kindly hosted me during a working visit to three universities in New Zealand in 2007. I would like to thank Jennifer Lawless and Sedat Bulgu for bringing the Turkish perspective into their chapter on Gallipoli. I have been most fortunate to have met all four of these authors, both in their home countries and in the UK, and to have benefited from their hospitality.

I first became aware of Cyndi Mottola Poole after she had written a review of the *History Wars* book. I had noted that she was able to appreciate the subtext of the 2012 work and was grateful when she agreed to write her USA chapter in this 2016 book.

I would like to thank Nazan Çiçek for help with translations, but would like to give special thanks to my son, historian Christopher Guyver, for his help with editing and proofreading during a time when I was unwell, and to my wife Margaret for tolerating my long absences both real and virtual while I inhabited the space created while this book was being constructed.

Introduction

Robert Guyver

The book's title

The title, *Teaching History and the Changing Nation State: Transnational and Intranational Perspectives*, explains in a nutshell the chief rationale for the book. Teaching history has in the past been strongly linked to the nation, with outcomes that have been both good and bad. Constructing history for an inclusive nation which seeks understanding not only across its own component groups – but also of its neighbours – can clearly be a force for good. However, constructing history for the exclusive nation, especially one which sets itself against its neighbours, is a dangerous force in the world. Often transnational perspectives, and indeed studies that examine the complexities of regionally intranational history within the nation, can enhance understanding of the nation itself. Patriotism is a linked concept which should not necessarily be seen just as the property of the political right, as there are patriotisms of the left and centre too (Bew 2011); also it has recently been subject to philosophical revision by such writers as Habermas (1995), Sternberger (1990) and Müller (2007) with their idea of 'constitutional patriotism'. In a similar vein, David Cannadine in his work on historian G. M. Trevelyan wrote about 'consensual patriotism' (Cannadine 1982: 114).

This book is aimed at teachers of history, at those involved in educating teachers and at historians themselves as well as any members of the public who find these matters of general interest. The twelve substantive chapters develop the four themes of the book in case studies which are transnational, intranational or comparative. An analytical 'discussant' chapter provides a synthesis for each of the book's parts.

Thus there are seven transnational studies (Palestine–Israel, Ukraine–Russia, Republic of Ireland–Northern Ireland, Turkey–Greece, Portugal–Brazil, Australia–Turkey and Australia–New Zealand), three intranational studies (England/UK, USA and Spain) and two comparative studies (South Africa–Rwanda and Australia–Russia).

The themes of the book

The four themes of the book were to some extent 'imposed' on the chapter authors by the editor, although it was agreed that they could be subsumed in order not to disrupt the flow of the chapters. There is some overlap between them, especially across the last two sets of themes, where 'landmarks' can also be shared histories or commemorations. Re-evaluating past denials is often associated with politics and the nation and can be directly linked to the notion of 'landmarks with questions'.

Pedagogy, democracy and dialogue

Where two or more authors have been involved in writing chapters the process itself has been one of dialogue. There has also been dialogue by email or personal contact between the editor and all chapter writers. In fact the three authors of Chapter 2, who live in the Netherlands, Ukraine and the Russian Federation, communicated by Skype before committing their thoughts to paper. I was able to meet the two authors of Chapter 1 because we all happen to live or work in the same city. We were dealing with jurisdictions which had different definitions of democracy, who were caught up in different political trajectories and where the working out of some rather undemocratic features could be seen in political attitudes to history education. In one case, Ukraine and Russia, there was a ground war taking place over the time that the authors were writing. In another, Palestine, a political stand-off, an occupation, was continuing to make life feel rather undemocratic on the street.

The role of history teacher associations and networks (national, international and transnational) emerges as significant in several ways, not least because it is not just historical knowledge but also pedagogy and the understanding of the discipline which underpins and indeed defines teachers' professionalism. As seen in chapters 2 and 11 EUROCLIO as a transnational organization has been involved in cooperative work with 'native' teachers in setting up new history teacher associations in Russia and elsewhere in Central and Eastern Europe. In England and Australia such associations, not directly connected with EUROCLIO but largely sharing the same aims, played an active role in curriculum reform.

The nation – politics and transnational dimensions

Simon Schama, the British-born historian and television presenter who works in the USA, said in a public meeting in England in May 2013 that history was about understanding other people, and in order to stress his point he referred to the work of Herodotus, who travelled widely across the ancient Greek world. Schama, who had already been involved in the curriculum debate in England, while declaring that he sought to dissolve identity politics was also accused of playing such politics by marking out winners and losers in the narrative of the nation. But to understand English or British history you had to look beyond the island shores and back to the time of empire. There could be no other explanation for large populations from South Asia and the Caribbean living in British cities.

In the chapter on Turkey and Greece the transnational dimensions of their shared histories are apparent in that current land-spaces in both countries were once either part of the Ottoman Empire or of the Byzantine or Eastern Roman Empire. Present-day politics in the relationship between Turkey and Greece draws constantly on this history. The relationship between Portugal and Brazil is at the same time both national and transnational as exploration, trade, colonization, empire and independence played out parallel narratives. The Spain chapter uses an interesting range of 'plurinational' vocabulary (centralist nationalism, peripheral nationalisms, co-existence) to analyse Spain's current dilemmas but in so doing offers some ideas for other situations which might apply to the United Kingdom or even to the Russian Federation, in time.

In Palestine national and international events like the first and second intifadas, UN resolutions and the Oslo Accords came together in the form of the Israeli–Palestinian Centre for Research and Information (IPCRI) to influence the shape and form of Palestinian school history textbooks. The identity politics underpinning this development is examined in Chapter 1, and the issue is summarized in the last paragraph. The Oslo Accord 'reframing' of Palestine was resisted only in the 'space' of education, flagging up a significant gap between historical framing and narrative 'which had been ignored by peace brokers ever since 1967 and depicted as an obstacle for peace'. The authors see this very gap as the reason for the conflict, a gap that IPCRI failed to breach (or bridge), indicating the need for a new framing, which to the minds of the authors only the narrative of the settler colonialist paradigm can offer. The experience outlined in Chapter 3 about the Republic of Ireland and Northern Ireland is an example of a reframing that hinges on increasingly shared pedagogies and shared understandings of a democratic but critical interpretation of citizenship. As a way out of conflict in these two jurisdictions (in Ireland, north and south of the border) there is a growing acceptance of multiple identities which underpins the new thinking about citizenship.

Landmarks with questions

This theme-title comes from a phrase used by Australian historian John Hirst when faced with trying to reconcile the wish of Prime Minister John Howard in the summit of August 2006 for a canon of events with the nature of historical investigation. All of the chapters in the book mention events which have over time been interpreted in different ways. In the chapters on the USA and on Portugal–Brazil the perspectives of Indigenous people are included, and these are also a key part of the Australia half of the comparative Australia–Russia chapter. The so-called 'Whig' interpretation of history raises its head in that chapter and in Chapter 9 on England, where there is a report on a debate about whether some events or developments should be celebrated as significant political or social landmarks, evidence of a system that allowed difference and division.

Shared histories, shared commemorations and re-evaluating past denials

The two chapters that focus on 'Gallipoli' are based on shared histories and a shared commemoration. The event, and the Anzac myth that underpins it, has been 'historicized' for various purposes including the creation of national identity, in Australia and New Zealand. The selectively partial understanding of the event especially in its broader context and effectively as an invasion of another nation is set alongside the use of film. Questions are asked about the relative significance of Gallipoli and New Zealand's own colonial wars between its government and the Indigenous Maori people in the mid-nineteenth century, evidence for which can be seen all over New Zealand. The existence of nearly 70,000 Turkish residents in Australia places a new burden of responsibility on teachers to include their perspectives, drawing on a growing number of freshly available Turkish sources. Similarly a Turkish presence in commemorations may be a matter for public concern, but reflects a more inclusive and democratic view of the nation.

The handling of a traumatic past is a feature in several chapters, but especially in the use of the concepts of remembering and forgetting in the comparison between South Africa and Rwanda. It is better to remember than forget when dealing with the psychological effects of trauma, and this can either be recognized and therefore built into a curriculum or it can be politically excised, as can be seen in examples given about Rwanda, Russia, and Israel's relationship with the inadequately 'reframed' Palestine. In Turkey and Greece too, a new approach to disputed histories is suggested where micro-histories are set against macro-histories to reduce the immediate impact of a politicized blame-game.

The four 'parts' of the book

These are the four parts of the book:

Part 1: Shared Histories in Transnational and Intranational Post-Conflict Settings
Part 2: Shared Histories in Post-Colonial Settings
Part 3: Comparative Settings – Federations, Shared Histories and Emerging Democracies
Part 4: Shared History as a Transnational and Intranational Landmark with Questions (Gallipoli, involving perspectives from Australia, New Zealand and Turkey)

These are attempts to put the case studies in groups, but there is a great deal of overlap as well as a possible misnomer-use in that Chapters 1 and 2 are hardly 'post-conflict' situations, and some of the chapters in Part 1 could just as easily be placed in Part 2 or elsewhere. The main dynamic in history education in England (given its curious position in the UK, where all of the UK's constituent parts have their own separate arrangements or curricula for school history) is not necessarily its 'post-colonial' status. Spain and Australia are clearly democracies that have 'emerged' quite differently to Russia. 'Shared histories' seems on the face of it to be a dominant theme in the book, although this notion is resisted in some places and this failure of mutual understanding is a feature of continuing conflict.

Each of these parts is followed by discussant chapters in which the problems and issues raised by the authors are discussed in a further analysis and synthesis by the editor. Connections are made to the constituent elements within each part and also to different chapters in the book.

The dialogic dimension in this work is experimental. It is, however, a necessary component which defines the very nature of transnational and intranational history. Writing this book has been about seeking to understand other people, but ironically in so doing it has also been about trying to understand the nation itself in a different way.

References

Bew, Lord (2011), *Schools: History Debate*, House of Lords, 20 October 2011, Hansard transcript, columns 428–9.

Cannadine, D. (1982), *G. M. Trevelyan: A Life in History*, London: HarperCollins.

Habermas, J. (1995), *The Normality of a Berlin Republic: Lesser Political Writings VII*, Frankfurt am Main: Suhrkamp Verlag.

Müller, J.-W. (2007), *Constitutional Patriotism*, Princeton: Princeton University Press.

Sternberger, D. (1990), *Verfassungspatriotismus* [Constitutional Patriotism], Berlin: Insel Verlag.

Part 1

Shared Histories in Transnational and Intranational Post-Conflict Settings

1

Palestine: Reframing Palestine in the Post-Oslo Period

Nadia Naser-Najjab and Ilan Pappé

Introduction and conceptual framework

The Oslo Accord signed between Israel and the Palestine Liberation Organization (PLO) in September 1993 brought to the world the Palestinian Authority (PA). This political body was meant to rule the areas within the West Bank and the Gaza Strip Israel evicted under the terms of the peace accord. The PA assumed roles and responsibilities in almost every sphere of life but was constantly monitored, criticized and curbed by Israel and the international community when it was alleged it exceeded its powers and ambitions. One of the most contested areas was education. Before that period, Palestinian education was under the control of Jordan in the West Bank and under that of Egypt in the Gaza Strip. In 1967, when Israel occupied the West Bank and the Gaza Strip, Palestinian education came under Israeli military control.

Immediately after the first textbooks were produced by the PA, they were condemned by official Israel and its friends in the United States as texts of incitement that undermined the peace process. The controversy that has surrounded the Palestinian curriculum touches upon themes and concerns that go well beyond the relatively confined field of education policy. As the subsequent engagement demonstrates, the development of a Palestinian curriculum evoked questions and concerns that correspond as much to the study of politics as to that of education. The question of education, far from being an uncontroversial or self-evident concern, was, in the Palestinian context, a politicized issue from beginning to end.

The battle over the orientation of the textbooks produced by the PA transcends a factual debate about truth: namely whether or not the books do incite against Israelis and Jews. It exposes the failure and internal contractions of the peace process between Israel and Palestine in general and that of the Oslo peace agreement in particular. Through a closer look at this issue one can appreciate the irrelevance of the peace process as a means of reconciliation between the two sides. The Israeli and international reaction to the textbook issue and the Palestinian response to it indicate the gap between two basic narratives and the framing of the origins, essence and ways of solving the conflict in Israel and Palestine.

In this chapter we are particularly interested in the criticism directed at the textbooks coming from the Israeli–Palestinian Centre for Research and Information (IPCRI), an allegedly liberal Zionist non-governmental organization (NGO), which even has Palestinian membership in it. Through the examination of this particular criticism we can relate it to a more general conversation about two possible perceptions of the relationship between power and education.

It seems that in this case two different perceptions of power are at play. The power of education over politics appears as a perception held by those criticizing the Palestinian textbooks, and the power of politics over education is the one we expose as lying behind the criticism, including when this power is exercised by an outfit allegedly promoting peace and co-existence. This second form of power is familiar from Foucault's deconstruction of the relationship between power and knowledge (Foucault 1991). The power in this second sense is not imposed directly but through a discourse of peace and democracy that denies the right for a Palestinian narrative in the name of these two noble ideals. Since part of the pressure was also articulated in the name of enlightenment and progress one can also see at play the power of cultural hegemony, in the Gramscian sense, in the attempt to silence a Palestinian educational voice in the name of cultural superiority, modernity and scholarship.

We are also examining this critique while recognizing a possible alternative way in which an NGO devoted to peace and reconciliation could have engaged with a Palestinian attempt to produce an educational narrative in the wake of the Oslo Accord (for instance by offering a Gadamerian fusion of horizons and creating a bridging narrative, rather than destroying the narrative of the occupied and dispossessed).

But above all, the inability of even a liberal Zionist NGO, with Palestinian members in it, to respect or even tolerate a Palestinian input in a future educational narrative for the sake of peace, is the inevitable outcome of the nature of the Zionist project in Palestine. Zionism, even in its liberal manifestation, is a settler colonialist movement and, as recent research has adequately shown, this ideological perspective informs its approaches to the native population and their national desires. As will be explained in this chapter, Zionist settler colonialism was able to impose politically and economically its will on the disempowered Palestinian leadership in the Oslo Accord – it failed to do so in the realm of education.

The Israeli criticism of the Palestinian textbooks focused on those sections that represented the Palestinian national narrative. This narrative was hardly visible in all the other aspects of the Oslo Accord. While the PLO was willing to surrender to an Israeli dictate in the overall political framework of the accord, this surrender could not easily be translated into a 'tamed' textbook that would have been acceptable to Israel and international observers.

Economically and politically, the post-Oslo reality was shaped by Israel's absolute control in every aspect of Palestinian life, even in areas which were allegedly ruled by the Palestinian authority (Area A and parts of the Gaza Strip, according to the Oslo II agreement). This left the Palestinian Authority in control of less than 40 per cent of the West Bank. Areas A and B were fragmented into more than 200 cantons, bisected by roadblocks, checkpoints, settlements and eventually the Separation Wall built in 2002. The Oslo Agreement, as an interim agreement, left the issues of Jerusalem, the

Palestinian refugees and Israeli settlements and border to the final phase within five years. Final status issues remain unsolved to the present time and the Israeli settlements are creating facts on the ground and compromising the possibility of establishing a contiguous Palestinian state with full sovereignty.

However, in the field of education, Israel found itself unable to exercise such power directly – hence the criticism from the Israeli official spokespersons. As we shall show in this chapter, the condemnation of the Palestinian Authority's attempt to allow its narrative to be fully displayed in its textbooks and curricula frustrated Israeli liberals and left Zionist NGOs and activists who assumed that the political and economic surrender was an act of peace that should have led the Palestinian educators to give up on their national narrative as part of the Oslo Accord.

The educational battle raged between the official Palestinian educational agency, committed to the Oslo Accord, and the most ardent supporters of the accord in Israel, NGOs like IPCRI, which we examine here more closely. This dispute exposes the gap between the framing of Palestine between the two sides of the conflict and it unpacks the charade of the Oslo Accord. The Israeli–Palestinian Centre for Research and Information was established in 1988 as a joint venture of Palestinian and Israeli peace activists, but in essence it was a front organization for the Zionist left in its search for a two-state solution.[1] It is a non-profit think tank that, in its own words, 'combines research with peacebuilding actions and advocacy across Israel and Palestine'.

Following the Oslo agreement, IPCRI was integrated into the 'People-to-People' (P2P) programme stipulated by the accord to support from below the diplomatic effort from above (Article VIII of Annex VI of the Oslo II Agreement): 'The two sides shall take steps to foster public debate and involvement, to remove barriers to interaction . . .'. The P2P activities were entrusted into the hands of Norwegian organizations assisted by funds from the European Union, USAID and Canada Fund, and other sources (Endresen 2001: 13; Hanssen-Bauer 2000: 35–40).

The bi-national nature of IPCRI should not mislead us. The hegemony in this outfit, as in all the Israeli–Palestinian NGOs springing up after Oslo, was Israeli. The impulse was noble: to advance reconciliation and co-existence through neutral venues which were supposed to be free from stereotypes and prejudice. But the political asymmetry between Palestinians and Israelis was reflected also in the relationship with the NGOs, as can be gleaned from Yifat Maoz's excellent analysis of them in 2000. The dominance of the Israelis was not only seen in joint NGOs but also in the overall imbalance between NGOs on both sides. The Israeli NGOs were more competent than the Palestinian ones. The Israeli side was more experienced in proposal-writing and seeking funds than its Palestinian counterparts, and this gave the Israelis a privileged position with the funding agencies (Maoz 2000). This dominance was recognized by the Norwegian P2P Programme Coordinator:

> When the People-to-People Programme began, Israelis dominated the dialogue in terms of the number of organisations involved, organisational efficiency, donor access, proposal writing, and willingness to [enter into] dialogue.
>
> Endresen 2001: 22

The alleged reason for leaving monitoring projects such as textbooks in the hands of Israeli NGOs was their professionalism. However, in reality, it was the same balance of power that dictated Israel's conception of peace to the Palestinians in the Oslo Accord that granted monopoly to the Israeli NGOs in the examination of textbooks.

The accord as a declaration of principles and as an expanded Norwegian and American exercise in reconciliation, as manifested in the P2P framework, did not attempt to bridge between two national narratives, or concerns and aspirations; it was an Israeli dictate to the occupied Palestinians, sanctioned by the Norwegians and the Americans and presented as a genuine peace treaty. It was in the field of education that the dictate was resisted (as it would be militarily, but unsuccessfully, resisted in the second Intifada in 2000 and with a greater measure of success, still to be seen, by the Hamas government in the Gaza Strip since 2006).

The framing reflects also two opposing conceptualizations of the conflict itself. The peace NGOs in Israel, such as IPCRI, view the conflict as one raging between two national movements. The two movements in this perception are very different in essence and quality. One is a European modernized force, Zionism, and the other, the Palestinian one, a more primitive form of nationalism working within the framework of an 'Arab' or 'Islamic' political culture. Therefore in every aspect of a reconciliation effort, the advanced side generously concedes some land, some rights and authority to the less reliable, developing national movement. This means that educational products such as textbooks have to be supervised and coached by Israelis devoted to the peace process. While the balance of power forced the Palestinian leadership to accept grudgingly, and probably wrongly, the Israeli imposition on their security, foreign policy, economy and social development, the Palestinians seemed to draw a line when it came to educational matters.

Geographically the liberal Israeli version frames Palestine as consisting of the West Bank and the Gaza Strip alone whereas in the Palestinian narrative Israel and the occupied territories are Palestine. In the liberal Israeli narrative demographically the Palestinians are only the people who lived in the occupied territories, whereas in the Palestinian one they include the Palestinians in Israel as well as the Palestinian refugees and exilic communities.

In the Israeli liberal view the narrative in post-Oslo textbooks should not dwell at all on the past, while at the same time it should recognize the ancient Hebrew past of the land and acknowledge the Holocaust. The texts were also expected to recognize Zionism as a national Jewish movement. The Palestinian narrative, as it appeared throughout the years and made its way into the textbooks, views Zionism as a settler colonialist movement that brought a catastrophe over the Palestinian people in 1948, in the Nakba, for which the Zionist movement would have to be accountable and the State of Israel responsible either in the form of compensation or of repatriation of the Palestinians who were expelled by Israel from the land in that year. The liberal Zionist narrative blamed the Palestinian and Arab leaders for what it described as a voluntary flight of the Palestinian population and absolved Israel from any responsibility for the deed.

Finally, the liberal Zionist narrative does not recognize the legitimacy of the Palestinian armed struggle and defines it as pure terrorism. The Palestinian narrative considers Palestinian resistance over the years, including after Oslo, as part of legitimate anti-colonialist struggle. The fact that the Palestinian leadership, the PLO, accepted the need to lay down their arms and negotiate and even accept a Palestinian state only in parts of Palestine does not negate the above framing of the land, its people and their struggle.

In every respect the Israeli narrative won the day on the ground, but failed to make an impact in the field of education. Conceptually, this imbalance raises some empowering references to the possible role of education among the world's most disempowered national movements and provides inferences as well to what the theoretical literature defined as feeble resistance. A way of navigating through an unwanted reality to empower, even slightly and even temporarily, and quite often individually, the sense of dignity, independence and liberation. In fact, we argue that the liberal Zionist NGO spearheading the criticism on the Palestinian textbook in the period under review included Palestinian members who joined it not because they accepted the Zionist narrative but because an Israeli-dominated NGO provided some freedoms otherwise absent in the lives of Palestinians in the occupied territories in the post-Oslo reality.

So which Palestine was supposed to appear in the Palestinian textbooks in the post-Oslo era? As Ali Jarbawi, one of the leading members of the Palestinian curriculum team put it:

> Which Palestine should we teach? Is it historical Palestine over its whole geographical area, or is it the Palestine that will emerge out of the political agreements signed with Israel? How to deal with Israel? Is it only a neighbour state or one that was established on Palestinian land?
>
> Palestinian Curriculum Development Center 1996: 454

The Palestinian mission

The Palestinian Authority (henceforth PA) first assumed formal responsibility for Palestinian education with its establishment in 1994. The creation of a Palestinian curriculum, an undertaking which touched upon questions of content, teaching methodology and the application of teaching materials, was a crucial stage, in both a symbolic and a practical sense, in the development of a Palestinian education system. As such, a Palestinian Curriculum Development Center (PCDC), in collaboration with UNESCO, was established, and mandated with the responsibility of developing teaching material with a strong emphasis upon the specificity of Palestinian culture, history and identity. It was committed to the basic chapters in the Palestinian national narrative as they appeared in the PLO's Declaration of Independence from 1988. That document accepted the partition of Palestine as a possible solution but stressed the need to recognize it as a necessary evil for the sake of peace, and one that does not alter what happened in history or the affiliation of all the Palestinians to the whole of Palestine. The PCDC was committed to promoting critical thinking and pedagogy alongside the national consciousness and orientation (Palestinian Curriculum Development Center 1996; Moughrabi 2001; Brown 2002).

The PCDC was willing for the curriculum to reflect the era of peace and reconciliation following the Oslo agreement. However, since the signing of the Oslo agreement the political reality was far from being peaceful and Palestinians faced grave predicaments on a daily basis. Israel continued building settlements in the West Bank which isolated Jerusalem, fragmented the West Bank and broke the connection with the Gaza Strip. According to Khalil Tufakji, Director of the Maps and Survey Centre, Orient House in Jerusalem, 'The Palestinian areas were being gradually transformed into agglomerations encircled by settlements and bypass roads' (2000: 54).

The situation deteriorated after 1996, following the election of Benjamin Netanyahu as Prime Minister. In September 1996, Netanyahu started to construct a tunnel beside the Al-Aqsa mosque/Al-Haram Al-Sharif. For the first time since the signing of Oslo II (1995) there were bloody clashes between Palestinians, including the Palestinian police force, and the Israeli army. In March 1997, Netanyahu's decision to build a new settlement on a site on Jabal Abu-Ghnaim in East Jerusalem created another crisis between Palestinians and Israelis.

There seemed to be some respite with new American involvement that produced the Wye River agreement of 1998.[2] But this was a limited arrangement that divided the city of Kahlil (Hebron) between the settlers and the locals. It was once again a memorandum catering solely to Israel's security's needs and perceptions (Aruri 1999: 18; Hanieh 2001).

When the time came allegedly to discuss the issues at the heart of the conflict, such as refugees, settlements, the fate of Jerusalem and the borders and sovereignty of the future Palestinian state it was clear that this was not going to materialize. The Camp David Summit in 2000 was broadcast as a summit for finalizing peace – in essence it was the last attempt to force Yasser Arafat to declare a total surrender to the Israeli peace dictate. He refused and in the volatile atmosphere that followed all that was needed was a spark to ignite the fire. The Israeli opposition leader at the time, Ariel Sharon, decided to visit the Al-Aqsa mosque in September 2000 and all hell broke out: the second Intifada began.

The Israeli response to the uprising caused the Palestinian reality to deteriorate even further. In the next decade the whole political scene would change. Hamas would take over the Gaza Strip, and the matrix of oppression and control of Israel over the West Bank would disrupt any remnants of normal life in the West Bank. It was hard to think of the textbooks as reflecting a different reality according to the demands of the Israelis or whoever supported them (Roy 2004).

This was particularly difficult as education was hit hard by these developments. In 2000, according to the UN, around 500 barriers restricted student movement across the West Bank. Collective punishments such as curfews contributed to the closure of schools, as did Israeli incursions. During the period from 2003 to 2004, a total of 1,152 schooldays were lost in the West Bank (Palestinian Monitoring Group 2005). The majority of Palestinian students faced challenges of considerable scope and intensity. These obstacles have in turn impacted significantly upon educational development, attendance and learning outcomes.

Schoolchildren and students within Area C were at risk of physical attack from settlers while some classes in these areas were conducted in caravans and tents due to the lack of available school space. There was a high dropout rate in these areas (which was particularly pronounced among female students) (UNICEF 2011). In some cases children had to walk more than five kilometres to get to their schools and in other instances they needed to cross the Separation Wall. Teachers also routinely encountered the same obstacles.

In East Jerusalem the problems were of a different nature. Students in East Jerusalem were under the Israeli Ministry of Education's authority. The censorship of Palestinian national identity was manifested in a well-publicized controversy, in which the Ministry's staff made a series of changes to Palestinian textbooks. As a consequence, the Palestinian logo was replaced with the logo of the Jerusalem municipality while the Palestinian flag was deleted; in addition, all sections related to Palestinian history and the Nakba were also removed. In some cases the censored pages were left blank.

The situation is still the same at the time in which we are writing this chapter. A total of 3,414 Jerusalem-based students are separated from their schools by the wall. There are currently 5,000 children who are not registered as students, due to a lack of teaching space; in addition, of those students who are enrolled, around 2,300 have been impacted by a lack of classroom space (UNICEF 2011: 6).

The construction of the Separation Wall and the sealing off of the city from the rest of the West Bank has significantly affected education in East Jerusalem. As a consequence of this action, around 150 communities (of a total of approximately 290,000 Jerusalem ID holders) are currently cut off behind the Separation Wall, a situation which is ultimately likely to further accelerate further decreases in East Jerusalem's Arab population (which has substantially declined under Israeli occupation) (UN OCHA 2013).

Worst hit was the Gaza Strip. In the latest attack on it in the summer of 2014, 118 schools were damaged and 22 schools completely destroyed, with 95 schools used as shelters for those who were displaced, numbering about 190,000 to 215,000. Moreover, according to the UN about 190,000 children needed psychological support as a result of the war and loss of family members and relatives. Before that, the education sector had suffered a shortage of about 200 schools (and this is despite the fact that schools operated on a double-shift basis) (UN OCHA 2014). So the Palestinian mission was both to remain loyal to Palestinian culture, heritage and identity and at the same time to reflect the reality on the ground if it wished to be relevant to the society whose education it wanted to serve.

The declared mission of IPCRI was 'to promote democracy, tolerance, peace and pluralism'. By implication, IPCRI asserted that education should 'develop students' skills in problem solving, conflict resolution [and] critical thinking, [thus enabling] them to deal with problems that have more than one correct answer'. Loyalty to Palestinian history and narrative and adopting a reflective view of the reality in which students lived did not, in the eyes of IPCRI, fall within the list of these noble aspirations. But it is impossible to understand the double talk and insincerity of IPCRI if one does not first describe how in general the Palestinian books were received.

The condemnations of incitement

The condemnation of the Palestinian textbooks began in pro-Israeli quarters in the United States. The reports by these organizations and individuals claimed that the Palestinian textbooks incited violence and hatred against Israeli Jews and thus did not promote the values of peace, tolerance and co-existence. These were used in Israeli propaganda and lobbying campaigns against the Palestinian Authority. Since the PA was dependent on external funding it affected the Palestinian efforts to recruit money to develop, among other issues, their educational system.

One of the leading figures in the USA condemning the textbooks was Senator Hillary Clinton. Following the failure of the Camp David summit in 2000, from her first Senate campaign Senator Clinton continued to criticize Palestinian textbooks. She declared: 'All future aid to the Palestinian Authority must be contingent on strict compliance with their obligation to change all the textbooks in all grades – not just two at a time' (Henry 2000).

Her position was supported by the Center for Monitoring the Impact of Peace (CMIP),[3] an American non-governmental organization, one of whose directors, from 1998 to 2000, Itamar Marcus, resided in an Israeli settlement in the West Bank (Moughrabi 2001; Brown 2002). He alleged that:

> Ever since the PA became responsible for education in 1994, Palestinian children have been learning from their schoolbooks to identify Israel as the evil colonialist enemy who stole their land . . . the new PA textbooks fail to teach their children to see Israel as a neighbour with whom peaceful relations are expected.
>
> CMIP 2000

Chris Patten, the British politician on the Foreign Affairs Committee of the European Parliament, who served as the EU Commissioner for External Relations from 1999 to 2004, rejected vehemently the accusation that his organization had effectively endorsed and promoted anti-Semitism. He stated: 'It is a total fabrication that the European Union has funded textbooks with anti-Semitic arguments within them in Palestinian schools. It is a complete lie.' In subsequently observing that 'some critics may not be particularly interested in the facts, preferring to try to fit reality to their theory rather than the other way round', he effectively summarized the essential matter at hand (Patten 2002).

Nathan Brown, Professor of Political Science at George Washington University, was to subsequently reiterate Patten's observations when he investigated the original claims. He explicitly stated: 'The Palestinian curriculum is not a war curriculum; while highly nationalistic, it does not incite hatred, violence and anti-Semitism. It cannot be described as a peace curriculum either, but the charges against it are often wildly exaggerated or inaccurate' (Brown 2002). According to Brown's review, by the omission of the Jewish narrative in the historical or the present context, the Palestinian curriculum avoided controversial issues related to the Oslo Agreement and the consequence of the facts on the ground including the Israeli settlements and the permit system that interrupts the contiguity of the 1967 land. So it seems that in some cases the condemnation was based on what was supposed to be in the textbooks, but was not necessarily there. Not that mentioning permits and contiguity is tantamount to anti-Semitism.

In 2000, a group called 'Jews for Truth Now' accused Palestinians of incitement against Israel in the Palestinian school curriculum. The group claimed that a Palestinian textbook entitled *Our Country Palestine* teaches Palestinian sixth-graders that Israel should be destroyed. The group announced this in the *Haaretz* newspaper, in the USA and in other countries. Khalil Mahshi (2000), then General Director of International and Public Relations at the Ministry of Education, investigated the matter and found that the reference supposedly found in that book did not exist. Moughrabi (2001) found similar results. Nevertheless, the claim found an unquestioning audience, and CMIP reprinted the accusation and published a report that was translated into several different languages. As a result, two main funding sources for developing Palestinian curricula decided to shift funding to different projects, one from Italy and another from the World Bank. According to Na'im Abu Hommos, the Palestinian Minister of Education, 'The World Bank officially told the Palestinian Ministry of Education that the money destined for books for 7, 8, 12 and 14 year-olds, as well as for teacher training for these same years, would be allocated to other activities' (Morena 2001).

The Palestinian Authority Ministry of Education (2001) responded to CMIP to refute the allegations and ascertained that mentioning Israel as an occupier is a fact accepted by the UN. The Ministry emphasized that it will not describe Israel as an occupier when peace is reached and occupation ends. More importantly, the Ministry urged:

> The donors and the other UN member states should be courageous to voice their honest opinion about reality here in Palestine as they learn it first hand through the presence of their representative bodies. They should not be coerced into silence by unofficial lobbyists from any side. We expect them to use due process before they take positions and pass judgments. The first step in this process is to seek and find out the truth. This requires talking to all parties concerned and not accepting one-sided and biased reports.

Despite suffering from what might, outside of the uniquely fertile soil of the Israeli–Palestinian conflict, be taken to be a terminal affliction (namely having no basis in actual fact), the allegations were to find a renewed life and impetus in subsequent years, a development which says as much about the politics of the conflict as the ostensible concern. Both Ariel Sharon (in 2004) and Benjamin Netanyahu (in 2013) repeated the allegations. Foreign donors, having been browbeaten and shrilly accused of effectively promoting anti-Semitism, were compelled to re-evaluate their own funding arrangements, with the consequence that prior funding arrangements were consequently rescheduled and realigned.

In 2004, Sharon stated that Palestinians should stop incitement against Israelis in the Palestinian media and in the Palestinian curriculum, as preconditions for negotiations (Mualem and Benn 2004). As a matter of fact, one of Sharon's fourteen reservations to the Road Map for peace in 2003 was that Palestinians stop incitements

(*Haaretz* 2003). Prime Minister Netanyahu repeated the same request in January 2014 (Keinon 2014).

IPCRI's mission

Thus IPCRI took upon itself, as part of its greater overall mission to solidify the peace process through promoting values of democracy and reconciliation, to look at the textbooks produced by both sides in the post-Oslo era. While the Israeli textbooks escaped unscathed, the Palestinian ones were severely criticized. Overall, the Palestinian textbooks exposed many samples of 'an ambiguous or negative approach toward pluralism/tolerance/peace'. The aim of the studies is to ensure that the curriculum teaches peace and pluralism to influence students and encourage reconciliation and co-existence. The IPCRI study included most Palestinian textbooks and different grades but only the first to the eighth grades of Israeli textbooks for one academic year.

The three IPCRI reports on the Palestinian textbooks were presented to the Public Office of the US Consulate General in Jerusalem (but it is not clear whether the reports on the Israeli textbooks were handed in as well). The reports covered the period from 2000 to 2005. The first report evaluated the newly completed Palestinian textbooks for school year 2000/1. The evaluation covered grades 1, 2, 3, 6, 7 and 8. The second report covered grades 4 and 9, school year 2003/4. The third report evaluated the fifth and tenth grades, school year 2004/5.

The books were analysed thematically and were considered as potential contributors to civil society, peace, tolerance and diversity. The evaluation thus studied the curricula of language, art, religious education, history, civil education and national education. The second report, which focused on the Palestinian books alone, included an examination of human rights and the relationship to the State of Israel and to Jewish people. The report on Israeli textbooks did not analyse the national Israeli narrative in relation to the Palestinian one because, and according to IPCRI, this topic is not covered in the selected textbooks. As we shall see below, the Palestinian textbooks were in particular criticized for not including the Israeli narrative, without considering the grade level.

The Palestinian textbooks were analysed for the 'content' and 'communication' of the messages conveyed. The second report focused more on the content and symbolic material in relation to the concept of civil society including peace, human rights and democracy.

The third report focused on history education and geography in relation to the region. The report paid special attention to the notion of Palestine, homeland and Jerusalem. Such attentions were meant to assess the image and representation of Israel and Jews in the textbooks, and whether they refer to the relationship with the State of Israel and the topics related to peace agreements.

Let us first look at the analysis of the Palestinian textbooks. Overall one can say that there were some positive attributes found, which we describe here as 'A for Effort', but the balance sheet was negative. The positive side was the aspiration to prepare proper textbooks; the negative side was the failure to implement these aspirations. This condescending attitude is of course reminiscent of lofty modernizationist attitudes and colonialist approaches to education in the non-Western world.

A for Effort

The reports concede that they have not found direct incitements or hatred. The curriculum was praised for its stress on the need to accept the 'other'. The problem, however, as the reports mentioned again and again, was that these general notions were not associated with Israelis and Jews.

The reports acknowledged that concepts of peace, democracy, pluralism, respect for other cultures and universal human values in general were highlighted and stressed in the Palestinian curriculum. However, such values were not extended to include Israel and Jews.

These relatively positive remarks were, it seems, a sideshow in the report and written by additional reviewers and not the main body of researchers. They were also not integrated into the major part of the analysis of the three reports. Hence, we have very little to add to this section if we want to represent faithfully the spirit and word of the reports.

F for Failure

The tone of the reports is set in the first of the three reports through an evaluation of an Israeli educator. He wrote:

> The reviewer pointed out the references (or lack thereof) to Israel, Israelis, Jews, Judaism, and Zionism that he found problematic from an Israeli point of view. Subsequently, a Palestinian and international team analyzed the textbooks keeping in mind the remarks made by the Israeli educator.
>
> IPCRI 2003: 20

Therefore it was explained the report was written in order to:

> serve as an incentive to implement reform in the educational system in the direction of multicultural and global education, much of which is included in the promising foundational dimensions and the five-year plan for the reform of the Palestinian educational system.
>
> IPCRI 2003: 20

In order to achieve that, according to the reports, the Palestinian curriculum has to be changed. At the time of the reports it was evaluated as both 'inclusive' and nationalist. The reports concluded that the curriculum, despite its effort to encourage respect of other cultures, religions and ethnic groups, failed to mention Jews in particular. For example, in teaching the Koran and the Hadith, tolerance towards other religions was encouraged but the reports criticized the Palestinian curriculum for not mentioning Judaism in this context. The report assumed almost a sinister plot behind the omission: 'This lack of reference is perceived as tantamount to a denial of such a connection, although no direct evidence is found for such a denial' (IPCRI 2004a: 4).

It is very clear that IPCRI did not wish to be identified with the more brutal condemnations of the book. Hence, it is not always clear whether the possibility of incitement, as above, is disguised cleverly by the Palestinians or is the unfortunate outcome of the sloppiness of the authors of the textbooks. So in general the reports stated that the curriculum did not incite explicitly for hatred or violence against Israel or Jews. However, one could not be blamed, so it seemed, if the books were to be considered inflammatory if one was to 'consider the calls to liberating the Palestinian land/territories as instances of incitement' (IPCRI 2004a: 7). That 'one' would be Israel and the world, and hence, even if the books did not incite they appeared to incite, which was bad enough.

In a similar vein the third report explicitly expresses a concern that the refugees' dream of return to their homeland was not sufficiently qualified or mitigated (IPCRI 2006: 35). The essential consideration was not therefore the rights per se, but rather their subsequent rearticulation and reconstitution within the context of a conflict resolution framework.

The technique should be clear to the reader by now. There is an impulse to respect others and peace in the Palestinian textbooks, but it was not applied specifically to Jews and Israel. It seems, however, that most of the attention was paid to the framing of Palestine in the books and how it was juxtaposed with what IPCRI feared would seem to be an incitement.

Framing Palestine: the right and wrong way

In several places, the bottom line of the report was given in clear language. In a more detailed analysis the formula was more vague and focused on the possibility that incitement would be inferred from the text, even if the intention to incite was not there. The first summary comes at the very beginning of the third report:

> In the treatment and coverage of the history and geography of the region, the new textbooks continue to show some elements of imbalance, bias and inaccuracy. In some textbooks the Arabs' exclusive claim to the ancient history of the region is emphasized and several passages including references that reflect a continuous Arab presence in the greater Middle East region, with a noted lack of reference to the historical and contemporary presence of the Hebrews/Israelites/Jews in the region.
>
> IPCRI 2006: 3

Whereas in the report itself an ambiguous way of saying the same thing can also be found:

> [the curriculum] cannot be described as a war curriculum. Neither is it a peace curriculum. The textbooks do not contain calls for the destruction of the State of Israel. However, students are exposed to texts that promote the religious and national duty of loving and defending the homeland and the Palestinian culture.
>
> IPCRI 2006: 63

Here are a few examples that all evolve around the way the Palestinian textbooks frame geographically, politically and even emotionally, Palestine.

The first example refers to Jerusalem. When mentioning Jerusalem, there is no mention of the Jews and Judaism or of the city as a capital of Israel. The reports criticized the curriculum for referring to Jerusalem as the capital of Palestine but not also as the capital of Israel. Thus, the history and historical facts covered were in the eyes of the report 'selective'. In the report on the Israeli textbooks, the reviewers claim they, for their part, displayed a diverse view on Jerusalem as they mentioned the Temple Mount and 'where the Dome of the Rock is located is holy to Jews and to Muslims'. Jerusalem thus constituted the core of the conflict between Israel and the Arab world in general, and between Israel and the Palestinians in particular (IPCRI 2004b: 68).

Moreover, the reports accuse the curriculum of not referring to the State of Israel clearly and state that 'in some contexts, Jews, in historical and modern-day contexts (occupation, Zionism, settlers) are negatively represented in Palestinian textbooks' (IPCRI 2003: 7). The reports found that Israel was referred to as an occupying power and cause of Palestinian suffering. The curriculum encourages students to liberate and defend their land. This was translated by the report as calling for violence.

The second one deals with the notion of homeland. The Palestinians were expected to present multi-perspective narratives instead of focusing on Arab and Palestinian identities when engaging with the concept of homeland. The homeland, according to the critique, was not defined in the context of the present political reality and within the guidelines of the UN resolution and the peace agreements signed with Israel. Report III gave examples of such vagueness in wordings and/or referring to the pre-1948 or historical Palestine. For example, the curriculum mentioned the establishment of the Palestinian National Authority in 1994 on parts of the West Bank and the Gaza Strip. When referring to the pre-1948 situation the report gave examples of mentioning villages destroyed by Israel and the refugee problem created. In Report III, the review considered the homeland concept as ambiguous because it addressed the issue of Palestinian refugees, their suffering and their dream to go back to homeland 'without qualifying it' (IPCRI 2006: 35).

It seems the report expected the Palestinian curriculum to ignore pre-1948 Palestine altogether. The second report was alarmed by the fact that the textbooks referred to Israeli cities such as Jaffa and Acre as part of the homeland and that Israel was not mentioned on any map; neither is Palestine. Report I explains this:

> The rationale for this approach, as explained by political officials and educators alike, is that Israel itself has not yet marked its borders and that no final agreement has been reached with the PLO and the PA as to the final status of the borders between the two political entities.
>
> IPCRI 2003: 39

But the report insisted that: 'This, however, does not mean that maps included in the textbooks should be left without labels that reflect the historical as well as the present-day political reality' (IPCRI 2003: 39). Report III admits that: 'Whereas physical geography is almost comprehensive', the 'political geography of the region still suffers from elements of vagueness and imbalance, especially as it relates to direct references to "the State of Israel" as a geographic and political entity' (IPCRI 2006: 7).

The report's prior criticism of 'vagueness' and a lack of clarity also failed to acknowledge that the broader peace process was itself predicated upon the principle of constructive ambiguity (a point which was vividly illustrated by the fact that the initial terms of agreement between the two sides essentially boiled down to an acceptance to undertake further negotiations). One could indeed make a strong case that it was precisely this 'vagueness' and lack of clarity which functioned as a condition of possibility for the peace process in the first instance.

Although Report I states that homeland in the present context is defined as the West Bank and Gaza Strip, and this is defined in dotted lines or coloured, the report on the Israeli textbooks explains the absence of Palestinian places or borders because the maps 'are presented mainly in the context of the new Zionist settlement in the Land of Israel' (IPCRI 2004b: 20). The reviewers further justify this by saying that the maps were about the geographical and not political borders or were not relevant to the period. For some reason this argumentation was not allowed in the Palestinian case.

The third example refers to present-day realities as they were reflected in the curriculum. The report mentioned critically that the curriculum referred to the policies of Israel in the occupied territory, such as restriction of movement, confiscating land, house demolitions and other measures. In fact these references were depicted as part of the negative aspects of the curriculum. So it rebuked the book for the way the present reality appeared there. 'Generally speaking, Israel, Israelis, Zionism and Zionists are depicted as occupiers, invaders, aggressors, infiltrators, usurpers, and oppressors' (IPCRI 2006: 14).

But again, this being a liberal Zionist report, it is stated that this could be inferred as incitement. Similarly, in the analysis of this theme the report states clearly:

> No evidence was found of direct calls for the destruction of Israel. Except for calls for resisting occupation and oppression, no signs were detected of outright promotion of hatred towards Israel, Judaism, or Zionism. If the lack of ample references to the State of Israel in the body of the texts and on the maps as denial of its existence [*sic*], no evidence was found that points to an intentional attempt to do so.
>
> IPCRI 2004a: 5

Report III also acknowledges that the curriculum encouraged dialogue and tolerance but non-Arabs are not included or mentioned; moreover, the report accuses the curriculum of being vague in calling for resisting the Israel occupation, and that might be perceived as a call for liberating historical Palestine.

The curriculum that should have been

The reports are very didactic in tone and offer an insight into the way liberal Zionists would have dealt with the issues at hand. The reports emphasized the significance of critical thinking and exploring in education which they failed to see in the Palestinian curriculum. Thus more information should be provided about Israel, Jews and peace agreements. One can conclude that, based on the evaluation of such reports, the Palestinian curriculum is expected to rebrand Israel and reframe Palestine. Report II, for example recommended: 'the struggle to end occupation should be used as a vehicle to teach students about peaceful and non-violent actions, conflict reconciliation and conflict resolution' (IPCRI 2004a: 38).

It further expected the curriculum to highlight the interactions and cooperation between Palestinians and Israelis in different fields such as education and health. All in all, the curriculum as far as IPCRI was concerned should be a song of praise for the Oslo Accord:

> The concept of peace with Israel is not mentioned in the textbooks. The peace process based on the Oslo Accords, the Wye River Memorandum and the Anti-Incitement subcommittee – whose purpose was to reduce tensions and create a positive atmosphere of positive cohabitation – are not referred to in the 5th and 10th grade textbooks.
>
> IPCRI 2004a: 27

This is also related to a negative review of how international peace efforts were reviewed in the textbooks. The curriculum was scolded for mentioning the UN resolution[4] without referring to the partition plan and the recognition of Israel's right to security and borders. It also wished to rewrite the Palestinian version of events of how the second Intifada erupted.

Overall, the reports suggested that the Palestinians should have adopted a more scholarly and professional approach to the text. Report I explained extensively the need to address the theoretical framework of intolerance, prejudice and discrimination. The report emphasized the role of education in changing attitudes. Moreover, Report III stressed that peace education should be part of the curriculum and that 'the challenge for educators, however, is to replace a belief in peacekeeping with a commitment to peace-making and peacebuilding strategies to address the multifaceted forms of violence that exist in the region' (IPCRI 2006: 28–9).

The lack of scholarly soundness in the books is pointed out also by the third report. It gave the impression that the Palestinian curriculum lacks accuracies in history education in opining that:

> textbooks should introduce objective, up-to-date, comprehensive, and historically accurate information and accounts free of inciting, inflammatory, and offensive language and rhetoric and of elements of bias and of stereotypical images and representations.
>
> IPCRI 2006: 41

Well, had these textbooks been written by the new Israeli historians and the states' post-Zionist scholars who today dominate the production of knowledge on Israel and Palestine worldwide, these 'inaccuracies' would have been endorsed by the updated and critical research.

The reports also recommended that the Palestinian curriculum should adopt a pedagogy that encourages critical thinking and exposes students to different perspectives and historical narratives. This is mostly specified as to include Jews and Israeli perspectives or to mention their historical roots.

And how should resistance to oppression be framed? The curriculum is criticized for rejecting oppression and occupation and encouraging resistance and defending the land. Report III refers to this as calling for violent resistance. The examples of peaceful resistance with reference to international models such as India and South Africa are considered isolated and not sufficient (IPCRI 2006: 34).

In short, the reports concluded that 'It is essential to promote a culture of peace, coexistence, cooperation, and tolerance in spite of all the adverse circumstances that prevail. These efforts should be concerted and should cover all aspects of life' (IPCRI 2006: 43). Therefore, the reports recommend that history education should teach about the other, emphasize the present political reality of post-Oslo and refer to the legitimate rights of Palestinians and Israelis. Needless to say, if the rights of the Palestinians would be mentioned in a hypothetical revised report the possibility that this would infer incitement would be raised once more.

To sum up, the report did have a bottom line, as mentioned before, and did not leave the final word in any ambiguity. The report concluded that representation of Israel and Jews was biased, especially in relation to the historical root of the Jewish in the Middle East. At best it seems the textbooks did not include the Jewish history at all, neither of ancient Israel (which in any way it was not meant to do as the textbooks were dealing with modern history) or in modern times (IPCRI 2006: 36).

The Israeli books under the microscope

In its report, IPCRI found little fault with the Israeli textbooks. One of its main explanations for this was the random selections it claimed to have used for both sets of textbooks. But somehow the random search of Palestinian books revealed incitement while the one on Israeli books saw little problem in them.

Thus the IPCRI report states: 'Because we examined the books that are intended for 1st–8th grades, the question of the national Israeli narrative and how it relates to the Palestinian narrative is not particularly relevant' (IPCRI 2004b: 3). If there were any criticisms it was a remark that concepts of peace, pluralism and reconciliation were not gleaned from Biblical stories.

The report accepted that Arabs in general did not make their way into Israeli textbooks on history or culture. This absence was justified in the following way:

> However, in view of the fact that these textbooks are designed for students in Jewish State-education elementary schools, they deal predominantly with the history of the Jewish People, with Zionism, and with Jewish settlement in the Land of Israel.
>
> IPCRI 2004b: 10

It is worth mentioning that any evaluation of Israeli textbooks was treated not only with bias but in favour of the Israeli curriculum. This is despite the studies available that found Israeli textbooks were racist and incite against Arabs and Palestinians. So while IPCRI found no fault with the Israeli textbooks, critical Israeli scholars were far less impressed. A study of 124 Israeli textbooks by Professor Daniel Bar-Tal of Tel Aviv University (1998) found that Arabs were described as 'hostile, deviant, cruel, immoral, unfair, with the intention to hurt Jews'. Nurit Peled-Elhanan's study of sixteen books on geography, history and civil studies (2012) found that Palestinians were represented as primitive, that the myth of *terra nullius* was uncritically reproduced, and that the Israeli massacres of 1948 were relativized as an unfortunate, although necessary, precondition for the establishment of Israel.

It is striking that the same standards recommended to the Palestinians, and the absence of which the reports lamented in the current textbooks, were not expected of the Israeli narrative. While the Palestinian narrative was condemned for being reductionist, in the report on the Israeli textbooks the simplified historical account was praised as evidence of encouraging good relations with neighbours. As a matter of fact, the examples referred to are not only inaccurate but also condescending.

The most astonishing part of the report on the Israeli textbooks is that obvious fabrications and distortions were repeated without any criticism. One of the stories the report referred to in the report on the Israeli textbooks was about a Zionist settler who avoided buying land close to Arab 'settlements', so as not to incur the envy of the Arab inhabitants (IPCRI 2004b: 12). The Zionist settler also permitted Arab neighbours to continue and use the spring water on 'his' land. Even when negative examples were given of the stereotyping of Arabs, positive examples were followed immediately and based on the reviewers' interpretations and would be considered as diverse images of Arabs (IPCRI 2004b: 14–16).

While the absence of Israel from the Palestinian textbooks was condemned, the absence of Palestine in the Israeli textbooks was justified. The reviewers related the absence to the grades studied and the period covered.

Conclusion

The attitude of IPCRI to the issue of the textbooks was very clear from the outset. In its eyes Palestinian education could not legitimize resistance or a struggle against occupation. Moreover, from IPCRI's point of view any reference to the resistance and struggle are framed as incitement. And thus if resistance or even a striving to change the status quo of a decades-long occupation and colonization is delegitimized as an educational mission, cherishing the status quo is what IPCRI expects to be the main object of the Palestinian educational system. As noted, politically and economically, the PA submitted to this logic of the 'peace process'; educationally even the most cooperative Palestinian educators found it very hard to accept.

The framing of references to a past or present struggle as incitement exposes an even more profound discord between the liberal Zionists of IPCRI and the Palestinian national educators. There can be no reference, in the eyes of IPCRI, to the core issues that produced the struggle in the first place. Therefore the criticism insinuates that existing Palestinian grievances are somehow artificial or induced. Palestinians are therefore denied political agency to the extent that they appear as unthinking receptacles, as an inert mass that can easily be cultivated and instrumentalized for purposes other than their own.

In closely engaging with each of these instances we get a sense of how the education debate (and the conflict resolution framework which it is part of) has become politicized. The instrumental adaptation of incitement appears, to this extent, as a means through which broader forms of violence are enabled, legitimized and enacted. State violence by Israel thus is not questioned in Israeli books, by IPCRI or anyone else condemning the Palestinian textbook in the post-Oslo era, but any form of Palestinian resistance is depicted as harming the chances of reconciliation. Peace therefore demands nothing of Israel in terms of struggle and violence, but insists it magically disappears from the Palestinian arsenal, even as the occupation continues (or in fact becomes worse, as was the case).

The critics focused on the pre-Oslo agreement chapters of the Palestinian textbooks and insisted these books should depict 1967, and not 1948 or let alone 1882, as the starting point of their narrative.[5] This meant in essence wiping out the Palestinian narrative through surveillance and control. There is no engagement with knowledge here for the sake of reconciliation or mutual understanding. As pointed out by Edward Said, 'The Palestinians are expected to participate in the dismantling of their own history at the same time' (Said 1984).

The examination of the textbooks, by IPCRI or by anyone else, condemning it as incitement is not based on any factual or professional scrutiny as the EU Commissioner for External Relations, Chris Patten (2002) explains:

> [I]t was alleged that we were funding textbooks [and] that [they] were untrue, we denied it. There was even a report by the EU Heads of Mission in Jerusalem refuting the allegations in terms, a report which is publicly available at the Council web-site! Did this change anything? Alas, no. The story comes back again and again and again with the regularity of clockwork.

The IPCRI reports were a far more complex examination than the explicit condemnation voiced by official Israel and the USA. But long reports have a bottom line and in this it was a verdict of bias that was translated by politicians into an accusation of incitement. Hence a supposedly more balanced, and academic, view carried at the end of the day the same message expressed more vulgarly and bluntly by politicians – the Palestinian textbooks and curricula are biased in a way that endangered peace and reconciliation.

The complex approach was framed in the following way. The textbooks and curricula were praised for an overall attempt to be loyal to principles of peace and pluralism, but failed to do that when they focused on history (the very essence of every national narrative). Take out a Palestinian version of the history of Palestine from the textbooks and they would have been praised for the positive impulse.

Palestine was reframed by sheer military, political and economic force in the Oslo Accord and has been ever since that failed peace attempt. The only space where this imposition was resisted, and therefore so harshly criticized, is education. The gap between historical framing and narrative has been ignored by peace brokers ever since 1967 and depicted as an obstacle to peace. In fact what the issue at hand proves is that this very gap is the reason for the conflict, and if it cannot be breached between the most moderate Palestinians and liberal Zionists we need a new framing, which to our mind only the settler colonialist paradigm offers.

Notes

1 President Arafat held a press conference on 14 December 1988 at which he denounced violence, accepted the UN Security Council Resolutions 242 and 338, and recognized the State of Israel and its right to exist.
2 Netanyahu and the PLO signed the Hebron Protocol on 15 January 1997 to prepare for the Israeli redeployment from the city.
3 Subsequently renamed the Institute for Monitoring Peace and Cultural Tolerance in School Education.
4 The reports refer to 'the UN resolution' without specifying which one or ones. They probably meant UN Security Council Resolutions 242 (22 November 1967) and 338 (22 October 1973). The reports thought that UN General Assembly Resolution 181 (29 November 1947) was missing, which concerns the partition of Palestine.
5 The first immigration of Jews from the diaspora (known in Hebrew as 'Aliyah') began in 1882.

References

Aruri, N. H. (1999), 'The Wye Memorandum: Netanyahu's Oslo and Unreciprocal Reciprocity', *Journal of Palestine Studies* 28 (2): 17–28.
Bar-Tal, D. (1998), 'The Rocky Road Toward Peace: Beliefs on Conflict in Israeli Textbooks', *Journal of Peace Research* 35 (6): 723–42.
Brown, N. J. (2002), *Democracy, History and the Contest over the Palestinian Curriculum*, an independent report prepared for The Adam Institute. Available online: http://home.gwu.edu/~nbrown/Adam_Institute_Palestinian_textbooks.htm (accessed 2 March 2015).
Centre for Monitoring the Impact of Peace (CMIP) (2000), *The New Palestinian Authority School Textbooks for Grades One and Six*, New York: CMIP.
Endresen, L. (2001), *Contact and Cooperation: The Israeli-Palestinian People-to-People Program*, Oslo: Fafo Institute for Applied Social Science. Available online: http://www.fafoarkiv.no/pub/rapp/659/659.pdf (accessed 3 March 2015).
Foucault, M. (1991), *Discipline and Punish: The Birth of a Prison*, London: Penguin.
Haaretz (2003), 'Israel's Road Map Reservations', 27 May. Available online: http://www.haaretz.com/print-edition/news/israel-s-road-map-reservations-1.8935 (accessed 2 March 2015).
Hanieh, A. (2001), 'The Camp David Papers', *Journal of Palestine Studies* 30 (2): 75–97. Available online: http://www.palestine-studies.org/jps/abstract/40908 (accessed 2 March 2015).

Hanssen-Bauer, J. (2000), 'The Israeli–Palestinian People-to-People Program: The Fafo Model of People-to-People', paper presented to the Helsinki Workshop on Evaluating Israeli–Palestinian Civil Society Cooperative Activities, 27–8 November 1999, 35–40, Helsinki: Civil Society Conflict Prevention Network KATU.

Henry, M. (2000), 'Hillary Clinton: Link PA to End to Antisemitism', *Jerusalem Post*, 26 September.

Israel/Palestine Centre for Research and Information (IPCRI) (2003), *Report I: Analysis and Evaluation of the New Palestinian Curriculum Textbooks – Renewing Palestinian Textbooks and Tolerance Education Program, March*, Submitted to: The Public Affairs Office US Consulate General Jerusalem.

Israel/Palestine Centre for Research and Information (IPCRI) (2004a), *Report II: Analysis and Evaluation of the New Palestinian Curriculum Textbooks – Renewing Palestinian Textbooks and Tolerance Education Program Grades 4 and 9*, Submitted to: The Public Affairs Office US Consulate General Jerusalem.

Israel/Palestine Centre for Research and Information (IPCRI) (2004b), *Examination of Israeli Textbooks in Elementary Schools of the State Educational System*, April 2004.

Israel/Palestine Centre for Research and Information (IPCRI) (2006), *Report III: Analysis and Evaluation of the New Palestinian Curriculum Textbooks – Renewing Palestinian Textbooks and Tolerance Education Program Grades 5 and 10*, Submitted to: The Public Affairs Office US Consulate General Jerusalem.

Keinon, H. (2014), 'Netanyahu: Palestinian Incitement Spurs Mideast Conflict', *Jerusalem* Post, 1 January. Available online: http://www.jpost.com/Diplomacy-and-Politics/Netanyahu-Palestinian-incitement-spurs-Mideast-conflict-337133 (accessed 2 March 2015).

Khalil, M. (2000), 'If You are for Truth, You Seek the Truth First', Available online: http://webcache.googleusercontent.com/search?q=cache:f2ihFw8ZHAgJ:www.miftah.org/Doc/Factsheets/MIFTAH/English/Jan30dy2k4.doc+&cd=1&hl=en&ct=clnk&gl=uk (accessed 2 March 2015).

Mahshi, K. (2000), 'The Palestinian Ministry of Education and Non-Governmental Organizations: Cooperation and Possible Partnership', paper presented to the International Conference on Palestinian Government/NGO Relations: Cooperation and Partnership, Ramallah, February 2000.

Maoz, I. (2000), 'An Experiment in Peace: Reconciliation-aimed Workshops of Jewish-Israeli and Palestinian Youth', *Journal of Peace Research* 37 (6): 721–36.

Morena, E. (2001), 'Israel or Palestine: Who Teaches What History? A Textbook Case', *Le Monde Diplomatique*, July. Available online: http://mondediplo.com/2001/07/11 textbook (accessed 2 March 2015).

Moughrabi, F. (2001), 'The Politics of Palestinian Textbooks', *Journal of Palestine Studies* 31 (1), Issue 121. Available online: http://www.palestine-studies.org/jps/fulltext/40982 (accessed 2 March 2015).

Mualem, M. and Benn, A. (2004), 'Sharon: PA's Real Test is Ending Incitement', *Haaretz*, 19 November. Available online: http://www.haaretz.com/print-edition/news/sharon-pa-s-real-test-is-ending-incitement-1.140687 (accessed 1 March 2015).

Palestinian Authority, Ministry of Education (2001), 'The Palestinian Curriculum and Textbooks: A Clarification', Ramallah, 12 May. Available online: http://www.miftah.org/Display.cfm?DocId=3060&CategoryId=21 and http://www.miftah.org/Doc/Factsheets/MIFTAH/English/Jan30ay2k4.doc (both accessed 2 March 2015).

Palestinian Curriculum Development Center (1996), *A Comprehensive Plan for the Development of the First Palestinian Curriculum for General Education*, 2nd Edition, Ramallah: Palestinian Curriculum Development Center.

Palestinian Monitoring Group (2005), *Trend Analysis, Education under Occupation: Disruptions to Palestinian Education Stemming from Israeli Military and Settler Activity, 1 September 2003–30 June 2005*, 30 October. Available online: http://www.pacbi.org/etemplate.php?id=104 (accessed 2 March 2015).

Patten, C. (2002) (Commissioner for External Relations), Statement to the Foreign Affairs Committee on EU Budgetary Assistance to the Palestinian Authority, Foreign Affairs Committee of the European Parliament, Brussels, 19 June 2002. Available online: http://europa.eu/rapid/press-release_SPEECH-02-293_en.htm (accessed 11 November 2014).

Peled-Elhanan, N. (2012), *Palestine in Israeli School Books: Ideology and Propaganda in Education*, London: I.B. Tauris.

Roy, S. (2004), 'The Palestinian–Israeli Conflict and Palestinian Socioeconomic Decline: A Place Denied', *International Journal of Politics, Culture, and Society* 17 (3): 365–403. Available online: http://link.springer.com/article/10.1023/B%3AIJPS.0000019609.37719.99 (accessed 2 March 2015).

Said, E. (1984), 'Permission to Narrate [Edward Said writes about the story of the Palestinians]', *London Review of Books* 6 (3), 16 February: 13–17.

Tufakji, K. (2000), 'Settlements: A Geographic and Demographic Barrier to Peace', *Palestine-Israel Journal of Politics, Economics and Culture* 7 (3/4). Available online: http://www.pij.org/details.php?id=254 (accessed 8 March 2015).

UNICEF (2011), *Occupied Palestinian Territory, Education in Emergencies and Post-crisis Transition, 2010 Report Evaluation*, June. Available online: http://www.educationandtransition.org/wp-content/uploads/2007/04/OPT_EEPCT_2010_Report.pdf (accessed 2 March 2015).

United Nations Office for the Co-ordination of Humanitarian Affairs (OCHA) (2013), *The Humanitarian Impact of the Barrier*, July. Available online: http://domino.un.org/UNISPAl.NSF/3822b5e39951876a85256b6e0058a478/ee597cde07fb400c85257ba30049e6a6?OpenDocument (accessed 2 March 2015).

United Nations Office for the Co-ordination of Humanitarian Affairs (OCHA) (2014), *Occupied Palestinian Territory: Gaza Emergency Situation Report* (as of 4 September 2014). Available online: https://www.ochaopt.org/documents/ocha_opt_sitrep_04_09_2014.pdf (accessed 8 March 2014).

2

Russia and Ukraine: EUROCLIO and Perspectives of Professional History Educators on Societies in Transition

Tamara Eidelman, Polina Verbytska and Jonathan Even-Zohar

Introduction

EUROCLIO, the European Association of History Educators, established in 1992, supports the development of responsible and innovative history, citizenship and heritage education by promoting critical thinking, mutual respect, peace, stability and democracy. It promotes a sound use of history education towards the building and deepening of democratic societies, connecting professionals across national, ethnic and religious boundaries. EUROCLIO believes that the past does not stop at national borders and that history education has a significant impact on how people look at the world around them. The Association propagates an approach to history education that deconstructs historical myths and negative stereotypes. While combating the instrumentalization of history education for petty political objectives, EUROCLIO's work fosters mutual understanding among Europe's citizens and beyond, and defends the acknowledgement of societies' cultural and linguistic diversity. EUROCLIO promotes the teaching of an attractive, engaging and relevant history, heritage and citizenship education, supporting a twenty-first-century knowledge-based and global society. It seeks to enhance the quality of history and citizenship education through capacity-building of history education professionals and producing and implementing innovative teaching tools.

Since its foundation, EUROCLIO has worked in many European countries and beyond, but a central focus has been on countries in political transformation and in particular those with inter-ethnic and inter-religious tensions such as Bulgaria, Estonia, Latvia, Romania, Russia and Ukraine. EUROCLIO's work brings together historians and history educators to share experiences, to implement innovative learning about the past, while also discussing sensitive and controversial issues and therefore creating new and inclusive historical narratives.

In both Ukraine and Russia, EUROCLIO supported the development of history education by working closely with history teachers as they founded history teacher associations, trying to develop and implement new pedagogical approaches, and learning all at the same time how they could support themselves and their colleagues to develop professionally.

In 2011, EUROCLIO obtained funding from the European Union's Eastern Partnership Programme for a large project. With a wider regional view, bringing together stakeholders from Armenia, Azerbaijan, Georgia, Moldova and Ukraine, and through additional peer-learning efforts by EUROCLIO, it also reaches out to Estonia, Latvia, Russia and Turkey. The publication and subsequent teacher training expected to arise out of this programme was organized over the course of 2015.

Part 1: Building a nation with history – political and transnational challenges

How have the political transitions since 1991 in Ukraine and the Russian Federation respectively affected the practice of history education? What were the main challenges?

The Ukrainian experience

With independence, the processes of constructing a new national identity and reconstructing historical and collective memory started. In the early 1990s a complete revision of the contents and methodology of history education in Ukraine was undertaken, and the whole generation of school history textbooks was overhauled. A 'science' of history education was to be developed, incorporating new concepts and methodological approaches. A scheme of Ukrainian history which became the foundation for history textbooks reflected a historical narrative from 'Princely' times (the ninth to the thirteenth centuries CE) to the present, and showed the continuity of history and the natural formation of Ukrainian statehood, seeking to secure in students' minds an integral vision of Ukraine's past.

Meetings discussing history education and history textbooks in the context of the challenges and demands of modern society have been held within the Ukrainian professional history education community in the two-and-a-half decades since independence in 1991, and the most significant contribution has been the work of the Monitoring Commission of School Textbooks in the History of Ukraine organized by the Ukrainian Institute of the National Memory in 2008. Textbooks were examined for the quality of their relationship to modern Ukrainian society, whether history was 'humanized', the sense of openness to 'the other' and to the world beyond individual communities, and whether critical thinking was encouraged.

The monitoring of textbooks organized by the Ukrainian National Memory Institute concluded that they do not present the necessary variant of the collective identity which would satisfy the needs of internal consolidation of modern Ukrainian society. The majority of textbooks stressed an ethnocentric vision of history leaving aside the multi-ethnic, multicultural and multi-faith dimensions which have been the priorities of school history education in open societies. The old priorities had reflected a false consciousness of Ukrainian ethnic, linguistic and religious unity. Criticism of this approach as inadequate would draw on these factors: the association of a monocultural community identity with a suppressed lower social strata; a pessimistic view of Ukraine's colonial status and inferiority complex; the representation of a bipolar world, and not a variety of social strata, interest groups and small communities.

One such variant of historic memory presented in modern history textbooks is reflected in a controversial mismatch between personal/family history memory and the official type of collective memory. The results of monitoring most Ukrainian textbooks showed a paradoxical disparity between the challenges of today and school textbooks, and this needed to be challenged urgently because schoolchildren were being taught something anachronistic, and would consequently experience problems identifying themselves with a common historical past in present-day Ukraine. The commission concluded that textbooks do not correspond either to the modern state of the discipline of history or to the needs of society or the state standards (Yakovenko 2008: 64–81).

A survey of school leavers conducted by the Nova Doba Association[1] in partnership with the Fund of Democratic Initiatives (DIF) (Nova Doba and DIF 2008) aimed at defining the dual dynamics of (a) the pedagogical influence within history education and (b) civic education, on the generation born in the year of independence, 1991. While analysing the educational factors influencing the development of civic virtues in young people a number of problems were revealed. The survey results indicated the low level of engagement with the main democratic values (human rights, pluralism, a multi-party system, a state where the rule of law applied, elections, the mass media). Also, the survey registered unwillingness to vote in elections, an alienation from the local community and a deficit in the skills needed to evaluate the related information critically. In the opinion of students, the uniting factors of Ukraine as a single nation were: the wish to build a better life in the country (50 per cent); equal rights of the citizens of Ukraine (34 per cent); patriotic feelings of the citizens (30 per cent); and a common history (25.3 per cent). Nevertheless – and worryingly – only 20.6 per cent of the whole sample felt a sense of belonging linked to Ukrainian citizenship, and this could be interpreted as testimony to a low level of their understanding of the concept of a political nation.

Many students want a strong power in Ukraine. The survey results indicate that students' level of knowledge and skills for co-existence in a modern democratic, multicultural society do not equate to the aspirations of a global information society, and this gap between life as it is and life as it might be demonstrates significant underlying psychological tensions in individual perceptions of these changes.

It shows that young people often have no awareness of the principles of various integrating life experiences and norms of behaviour. The necessary mutual complementing of personal autonomy and accepted social norms has decreased. The danger of this phenomenon is that self-identification has become a dominant force and consists not only in the fact that new forms of social development have not always received proper educational support, but also, as changes increased, these were accompanied by negative (and intolerant) perceptions of representatives of other cultures and religions, and other ethnic and racial groups, reflecting growing social and cultural differences, with unfortunate characteristics. In particular a failure to adapt to these differences can be seen in attempts to deny them, and this dominant self-identification involves both individuals and their peer groups in setting up their exclusive perception of 'our people' in opposition to strangers.

Indeed, recent events give many examples of Ukraine's emergence from its totalitarian past but nevertheless testify to increasing intolerance and violence. That is why human rights constitute an important aspect of historical memory in Ukraine. It is important to emphasize that during the current war in Ukraine human rights are greatly threatened. Thus, a special focus should be given to the history lessons of the twentieth century, the Second World War, the Holocaust, other genocides, conflicts, deportations, confrontation and collaboration, and their lessons, which can provide a much-needed background commentary to these contemporary processes which are marked by an increase in intolerance and violence, especially among the young generation.

The Russian experience

Political changes affected Russian education so much that, some time at the end of the 1980s, history teachers were asked to abandon textbooks as old books contradicted the new information coming from mass media, and new books were not readily available. The history exam was also postponed for one year. The main focus of interest was on the history of the twentieth century, which has since been the most controversial part of the history curriculum. At the beginning of the 1990s a liberal version of history was the most popular, Stalin's rule was criticized, and liberal ideas were promoted. Many educational practices that were used by teachers in the 1920s, and forgotten since then, were revived in classrooms. At the same time most textbooks remained traditional from a methodological point of view, concentrating mostly on facts and knowledge, and Western practices were almost completely unknown. Many new methodological ideas were introduced, but usually in teaching Ancient and Medieval History, which was aimed at younger children, while Russian history, considered as a more 'serious' topic and part of a controlled examination system, was usually taught in a more traditional way. Textbooks printed in the 1990s by the MIROS Institute (Moscow Institute for Development of Education Systems) showed completely new ways of teaching European and world history, but Russian history was excluded from these innovative approaches.

Connections with Europe through cooperation with Western teachers, and especially the EUROCLIO projects in Russia (*Uroki Clio*, '*Lessons from Clio*', 1997–2000; and *Mosaics of Culture*, 2003–5), introduced many teachers to new pedagogical ideas. Unfortunately, in the first decade of the new century, the political and educational situation started changing dramatically.

What place did historical issues have in the post-1989/1991 society – collective memory, identity and cultural history, as well as new issues addressed and archives?

Ukraine

The experience of transition in Ukraine caused history education to face some problems and challenges. For example, the official version of the national history of each community is reflected in school curricula and history textbooks and is handed down to the following generations. But in the oral history of a family, community or other groups of society unofficial memory is preserved, which provides another version of certain events, different from the official one. The distinctive nature of Ukrainian society is characterized by the co-existence of different and potentially controversial types of historic memory. The Ukrainian historian Natalia Yakovenko has categorized these parallel types of memory:

> 1. The romantic historiography of the early-middle nineteenth century representing the Cossack vision of the past, mostly cultivated in central Ukraine.
> 2. The populist academic historiography of the late nineteenth to the early twentieth centuries perceiving the past as a battle between the twin Slavic nations Ukraine and Russia against enemies (Poles, Tatars, Turks etc.) to preserve the Orthodox religion and ethnic rights.
> 3. The nationalist historiography of the twentieth century, mostly originating from the diaspora – a version of the past coloured with strong nationalistic aspirations, in particular with the cult of heroes from the OUN-UPA (Organization of Ukrainian Nationalists – Ukrainian Insurgent Army) as fighters for Ukrainian statehood, operating in the Western Ukraine and partially in Volyn.
>
> Yakovenko 2008

The memory of the Second World War is one of the most controversial historical episodes in the Ukrainian collective memory. The lack of social consensus under the present circumstances in Ukraine as a post-totalitarian country allows different political forces to politicize the same past.

Between about 2005 and 2015 this conflict was deepened because of an inconsistent historical memory policy. Let us illustrate this with a few examples. During Viktor Yushchenko's presidential term (2005–10) the restoration and preservation of the national memory of the Ukrainian people, and reflecting the third model in the list above, was declared as state policy and this was reinforced in the completion of a range of activities at state level as it was through history education that the tragic events in Ukraine's history would be commemorated: the Holodomor (the 1932–3 famine genocide); Stalin's purges and the national liberation movement; the role of the Ukrainian Insurgent Army (UPA) in the Second World War; the role of the Organization of Ukrainian Nationalists (OUN) and its (controversial) leader Stepan Bandera (1909–59). In 2010, Viktor Yanukovych became president.[2] He advocated a positive revision of the common Soviet past with Russia. Under his policy of historical memory in 2010–13 the rudimentary Soviet discourse came to the fore, expressed in the denial of the Holodomor as a genocide, a pompous celebration of Victory Day (originally 9 May 1945), and a vision of the Second World War as the shared accepted interpretation for both Ukraine and Russia.

Meanwhile political forces after these changes were at work to influence the process of the forming of historical memory through education as well. The fact that history was being rewritten received increasing attention during the last decade in the debates of scholars, politicians and politically minded citizens. For instance in the autumn of 2011 (at the beginning of Yanukovych's presidency) changes were introduced to textbooks for the 11th grade. The reason for this was the decision taken in 2010 to return to an eleven-grade system after some time with a twelve-grade system. It involved the shortening of all syllabi. On the other hand textbooks on history not only became shorter, but they had also undergone a shift of emphasis – from the previous attention given to national liberation movements to a classical Soviet historiography scheme. For instance, in previous history textbooks for the 11th grade the first chapter had been called 'Ukraine during World War II', and in the new textbook it would be entitled 'The Great Patriotic War'. The OUN had received substantial attention in the textbooks of previous years, and in the modern textbook it receives scant attention. The information on OUN-UPA and russification would be curtailed, and the Orange Revolution allotted a few sentences.

The new textbooks of 2011, unlike the textbooks of the previous years, became less emotionally coloured and more generalized, and after reading the summaries proposed by the authors a student cannot always understand the tragedy of the society or recognize a country with a three-dimensional personality. The narrative text in them is confined to the most essential facts which are given without analysis and emotional colouring. Kasyanov (2011) confirmed this view by stating:

> It is not difficult to notice that the problem of history education and the content of textbooks aggravates each time with the change of political power. It was so in 2005, and the same happened in 2010. However, all the 'shaman dances' of politicians around history textbooks do not influence the resolving of real problems in the least – they remain the same as they were 10–15 years ago. Our textbooks, especially in history of Ukraine, still contain elements of xenophobia, cultural and ethnic intolerance, and gender chauvinism.
>
> Kasyanov 2011

Parallel experiences in the Russian Federation

Historical issues were very important in Russian society in the 1990s. Completely new information became available for teachers as well as for students. Many names and events of twentieth-century Russia were completely or partly reconsidered. Many documents from archives which were closed in Soviet times were now open and yielded a haul of materials for researchers and for teachers too. The NGO 'Memorial', an international historical, educational, human rights and charitable society, founded on 28 January 1989 to commemorate the victims of Stalin's repressions, collected oral history, helped survivors of Stalin's camps and organized school history contests. Soviet history became increasingly popular.

It is clear that these new assessments of political persons were strongly related to a new political situation at that time in Russia. Some important personalities from previous centuries – Peter the Great, Ivan the Terrible – were also often looked at from the seemingly new perspective. All Russian history was considered to be a source of discussion about Russian destiny and the Russian future.

Strong debates went on for more than two decades, reassessing Russian history. Many people were, however, beginning to consider new information about 'black pages' of Russian history as humiliating and destroying national identity. Demands were being made (and have increased in recent years) to 'save students at school' from 'libellous' information. Sometimes these facts are admitted to be true, but students are supposed 'not to be ready' or it is feared that 'they will be too disappointed' and will 'lose national pride'. As Karen Shakhnazarov, a famous Russian film director, has commented controversially in several interviews: 'You cannot say to a child that his father is alcoholic and his mother a prostitute' (e.g. Shigareva 2013).[3] This is social denial of a past that has had to be re-evaluated with the new evidence, and reflects an identity crisis which often follows a change in political status and orientation. It also touches on a psychological debate about whether it is better to remember or to forget.

In the 1990s, though, history started losing its appeal. People got tired of politics as well as of history. Terrible images from the past, that had been new to them in the 1980s, became boring. Ethnic conflicts and terrorist attacks in the present seemed more terrifying. Meanwhile a new trend of rehabilitation of the Soviet period emerged. Society was so shocked by historical truth, as well as by the collapse of the USSR, that people needed to find something to believe in. Unfortunately, neither historians nor politicians managed to provide people with a positive image of the past and present. It seemed impossible to find a reasonable balance between 'telling people all the truth, no matter how terrible it was' and 'not disappointing people and destroying their national pride'. The truth had been told about Stalin and the Soviet past, and this was very important. But the political and the historical trauma had been much stronger than had been thought, and nobody cared to provide people with ideas about Russian history that were both positive and truthful!

National euphoria after the annexation of Crimea in March 2014 was very correctly labelled by psychologist Lyudmila Petranovskaya (2014) as an example of the 'Weimar Syndrome' – a paradigm associated with a search for a new source of pride after national humiliation, as in the case of Germany following its defeat in the First World War, especially after the harsh conditions imposed by the Treaty of Versailles in 1919 – with all their possible future implications.

Pressure to incorporate ideas of national pride to be impressed on children with the help of history teaching, is, unfortunately, increasing. Images of 'strong power', of military victories, of Russian supremacy are getting more and more popular. Terrible misuse of history has happened recently since the annexation of Crimea, when Crimean and Ukrainian history have been distorted to serve the political aims of the Russian government, and it has to be admitted, unfortunately, that so far this falsified history has been manipulated very effectively to create a new identity built on a wrongly understood national pride.

What has been the role (and mutual relationship) in Ukraine and the Russian Federation of civil society and the professional education community?

Ukraine

In schools, there is an urgent need to address controversial historical memory in Ukraine by forming a distinctly democratic collective image of society in the students' perception, in helping pupils to become active members of this democratic society, and enabling them to make a positive contribution to that society. History must not be used to indoctrinate them into a given set of beliefs and attitudes. This involves developing the pupils' critical thinking, as well as introducing an innovative methodology.

The Constitution and other laws of Ukraine reflect a positive view of both public opinion and the professional community, as seen in the Standards of Secondary Education and in examples of positive cooperation between Ukrainian and European institutions in the process of democratizing history education. Cooperation between national bodies, historians, history teachers with European institutions and educators has played a crucial role in introducing new approaches to history education in Ukraine, and the cooperation between the Ministry of Education and associations of teachers with the Council of Europe, EUROCLIO and EUSTORY are examples of this.

Aiming to support a more multicultural approach to school history teaching, the Directorate of School Education of the Council of Europe (this 'Programme of Cooperation between the EU and the Council of Europe' is entitled 'Encouraging the Human Rights Culture in Ukraine and South Caucasus') has held seminars in Ukraine about the problem of showing links between national identity and cultural diversity in curricula, textbooks and manuals, and also in the practice of teaching. Different conceptual approaches were discussed as well as ways of introducing an intercultural approach into the educational process. The national curricula were analysed with the aim of further improvement and development. In this partnership the Ministry of Education has played an important part, as it gives such a discussion a legalized status, thus stimulating the improvement of the process.

The innovative approach to history introduced by Ukrainian scholars and teachers of history in their cooperation with European organizations such as the Council of Europe and EUROCLIO can be seen in their work in demythologizing the discipline, methodology or science of history, examining pedagogical aspects of history education by disseminating this through schools and mass media (responding to the needs of history educators, researchers and journalists). The purpose of this dialogue with external bodies is to shun Ukrainian ethnocentrism and to give children of different nationalities the possibility to realize their belonging to a common but diverse past.

There is a need at both school and university level to have choice within the learning of history of different historical interpretations and hypotheses, underpinned by a critical awareness of the role of myth in history but where no historical version is formulated as the only true one. Such an approach is important for teachers, textbook authors and university students. School history is transformed to become a 'site' where humanistic values and human rights (individuals' rights to life, freedom and independent opinions) are nourished. Through this citizens are nurtured who consciously choose their position, respect other people's choices and promote the aim of reaching a consensus in society – through empowering and meeting the needs of those who make up society, including parents, local community representatives and even journalists.

The image of neighbours in history textbooks became a key focus of the Ukrainian–Polish Commission. A meeting on improving school textbooks of history and geography took place in Katowice (Poland) from 25 to 28 September 2012. Its recommendations worked out the following issues: more balanced presentation of controversial issues in the history of both nations (events such as the Volyn tragedy, 1943–4; operation 'Visla', the Soviet repression of Polish people, involving expulsions in 1947; and the Katyn Massacre of 1940). It was concluded that the Ukrainian evaluation of Polish people and Ukrainian appreciation of the contribution of Polish culture to the Ukrainian culture is at a very low level. At the same time Ukrainian scholars pointed out that Ukrainian subjects in Polish textbooks are presented as fragmentary, discrete and are discussed only in connection with the world wars.

As a result of these discussions new approaches to teaching history have been introduced in the new version of the Basic and Secondary Education Standard, the sphere of 'Social Sciences'. Unlike in the previous version of the Standard, the historical and social sciences components have been clearly separated, not only in the construction of their content, but also in the way that their aims and objectives have been defined to reflect more precisely the role of history as the main identity-forming subject, which teaches students dignity, human rights and democracy, and develops their positive attitude towards common European values. According to the new Standard the following modern methodological demands have been introduced into history teaching and learning:

1. critical thinking development;
2. possibilities for various interpretations and evaluations of historical events, phenomena and processes;
3. teaching controversial and sensitive areas;
4. paying attention to everyday life history and the history of ideas;
5. combining global (European, national, regional) and local history on different levels; and
6. putting forward a 'problematic-thematic' approach to content formation.

(Cabinet of Ministry of Ukraine 2011)

The historical component of the Standard plays the leading role in forming students' identity and their sense of dignity as a result of examining the social and moral experience of previous generations as well as understanding the history and culture of Ukraine in the context of historical processes. The modern approaches to school history education have been introduced into the new version of the Standard: the 'anthropological' approach, which means making history more personal, showing historical events, phenomena and processes from the point of view of ordinary people, reducing the volume of political history with preference given to socio-economic history, everyday life history and the history of ideas – that is why this correlation should become the basis for forming the new content. Besides this there is the 'competence' approach, which means reducing the volume of knowledge for the benefit of forming students' skills and abilities. Teaching history foresees using the problematic-thematic method combined with general, thematic and deep learning, and synchronic teaching of the interconnected courses of history of Ukraine and world history. The achievement of the historical component of the Standard is its authors' aspiration for a gradual increase in demands to students' academic achievements at each stage of history education. Since this history curriculum is based on the linear-chronological principle, successive historical periods are taught in respective grades (school years) and the content load grows gradually with every year (grades 8 to 11).

In the New Standard, history education content is based on the following principles: simultaneous study of two interrelated courses – history of Ukraine and world history; linear and chronological construction of educational historical information; a problem-thematic approach to the content; multi-aspectivity, multi-perspectivity, a balanced presentation of national, regional and local history; and a combination of review, thematic and in-depth study.

External Assessment has been introduced since 2006 at the state's final testing arrangement in school and as an entrance examination for Higher Educational establishments. According to the order of the Ministry of Education and Science of Ukraine and in support of students' wishes the tested topics are the history of Ukraine from ancient times to present time and world history in the twentieth century. There are all types of test tasks: choosing the right answer; matching suitable answers; tasks with a map and sketch-map, photos, cartoons; and work with a history source, as well as the essay.

The Russian Federation

The professional history education community has been strongly divided in Russia. Many teachers, especially elderly ones, were often shocked by new information and sometimes even refused to work in high schools – although teaching twentieth-century history had before been considered to be the most prestigious part of the history teaching syllabus. At the same time many younger teachers enjoyed this new opportunity, introduced their students to new archive sources, tried to make them aware of new information and taught them how to be active history learners – this innovation in the teacher–student approach can be considered as part of the formation of civil society as many students followed the model of their teachers and later became active citizens, even if not professional historians.

In addition, NGOs played an important part in the Russian situation in the 1990s – Memorial has already been mentioned. Several history associations in Moscow, Arkhangelsk, and even Khabarovsk (on the very far eastern side of the Russian Federation) were founded and sought to connect teachers from different parts of Russia. But even in the 1990s these associations did not get any state support and thus remained isolated. They developed their own horizontal links and networks, strongly supported by EUROCLIO, connecting many committed educators from across Russia. But at the same time state policy gradually turned from 'neutral' to 'negative', which made the life of these associations extremely difficult.

The role of EUROCLIO

Between 2002 and 2005 EUROCLIO, together with the Moscow History Teachers Association, developed a project entitled *A Mosaic of Cultures*, having identified a key problem in the Russian Federation, thus:

> The Multicultural character of the Russian Federation is not reflected in the history education which has a strong Russocentric approach. History education provides no answers or understanding for the multicultural society in Russia, neither for the ethnic conflicts and tensions at hand.

To address this problem various objectives were identified, among which were:

1. To discuss openly the merits and drawbacks of national self-determination, using facts and arguments instead of myth and ideology.
2. To diminish the ethnocentric Russian approach in history education.
3. To initiate a balanced multicultural approach in Russian history education.

With the financial support of the Dutch Ministry of Foreign Affairs MATRA-Programme[4] new educational materials were published and disseminated, teachers were trained and networks were strengthened. The final report however states that 'The cooperation with the target group of history and history teacher trainers is very positive till now, although only a limited group was involved.' The civil society-based strategy to sustain the results was described thus:

> The project is mainly focusing on transferring knowledge and skills and gaining experience, both in the educational and the management field. The target group consists of educators, which are all multipliers. The professional development of teachers as a result has a long-lasting impact on their teaching, reaching out to all their pupils. The training of teacher trainers is even wider reaching. To sustain this multiplier effect the associations of history educators in Russia are also supported by developing management and organizational skills. It is envisaged that new professional associations will emerge in several of the cities where teacher training is taking place. These associations can and will continue the professional development of teachers and the dissemination of project results also after the finalization of the project.
>
> Eidelman 2005

How this was reflected in the Russian Federation

Two EUROCLIO projects, *Uroki Clio* (Clio Lessons) (1997–2000) and *Mosaics of Culture* (2003–5), showed many educators what kind of relations between NGOs and civil society should and could be. During these projects, and in great part because of them, the Moscow Teachers' Association was given support in its organization and had its best decade so far. Association members participated in seminars linked with the projects, attended EUROCLIO events, and Association board members got valuable managerial experience from EUROCLIO. The Association managed also to organize not only small events and seminars for its own members, but also attended several international conferences where educators from many countries of the former USSR made contributions. Seminars all over the country with the participation of Russian and Western experts helped teachers from different parts of Russia to know each other and to become aware of EUROCLIO activities. A lot of contacts between educators all over Russia and outside Russia were made, and it was really a 'grassroots movement' that could have developed even further with stronger links and greater organization.

But from the beginning of the 2000s the situation deteriorated. An incredible increase of red-tape procedures started to weigh heavily in many spheres of Russian society, including education. Legislation against 'foreign agents', organizations which get money from abroad, made the existence of many NGOs problematic. Congresses of teachers and teachers' associations that are sponsored, organized and ruled by the state pretend to have some kind of independence, although this is just a facade. Links between different teachers and educators in Russia still exist at an individual level, but real activity is very feeble.

Part 2: Pedagogy, democracy and dialogue – history educators try to address the challenges

How did the role of history teachers change after 1989/91?

Ukraine

Discussions about the mission of history education still continue and focus on ways that history education can be developed, the methodological principles of textbook writing, the need to approach the principles of pedagogy and the discipline and nature of history in the education of the young generation, as well as the need to address the teaching of controversial and sensitive issues related to national history memory.

The gap between the aims of history education as implemented in Standards, in the curriculum, in external assessment demands and in textbooks and the actual practice of teaching practice is obvious and should be the subject of an appropriate set of interventions. Among the challenges are the overloaded content of school history, a lack of time for the development of competences, and problems of school testing regimes based mainly on knowledge-based assessment where skills are neglected. This gap between the volume of knowledge and an absence of skills (which are nevertheless demanded for external assessment) needs to be addressed, and this requires a re-evaluation of the structures of school courses and the kinds of demands being made to support students' achievements. This situation is compounded by a lack of methodological literature, and a shortage of reported and disseminated cases of pedagogical practice addressing history-related competences development. Resistance to these stultifying factors is made more difficult by the state monopoly of in-service teacher training provision, which influences the quality of teachers' professional growth, and there is an urgent need to hold regular discipline-based and practical conferences/seminars for teachers of history to encourage innovative teaching methodology.

The demands of external assessment in history have as a prerequisite a special preparation for students, for which no additional educational time is given at school and little appropriate teacher training is available. This is important because any theoretical discussion would be useless without practical implementation in teaching. The teacher's willingness and readiness for social dialogue is very important, as well as their critical thinking, professional and civic competences, civic culture and ability to organize such a dialogue at different levels. Teachers of history should create the possibilities for the young generation to acquire competences of critical thinking, to educate citizens who evaluate the past and present of their own nation soberly, who are ready for a dialogue with others and are able to make a conscious choice and identify manipulations with consciousness.

So, taking into account modern challenges and the needs of a global multicultural information society, to prepare the youth for life in such a diverse society, education needs a flexible system of introduction to the content and methodology of history teaching, in-service teacher training, the creation of practical tools and recommendations of taking into consideration these aspects in the educational process.

Forming such abilities and the willingness to assimilate actively in situations of social change, social and political choice, and positive adaptation to changes in social environment and culture can be reached by strengthening experiences of social constructivism through the mutual completion of tasks and partnership with socially interacting participants. In this respect associations of teachers are in a position to be influential instruments of dissemination of new ideas to transform innovations into shared good practice, reaching a widening audience of teachers and students. The partnership between Nova Doba and EUROCLIO plays a significant role in the practical implementation of innovative approaches in history teaching, curriculum and textbooks. This cooperation is important because it provides opportunities for introducing high educational standards, good practice and modern approaches to evaluate practice critically, to initiate national discussions on these topical issues; and the important outcome of such seminars is the preparation of trainers, who can disseminate the knowledge and skills thus acquired at different levels in the various regions of Ukraine.

So, taking into account modern challenges and needs, and to prepare youth for life in a global multicultural and diverse information society, education needs a flexible system of introduction to the content and methodology of school history, in-service teacher training, and the creation of practical tools and recommendations for taking into consideration these aspects in the overall educational process. These new approaches to history teaching were developed in cooperation between Nova Doba and EUROCLIO and were aimed at:

1. educating students to respect basic human rights;
2. enabling school students to free themselves from stereotypes, discrimination and xenophobia towards other social, cultural and religious groups;
3. learning about alternative opinions and the language of self-expression, tolerance to others as a norm of social behaviour, about the principle of personal autonomy and fundamentals of civic solidarity;
4. teaching students how to develop a friendly attitude to others and to perceive their needs and their culture open-mindedly;
5. basing teaching and learning on the ideas of multi-perspectivity;
6. anticipating interaction between various cultures in a school, local community, country;

7. introducing students to the content and methodology of school history, in-service teacher training, practical tools and recommendations of how to incorporate all the above-mentioned objectives into the educational process (for target groups of teachers, university lectures, textbook authors, specialists of methods of in-service teacher training institutions, university students);
8. developing a tolerant approach and enabling participants to challenge public opinion in local communities to promote mutual understanding and stimulate the combating of hate language in the self-expression of mass media (the need to involve parents, local communities and journalists).

Strengthening the mission of education within a process of European cooperation reinforces the role of history education, and history educators as well as international professional non-governmental organizations such as EUROCLIO play a crucial role. EUROCLIO promotes the sound use of history education towards the building and deepening of democratic societies and therefore tries to connect across the boundaries of countries, ethnicities and religions.

In view of the above problems Nova Doba was looking to provide suitable solutions relevant to the existing social and education demands, and its activities aimed at:

1. educating students to respect basic human rights;
2. promoting tolerance for combating racism, xenophobia and other forms of discrimination; and
3. introducing innovative European approaches and a methodology of history education into the educational process.

The main goal of Nova Doba activities is to facilitate a public discussion about how the role of history in post-communist societies can be reconsidered, and to identify new opportunities for building a multicultural image of Ukrainian society based on the European democratic approach to education. In particular: to replace a traditional ethnocentric approach with new multicultural and multi-layered approaches to the development of history education, both in its content and its methods of teaching in school curricula and textbooks; to introduce innovative models of teaching and developing an open-minded education focused on the multicultural approach at the pre-service and in-service stages; and to promote the practice of engaging young people (school and university students) in various activities in local communities that will assist in developing their tolerance of and respect for social differences, as well as their civil responsibility.

Cooperation with EUSTORY (The History Network for Young Europeans) brought Ukraine solid experience in implementing activities for young people, in organizing a contest for young history researchers, *Looking Back into History*, which was aimed at encouraging students to investigate history in their nearest environment, the local community. The process of research involved considering history from different perspectives where young people would develop critical thinking and civic responsibility, promoting reconciliation and dialogue at a local level. Winners of the contest get an opportunity to participate in the international EUSTORY academies as members of the wider European network of youth researchers.

The role of Nova Doba

Thus, on the one hand, the historical memory policy and, on the other hand, the problems of curricular content overloading and the lack of teachers' competences influence the elucidation of these issues in history teaching. The solid impetus for enhancing teachers' knowledge and skills in introducing new methodology is given by informal education and NGOs. *A History of the Epoch from the Eyes of an Individual* and *Together in One Land: A Multicultural History of Ukraine* are textbooks developed by members of Nova Doba in close partnership with EUROCLIO and were aimed at meeting these challenges: (i) the conflict associated with historical memory in Ukrainian society; and (ii) bridging the gap between standards, new visions of history educators and innovative methodology, based on European approaches to history teaching.

A new Nova Doba textbook, *Together in One Land: A Multicultural History of Ukraine*, was published to help students understand the essence of a shared historical heritage of ethnic and cultural diversity in the historical dimension. The main criterion of the teaching materials is common human values (tolerance, respect for human rights, mutual understanding, solidarity, freedom, civil responsibility) aimed to help in overcoming stereotypes, prejudices, xenophobia, violence and hatred. As a result, the teaching materials laid the basis for the development of young people's critical thinking, curiosity, creativity, historical imagination and empathy. The book focused on several approaches: problem-based topics (to develop understanding of issues of multiculturalism in certain contexts); multi-perspectivity (looking at historical events from the point of view of different subjects and different historical interpretations); a multi-layered approach (different dimensions of history: ethno-social, cultural, religious, political, gender, etc.); and an intercultural approach. The problem of a dialogic approach embracing the interaction of cultures and an intercultural dialogue is the leading idea of the manual and a strand which runs throughout the whole book.

The main focus is devoted to methodological materials – a system of questions and tasks – that are intended to give formative advice on the path to the summative sections with key questions. The themes – reflecting various images of the world, cultural diversity and intercultural contacts – are presented in the content of the historical sources. The concept of organizing the manual's educational material is based on overcoming stereotypes, reinterpreting the experience of past interrelations not only of ethnic and religious communities on the territory of Ukraine, but also with the neighbouring nations. To a certain extent, this task is realized by the specialized course and manual, *New Approaches to History Education in Multicultural Environment Conditions* for students in the History subject departments of pedagogical universities.

A special focus in Nova Doba activites is given to the tragic events of the Second World War. The round tables organized by Nova Doba in 2012 and 2013 were aimed at sharing the historical experience of Central–Eastern Europe during the war. These were devoted to the Holocaust and genocides, collaboration and resistance, and were aimed at discussing the most topical issues of history and historical memory about the Second World War with special emphasis on searching for national (inside Ukraine) and international (inter-state) consensus on preserving memory about the conflict. On the basis of these round-table materials a scientific-methodological resource, *The Modern Discussion of World War II*, was written as a basis for further development of manuals for school and university education. This is the content of the three round tables.

Human rights

Human rights constitute an important aspect of historical memory about the Second World War. In 2013 Nova Doba organized a youth research contest and discussion titled *Human Rights: Lessons from the History of the Twentieth Century*. It has provided the opportunity for the young generation to extend their knowledge and ability to analyse and discuss complicated and contradictory pages of twentieth-century history from the point of view of compliance with human rights and protection of human dignity.

Sharing history – cultural dialogues

This was designed to promote mutual understanding, tolerance and intercultural dialogue through capacity-building and methodological training of informal and formal educators and their associations in the field of culture in Armenia, Azerbaijan, Georgia, Moldova and Ukraine. It sought to develop educational materials that would promote the core ideals of the project: tolerance, mutual understanding, understanding of diversity and democracy through the creation of critical thinking exercises, encouraging multi-perspective analyses of evidence and creating a learner-centred approach to cultural education.

What were the obstacles for innovation?

Although Ukraine has quite a modern curriculum for history education which is in accordance with international guidelines, it is hardly implemented at the classroom level. The key problems preventing this are lack of time and overloaded curricula, and as a result the inability to reach the level required by evaluation criteria; decreasing students' motivation for study, focus on 'factual knowledge' (as required by 'IIE' – internal independent evaluation), and fragmented work with documents or other original sources, which depends on the professional level and motivation of individual teachers. The task of developing critical thinking is not realized in practice because of the unpreparedness of most teachers to teach controversial and sensitive issues (despite the efforts and successes of informal education). In senior grades political and military history prevails. Little attention is paid to aspects of everyday life history, 'a human being in history', including such factors as gender etc. There is a lack of special courses in history, and an introduction to new methodologies needs to be provided. The existence of the state order for educational literature contributes to the absence of free competition for textbooks. There are not enough instructional materials for teaching history (sets of texts, audio and video materials, albums, illustrated guides in history of culture, science and technology, collection of videos – feature and documentary films, TV programmes, etc.).

Russia

History teachers at the time of perestroika (initially 1985 to 1987 and continuing under the presidency of Mikhail Gorbachev[5]) became really important people. The history teacher has always been considered as an influential person in education. In Soviet times it was usually an ideological job, and history teachers were supposed to be party members – often they were heads of the school-based (communist) party organization, and often a history teacher could eventually become a headteacher, and in the 1980s history teachers in many schools could bring the spirit of perestroika into classrooms. At a time when political discussions and clubs were organized at schools, when impressive new material became available for teachers as well as for students, the role of the history teacher became more and more important.

Many history teachers have proved to be capable not only of teaching but also of organizing their students' activities in connection with history – for example historical competitions such as those organized by Körber Stiftung and the Moscow History Association, by Memorial, by the Moscow History Teachers Association, by *Uchitelskaya Gaseta* (the teachers' newspaper), and by other organizations showed that many teachers and their students were and are still interested not only in exam results, but also in understanding modern Russian history, in studying the histories of their families and connecting these to the history of the country.

Teachers who participated in the *Uroki Clio* and in the *Mosaics of Culture* projects (Crijns 2005; Eidelman 2005), stressed that their students were usually happy to approach history in an innovative way and to discover that history is not only about facts, but is also a great field for intellectual activity. At the same time, we should sadly admit that at the moment history teachers in Russia cannot be proud of their role. Many of them are responsible and creative and do wonderful work. But the whole situation is not favourable for teachers as leaders. Low salaries, constant bureaucratic pressure, social disrespect, long working hours, burdensome responsibilities and the constant fear of dismissal all make most teachers just people who prepare students for final exams.

When state exams became compromised by constant charges of corruption, teachers lost the last vestiges of their prestige. If answers to state exams can be bought, there is no reason for students to care about their classes. Social websites have shown several videos where students humiliate and even beat their teachers. Of course, there are still great schools and impressive personalities among history teachers, but the situation is desperate. It becomes increasingly difficult for good teachers to teach, and even more difficult for teachers to play a role in the social life of their communities. Teachers have been used in recent years to support the most demeaning and disgusting state actions to falsify election results (as many teachers are traditionally members of election committees). When the state organizes a pro-governmental meeting, or an anti-Ukrainian march, teachers (along with other state-paid workers) are made to participate. Special orders are sent to schools, dictating how many teachers should turn out at these so-called 'people's events'. It all shows that teachers are being treated by governmental bodies as really insignificant people. Teachers do not have any powerful organization. The independent trade union 'Teacher' is a small association and several teachers have already encountered problems because of their membership. The Moscow Teachers' Association has no resources and no official help, as any organization which wants to be influential now in Russia needs state support.

Education in general in Russia is in great danger at the moment, which makes teachers' place in society even more problematic than usual. Still, if anything good can happen here it will not happen without the participation of responsible and creative teachers, who – it must be stressed – are still present in Russian education.

Conclusion: where history is not history but the present – a responsible community of educators

In Ukraine the processes of research, preservation and teaching history serve a crucial role in the development of public opinion and civic culture. In fact, history is often the tool for politics and serves in an environment of xenophobia and human rights violations. Accordingly, strengthening the role of civil society in promoting human rights, democratic reforms and peaceful reconciliation are the specific objectives for which educational initiatives are needed to promote tolerance and mutual understanding through history education.

Despite the success of informal education, most teachers are not ready to teach controversial issues. Thus, on the one hand, the historical memory policy and, on the other hand, the problems of curriculum content overloading and lack of teachers' competences influence the elucidation of these issues in history teaching.

Forming the ability and willingness to be involved in the active assimilation of situations leading to social change, social and political choice, as well as positive adaptation to changes in the social and cultural environment, can be reached by strengthening situations where there is mutual completion of tasks and the setting up of grassroots partnerships of socially interacting participants.

In early 2011, Nova Doba and the Petro Jacyk Programme for the Study of Modern Ukrainian History and Society created 'Historical Initiative' – a public movement of professional historians and teachers of history from all regions of Ukraine that strives for historical reconciliation through dialogue and cooperation with professional historians, teachers, mass media and all active and responsible citizens of Ukraine (Ukrainian Pravda: Historical Pravda 2011). To that effect, this group planned several meetings and the preparation of new textbooks. And since the memory of the Second World War is the most divisive topic in Ukraine, this issue has had to be specifically addressed, in cooperation with the academic community of the neighbouring and the EU countries.

One year has now passed since the tragic events not only in Kiev at Euromaidan but also in different cities and villages of Ukraine where Yanukovych's powers killed people protesting for their right to live in a free democratic country. Euromaidan proved the will of the young generation of Ukraine to defend democratic values, and Ukrainians paid a high price for exercising this freedom of choice. The war in Ukraine is the next step in defending Ukrainians' sovereignty while Putin's regime is attempting to hamper democratic development in Ukraine. War is a new phenomenon which has invaded people's lives. This war has been waged by the Kremlin in significant and new ways: Putin's measures of influence in Ukraine have taken the form of hybrid war supported by an information war.

These are extremely influential means which influence the consciousness of vulnerable Eastern Ukrainians who have tighter contacts with Russia, but who, like other post-Soviet citizens, are experiencing not only difficult problems with choices but also disorientation caused by the propaganda conditions. The construction of historical myths plays an influential role in the way that propaganda is used.

Thus responsible history educators are of paramount importance in both Ukrainian and Russian societies. The Ukrainian community distinguishes between democratic-minded Russians, who support peace and recognize Putin's aggression in Ukraine, and Russians who are victims of propaganda disseminated by the Kremlin media for Putin's regime which is not only leading the war in Ukraine but also supporting terrorism and aggression, using the language and weapons of hate.

In February 2015 Nova Doba organized seminars in different regions of Ukraine (Dnipropetrovsk, Odessa, Kharkiv, Poltava, Kiev, Ternopil, Kherson, Lviv, Bila Tserkva, Vinnytsya, Chernivtsi, Sumy, Mykolaiv, Ivano-Frankivsk and Cherkassy) aimed at strengthening professional networks and communication, supporting the process of mutual understanding and reconciliation in Ukrainian society. The organization was deeply impressed by their desire to communicate, to learn and understand the situation, and their willingness to solve the problems.

As an outcome of Nova Doba's communication with teachers from different regions many questions were raised, such as:

1. how to work with students arriving from war regions;
2. how to overcome the difficulties in relationships between students from different regions in one class;
3. how to encourage a sense of positive identity and stimulate an integration process;
4. what is the responsibility of teachers in this difficult period?

The ideas presented through the workshops and the associated developed materials were those of critical thinking, multi-perspectivity, intercultural dialogue, tolerance, integration and respect for different opinions. These ideas are not only welcome, but also appear to be like a breath of fresh air for professionals today.

Responsible networking at grassroots level is the best means of taking action against violence and war. The community of history educators should unite their efforts against war, terrorism, propaganda and hate, proposing effective tools based on new methodologies in history education and European values. That is why the role of European institutions – the Council of Europe, EUROCLIO, EUSTORY – have become of great importance. The integration of professional communities and the introduction of democratic ideas into classrooms are our answers and our contribution to the stability and democratic sustainability of Europe. In spite of challenges the history community all over the world should be united, especially the Ukrainian and Russian community, in supporting democratic values, integration and freedom as the fundamental values of a democratic society.

Finally we would underline the strategy of EUROCLIO as being right because its association has not been restricted by the membership of the EU and it is disseminating innovative and democratic teaching strategies all over the world.

Notes

1 Nova Doba represents all Ukraine and its full title is 'Nova Doba – the All-Ukrainian Association of Teachers of History and Civic Education'. *Nova doba* in Ukrainian literally means 'new era'.
2 Victor Yanukovych relinquished power in February 2014.
3 The theme of number 24 of the weekly newspaper, *Arguments and Facts*, was 'What should be the ideal Russia?
4 MATRA is a Netherlands bilateral assistance programme. MATRA stands for **Ma**atschappelijke **Tra**nsformatie (Social Transformation). It is a Funding Programme of the Dutch Ministry of Foreign Affairs which was aimed at supporting social transformation in the formerly communist and socialist countries of Europe, among others, through education. EUROCLIO has received funding for various projects related to this programme.
5 Mikhail Gorbachev was General Secretary of the Central Committee of the Communist Party of the Soviet Union from 11 March 1985 to 24 August 1991; he was President of the Soviet Union from 15 March 1990 to 25 December 1991. 'Perestroika means restructuring'.

References

Cabinet of Ministry of Ukraine (2011), *The Decree of the Cabinet of Ministry of Ukraine on Approval of the State Standard of Basic and Full General Secondary Education*, 23 November, No. 1392, Kiev. Available online: http://zakon.nau.ua/doc/?uid=1053.24.0 (accessed 24 July 2015).

Crijns, H. (2005), *EUROCLIO Matra Project: Mosaic of Cultures, Final Report*, The Hague: EUROCLIO.

Eidelman, T. (ed.) (2005), *EUROCLIO Matra Project: Mosaic of Cultures, Teaching the Multicultural Society in Russia, Educational Materials*, The Hague: EUROCLIO.

Kasyanov, H. (2011), 'Our Textbooks are the Subject of Ideological Manipulation', in D. Rybakov (ed.), *Why and How to Rewrite the History of Ukraine*. Available online: http://www.istpravda.com.ua/articles/2011/01/31/20201/ (accessed 9 February 2015).

Nova Doba (2012a), *Modern Discussions on World War Two*, Lviv: Western-Ukrainian Publishing House. Available online: http://www.novadoba.org.ua/ukr/contemporary-debates-book (accessed 9 March 2015).

Nova Doba (2012b), *Together in One Land: A Multicultural History of Ukraine*, Lviv: Western-Ukrainian Publishing House. Available online: www.novadoba.org.ua/together-on-the-same-land-book (accessed 9 March 2015).

Nova Doba (2013), *Sharing History: Cultural Dialogue*, Lviv: Western-Ukrainian Publishing House. Available online: http://www.novadoba.org.ua/ukr/common-history-book (accessed 9 March 2015).

Nova Doba and EUROCLIO (2004), *History of the Epoch through the Eyes of an*

Individual: Ukraine and Europe in the First Half of the 20th Century, Kiev: Nova Doba and EUROCLIO. One chapter can be found online: http://www.forumhistoriae.sk/euroclio/documents/how/01_How_to_work_with_textual_sources.pdf (accessed 9 March 2015).

Nova Doba and the Fund of Democratic Initiatives (DIF) (2008), 'A survey of school leavers', 10 December. Available online: http://dif.org.ua/ua/polls/2008_polls/rovesniki-nezalezhnoi-ukraini-dumki_-interesi_-gromadjanski-pozicii.htm (accessed 27 July 2015).

Petranovskaya, L. (2014), Blog entry, 28 June. Available online: http://ludmilapsyholog.livejournal.com/235045.html (accessed 9 March 2015).

Shigareva, J. (2013), 'Karen Shakhnazarov: "Enough to Drag Everything from the West – it's Time to Live your Mind"', *Arguments and Facts* 24, 6 December. Available online: http://www.aif.ru/society/44159 (accessed 14 March 2015).

українська правда: історична правда [Ukrainian Pravda: Historical Pravda] (2011), '28 українських істориків заявляють, що "не віддадуть" минуле та майбутнє України в руки політиків [28 Ukrainian historians claim that [we should] "not give" the past and future of Ukraine into the hands of politicians]', 24 January. Available online: http://www.istpravda.com.ua/short/2011/01/24/17727 (accessed 31 July 2015).

Yakovenko, N. (2008), 'The Image of Self: The Image of the Other in School History Textbooks', in N. Yakovenko (ed.), *School History through the Eyes of Scholars–Historians*, 64–81, Kiev: Olena Teliha Publishing House.

3

Republic of Ireland and Northern Ireland: Eroded Certainties and New Possibilities

Fionnuala Waldron and Alan McCully

Introduction

Since the nineteenth century history teaching in Ireland has been buffeted by political turbulence and conflict. From a common base under British rule, partition in 1921–2 led to divergence as each jurisdiction, the Irish Free State and Northern Ireland respectively, sought to consolidate statehood through fostering the allegiance of their young. In such circumstances the messages were of conformity and certainty, with little room for those who questioned the legitimacy of each state from within. From the second decade of the last century each territory followed a separate path governed by its own, frequently oppositional, political prerogatives. It is only in the last thirty years or so, when stability on the island was again threatened by violent forces, that common purpose has resurfaced in curriculum policy, including the teaching of history. Thus, traumatic events associated with conflict and its aftermath have challenged old certainties and, prompted by the recognition that conflict-sensitive education which contributes to peace-building requires real engagement with politics and the psychology of conflict, there has been a move on both sides of the border towards a more inclusive canon and pluralities of histories. The desire for reconciliation emanating from the Northern Ireland peace process, allied to greater political maturity in government and the influence of global educational trends, have converged in ways which open up possibilities for creative synergy between the northern and southern history education communities (McCully and Waldron 2013). This chapter briefly traces these developments but then examines the implications for history teaching's extrinsic aims – its aspirations to contribute to societal change and the consequent implications for its relationship with the democratic citizenship programmes which exist within the curricula, north and south. Finally, it asks whether the current focus on the local dimensions of post-conflict community relations in existing curricula needs to be broadened to meet the global challenges of the twenty-first century.

Politics and transnational dimensions: divergence, convergence and eroded certainties

Prior to partition Ireland's national system of education was overseen by a National Board. The original multi-denominational character envisaged for its structures at its establishment in 1831 had long since given way to denominational interests but the Board continued to control the curriculum offered in all its schools through approved textbooks. Initially excluded on the grounds that objectivity was problematic, history (local, British and Irish) was introduced in 1900 using sanctioned texts. Despite tensions in the revolutionary period after the 1916 rebellion the Revised Programme remained in place until partition in 1921–2 (Coolahan 1981; McCully and Waldron 2013: 146).

Partition represents an obvious watershed in that education was reconstituted under two systems premised on different political ideologies and religious identifications. In the Free State the system slipped quite seamlessly into the sphere of influence of the Catholic Church. In Northern Ireland the Church resisted the new government's initial moves to centralize and move towards a multi-denominational approach. Opposition from the Protestant churches also emerged, ensuring that, structurally, the education system was organized on clear sectarian lines. Ideologically, then, the two fledgling jurisdictions in Ireland were bound to go their separate ways, but politically they had similar priorities. Both were new entities born out of violent upheaval and both faced enemies from without and within. Therefore, both conceived of education, and history teaching, as a way of generating loyalty by closing ranks around their respective dominant identities.

In the south the teaching of history was essentially a state-building project, particularly in the context of primary education. Prior to the introduction of free post-primary education in the 1960s, the majority of children completed their compulsory schooling in national primary schools. The primary sector, therefore, presented the best opportunity for the realization of that distinctively Gaelic identity on which the foundational 'imagined community' of the Irish Free State was premised (Anderson 1991; O'Callaghan 2009: 19). In general, national curricula during this period were characterized by cultural nationalism (Coolahan 1981). At primary level in particular, the revival of the Irish language was prioritized and Irish became the medium of instruction for subjects such as history, even in areas where it was not children's first language. Thus, the conflation of Irish identity with both the Irish language and with Catholicism was inherent in the nationalist ideology which permeated the primary curriculum (McCully and Waldron 2013: 149–50). The post-primary sector in the Free State was small in size, private and denominational. While the history curriculum was broadly consistent with the political agenda of Gaelicization, O'Callaghan (2011) argues that the Catholic ideology that dominated the sector was even more influential. While these curricula and practices were contested for their inherent sectarianism and nationalistic bias, criticism of the system had little effect prior to the 1960s (McCully and Waldron 2013; Jones 1992; Doherty 1996).

From the outset the northern state's priorities were to contain the nationalist threat to its existence. It used its power over finance, school structures and curriculum to promote positive attitudes towards the United Kingdom and to guard against potential nationalist agitation in schools under the influence of the Catholic Church; in time, its social policy, including education, was focused on gaining parity with the rest of the UK. History education, an option only in the final three years of elementary education, but a compulsory component of secondary provision, raised a dilemma. There was a desire to expose children to an 'Ulster as British' narrative but also unease that emphasis on a local dimension might legitimize the claim from Catholic schools to teach about Ireland's past. Consequently, a watching eye was kept on the endorsement of suitable textbooks, while in the primary school a lack of attention to history was more desirable than encouraging teaching which might be subverted by a nationalist agenda. In the north, too, there were occasional voices of dissent emanating either from the nationalist community or from those with premonitions that the deeply partisan and partial histories learned in the street were an ingredient for trouble in the future (McCully and Waldron 2013: 145–6).

Landmarks with questions? From the single to the plural

North of the border there was no prescribed statutory curriculum prior to the outbreak of violence in the late 1960s, or indeed until 1991. This, perhaps, gave schools some leeway to pursue their own agendas with regard to history teaching at primary and lower secondary levels. However, the dominant influence of external examination syllabi at ages fourteen, sixteen and eighteen which concentrated on European and British history ensured that learning remained content-focused and that Irish history was often marginalized. In the early years of the Troubles, when concerned educators sought to address communal division through the formal curriculum, it was frequently history teaching that was placed under the spotlight. There was a strong perception that it had been used by both communities in their respective segregated school systems, in one way or another, to prop up dominant and exclusive group identities (Magee 1970). Mutually exclusive identities between the unionist and nationalist populations were acknowledged as at least one major driver of conflict, and references to historical events were often used to illuminate past wrongs or justify actions in the present (Walker 1996). Influenced by exciting developments taking place in England, committed history educators saw the potential for adapting the Schools Council History Project's emphasis on the subject as a disciplinary process to enable teachers in Northern Ireland to take a more objective and enquiry-based approach to contentious issues in history (McCully, forthcoming). This emphasis on process, cognition and objectivity was carried through to the introduction of the first, statutory Northern Ireland Curriculum in 1991, which succeeded in ensuring that for the first time all primary and secondary pupils would address common aspects of Irish history. The 5–14 history curriculum was structured to allow primary pupils to gain an understanding of history as evidence-based, and open to different perspectives and interpretations, through studying largely benign aspects of family and social history. In turn, these could then be applied to increasingly contentious issues from Ireland's past as students progressed through secondary school.

The work of Barton (2001a, 2001b) and Barton and McCully (2005, 2007, 2012) indicates that a multi-perspective, disciplinary approach had strengths not only in opening students to alternative viewpoints but also in signalling the limitations as to how far this moved them beyond their dominant community positions. There was frustration on the part of the curriculum authorities (Council for Curriculum, Education and Assessment (CCEA) 1996) that learning in history continued to be too content-driven and that teachers were not exploring its potential for impact on community attitudes. This led to more explicit guidelines in which aspects such as the relationship between history and national identity were given greater emphasis. Generally, even innovative teachers were more comfortable with the cognitive aspects of the disciplinary approach than making direct connections between the past and contemporary cultural and political issues (Kitson 2007).

In the Republic, reform of the history curriculum began in the mid-1960s with the establishment of a Study Group on the Teaching of History in 1966 by the government of the day; the ensuing recommendations included a focus on historical concepts and processes, on the link between past and present and on the inclusion of social, economic and local history. Informed by a broader project of modernization, which linked the economic future of the country to the quality of its education system, the state agenda in education went beyond a consideration of history and, over the course of five years, included structural reform at post-primary level and the launch of a new Primary School Curriculum in 1971. Premised on the principles of constructivism and underpinned by a child-centred ideology, the 'new curriculum', as it was colloquially termed, located history, along with geography, civics and elementary science, in the context of a broader subject of Social and Environmental Studies (Department of Education (DoE) 1971: 87). While Tormey (2006) characterized the 1971 curriculum as continuing to draw on the rhetoric of 'virtuous patriotism', there is also evidence of a broader conceptualization of history and an emergent focus on the process of historical investigation through 'exploration and discovery' and through an emphasis on project work (DoE 1971: 87, 92). Despite these reforms, however, and notwithstanding some increase in project-based work, traditional teaching approaches continued to dominate practice, resulting in textbook-led teaching and little engagement with the local environment or with historical sources (Motherway 1986; Irish National Teachers Organisation 1996).

Nonetheless, the beginning of the Troubles in Northern Ireland in the late 1960s had thrown the nationalist rhetoric and ethnocentrism associated with history teaching in the south since the foundation of the state into sharp relief. Although attempts were made to progress a reform agenda at primary level through the creation of guidelines for textbook publishers, real change at curricular level did not occur until the 1990s, when the Republic entered a period of educational reform (McCully and Waldron 2013). The Primary History Curriculum (National Council for Curriculum and Assessment (NCCA) 1999a) that emerged from that process incorporated the southern state's response to a range of influences, educational, political and ideological. Similar to developments in Northern Ireland, the curriculum, which is still in use, was strongly influenced by enquiry-based approaches emanating from the UK. Conceptualized as 'working as a historian' (NCCA 1999a) it emphasizes engagement with historical sources, the development of historical concepts, recognition of multiple perspectives and the provisional and constructed nature of historical knowledge.

Understanding how the past has influenced the present is a key objective of the curriculum, including how past events have shaped current attitudes and behaviours (NCCA 1999a: 13). Unlike the NI primary curriculum, and consistent with its historic practice, the southern curriculum includes a focus on political history in the later years of primary when the key 'landmarks' of Irish and European history are introduced. Yet, while the familiar canon of national history characteristic of earlier curricula is evident, it is premised on an ideological frame which embraces the idea of multiple perspectives and identities, and promotes openness to and respect for others (McCully and Waldron 2013; Ross and Faas 2012; Tormey 2006; Waldron 2004). Described by Waldron (2004) as 'relentlessly post-nationalist' (217) and by Tormey (2006) as 'globalised' (312), the 1999 history curriculum can be seen as embodying the Irish state's educational response to the peace process and to the globalization and increased diversification of Irish society characteristic of the Celtic Tiger period of the mid to late 1990s. It recognized the challenge both processes presented to historic presumptions of cultural homogeneity on the island (McCully and Waldron 2013).

While history has been a compulsory subject at primary level since the foundation of the southern state, at post-primary level it has been compulsory for the majority of schools in the initial phase of schooling to Intermediate or, latterly, Junior Certificate examination level only, after which it is subject to student choice. The effect of this has been that most students studied history to the age of fifteen years, after which approximately 17 to 18 per cent continue its study to Leaving Certificate level (Department of Education and Skills (DES) 2014). Constrained by a systemic focus on state examinations, curricular reform at post-primary level has been limited (Coolahan 1981: 135). The first major reform occurred during the 1980s with the introduction of the Junior Certificate syllabus in 1989, which endorsed a 'new history' approach, focusing on the development of historical skills and concepts and on the role of evidence in the construction of historical knowledge (Crowley 1990). The syllabus, however, showed little evidence of the explicit engagement with issues of identity evident in the primary curriculum (McCully and Waldron 2013). More recently, efforts to 'rebalance' the history curriculum (NCCA 2008) have been overtaken by a more fundamental reform of the Junior Cycle outlined below. At senior level, reform has seen an increased emphasis on disciplinary-based procedural knowledge, with the introduction of document-based work and individual source-based research projects in the most recent revision of the syllabus (DES/NCCA 2004).

In summary then, over recent decades the teaching of history at primary level in the Republic of Ireland has undergone significant reform in response to a range of key influences: the critical interrogation of the dominant nationalist narrative in the context of the Troubles and the emerging peace process; the increasing diversification and globalization of Irish society, which challenged notions of cultural homogeneity and of singular and fixed identities; and new ideas in history education which saw children as actively engaged in the construction of knowledge rather than as passive learners of received narratives. While reform of the subject at post-primary level has been more gradualist and constrained, the historically dominant ideologies of nationalism and Catholicism have long been replaced by a commitment to the study of history as an academic discipline. In Northern Ireland the commitment to a disciplinary approach at all levels came a little earlier, partially stimulated by the same constructivist educational trends at work south of the border. Here, its potential to generate alternative perspectives was both a strength and a constraint. While embraced at policy level, the sensitivities of a divided and violent society meant that many teachers shied away from the harder challenges it posed, leaving the 'risk-takers' to occupy the contested space of history's contemporary relevance (Barton and McCully 2007; Kitson and McCully 2005; Kitson 2007).

Recently, for both parts of the island, the contemporary relevance of history has been heightened by the politics of commemoration. The period from 2012 to 2022 in Ireland has been named the 'decade of centenaries' as it represents a period during which key historical events associated with the Irish struggle for independence and the First World War will reach their centennial years. The decade has been identified as significant in terms of promoting discussion on identity, conflict and reconciliation in the context of the ongoing peace process and prompting renewed critical engagement with these events and their legacies. In an educational context, much of this work resides at the nexus between history and citizenship education and requires a strong, dynamic and sustained relationship between the two subjects. How ready is either jurisdiction for this engagement?

Pedagogy, democracy and dialogue: history, citizenship and post-conflict Ireland

The relationship between history and citizenship is well documented, if somewhat contested (for example Wrenn 1999; Arthur et al. 2001; Lee and Shemilt 2007). Although Lee and Shemilt (2007: 15), for example, argue that the case for a 'more systematic relationship between history and citizenship is compelling', they nonetheless see that relationship as potentially problematic, while Harris (2011: 186) describes them as 'uncomfortable bedfellows'. Lee and Shemilt (2007) put forward three potential relational models, i.e.:

1. the cornucopian model (where history's intrinsic contribution to citizenship needs no further elaboration);
2. the carrier model (where history content is chosen for its potential to meet the needs of citizenship); and
3. the complementary model (where history's unique contribution to citizenship lies in the development of historical consciousness, which includes temporal orientation).

Drawing on the theories of Jörn Rüsen, the capacity to orient in time (seen by Rüsen (2005) as the 'practical function' of historical thinking) supports an understanding of the 'contingency and fragility' of democratic structures and culture (Lee and Shemilt 2007: 18). For Barton and Levstik (2004), the relationship between history and citizenship is more fundamental. Closer to, but going beyond the idea of a 'carrier' relationship, education for democratic citizenship provides the justification for history's place on school curricula in the first instance, supporting the development of 'reasoned judgement about human affairs', 'an expanded view of humanity' and 'deliberation over the common good' (2004: 36–40).

The potential synergy between history and citizenship education is illuminated further by Davies (in Arthur et al. 2001) when he identifies three key connections between the subjects at the level of curriculum design; these are the knowledge dimension, the development of skills of enquiry and communication, and skills of participation and responsible action (Arthur et al. 2001: 29–43).

Davies sees history's knowledge contribution as focusing on first order conceptual understanding, allowing students to grasp the historical context of ideas such as democracy, communism and human rights. History should help students to grasp the evolution of government and political life and provide a background in national history. Thus they are better placed to understand the contemporary political world. History's second contribution is through the development of enquiry and communication skills underpinning the disciplinary approach. These he regards as essential for the young person to engage in critical decision-making. As regards the third contribution, that of skills of participation and responsible action, history can provide insight into effective (and ineffective) actions in the past, for example in relation to the abolition of slavery or the campaign for factory reform. Students might also be directly engaged around community interpretations and memorializations of past events, thus developing and refining historical consciousness as envisaged by Lee and Shemilt (2007).

The relational models put forward by Lee and Shemilt (2007), combined with the three key dimensions of learning indicated by Davies (in Arthur et al. 2001) provide a productive lens through which the relationship between history and citizenship at curricular level in Ireland, north and south, can be viewed.

Citizenship and history education in Northern Ireland

As already outlined, the evolution of the history and citizenship curricula in Northern Ireland over the last forty-five years has taken place in very particular circumstances. First there was the context of a divided society experiencing communal violence and, more latterly, a post-agreement society struggling to emerge from conflict. Educational responses to conflict in Northern Ireland have been documented in detail elsewhere (Gallagher 2004; Richardson and Gallagher 2011) but, inevitably, history and citizenship education, as two areas of the curriculum directly impinging on the political, cultural and social attitudes at the core of division, were bound to be shaped, at least to an extent, by the prevailing tensions in the wider community.

There was no explicit tradition of citizenship education in Northern Ireland prior to the Good Friday Peace Agreement, 1998, even in the more restricted guise of informing young people of political processes through civic education. Aside from history, when addressing communal division in the early years of the conflict, attention usually focused on extra-curricular activities involving relationship-building through cross-community contact and prejudice reduction.

Two curricular initiatives specifically directed at addressing conflict did emerge in the 1970s, supported by both philanthropic and state funding. These were the Schools' Curriculum Project (SCP), led by John Malone and based at Queen's University, Belfast, and the Schools' Cultural Studies Project (SCSP), initiated by Malcolm Skilbeck at the New University of Ulster, Coleraine (Skilbeck 1973; Crone and Malone 1979; Robinson 1983; McCully and Emerson 2014). Both had a radical edge. Malone, a former headteacher, argued for the creation of classroom materials on a range of local and related international issues as the basis for young people discussing sensitive issues on a cross-community basis. Skilbeck's SCSP produced a clear curricular model for addressing social division through a reconstructionist framework. He argued for 'the renewal of the school curriculum directed towards the sensitive and vital areas of attitude formation, values and moral-civic behaviour' (Skilbeck 1973). Neither initiative shirked tough conversations which tackled community divisions. The SCSP, particularly, had been underpinned by principles of enquiry and evidence drawn from the social sciences but was more driven by the imperative of improving individual and group relationships, and challenging the use of violence as a political tool, than overtly fostering the concept of citizenship. Unfortunately, the work of the SCP and the SCSP failed to find a secure place within most traditionally oriented schools of the time. Indeed, to date, any experimental programmes which have sought to raise controversial social issues in Northern Ireland have struggled either to fit into existing subject boundaries or to create new space. Thus, they have lacked status in the eyes of teachers and, often, students (O'Connor and Niens 2009).

A policy outcome did arise from the groundswell of practitioner commitment to community relations work in the formal education sector. When a statutory Northern Ireland Curriculum (NIC) was introduced in 1991, two of its cross-curricular themes were Education for Mutual Understanding (EMU) and Cultural Heritage. (The two were 'conjoined' in 1996.) The former was important in that it brought the language of community relations into the mainstream curriculum for the first time and impressed on all schools and teachers that they had responsibilities in this area (Smith and Robinson 1996). However, this broad cross-curricular approach was a weakness in that the priorities of subject teaching inevitably trumped obligations to examine objectives such as 'cultural understanding' or 'understanding conflict'. Further, EMU was essentially about relationship-building and was frequently compartmentalized as engaging in cross-community contact outside the formal curriculum (even though this was not a statutory aspect of its provision) (Smith and Robinson 1996; Smith 2003: 8; Arlow 2004: 282–3; Richardson and Gallagher 2011). In fairness, EMU did impact on NIC History more than on other subjects, not least in the inclusion of key aspects of Ireland's past and the importance placed on considering 'points of view' and empathetic understanding (Department of Education Northern Ireland (DENI) 1991).

Smith's critique of EMU coincided with a resurgence of interest in citizenship education at international and national levels. The Council of Europe was taking an active role in promoting democratic citizenship in the countries of eastern and central Europe emerging from the communist bloc. The Civic, Social and Political Education (CSPE) programme in the Republic (see below) and the Crick Report (Qualifications and Curriculum Authority (QCA) 1998), a catalyst for a statutory citizenship initiative in England, provided further impetus. At home the Good Friday Agreement, 1998[1] made it an imperative that society move away from violence towards sustainable democratic politics. Smith (2003) advocated a civic education programme which dealt with underlying social inequalities, examined issues through the lens of social justice and allowed young people to explore the complexities of contested national identities in the context of cultural pluralism. He argued for a timetabled political education programme underpinned by a human rights framework – and recommended that this should be accompanied by opportunities for young people to develop historical understanding of the nature of conflict in Northern Ireland.

Over the next few years his initial ideas went through several iterations before Local and Global Citizenship was incorporated within the revised NIC in 2007 (Arlow 2004; CCEA 2007). The latter marks a radical shift from what preceded it. Its 'Big Picture' structure puts emphasis on broader areas of study beyond individual subject disciplines. It is outcomes-based and stresses the importance of making connections across the curriculum to ensure that students' learning is a holistic experience (CCEA 2007). In the primary school pupils follow Personal Development and Mutual Understanding (PDMU). This integrates a foundational citizenship strand with health issues, personal development and relationship-building, though with some opportunity in the latter years to explore potentially contentious community issues. Local and Global Citizenship operates at secondary level. It is structured around a conceptual framework – Diversity and Inclusion, Equality and Social Justice, Democracy and Active Participation and Human Rights and Social Responsibility – and places emphasis on active and participatory learning and teaching approaches. The global dimension is an important addition in encouraging young people to see beyond the parameters of Northern Ireland. It allows core concepts to be explored in a range of contexts and opens students up to 'multiple citizenship' (Heater 1999: 115–54).

The progress of Local and Global Citizenship since its inception has been mixed. As with citizenship initiatives in other jurisdictions it has wrestled with issues of status at the implementation stage. An evaluation in 2009 reported that it had positively influenced pupils' confidence, attitudes, values, skills and behaviours in relation to citizenship issues and raised expectations of democratic practice in schools. However, the report also highlighted failures: to provide real opportunities for active pupil engagement; to appreciate wider aims and purposes; and to map the potential contribution of all subjects to exploit professional collaboration and networking (O'Connor and Niens 2009: 12).

The status issue is a significant barrier. Arguably, by placing citizenship education at Key Stage 3 (aged 11–14) within the Learning for Life and Work area of study as a strand alongside Personal, Social and Health Education and Employability, it became identified as on the fringe of the curriculum. The original intention was to position it in Environment and Society in relationship with history and geography, two subjects with which it has clear knowledge links. O'Connor and Niens (2009: 11) point to the positives of drawing on a committed teacher base from a wide range of backgrounds, including the creative arts, but this can also result in reluctant conscripts with little aptitude for the challenge. It is argued that a deficit in teacher knowledge has led to a corresponding lack of rigour in student learning (McCully and Emerson 2014). The

Education and Training Inspectorate report that the expectations, generally, in relation to interconnected learning have yet to be realized and citizenship education has not become the fulcrum for interdisciplinary work that was initially envisaged (CCEA 2007). Consequently, the potentially close relationship between history and citizenship has not been fully explored.

History in the NIC seems well positioned to interact positively with Local and Global Citizenship education. While its revised 2007 incarnation continues to promote the expectation that aspects of contemporarily relevant Irish history will be studied in depth it has both freed up content selection to encourage innovative choices and has significantly strengthened its extrinsic objectives to prepare young people to be 'contributors to society' (CCEA 2007). For instance, in pursuit of this, students are required to investigate how history has affected personal identity, culture and lifestyle; how it has been selectively interpreted to promote stereotyping; how it has been used and abused to justify particular views and actions; and how historical figures have behaved ethically, or unethically, in the past. Yet positioned against Davies's three indicators the picture is mixed. First, there is little evidence that citizenship and history teachers plan together to map and exploit the obvious knowledge conduit between them. Second, more positively, history teachers, despite limitations in practice, do endeavour to promote critical and discursive thinking and are conscious that these attributes have utility beyond the history classroom. Third, with reference to skills of participation and responsible action, some departments have used the freedom of the new curriculum to align their subject content to aspects of the past, like the US Civil Rights movement, that illustrate human agency to effect change – and, particularly in the context of the First World War, interesting work is emerging which explores different community perspectives on remembrance and commemoration. However, the explicit linking of past with present to explore contemporary relevance is only slowly developing.

The lack of symmetry features at both primary and secondary levels. In primary history pupils are unlikely to meet political ideas in any shape or form (McCully and Waldron 2013). In history, generally, not enough emphasis is placed on content areas which exemplify the evolution of democratic government and practices and, indeed, students are more likely to encounter democratic inadequacies as illustrated by the Weimar Republic and the Northern Irish state between 1921 and 1972. As critical historical study this is healthy, but it is also important that students are motivated by those in the past who have pursued the common good (Barton and Levstik 2004). Although there is no obligation to do so, schools usually restrict themselves to national and European topics, rarely exploring aspects like the legacy of empire, thus limiting the contribution history might make to the global dimension of citizenship. In the other direction, the citizenship curriculum, influenced by the legacy of conflict, concentrates on issues of equality and social justice, and the causes, implications and prevention of sectarianism and racism. Students are encouraged to express views and even take forms of direct action but there is little attention paid to the structures and dynamics in which formal politics operates. In England the Crick Report insisted that the citizenship programme had a 'political literacy' strand. Crick defined this as 'pupils learning about how to make themselves effective in public life through knowledge, skills and values' (QCA 1998). As Wrenn (in Arthur et al. 2001: 70–87) points out, to become an effective citizen you must go 'beyond knowledge' to understand that knowledge in action. The omission of a similar strand in Northern Ireland has had two unfortunate consequences. It was a lost opportunity to demonstrate citizenship's rigour to a sceptical audience and it removed obvious common ground where history and citizenship might complement each other.

Thus, despite the clear need for Local and Global Citizenship in a still fractured society its position in schools remains precarious. Potentially, a stronger alliance with history could boost its standing and give its teachers renewed confidence – and provide history teachers with a clear rationale for relevance. Two recent projects, *Facing Our History, Shaping the Future* (FHSTF) and *Teaching Divided Histories*, both dedicated to addressing societal differences through reference to the past, have appealed to both history and citizenship teachers. Both have succeeded in galvanizing (sometimes) cautious practitioners into innovative risk-taking, particularly related to issues associated with the more recent contentious past. Both projects have history and citizenship dimensions. Yet neither initiative has explicitly articulated the respective contributions of each, thereby potentially fudging the disciplinary procedures of history with aspects of moral education and prejudice reduction. This risks 'presentism', making sense of the past through the present (Lee and Shemilt 2007), or as Wrenn (in Arthur et al. 1999: 103) warns, 'As soon as we start trying to use history to engineer a change in pupils' values and attitudes, and get them to arrive at a pre-determined conclusion, it stops being history and becomes something else'.

Much work is required if history in Northern Ireland is to effectively complement citizenship education as envisaged by Lee and Shemilt (2007). On the one hand, history has not faced up to its obligation to inform contemporary debate. On the other, citizenship has not been direct enough in developing young people's political consciousness.

Citizenship education in the Republic of Ireland

Similar to history education, and to experiences in Northern Ireland, questions around citizenship and citizenship education in the Republic of Ireland were given urgency by the social and political events of the 1990s and early 2000s which generated a discourse of inclusion and respect for diversity with regard to historic divisions and to the adoption of interculturalism as the state's educational response to more recent patterns of migration. Unlike Northern Ireland, the Republic already had a tradition of civic education as part of the formal curricula from the mid-1960s which was influenced by the modernization agenda and by Ireland's growing engagement with Europe. Predicated on the conflation of Catholic virtue with the 'cultivation of good habits' and dutiful citizenship, however, the focus of civics at primary level continued to be predominantly national and fundamentally theocratic (DoE 1971: 115; Waldron 2004). At post-primary level it was led by values such as 'civic responsibility, moral virtue and adherence to the law', although strongly allied in practice with religious education (Gleeson 2008). While it remained a required subject, the 1970s and 1980s saw a decline in interest in civic education, a decline that was halted to some extent by the introduction of CSPE as part of the post-primary curriculum in the mid-1990s.

Since the introduction of the new syllabus in 1996 CSPE has been a required course at Junior Cycle level. Beyond that, it lingers for one more year as part of Transition Year, before giving way to the exam-oriented senior cycle programme. The current programme puts forward a view of 'active participatory citizenship' informed by the following seven concepts: rights and responsibilities; human dignity; law; development; interdependence; stewardship; and democracy (DES/NCCA 2005). The idea of participation is given a concrete value through the action project, which students are required to complete for examination. In addition, active learning methodologies are seen as integral to the subject (DES/NCCA 2005: 7).

Despite ongoing issues of status and lack of adequate resourcing, CSPE has been characterized as offering 'scope and hope' for citizenship education (Jeffers 2008). On the other hand, Jeffers (2008) criticizes its failure to engage with issues of power and notes also the tensions inherent in promoting citizenship across the curriculum in a system which privileges subject disciplines and teacher autonomy. Others have commented also on its 'Cinderella' status within the curriculum (Bryan and Bracken 2011: 23; Gleeson 2008) and on its failure to problematize state policies in relation to the global South (Finlay 2006). In terms of identity, it has been described as seeking to construct a post-national identity with a strong European dimension (Keating 2009; O'Connor and Faas 2012). For Keating (2009) the view of Europe embodied in CSPE is geographically limited, ahistorical and with little that would support the development of affective ties. Indeed, it is notable that beyond a single mention of 'origins' with regard to communities (DES 2015a: 12) the CSPE syllabus does not acknowledge any relationship between history and citizenship apart from general statements recognizing the contributions of other subjects.

This failure to articulate structural links is not confined to citizenship. As outlined below, the Junior Cycle is in a process of transition with a new 'rebalanced' history curriculum scheduled for introduction in 2019 in the final wave of reform of the curriculum. The current syllabus, which has been in place for a number of decades, eschews any engagement with issues of identity and, while it justifies its inclusion of Irish history by reference to the 'importance of education for citizenship and of developing an understanding of contemporary life in Ireland' (DES 2015b: 2) there is no reference to citizenship thereafter. Rather, it focuses on introducing 'young people to the job of the historian' (p. 2) and the values and attitudes it seeks to develop are predominantly within that domain. Thus, while referencing citizenship and acknowledging the importance of linking the past and the present, the current syllabus offers little beyond a disciplinary focus.

The recent reform agenda within education in the Republic has included a re-envisioned curriculum framework at Junior Cycle. Similar to the 'Big Picture' approach associated with Northern Ireland, the new framework has been generally hailed for its re-orientation away from a subject-centred curriculum to one focused on student learning outcomes and from a systemic preoccupation with summative assessment through national terminal examinations, towards a more school-based holistic assessment-for-learning approach. The reforms have not been well received in all instances, most notably for this chapter in relation to the proposal to remove history and CSPE from the list of core or mandatory subjects. While history can still be selected as an optional subject or can become the focus of a range of 'short courses' that have been incorporated into the framework, the decision has been strongly contested by history teachers and by professional historians who have campaigned heavily for the decision to be reversed. On the other hand, CSPE has been reconceptualized as belonging to a broader area of learning named 'Wellbeing' and while it remains a separate examinable subject until 2018, its content beyond that remains uncertain.

Paradoxically, at senior level, one could argue that the fate of citizenship and its relationship with history is more positive. Current plans to introduce Politics and Society as a subject will see the space for citizenship extended, and, while history at Senior Cycle is strongly disciplinary in its orientation, it is the syllabus which most explicitly references the wider social purpose of history. Its aims and objectives, for example, include specific reference to 'preparation for life and citizenship' and enumerate associated dispositions, values and critical thinking skills (DES/NCCA 2003: 3, 4). Nonetheless, in general there is little recognition of the links between citizenship and history evident in post-primary syllabi and, similar to Northern Ireland, Davies's trilogy of connections remain largely unrealized. The potential of history to contribute to conceptual understanding and knowledge and to promote insight into human agency remains implicit in a 'cornucopian' history syllabus (Arthur et al. 2001; Lee and Shemilt 2007). Evidence also suggests that the kinds of inquiry-oriented and deliberative teaching approaches that can contribute to citizenship education are not yet embedded in practice (McCully and Waldron 2013). From an identity perspective, despite the focus on multi-perspectivity and on multiple identities in both curricula, identity within citizenship is ahistorical and unproblematized. Does primary education fare any better?

Premised on a social constructivist epistemology and underpinned by the ideology of child-centred education, the current Primary School Curriculum has been identified as facilitating intercultural and rights-oriented practice (Ross and Faas 2012; Ruane, Horgan and Cremin 1999). It is explicitly values-based and underpinned by values such as respect for diversity, the promotion of equality and social justice and solidarity with others. The curriculum also recognizes its role in identity construction across a range of intersecting identities, and to children's development as 'citizens of a global community' (NCCA 1999b: 26, 27).

Citizenship education itself is located within Social, Personal and Health Education (SPHE) as part of a broader strand entitled 'Myself and the Wider World'. Its aims reveal its civic republican roots, focusing on the development of social responsibility, commitment to active citizenship and appreciation of democracy as a mode of living (NCCA 1999c: 9). Although acknowledged for its focus on children's engagement in democratic processes, its commitment to equality-related values and issues and its recognition of multiple identifications, SPHE has also been criticized for its overarching conceptualization of children as duty bearers with regards to the rights of others rather than rights holders, and for its narrow conceptualization of children's participation, which does little to challenge traditional adult–child power relations (Waldron et al. 2014). In addition, while it is fair to say that it supports the idea of multiple identities those identities are largely ahistorical and devoid of any critical focus.

In practice, citizenship education at primary level is seen as limited by the constraints of the system, which include lack of resources (including time), large class sizes and teacher dependence on textbooks (NCCA 2008). Research has also found Irish primary teachers to have low levels of knowledge regarding human rights and, consistent with the curriculum itself, a tendency to prioritize responsibilities over rights (Waldron et al. 2014). In addition, and similar to systems elsewhere (Mejias and Starkey 2012), the education system in Ireland is highly dependent on external agencies, both state-sponsored bodies and non-governmental organizations, for citizenship-related programmes and initiatives (Hammarberg 2008). This dependence explains to a large extent the influence of award-led competitive programmes within the system which can serve to separate citizenship education from children's everyday learning and militate against its integration with other curriculum areas despite commitment at curriculum level to a whole-school, cross-curricular approach (Waldron et al. 2014).

The curriculum supports the integration of SPHE with 'relevant subject areas' and structurally it shares a strand on environmental care with both science and geography (NCCA 1999c: 11). Yet, despite an explicit focus on identity construction at personal, local, national, European and global levels, history is largely unreferenced. More mention is made of history in the Teacher Guidelines, where history is identified as contributing to the development of empathy, understanding change and what shapes communities, investigating the contributions of diverse groups to society and looking at self and family (NCCA 1999d: 38). The exemplars outlined, however, locate history very firmly within a local context (p. 49). Similarly, when integration is viewed through the lens of the Primary History Curriculum, citizenship is explicitly mentioned only in the footnotes and only in relation to the local dimension of citizenship.

There is a consistent failure across both curricula to explicitly link history and citizenship education, except where local history is concerned. Within the history curriculum itself, serious attention is given to the role of history in enabling children to link the past and the present; understand the historical contribution of diverse groups; recognize different perspectives; respect different traditions; and recognize that people belong to multiple communities and have a range of identities (NCCA 1999d: 13). In the Guidelines, history is seen as 'fostering local, national and European identity', a critical awareness of Irish and European heritage and a 'sense of citizenship' (NCCA 1999e: 29). Yet SPHE remains unreferenced within both documents except in so far as it relates to personal and local history. Despite a shared concern with identity construction and with understanding how society works, history and SPHE, at the level of curriculum, occupy two parallel paths with very few structural connections between them.

Parallel paths, failed connections and unrealized potential

Curricula, north and south, espouse democratic citizenship programmes, yet in neither instance has the relationship between this and history teaching been adequately articulated. Indeed, while curricula in general recognize the extrinsic aims of history education, and provide also for fairly robust citizenship education programmes, neither provide the kinds of structural links between history and citizenship that are required if education is to meet the challenges posed by the complexity of post-conflict, multicultural contexts. While there are similarities in the challenges faced by both jurisdictions, their divergent educational pathways over much of the twentieth century, coupled with differences in their experiences of and responses to conflict, mean that the sites of disjuncture between history and citizenship at curricular level are not identical.

You could argue that the relationship between history and citizenship in Northern Ireland displays elements of all three of Lee and Shemilt's (2007) relational models. In terms of its conceptualization, the NIC supports the complementary model. Its architects envisaged that pupils would learn by making connections across subject boundaries and by developing sets of generic skills which could make sense of common themes. So far, those subject borders have remained resolutely intact and any hope that a history/citizenship collaboration might be a catalyst for change has yet to materialize. Differences in status and the continued compartmentalizing of knowledge by hierarchy of importance work against a more holistic view of the curriculum despite its designers' intentions. In practice, then, the cornucopian model seems dominant. There are outstanding history and citizenship teachers who warrant Skilbeck's title (1973) as 'change agents', especially in the context of a transitional Northern Irish society. However, even these practitioners usually choose to work in one area or the other, thus limiting the potential for young people to develop a criticality which challenges political orthodoxy at a local or global level. For some community relations practitioners (usually from a non-history background), on the other hand, the subject is seen as a 'carrier' and social utility is prioritized at the expense of the discipline. This approach is often encountered in non-formal youth and community work and, as indicated, recent history curriculum-focused projects funded through 'peace-building' sources feature individual attitudinal change strongly in their intended outcomes (FHSTF 2015; Nerve Centre 2015).

Despite the acknowledgement of the relevance of history to citizenship education at primary level in the Republic, the structural links never stray beyond the surface. Where explicitly identified, they reside at the local level only, placing national, European and global citizenship in a curiously free-floating, ahistorical and decontextualized space. Similarly, at post-primary level, there is little to connect history and citizenship other than isolated references that generally fail to move beyond the level of platitude. The newly imagined Junior Cycle framework may in the future support more boundary-crossing between subjects. Currently, however, given the lack of connectivity between history and citizenship education in both primary and post-primary curricula, it seems that in the Republic the relationship between them conforms at best to the cornucopian model; the potential of history to contribute to citizenship is never realized while citizenship fails to engage with the historical roots of current institutions, structures and identities. This is problematic from a number of perspectives, some of which have a stronger resonance with the Northern Ireland context than others.

Firstly, and reminiscent of Davies's dimensions of knowledge and action (Arthur et al. 2001), the failure to connect young people's historical learning with their understanding of democratic structures, institutions and modes of living compromises their understanding of how democratic change (or its opposite) occurs, and the role of human agency in effecting change.

Secondly, there is evidence in the Republic's curricula of a shying away from issues of identity. While it is possible that this stems from an understandable fear of reinforcing or rejuvenating older narratives, the consequences are a failure to problematize identity within history and an ahistorical view of identity in citizenship education. Thus identities, whether multiple or not, are seen as having either benign roots or appearing fully formed in the present. In the 'emerging from conflict' context of Ireland, there is an evident need to re-examine aspects of contested historic identities. In the context of evidence which suggests that children in Ireland are constructing identity-based views from a young age (Waldron and Pike 2006; Connolly 1998), providing opportunities for sustained and critical engagement with those identities would seem advisable.

Finally, while the impetus towards multiple identifications and perspectives is evident in history and citizenship curricula north and south, it is questionable whether such multiplicity takes sufficient account of communities beyond the traditional unionist and nationalist divide or whether, in the context of globalization, enough attention is given to issues and questions which pertain to all of humanity in the twenty-first century.

Concluding thoughts: From shared histories to big histories

Recent decades have presented serious challenges to historic identities in Ireland, and the idea that there is a shared understanding of events within any one community is itself open to question. Also, limiting the focus to those communities traditionally associated with conflict raises the question as to whether either jurisdiction continues to conform neatly to this duality. While acknowledging the need for ongoing engagement with the post-conflict context of historically divided communities, this is no longer a sufficient recognition of the plurality of communities on the island, some of which lay claim to deep historical roots and others which are more recent. Furthermore, confining the discussion to historic communities and historic divisions foregrounds the ideology of nationalism while masking other equally problematic ideologies such as those relating to class, gender, ethnicity and global capitalism. At the very least, we need to be moving towards a conceptualization of history education such as that proffered by Nordgren and Johansson (2015). Building inter alia on the work of Rüsen (2005) on historical consciousness and Byram, Nichols and Stevens (2001) in relation to intercultural competence, they present a model for intercultural historical learning which moves beyond the national space, even where that space is conceptualized as multicultural, to consider meta-narratives such as migration and to 'decentre' and reframe curricula away from Western-centric definitions of what is historically significant.

Also, given the existential threat posed by climate change, the economic and political dominance of transnational corporations and supranational organizations and the continuing structural inequalities which characterize global relations, is there a possibility that in focusing on the 'local' (even the re-imagined 'local' of plural identities), history education is in danger of missing the big picture? At the very least, it could be argued that neither jurisdiction provides sufficient opportunities for developing an understanding of the historical roots of inequalities of wealth and power between the global North and South; yet such understanding is critical to the recognition of the responsibility of the global North in creating such inequalities in the first instance and of the ongoing complicity of Northern citizens in maintaining them. While such engagement is necessary, however, it is probably not a sufficient response to contemporary global issues.

Writing in 1991, David Christian characterized historical scholarship as 'fragmented and parochial'. Submerged in the detail of archival study, it needed to 'search for larger meanings in the past' (p. 227). Christian made the case for 'big history' which sees 'the appropriate time scale for the study of history' as 'the whole of time'. Such a timescale allows for 'very large questions' to be asked, questions which place our relationship with the planet and with other living things at the heart of historical investigation. More recently, Kate Hawkey argued for 'a new look at big history' (Hawkey 2014). Placing human relations with the planet at the centre of historical study, she articulated the 'need for a more porous boundary between natural and human factors in historical explanations' (p. 167). While the decades between Christian's article and now have seen a growth of interest in environmental history and the history of climate change, few would argue that its pace is commensurate with the urgency of its project and questions relating to humankind's relationship with the earth remain on the margins of historical scholarship and history education.

There is a strong argument, then, that while the shift in focus from a history education narrowly focused on a desired national identity towards one that is more open, critical and plural is a welcome one in the context of post-conflict Ireland, by maintaining a 'local' as opposed to a 'global' focus it falls short of what is required to meet the challenges of the twenty-first century when more fundamental questions relating to human life on earth will need to be addressed.

Note

1 The Belfast or Good Friday Agreement 1998 was endorsed by the British, Irish and United States governments and was signed by all but one of the main political parties in Northern Ireland. It provided for a power-sharing Executive and the decommissioning of paramilitary weapons.

References

Anderson, B. (1991), *Imagined Communities: Reflections on the Origins and Spread of Nationalism*, London: Verso.

Arlow, M. (2004), 'Citizenship Education in a Divided Society: The Case of Northern Ireland', in S. Towel and A. Harley (eds), *Education, Conflict and Social Cohesion*, 255–314, Geneva: International Bureau of Education, UNESCO.

Arthur, J., Davies, I., Wrenn, A., Haydn, T. and Kerr, D. (2001), *Citizenship through Secondary History*, London: Routledge-Falmer.

Barton, K. C. (2001a), '"You'd be Wanting to Know about the Past": Social Contexts of Children's Historical Understanding in Northern Ireland and the United States', *Comparative Education* 37: 89–106.

Barton K. C. (2001b), 'A Sociological Perspective on Children's Understanding of Historical Change: Comparative Findings from Northern Ireland and the United States', *American Educational Research Journal* 38: 881–913.

Barton, K. C. and Levstik, L. S. (2004), *Teaching History for the Common Good*, London: Lawrence Erlbaum Associates.

Barton, K. C. and McCully, A. W. (2005), 'History, Identity and the School History Curriculum in Northern Ireland: An Empirical Study of Secondary Students' Ideas and Perspectives', *Journal of Curriculum Studies* 37 (1): 85–116.

Barton, K. C. and McCully, A. W. (2007), 'Teaching Controversial Issues Where Controversial Issues Really Matter', *Teaching History* 127: 13–19.

Barton, K. C. and McCully, A. W. (2012), 'Trying to "See Things Differently": Northern Ireland Students' Struggle to Understand Alternative Historical Perspectives', *Theory & Research in Social Education* 40 (4): 371–471.

Bryan, A. and Bracken, M. (2011), *Learning to Read the World? Teaching and Learning about Global Citizenship and International Development in Post-Primary Schools.* Dublin: Irish Aid/Identikit.

Byram, M., Nichols, A. and Stevens, D. (2001), 'Introduction', in M. Byram, A. Nichols and D. Stevens (eds), *Developing Intercultural Competence in Practice*, 1–8. Clevedon: Multilingual Matters.

Christian, D. (1991), 'The Case for "Big History"', *Journal of World History* 2 (2): 223–38.

Connolly, P. (1998), *Early Years Anti-Sectarian Television*, Belfast: Community Relations Council.

Coolahan, J. (1981), *Irish Education: Its History and Structure*, Dublin: Institute of Public Administration.

Council for Curriculum, Education and Assessment (1996), *Northern Ireland Curriculum: History Guidance*, Belfast: CCEA.

Council for Curriculum, Education and Assessment (2007), *Environment and Society: History*, CCEA. Available online: http://www.nicurriculum.org.uk/docs/key_stage_3/areas_of_learning/statutory_requirements/ (accessed 11 February 2015).

Crone, R. and Malone, J. (1979), *Continuities in Education: The Northern Ireland Schools' Curriculum Project*, Windsor: NFER.

Crowley, N. (1990), 'The History Syllabus', in T. Crooks (ed.), *The Changing Curriculum: Perspectives on the Junior Certificate*, Dublin: O'Brien Educational.

Department of Education (1971), *Curaclam na Bunscoile: Primary School Curriculum*, 1, Dublin: The Stationery Office.

Department of Education and Skills (2014), *Education Statistics Database*. Available online: http://www.education.ie/en/Publications/Statistics/Education-Statistics-Database/ (accessed 11 February 2015).

Department of Education and Skills (2015a), *The Junior Certificate Civic, Social and Political Education Syllabus*, Dublin: The Stationery Office.

Department of Education and Skills (2015b), *The Junior Certificate History Syllabus*, Dublin: The Stationery Office.

Department of Education and Skills/National Council for Curriculum and Assessment (2003), *Leaving Certificate History Syllabus*, Dublin: The Stationery Office.

Department of Education and Skills/National Council for Curriculum and Assessment (2004), *History: Leaving Certificate Guidelines for Teachers*, Dublin: The Stationery Office.

Department of Education and Skills/National Council for Curriculum and Assessment (2005), *Civic, Social and Political Education: Guidelines for Teachers*, Dublin: The Stationery Office.

Department of Education Northern Ireland (DENI) (1991), *Northern Ireland Curriculum Programme of Study: History*, Bangor: DENI.

Doherty, G. (1996), 'National Identity and the Study of Irish History', *The English Historical Review* 111 (441): 324–49.

Facing our History Shaping the Future (FHSTF) (2015), *The Approach*. Available online: http://www.fohstf.co.uk/#/the-approach/4550813929 (accessed 11 February 2015).

Finlay, G. (2006) 'Popular Development, Moral Justification and Development Education', *Policy & Practice: A Development Education Review* 3: 5–13.

Gallagher, A. (2004), *Education in Divided Societies*, Basingstoke: Palgrave Macmillan.

Gleeson, J. (2008), 'The Influence of School and Policy Contexts on the Implementation of CSPE', in G. Jeffers and U. O'Connor (eds), *Education for Citizenship and Diversity in Irish Contexts*, 74–95, Dublin: Institute of Public Administration.

Hammarberg, T. (2008), 'Report by the Commissioner, Mr Thomas Hammarberg, on his visit to Ireland', Strasbourg: Council of Europe.

Harris, R. (2011), 'Citizenship and History: Uncomfortable Bedfellows', in I. Davies (ed.), *Debates in History Teaching*, 186–96, London: Routledge.

Hawkey, K. (2014), 'A New Look at Big History', *Journal of Curriculum Studies* 46 (2): 163–79.

Heater, D. (1999), *What is Citizenship?*, Cambridge: Polity Press.

Irish National Teachers Organisation (1996), *Primary School Curriculum: An Evolutionary Process*, Dublin: INTO.

Jeffers, G. (2008), 'Some Challenges for Citizenship in the Republic of Ireland', in G. Jeffers and U. O'Connor (eds), *Education for Citizenship and Diversity in Irish Contexts*, 11–23, Dublin: Institute of Public Administration.

Jones, V. (1992), 'The Attitudes of the Church of Ireland Board of Education to Textbooks in National Schools, 1922–1967', *Irish Educational Studies* 11: 72–98.

Keating, A. (2009), 'Nationalizing the Post-National: Reframing European Citizenship for the Civics Curriculum in Ireland', *Journal of Curriculum Studies* 41 (2): 159–78.

Kitson, A. (2007), 'History Education and Reconciliation in Northern Ireland', in E. A. Cole (ed.), *Teaching the Violent Past: History Education and Reconciliation*, Lanham, MD: Rowman & Littlefield, 2007.

Kitson, A. and McCully, A. (2005), '"You hear about it for real in school". Avoiding, Containing and Risk-taking in the History Classroom', *Teaching History* 120: 32–7.

Lee, P. and Shemilt, D. (2007), 'New Alchemy or Fatal Attraction? History and Citizenship', *Teaching History* 129: 14–19.

Magee, J. (1970), 'The Teaching of Irish History in Irish Schools', *The Northern Teacher* 10 (1): 15–21.

McCully, A. (forthcoming) 'Northern Ireland: Taking History Education Forward in a Divided Society', in L. Cajani, S. Lässig and M. Repoussi (eds), *History Education Under Fire: Curricula and Textbooks in International Perspective*, Braunschweig: Georg Eckert Institute for International Textbook Research.

McCully, A. and Emerson, L. (2014), 'Teaching Controversial Issues in Northern Ireland', in T. Misco and J. de Groof (eds), *Cross-Cultural Case-Studies in Controversial Issues:*

Pathways and Challenges in Democratic Citizenship Education, Tilberg: Legal Wolf Publishers.
McCully, A. and Waldron, F. (2013), 'A Question of Identity: Purpose, Policy and Practice in the Teaching of History in Northern Ireland and the Republic of Ireland', *International Journal of Historical Learning, Teaching and Research* 11 (2): 138–51.
Mejias, S. and Starkey, H. (2012), 'Critical Citizens or Neo-Liberal Consumers? Utopian Visions and Pragmatic Uses of Human Rights Education in a Secondary School in England', in R. Mitchell and S. Moore (eds), *Politics, Participation and Power Relations*, 119–36, Rotterdam: Springer.
Motherway, A. (1986), 'The Textbook Curriculum: The Status and Role of the Textbook in the Teaching of History and English at Senior Primary Level', *Irish Educational Studies* 6 (1): 193–203.
National Council for Curriculum and Assessment (1999a), *Primary School Curriculum: History*, Dublin: The Stationery Office.
National Council for Curriculum and Assessment (1999b), *Primary School Curriculum: Introduction*, Dublin: The Stationery Office.
National Council for Curriculum and Assessment (1999c), *Primary School Curriculum: Social, Personal and Health Education*, Dublin: The Stationery Office.
National Council for Curriculum and Assessment (1999d), *Primary School Curriculum: Social, Personal and Health Education: Teacher Guidelines*, Dublin: The Stationery Office.
National Council for Curriculum and Assessment (1999e), *Primary School Curriculum: History: Teacher Guidelines*, Dublin: The Stationery Office.
National Council for Curriculum and Assessment (2008), *Junior Certificate History: Draft Syllabus for Consultation*, Dublin: NCCA. Available online: http://www.ncca.ie/uploadedfiles/Junior%20Cycle%20Review/History_syll(2).pdf (accessed 11 February 2015).
Nerve Centre (2015), *Teaching Divided Histories*. Available online: http://www.fohstf.co.uk/#/the-approach/ (accessed 11 February 2015).
Nordgren, K. and Johansson, M. (2015), 'Intercultural Historical Learning: A Conceptual Framework', *Journal of Curriculum Studies* 47 (1): 1–25.
O'Callaghan, J. (2009), *Teaching Irish Independence: History in Irish Schools, 1922–72*, Newcastle upon Tyne: Cambridge Scholars Publishing.
O'Callaghan, J. (2011), 'Politics, Policy and History: History Teaching in Irish Secondary Schools 1922–1970', *Études Irlandaises* 36 (1): 2–13.
O'Connor, L. and Faas, D. (2012), 'The Impact of Migration on National Identity in a Globalized World: A Comparison of Civic Education Curricula in England, France and Ireland', *Irish Educational Studies* 31 (1): 51–66.
O'Connor, U. and Niens, U. (2009), *Evaluation of the Pilot Introduction of Education for Local and Global Citizenship into the Revised Northern Ireland Curriculum: Final Summary Report*, Coleraine: University of Ulster.
Qualifications and Curriculum Authority (QCA) (1998), *Education for Citizenship and the Teaching of Democracy in Schools: Final Report of the Advisory Group on Citizenship*, London: QCA.
Richardson, N. and Gallagher, T. (eds) (2011), *Education for Diversity and Mutual Understanding*, Oxford: Peter Lang.
Robinson, A. (1983), *The Schools' Cultural Studies Project: A Contribution to Peace in Northern Ireland*, Coleraine: New University of Ulster.

Ross, W. and Faas, D. (2012), 'Identity, Diversity and Citizenship: A Critical Analysis of Textbooks and Curricula in Irish Schools', *International Sociology* 27 (5): 574–91.
Ruane, B., Horgan, K. and Cremin, P. (1999), *The World in the Classroom*, Limerick: Mary Immaculate College.
Rüsen, J. (2005), *History: Narration, Interpretation, Orientation*, New York: Berghahn Books.
Skilbeck, M. (1973), 'The School and Cultural Development', *The Northern Teacher* 11 (1): 13–18, reprinted in M. Golby, J. Greenwald and R. West (eds) (1975), *Curriculum Design*, 27–35, London: Croom Helm/Open University Press.
Smith, A. (2003), 'Citizenship Education in Northern Ireland: Beyond National Identity?', *Cambridge Journal of Education* 33 (1): 15–31.
Smith, A. and Robinson, A. (1996), *Education for Mutual Understanding: The Initial Statutory Years*, Coleraine: Centre for the Study of Conflict, University of Ulster.
Tormey, R. (2006), 'The Construction of National Identity through Primary School History: The Irish Case', *British Journal of Sociology of Education* 27 (3): 311–24.
Waldron, F. (2004), 'Making the Irish: Identity and Citizenship in the Primary Curriculum', in C. Sugrue (ed.), *Curriculum and Ideology: Irish Experiences International Perspectives*, 209–38, Dublin: Liffey Press.
Waldron, F. and Pike, S. (2006), 'What Does it Mean to be Irish? Children's Construction of National Identity', *Irish Educational Studies* 25 (2): 231–51.
Waldron, F., Ruane, B. and Oberman, R. (2014), 'Practice as Prize: Citizenship Education in Two Primary Classrooms in Ireland', *Journal of Social Science Education* 13 (1): 34–45.
Walker, B. (1996), *Dancing to History's Tune: History, Myth and Politics in Ireland*, Belfast: Institute of Irish Studies, Queen's University Belfast.
Wrenn, A. (1999), 'Build it in, Don't Bolt it on: History's Opportunity to Support Critical Citizenship', *Teaching History* 96: 6–12.

4

Turkey and Greece: Reconstructing a Shared Past

Gülçin Dilek and Eleni Filippidou

Shared histories, shared commemorations and re-evaluating past denials

The two neighbouring countries Turkey and Greece have a common past that has extended over centuries. The relationship between the Greeks and the Turks started with the coming of the Seljuks, Muslim Turks, to Anatolia/Asia Minor in the eleventh century. In the following years, the Turks gradually settled in Anatolia, becoming a border neighbour of the Byzantine Empire, and after the foundation of the Ottoman Empire in 1299–1302[1] established a relationship which lasted for centuries. In the early Ottoman Empire period this continued through the wars with the Byzantine Empire and the struggle for sovereignty. Sometimes this involved military aid for other states, and diplomatic marriages led to the sharing of even more common ground with expansion of the Ottoman Empire into Balkan lands and the conquest of İstanbul (the fall of Constantinople) by the Ottoman Empire in 1453. Military expansion continued even further into the Balkans and through the settlement of the Muslim Turks in the places they captured. Therefore, the Greeks, like many other Balkan peoples (Albanian, Bulgarian, Serbian and Montenegrin, etc.), lived under the sovereignty of the Ottoman Empire until the nineteenth century when they started to achieve independent statehood. The breaking-up period of the two nations, starting with the independence of Greece (1821–30) and a series of struggles against the Ottoman Empire, continued with the Balkan Wars (1912–13) and deepened with the invasion of Western Anatolia, especially İzmir (Smyrna), by the Greeks (1919) and with the final phase of the Greco-Turkish Wars (1919–22). These events form the parameters within which a traumatic common past has been constructed.

The relationship between the Turks and the Greeks over a thousand years includes some key periods including the Byzantine past, 400 years under Ottoman sovereignty, and just under 200 years (185 years) as part of the history of modern Greece (Kalelioğlu 2008). These periods can be summarized under a number of headings, including togetherness/co-existence, alienation, otherization and cautiousness. The period starting with the conquest of İstanbul/Constantinople by the Ottoman Empire (1453) and continuing with the expansion and domination of the Ottomans into the Balkans can be defined as togetherness/co-existence because it was the period during which the two peoples lived together under the same empire (the Turks/Muslims and the Greeks/Rums/Christians). Rums is the name for the Christians who were considered to be the last remnant of the Roman Empire, as the Byzantine Empire was called at that time. When mentioned for some areas like Pontus or Anatolia the name is used to refer to the Christian Orthodox population which was mainly of Greek origin. But when it is mentioned for other parts of the Roman Empire it is also used to mean 'other people'. In this chapter the word Rum is used because, at the time of the events that we describe, the word 'Greek' was used only by the West and not by Greeks themselves. We also decided to use this term because the word 'Rum' is used in Turkish schoolbooks, thus it is therefore also mentioned in places where we describe the Turkish perspective.

The period during which the Balkan peoples defined themselves through ethnicity and gradually seceded from the Ottoman Empire with the help of nationalist movements in the West can be defined as alienation. The period from 1820 to 1923, starting with the revolutions of 1820–21 and following on from 1829/30, when Greece gained independence and separated from the Ottoman Empire, continued through the Balkan Wars (1912–13) and the Greco-Turkish Wars (1919–22) to when Turkey became a nation state in 1923, and this era can be defined as one of otherization. The recent past, when political issues, both those inherited from the past and those that have arisen much more recently, can be defined as a period of cautiousness. This period can be characterized as an intricate and sometimes binary network of experiences – such as friendship/hostility, approaching/avoiding, forgetting/remembering – that accompany the efforts to form friendly relations. These can intertwine and be changeable, justifying the definition of 'cautiousness' because the political issues which demand a solution need to be treated with caution in the context of their potential for tension and conflict.

Considering the terminology of a common past, it is possible to see the traces of a dramatic common memory. The victory of one side is the defeat of the other; the achievements of the one are the losses of the other. For example, the city that the Turks took and made their capital was correspondingly lost by the Greeks: the 'Conquest of İstanbul' is the 'Fall of Constantinople'. In the places where the Turks faced a rebellion against the state, the Greeks were fighting for independence: the 'Greek Rebellion' (as it appeared to the Turks) is the 'Greek War of Independence' of 1821. When the Turks encountered the Greeks who invaded their territory, the Turks, at the time, made efforts to gain independence and achieved it, and the Greeks faced defeat and destruction: the 'Turkish War of Independence' is for the Greeks the 'Disaster of Asia Minor'. The event which the Turks call the 'Cyprus Peace Operation' is the 'War of Cyprus' for the Greeks.

From 'otherness' to 'us'

What was more effective in determining the path of the relationships but much shorter in comparison with the period of co-existence (approximately 400 years in the context of Ottoman sovereignty) is the common past in the centre of which there was dissociation and conflict (nearly 200 years). In addition to the traumatic experiences caused by this past, the problems arising – some of which have not been totally solved – affect the present in the same way as they determine ways in which the significance of the past is seen at both national and international levels. On 30 October 1930 a Treaty of Friendship, Neutrality and Reconciliation was signed between Turkey and Greece, and Atatürk, the leader of the Turkish War of Independence and Turkey's first President, and Venizelos, the Greek Prime Minister, made efforts to constitute friendly relations between the two countries. This friendly relationship became more tense due to the disputes over Cyprus from 1954 and the Aegean Islands from 1974. After some positive steps, the breakthrough in Turkish–Greek relations occurred with the 1999 earthquakes. The sense of mutual solidarity brought about by these earthquakes took on a functional role in converting 'otherness' to 'neighbourliness' (Tılıç 2010: 205). According to Tılıç, who traced the conversion in media language from 'otherness' to 'us', the news about Greece in the Turkish media was in harmony with the official discourse, which had been shaped in line with diplomatic relations. On the other hand, Ünay (2007: 4) argues that it would be more correct to evaluate the atmosphere of dialogue between the two countries starting in the second half of 1999 as the moderation of relations rather than convergence; hence, with the start of dialogue, the issues that were of secondary rather than primary diplomatic importance were dealt with and several agreements on economy, tourism and the environment were signed; the three remaining difficulties – the minorities in Greece and Turkey; Cyprus; and the status of certain islands in the Aegean Sea – were left unresolved.

At this point, the collaborations and convergences on secondary issues can be evaluated as promising steps undertaken by two countries who share a common past and memory, and who were beginning to solve together the problems of prime importance. However, it is not surprising that diplomatic relations between the two countries bearing the weight of such a long and common past should be potentially fragile.

The nation – politics and transnational dimensions

Re-inventing Turkey and Greece after the separation from the Ottoman Empire

Greece and Turkey, in the process of constituting their national identities and becoming nation states, share some common experiences such as the rupture from the Ottoman past and otherization of this past after a certain interval of time. Özkırımlı and Sofos (2013: 36) argue that the developmental process in which nationalism movements appeared and were shaped in these two nations is extremely complicated and multi-dimensional and indeed quite different from the normal nationalist history narrative. At the same as the Ottoman Empire was in a state of terminal weakness, Greece totally separated; Greek nationalism was based on the civilization of Ancient Greece, combined with the Neo-Hellenistic Enlightenment movement which started in the eighteenth century. With the help of the European great powers (Britain, France and Russia) a small Greek nation state had emerged by 1830.

The Turks, on the other hand, tried to shore up the collapsing Ottoman Empire with a series of ideologies: Ottomanism, Pan-Islamism and Turkism. The Turkish elite adopted the nationalistic ideology of Turkism which was in harmony with other nationalistic doctrines associated with the founding of unitary states. In the same way as Turkey's rupture with the Ottoman past led to a re-engagement with supposed ancestral links with Central Asia to achieve legitimacy for the new nation state in 1923, so too did Greece look to the distant past of Ancient Greece to fictionalize its project of nationalism. The nationalist elite of Greece held the conservative, puritanical and religious Byzantine Empire responsible for all the negative experiences in Greek society from the fourth century, and then blamed the Ottoman Empire for the prolongation of that suffering (Millas 2004: 166; 2006). However, in the second half of the nineteenth century the Byzantine past was rediscovered under the historical conditions that changed for Greece, and thus the narration of the past dating back to the Ancient Greek period was constructed as a non-stop process of three thousand years with the inclusion of the Byzantine past (Millas 2004).

The Greco-Turkish Wars (final phase 1919–22)

The Greco-Turkish Wars, which had their origins in the nineteenth century and continued with intervals until 1922, contributed to both countries' projects of nationalism through mutual otherization. As might have been expected, both nations fictionalized their national narrations and identities in the context of this otherization discourse. Nevertheless, Heraclides reflects critically on how this national past fiction was nourished by otherization: 'I think we need "barbarian" Turks today just as much as we did in the past, otherwise the self-esteem of Greeks is imperilled. The love towards our homeland Greece and the hatred against Turkey move hand in hand and form the two faces of a coin' (Heraclides 2003: 70).

The foundation of modern Turkey was realized as the consequence of a series of wars with the Greeks. Accordingly, it has proved to be easy to allot a place for this interpretation within the traditional discourse of Turkish historical writing, with a sequence of military events: that the battle of Malazgirt/Manzikert (1071) opened the doors of Anatolia to the Turks; moreover, the sovereignty of Turks in Anatolia was accepted with the battle of Myriokephalon (1176); and their survival in Anatolia was guaranteed with the battle of Dumlupınar (1922). In one of the present history textbooks these battles are referred to in succession as 'homeland founder', 'homeland keeper' and 'homeland saver'; it is emphasized that the three battles are of great importance in Anatolia becoming a Turkish homeland (Önder 2014: 172). Copeaux (2013: 78) also suggests that Turkish–Anatolian history is founded on two of these three victories (Malazgirt/Manzikert and Dumlupınar), and that because these two battles were fought against Greeks, Greeks have been regarded as the main enemy throughout history.

In Greek textbooks the period from 1919 to 1922 is described in detail (five chapters). Its causes are explained by the end of the First World War and the decisions of the Entente Powers. Although it is not clearly mentioned, the student can understand that Greece had expansionist ambitions for the regions of north and south Anatolia. The relationship between Mustafa Kemal and the Sultan is also described in detail. The failure of the Greek administration in İzmir/Smyrna, the Greek–Turkish war and the population exchange are considered to be the result of the conflict between the King of Greece and Venizelos (1864–1936) (Louvi and Xifaras 2007: 102–10).[2]

The failure of the *Megali Idea* and the end of the wars

By the start of the twentieth century, the *Megali Idea*, the 'great idea', of a Great Greece was a vision of a Greek empire which included historic Greek settlements which had existed from ancient times into the Byzantine and Ottoman periods. This vision of a Great Greece developed during a time of great political instability in Greece, which peaked in 1917 with the National Schism between Prime Minister Venizelos in Thessaloniki and King Constantine in Athens. The *Megali Idea* was an attempt to hold on to and enhance ethnic Greek (or Rum) enclaves in Anatolia. It was complicated by the wish of Rum populations in the Russian areas around the Black Sea to leave at the outset of the Russian Revolution. There were serious clashes in different parts of Anatolia, including the Aegean coast and the Pontus region, and even claims of massacres; where there was an absence of concrete evidence about these claims, they would have to fall into the category of disputed history. Greece was thus at war with Turkey in the last years of the Ottoman Empire before Turkey became a Republic. In the end, after the decisive battle of Dumlupınar the situation was resolved by the Treaty of Lausanne.[3] The treaty came into force on 6 August 1924, when the instruments of ratification had been officially deposited in Paris, France, and yet another population movement of Greeks/Rums was agreed whereby the Anatolian and Pontus Greek population were moved to Greece. In similar moves the Turkish population living in Crete and parts of mainland Greece moved back to Turkey. Turkish textbooks have the objective of being able 'to comprehend the expansionist wishes of Greece for Anatolia', and the policy of the *Megali Idea* is one of these teaching objectives. Therefore, in Turkish teaching programmes and textbooks today there is emphasis on this *Megali Idea* and it is suggested that Greece had designs on the lands of Turkey. These Greek claims on Turkish territory are described by the Turkish teaching programmes and textbooks as groundless.

Turkish textbooks express surprise that Greek and Turkish populations failed during this period to continue the neighbourliness of the past, and accuse Greek/Rum gangs of starting the massacres in İzmir/Smyrna and the Pontus region, and the Greek/Rum population as a whole of ingratitude (Komisyon 2014). This is best seen, however, in the much wider context of the changes that were affecting both Greeks and Turks as the old Ottoman imperial structure (along with other structures in Europe such as the Habsburg Empire), which had allowed a certain amount of multiculturalism and plurality, gave way to strong forces of nationalism underpinned by an aggressive, indeed exclusive, stance on ethnicity. Whereas Turkish textbooks often mention the *Megali Idea*, Greek textbooks approach it with caution or sometimes omit it altogether because of its irredentist connotations, and a straight narrative is considered as being best avoided in this context.

In this dialogue between history educators only the official interpretations have been outlined here, and clearly this topic of conflict is controversial in both counties' history teaching. The focus has been on how to overcome these areas of conflict and similar issues through history teaching. What makes this particularly difficult is that both sides blame each other for the massacres (such as were experienced in the Pontus region and in İzmir/Smyrna) based on historical evidence.

The Pontus massacres are mentioned in the Greek school history books of the sixth grade of primary school, the third grade of junior high school and the third grade of high school. Turkish textbooks on the other hand place the blame for the massacres on Rum gangs and argue that Venizelos had massaged the figures of Rums who lived there (and who they say were encouraged by him to settle there before 1914) (Turan et al. 2014: 166–9). Another of the Turkish history textbooks (Komisyon 2014: 30)[4] asserts that the Greek claims about the Pontus massacres (1915–22) are delusive and wrong, while claims that 'the massacres committed by the Rums were proven after investigations and excavations' are included. The conflicting recent past becomes obvious in the teaching of history through the claims of massacre which both countries direct at each other, and at this point it seems hard to overcome the nationalistic perspective and show an objective stance. According to Saray (2005: 103), the purpose in including the Pontus problem was not to create hostility but to raise awareness by showing that Turkey was protecting itself from external threats, and for this reason these issues have to be dealt with carefully.

The Turkish–Islamic synthesis – 1970s to recent times

The common other of both nations is the Ottoman past. Just as significantly, these two nations also have in common the separation from their Ottoman pasts in the name of realizing their own nationalistic projects. In Greece, the previous tendency to ignore or negate the Ottoman past seems now to have evolved into a perspective of relative objectivity, especially in a pedagogical context; while in Turkey the tendency immediately after the foundation of the Republic to internalize the westernizing and secularist values of the new nation state, pushing the Ottoman past to one side, has today been replaced by a new trend of embracing the Ottoman heritage.

The Turkish–Islamic synthesis started in the 1970s and has intensified more recently thanks to political manipulations, along with the 1980 coup and the wider context of the Cold War. The discourse that the Turks were the defenders of Islam in the past is now emphasized in history textbooks (Önder 2014), and the expansion into Anatolia and from there into the West (conquests/expeditions in Turkish literature) is claimed to have the purpose of 'preventing danger' heading for Islamic countries. Therefore, the Turkish–Islamic synthesis, which has been a vital ingredient of history textbooks since the 1980s, has provided another layer for fictionalizing the identity of the nation. As with Islam, the present-day textbooks do not give room for any doubt on the matter of Turkishness. Accordingly, in *History Textbook Ten* (Turan et al. 2014: 10), the Western historians H. A. Gibbons and Arnold Toynbee, not having used the primary sources, are said to have introduced into Western literature the theory that the founders of the Ottoman Empire were the 'Rums [Christian Greeks] who accepted Islam'. The students are instead expected to learn that the founders of the Ottoman Empire were in fact Turks. The nation state perspective, which underpins history teaching, still sees its own mission as to present a homogenous identity.

Textbooks and their effects on minority groups

There were news reports in 2012 of possible threats to a minority group of Turks living in Greece. Western Thracian Turks felt uneasy with the content of new Greek textbooks which had been altered to include more hostile depictions of Turks (Berberakis 2012). In contrast to the 2007 sixth-grade Greek textbook, which included more amicable expressions about Turks, the new Greek textbooks, with effect from 2013, would include assertions about the Turks/Muslims' setting fire to the Rums' and Armenians' settlements in İzmir, murdering the Metropolitan bishop Chrysostomos, plundering, killing and expelling the Greeks from Anatolia in 1922. Because of the potential to stimulate hostility against Turks, these revised inclusions were uncomfortable for the Turkish minority living in Greece. Such a unilateral perspective may work to reinforce nationalist perspectives in both societies.

In the following two sections, we shall discuss the existing political issues and how the common past can be subjected to rereading on pedagogical grounds despite the dominance of nation state viewpoints in both Turkey and Greece.

Pedagogy, democracy and dialogue

Education has a privileged position in the ideology and social engineering of any nation state. Correspondingly, the tendency to construct a long and continuous past to trace the genealogy of nation states sets historiography to work as a means of fictionalizing this past, while in schools history is prized as a means of communicating this past to the masses. History teaching in both Turkey and Greece is still prone to this tendency. The official history fiction conveyed through schools has been responsible for the widespread construction and direction of the perceptions of the peoples of both countries towards each other. All in all, the narrative and discourse framed in textbooks are articulated in the light of a mixture of problems from the past and of policies which have been inherited from these problems. On some occasions the common past can be presented in a manner that aimed at creating more amicable relations (as in the aftermath of the 1999 earthquakes), and changing dynamics in diplomacy as well as other political agencies can be elements in this process (like the role of the European Union in resolving the problems between the two countries).

On 20 April 1951 Turkey and Greece agreed to exclude hostile statements in school textbooks.[5] The agreement stated that a committee of ten members (five from Turkey and five from Greece) should ensure that there were no misunderstandings in the schoolbooks that would lead to the creation of hostile emotions against the other country. As a result, the vocabulary which had been commonly included in Turkish and Greek textbooks was revised. Examples in Turkish textbooks were expressions such as 'to disembowel', 'to slaughter', 'to kill ruthlessly', 'to kill viciously', 'corrupt and dishonest enemy', 'vicious enemy', 'Greek ramblers' and 'Greek flocks'. Similarly, pictures portraying the ruthless behaviour of Greeks towards Turks were expunged from the textbooks (for example, the 1921 painting by Vittorio Pisani depicting the Greek landing at Smyrna in 1919) (Ata 2005: 84). Yet one can see that the exclusion of actively hostile statements in textbooks published since then does not necessarily mean that the dominant presentation is of a common past free from nationalistic, one-dimensional viewpoints. The way of handling the common past in the textbooks makes it possible to trace how national identity is still fictionalized.

Accordingly, the conquest of İstanbul by Turks (the fall of Constantinople) is one of the important common events in the past of the two countries and it therefore attained an established place in the textbooks. This event, accepted as the turning point of Turkish history, is also one of the most popular subjects of Turkish historiography. It is regarded as a beginning of the new age, a great success achieved by Turks, an important stage in extending the Ottoman Empire. Öztan (2014), who has studied how this significant historical event (often accepted to have closed the Middle Ages and opened the Early Modern era) is reflected in children's literature, shows the several phases of the narrative. First, in the early Republican era of the 1920s and 1930s it was fictionalized from a nationalistic-militarist viewpoint, when a distance was put between Turkey and the Ottoman past. Later, in the 1950s, interest in the Ottoman past increased. Following this, in the 1960s and 1970s the perspective of the Turkish–Islamist synthesis (when Turkishness was on a par with religious causes) gradually had more influence. In the 1980s, and rising greatly in the 2000s, the Islamist perspective came to the fore when there was a virtual explosion in religious-themed conquest books in parallel to the rise of political Islam.

Öztan (2014) shows that the stereotypes of the conquest have a structure which resists change from whichever perspective the conquest is fictionalized. For example, the image of the Byzantine Empire has not changed in textbooks and it is still seen as a period of intrigue, degeneration and weakness. Copeaux (2006: 381–5) argues that Byzantine history was dealt with as an axis of Turkish history in the past, but that there was much hesitation when deciding whether to define Byzantium as a civilization of the East or the West. The criterion for judgement was on the quality of its contribution to fictionalizing the Turkish past. Thus the Anatolian past was approached selectively and, in this sense, that Byzantine heritage which Turkish educators regarded as associated to the Greeks was rejected. Millas (2011: 196) complains about the diminishing of the role of Byzantium in Turkish textbooks.

Nevertheless a comparative study made by Filippidou and Özbaş (2014), focusing on how the subject of the conquest of İstanbul/fall of Constantinople is handled at primary school level in old and new Greek and Turkish textbooks, has shown that while the textbooks in both countries still have a unilateral point of view and do not encourage empathy and perspective-taking, the historical method, language of the text and the resources used are now more favourable and the approach is more pacific.

One theme within official history discourse in Turkey contributes to the fictionalization of an idealized Ottoman Empire: in Turkish historiography and textbooks the concept of 'religious tolerance' together with the Ottoman 'nation system', where the Sultan's subjects were classified according to their religious beliefs, and the community leader was entrusted with religious and executive authority, is central to this idealization. In the tenth grade history textbook, religious tolerance and the nation system are mentioned together seventeen times (Turan et al. 2014). In this discourse the 'Rescuing Ottoman' accompanies the 'Tolerant Ottoman': the Orthodox Greeks were rescued from the domination of the Catholic Church and Byzantium. In the presentation of the attitude of the Ottoman Empire towards all non-Muslims in general, and towards Greeks in particular, the discourse about the idealized living conditions and political/social status of non-Muslims was always fictionalized through the lens of the ruler/ruled dichotomy. The images of benevolent, tolerant and fair rulers, and loyal non-Muslims contented with their lot, are the common themes of all Turkish textbooks.

This idealized fiction is problematic for two reasons. First, the limited narrative about the role of non-Muslims in political and social life narrows and objectifies them. These statements also aim to prove how comfortable they were under Ottoman governance (e.g. that the Greeks freely engaged in commerce and undertook official tasks as translators). However, a rather different approach would take this beyond what is in fact rather a monolithic discourse. This could be achieved through a historical narrative in which the active participation of the Greeks in political and social life is revealed. Greeks/Rums could thus be presented as the subjects of history in their own right, not merely as contributory factors in constructing and reinforcing an image of the Ottoman past.

Secondly, the non-Muslims presented as living in such comfortable conditions rose up against the Ottoman Empire in several periods. The story of Greeks in the Turkish history narrative is quite simple: these Orthodox Christians, having some freedom and living quite comfortably under the Ottoman sovereignty, rebelled against the empire while under the influence of Western movements like nationalism and Western power groups (Russia, Britain, France), and in due course they became an enemy with expansionist desires on the territory of the Ottoman Empire.

That 'the archetypal sins of Rums are ingratitude' is inherent to this story of toleration (Millas 2011: 207). For example, in the current history textbook for high school grade ten, the Ottoman Empire's allowing the Greeks in the civil service to be translators, meaning that they had the most privileged place among the minorities, and that they had freedoms in their religion and language, is given in the section of the 'Greek Rebellion' (Turan et al. 2014: 164). One of the frequently repeated discourses in the history textbooks is the agency of the European powers in provoking the Balkan nations to rise against the Ottoman Empire. The historian Millas, born in Ankara but of Greek ethnicity and living now in Athens, finds it troublesome to give students the impression that the Greeks living in the Peloponnese (Morea) or elsewhere had nothing to complain about, especially if the wish to become a nation state is only attributed to the interference of these great powers, without any reference to the national will of the Greeks themselves. He criticizes the Turkish textbooks for giving no other reasons for the Greeks' desire for an independent state.[6]

Again, the selectivity in the chosen narrative of textbooks highlights the concepts of justice and freedom of religion, and blurs the fact that non-Muslim people suffered discrimination in comparison to the Muslims, and they did not get the benefit of the same rights (Özkırımlı and Sofos 2013: 41; Millas 2006: 107). Greek textbooks stress that the 'Greek War of Independence' (1821–30) was influenced by values such as independence and freedom coming from the European Enlightenment, and that, thus inspired by the ideas of Voltaire and Kant, the Greeks, especially those living outside the borders of the Ottoman Empire, wanted independence. Following this narrative, the split from the Ottoman Empire and independence of Greece were welcomed as redemption after a long struggle (Skoulatou, Dimakopoulou and Kondi 1995: 225–50; Margaritis et al. 1999: 61–5; Louvi and Xifaras 2007: 23–40; Aktipis et al. 2008: 81–136).

In comparison to previous presentations of the common past in Greek history teaching, current textbooks are more objective. According to Stathis (2013: 133), who studied the high school grade three history course books published in Greece from 1955 to 1992, 'In Greek textbooks the Turk is the national other who existed for over 400 years.' Stathis reveals that Turks were presented generally with negative judgements and images (conqueror, oppressive, barbarian) in the books published before 1984, and argued that Turks should be approached more objectively, though while some steps were taken in the textbooks dated between 1984 and 1992 to present a more positive image of the Turks, alluding to any concord between the two countries was still not possible (Stathis 2013: 126–8). However, in current Greek history textbooks a whole chapter is devoted to a detailed description of Ottoman rule. They mention that although in the first centuries of Ottoman rule (*turkokratia*) the conditions in which Greeks lived were harsh because of the *devşirme*[7] and taxation, by the seventeenth century the Greeks had negotiated privileges that helped them live a prosperous and civilized life. The fact that the Sultan had given not only religious but also administrative authority to the Orthodox Patriarch of Constantinople had helped the Ottoman-Greeks to establish schools, to conduct trade and to take important positions in the administration of the Balkans. In the new schoolbooks the period of *turkokratia* is approached in a 'neutral' way (Dimitroukas and Ioannou 2008: 133–9; Aktipis et al. 2008: 27–46).

Landmarks with questions

Two parallel constructions

The past as a site of memory is important in the fictionalization of national identities from nationalistic perspectives. Events, phenomena and experiences all shape not only national memories but also national identities, but there is inevitably some experience of fracturing of both memories and identities when these are seen through the prism of current policies and perceptions. The period between 1821 and 1923, and indeed other periods before and after, can be seen as interactive years of two parallel constructions. The past builds up the present and vice versa, drawing on the identity of other communities with whom at the same time a common past is shared and with whom a common memory is built up correlatively. How common memory is constructed in Turkey and Greece is and has been highly problematic, as relations have been generally hostile since the nineteenth century, and although a better relationship has been established more recently, both countries have experienced their own internal political problems. It is worth considering which criteria can contribute to a different kind of common history that goes beyond a past that has been shared only superficially.

The historical actors' points of view

Is it possible to reread our common past from different perspectives despite the impositions of official history? One approach can be to present these efforts at rereading from the historical actors' point of view in their historical contexts and by paying attention to the layered structure of the events. To this can be added the different interpretations of historians.

Karpat (2004), for instance, argues that the Orthodox Patriarchate in Constantinople (İstanbul), having undertaken important political and religious functions in the Ottoman Era, opposed the Greek national struggle. By acting in concert with the elite of the Greek population from the Fener (or Phanar)[8] where the Patriarchate was based, it aimed to reanimate the Byzantine Empire and to gain status within the Ottoman Empire. But, in spite of this opposition, these elite Phanariots were held responsible for the 1821 Greek Rebellion by the Sultan, and the Patriarch was executed alongside those involved in the Morea rebellion. Karpat's research (2004: 102–7) reveals that the uprising in the Morea in particular had a complicated and layered structure. Here, the actors in the field of struggle were not simply the Ottomans against the Greeks, but Greeks against other Greeks, between lower and upper clergy, between ship owners and land owners, between harsh chieftains (who were in fact gang leaders or ringleaders) and the Phanariots, between leaders of the Church and rulers, local chieftains and ship owners.

These findings are important since they challenge the simplified monolithic narrative still seen in Turkish textbooks. For instance, when the events of 1821 are handled in current textbooks, the Patriarchate is still at the centre (Turan et al. 2014: 164). Yet, as Karpat suggests, the Patriarch preferred the Ottoman status quo and did not support the uprising, as it was not in line with its interests of the Patriarchate. The Patriarchate was excluded from the political arena by Greece in the period of setting up a nation state, but 'in fact history showed that Greece and the Greek national Church acted as the heirs of Patriarchate' (Karpat 2004: 109). The role of the Patriarchate in the Greek uprising is disputed in Turkish historiography. Historians are divided over the Patriarchate's involvement. In turn, Greek nationalists excluded the Patriarchate. However, its politics, ideals and heritage (such as re-establishing the Byzantine Empire, later developed into the *Megali Idea*) were taken over by Greek nationalists. Furthermore, ironically the executed Patriarch Gregorios V was nevertheless proclaimed as a 'national martyr' in order to arouse the public support by some Greek revolutionists while constructing the nation state (Karpat 2004: 102–9). For example, according to Zallones (a Greek nationalist) the Patriarchate was not against the Greek revolution; the traitors who reported the design for the revolution to the Ottoman rulers and caused the Patriarch's execution were the Phanariots (Millas 2006: 174). What really happened? Greek nationalists' tendencies towards the Patriarchate differ according to political events in those times and also include some dilemmas.

Millas (2006: 112) does agree with Karpat that it is misleading to think that the clergy and all the Phanariots supported Ottoman rule, stating that the Phanariots had always been independent and this had manifested itself even through their adopting different strategies from one another. These explanations reveal another dimension of the complicated and layered structure of the events. If contradictory information and interpretations presented by primary and secondary sources are added to this, it is more difficult to come to a judgement about the events but it yields a perspective towards the past that is nevertheless enlarged and enriched. The presentation of the events with such an approach can carry the common past beyond the reductionist, selective and fictional stance of nationalistic perspectives. This requires the critical thinking skills of an interrogator, and although there are more obstacles preventing a simplistic judgement, the student is nevertheless invited to adopt plural and empathic perspectives.

Social differences across borders

Another approach in overcoming the unilateral narration of the development of the nation state is to examine the social class differences across borders in the past. For instance, Turkish textbooks often neglect to mention that, while the Rums had a secondary status like other non-Muslims, and were forbidden from growing beards and from riding horses, among other bans, and had to seek permission to wear furs, ethnic Rum interpreters from the Phanar were allowed to ride horses, grow beards and wear furs, and those in the employ of the chief translator were exempt from the poll tax (*jizya*) which the non-Muslims paid (Aydın 2007: 58). It is possible 'to divide the Rums under the Ottoman rule into three main groups such as governmental officials who were Rums from the Phanar (Greek aristocracy, Patriarchate and its circle, interpreters); rich traders, sailors and land owners; and peasant *reaya*[9] engaged in agriculture' (Seyitdanlıoğlu 2004: 51), and it is thus clear that the elite social class had a privileged position. These examples that can be multiplied reveal the importance of regarding the past by considering different social classes, societies and of course genders. Similarly, Akgönül (2012: 41) states that the Rum Orthodox community in the Ottoman Empire, although not divided by sharp lines, could be classified into four groups, in accordance with the geographical districts where they lived. Akgönül (2012: 44) does not doubt that the nationalist Rums who lived especially in Smyrna (İzmir) supported the military action taken in the course of the Greek invasion of 1919, but doubts that all Rums showed the same response to this invasion. According to Akgönül, it is extremely hard to make a certain list of the Rums' reactions and feelings about the military action. Yet the dilemma of the Rums of Asia Minor is that all of them without exception were accused of collaborating with Greek forces by nationalist Turkish authors, but nevertheless accused of not collaborating enough by the Greek authors and ultimately of contributing to Greece's defeat.

As can be seen in this example, the reactions of historical actors to the events can vary to the extent that they cannot be reduced to one single dimension. So, instead of over-generalizing about historical actors, presenting them in this multilateral light can help with the examination of traumatic events more calmly and from a certain distance.

Universal dimensions of traumatic events

An approach to follow when we try to reread the conflicting past beyond the nationalistic perspective can be to consider the universal context besides local and national contexts in interpreting traumatic events. For instance, one of the most severe and traumatic effects of war is sexual violence against women in war, not in any particular country or period, but in many battles across the world and in any historical period, and there is literature analysing this phenomenon in the context of gender history (see Yuval-Davis 2003; Enloe 2006; Saigol 2004; Akgül 2011). A specific example of this can be found in a statement in the high school textbook *The Republic of Turkey: Revolution History and Atatürkism* (Akdin, Çakmak and Genç 2008: 30) that most of the rapes were perpetrated by the Greeks during the Greek invasion (1919–22) (cited in the fifteenth clause of the report by Admiral Bristol).[10]

To benefit from academic research, to realize the universality of such events, and to consider these from a standpoint both of gender (for instance, the consubstantiation of women and nations, the violation of women in enemy territory being equivalent to gaining the territory, etc.) and of universal human rights, can transform the evaluation of historical events, even if the utmost sensitivity is necessary to evaluate such painful memories, taking it beyond national hatred to a more universal viewpoint. It is a delicate question which approach can most faithfully serve the purpose of breaking down a tendency to reinforce nationalistic prejudices, and this can be extended to consider whether on the one hand the events should be mentioned at all – in the interest of not stirring up hostility, or on the other if placing them in a universal context and benefiting from the relevant academic work, by taking care to use the right methods, can be regarded as the best way of presenting sensitive, contradicting and contested issues. However, to deal with these traumatic events from a narrow, nationalistic perspective (the harm done by the 'other' to 'us') risks creating a fault line in the construction of common memory.

Empathetic perspectives

Reflecting on conflicts and tensions from both countries' perspectives can help reread the past from an empathic perspective as well as a contextual one. Accordingly, the common past can be presented by giving both concepts, used by both countries (e.g. Greek Rebellion/Greek War of Independence), and by explaining how the opposite side interprets the events.

A functional approach can combine political history with a socio-cultural historical approach in rebuilding the common past. For instance, the Protocol of Turkish–Greek Population Exchange signed on 23 January 1923 at Lausanne between Turkey and Greece, and the period of population exchange, are handled in Turkish textbooks mainly from a political point of view, yet the books do not include any sources, materials or activities that will help students understand the feelings and thoughts of people who were exchanged in this period; whereas to understand the experiences of both sides and to show empathy towards those who left their homelands can be very meaningful in terms of understanding and concentrating on people in history beyond nationalities. Primary sources which reflect intellectual and actual experiences, dealing with the problems at individual (microcosmic) as well as national and transnational levels (macrocosmic), can have a serious functional role in the construction of a common past. Among these sources will be photographs, documents, memoirs, autobiographies and oral history studies (see Meydan 2012 for a classroom activity example).

Whereas Turkish textbooks only deal with the high politics behind the population exchange, Greek textbooks likewise do not describe the population exchange in detail although it is mentioned that the refugees brought their 'civilization' with them as well as new methods in agriculture and science. Besides this, people who had higher educational qualifications had an influence by re-establishing in Greece educational institutions with features influenced by their time in Asia Minor, thus providing a new *Zeitgeist* in education and the sciences (Louvi and Xifaras 2007: 121–2; Aktipis et al. 2008: 221–2).

It can be very helpful in understanding the pains of building the nation state in ways which show how the exchange influenced people's lives. Moreover, focusing on human feelings and experiences contributes to an empathetic evaluation of a common past through intellectual and affective exchange. On the other hand, the presentation of conflicting events and narratives together with the experiences in the axis of mutualization/friendship/neighbourhood (e.g. just as between Greek and Turkish neighbours during the invasion of İzmir/the landing at Smyrna) can both allow an activation of the human dimension in history and facilitate a journey which goes beyond not only binary opposites such as good–bad, but also outside and away from nations and politics.

Neyzi's oral history of İzmir/Smyrna 1922

Contrary to the monolithic narrative of official history which directs readers to identify with the country they belong to, oral history's value lies in making visible multiple dimensions and perspectives, in centring on humanity beyond nations and states, in questioning official narrations, and in realizing the relationship between retrospective and current interpretations. Neyzi (2013: 82), who made an oral history study about the 1922 fire in İzmir/Smyrna, for which Greeks, Armenians and Turks held one another responsible, tells us that she is interested in what the narratives and interpretations of the event would say to us about history, memory and identity beyond revealing which particular narrative is correct. She (Neyzi 2013: 83) argues that oral history is mostly presented as an alternative to official/national/public narratives; but the very complexity of the interplay between national and local narratives in her study confirms the strength of oral history, as it includes many different narratives and draws on several resources.

Traditional historians are suspicious of oral history because of its subjectivity, but Neyzi (2013: 84) believes that its subjective narrative structure is useful for studying how the past is understood and interpreted in the present. All these opinions are inspiring about developing some highly useful methods that can be implemented in teaching the process of reconstructing the common past. Accordingly, if history writing, in its postmodern sense, is an act of continual interpretation and fictionalization of the past, it can nevertheless be studied through oral history, through asking how and by whom the events are remembered, how they are interpreted by the individual, and how individual, local and national experiences all interact in this interpretation and construction of memory. Oral history studies that focus on a conflicting past are an important starting point in realizing how people coped with traumatic experiences, and in realizing the multi-layered nature of the events based on the differentiated stories of individuals, tempered by the discipline of history. This approach can be more constructive and realistic than fictionalizing a selective past. It avoids not only generalizations but also the worst aspects of 'nationalist/official' history.

Towards a 'democratic multinational state' Ottoman-style according to Rhigas Velestinlis/Pheraios (and Millas)

Millas (2006: 110, 174) suggests that the Greek Rhigas Velestinlis (or Rhigas Pheraios) (1757–98), who aimed to build up a multinational order in which laws, freedom and equality would dominate, can be regarded as the first of the Ottoman elite to oppose monarchic rule and to propose republicanism, and to predict a bourgeois revolution within Ottoman society. Seeing the Ottoman past through this figure is important because this past can be considered from a multicultural viewpoint in which other peoples apart from the Turks were made apparent. Studying Rhigas Velestinlis can help break down the artificial barriers of the rigid nationalist narrative and can make positive contributions to the construction of a common history as well as providing an alternative fictionalization of a richer, more holistic Ottoman past.

Conclusion

As long as history is manipulated as a means of fictionalizing identity, it seems inevitable that past events will continually be reconstructed from several political perspectives, be they stable or changeable, and history textbooks will be affected. This perpetual cycle needs to be broken. Historians, history educators and teachers should adopt both a pluralist and an interpretative approach which reflect the nature of history, and this will enable them to go beyond the monolithic nationalist/official narratives. Also, in such a shared enterprise towards rejecting a monolithic narration, we must reveal the multilateral roles, dilemmas and conflicts of historical actors and institutions in the historical contexts in order to reflect the events from different historical actors' viewpoints and to subject all of these materials to a multilateral analysis.

The historian Gerda Lerner (1979) once said that history has been seen with only one eye. We believe that now it is time to see history with both eyes.

Notes

1 The traditional date is 1299 but historian Halil İnalcık argues that it is 1302. So both dates have been used together.
2 He was elected several times as prime minister: 1910 to 1920 and from 1928 to 1932. Kings of Greece (Glücksburg Dynasty) were as follows: Constantine I (reigned first 1913–17); Alexander I (reigned 1917–20); Constantine I (reigned second 1920–22);

George II (reigned 1922–4; 1935–47). The Second Hellenic Republic was from 1924 to 1935.

3 The treaty was ratified by Turkey on 23 August 1923, Greece on 25 August 1923, Italy on 12 March 1924, Japan on 15 May 1924 and Great Britain on 16 July 1924.

4 In the Komisyon, Saray and Ata titles (which relate to textbooks), 'the Revolution' refers to the foundation of the Republic (1923) and the reforms that ensued.

5 Official Gazette, 23 April 1952, No. 103, available online at http://6dim-diap-elefth.thess.sch.gr/Greek/Diapolitismiki_Ekpaidefsi/NomothesiaDiapEkpshs/08_MorfwtikesSymfwnies/elladas_tourkias.pdf (accessed 22 April 2015).

6 See interview with Millas, available online at http://balkansbg.eu/en/inquiries/497-hercules-or-herkul-or-iraklis-millas.html (accessed 22 June 2015).

7 The *devşirme* was a 'blood tax' or 'tribute' where the sons of Christians in the conquered lands, especially in the Balkans, were taken from their families and educated to be high-ranking soldiers or bureaucrats. The practice was in decline by the middle of the seventeenth century.

8 The Fener (or Phanar) is a district of İstanbul.

9 The *reaya* were non-Islamic subjects of the Ottoman Empire.

10 Rear Admiral Mark L. Bristol was the US High Commissioner (and then the first US Ambassador) to the Republic of Turkey between the years of 1919 and 1927. The report referred to here would seem to be among his papers in boxes 74 and 75 stored in the Library of Congress in Washington: http://rs5.loc.gov/service/mss/eadxmlmss/eadpdfmss/2013/ms013044.pdf (accessed 12 March 2015).

References

Akdin, İ., Çakmak, M. and Genç, M. (2008), *Türkiye Cumhuriyeti İnkilap Tarihi ve Atatürkçülük Lise 3 Ders Kitabi* [Republic of Turkey History of Revolution and Atatürkism High School 3 Textbook], 4th edn, İstanbul: MEB.

Akgönül, S. (2012), *Türkiye Rumlari* [The Rums of Turkey], 3rd edn, trans. Ceylan Gürman, İstanbul: İletişim.

Akgül, Ç. (2011), *Militarizmin Cinsiyetçi Suretleri Devlet Ordu ve Toplumsal Cinsiyet* [Sexist Faces of State Militarism: The Military and Gender], Ankara: Dipnot.

Ακτύπης, Δ., Βελαλίδης, Α., Καΐλα, Μ., Κατσουλάκος, Θ., Παπαγρηγορίου, Γ. & Χωρεάνθης, Κ. (2008), *Στα νεότερα χρόνια. Ιστορία Στ΄ Δημοτικού*, Αθήνα: Οργανισμός Εκδόσεως Διδακτικών Βιβλίων [Aktipis, D., Velalidis, A., Kaila, M., Katsoulakos, T., Papagrigoriou, G. and Choreanthis, K. (2008), *In Recent Years: History Sixth Grade Primary School*, Athens: OEDV].

Ata, B. (2005), 'Tarih Pedagojisine Uygun Türkiye Cumhuriyeti İnkilap Tarihi ve Atatürkçülük Dersi Nasil Olmalidir? [What Should the Course for the History of the Revolution of the Turkish Republic and Atatürkism that is in Accord with the Pedagogy of History Look Like/Be Like?]', in M. Saray and H. Tosun (eds), *İlk ve Ortaöğretim Kurumlarinda Türkiye Cumhuriyeti İnkilap Tarihi ve Atatürkçülük Konularinin Öğretimi: Mevcut Durum ve Çözüm Önerileri.* [Teaching the History of the Republic of Turkey – The Revolution and Atatürkism in Secondary Education: The Current Situation and Solutions], 73–85, Ankara: Atatürk Araştirma Merkezi.

Aydın, B. (2007), 'Divan-i Hümayun Tercümanlari ve Osmanli Kültür ve Diplomasisindeki Yerleri in [Interpreters of the Divan-i Hümayun Imperial Council and their Roles in

Ottoman Culture and Diplomacy]', in H. İnalcik, İ. E Erünsal., H.W. Lowry, F. Emecen and K. Kreiser (eds), *Osmanli Araştirmalari* [The Journal of Ottoman Studies] 29: 41–86.

Berberakis, T. (2012), 'Okul Kitabinda Türkler Yine Düşman Oldu [In the Textbook Once Again the Turks Became the Enemy]', *Milliyet*, 4 April. Available online: http://www.milliyet.com.tr/okul-kitabinda-turkler-yine-dusman oldu/dunya/dunyadetay/26.04.2012/1532730/default.htm (accessed 23 February 2015).

Copeaux, E. (2006), *Türk Tarih Tezinden Türk İslam Sentezine* [From Turkish History Thesis to Turkish-Islamic Synthesis], trans. Ali Berktay, İstanbul: İletişim.

Copeaux, E. (2013), 'Türk Kimlik Söyleminin Topografyasi Ve Kronografisi [Topography and Chronography of the Turkish Identity Discourse]', *Tarih Eğitimi ve Tarihte Öteki Sorunu* [History Education and the Issue of the Other in History], 2nd edn, 70–84, İstanbul: Tarih Vakfi Yurt Yayinlari.

Δημητρούκας, Ι. & Ιωάννου, Θ. (2008), *Μεσαιωνική και νεότερη ιστορία. Β΄ Γυμνασίου*, Αθήνα: Οργανισμός Εκδόσεως Διδακτικών Βιβλίων [Dimitroukas, I. and Ioannou, T. (2008), *Medieval and Contemporary History: Second Grade Junior High School*, Athens: OEDV.]

Enloe, C. E. (2006), *Manevralar: Kadin Yaşaminin Militarize Edilmesine Yönelik Uluslararasi Politikalar* [Manoeuvres: The International Politics of Militarizing Women's Lives], trans. Serpil Çağlayan, İstanbul: İletişim.

Filippidou, E. and Özbaş, B. Ç. (2014), '"The Conquering or Fall of İstanbul": Analyzing of the Conquering or Fall of İstanbul Topic in Turkish and Greek History and Social Studies Textbooks', *Türk Tarih Eğitimi Dergisi* [Turkish History Education Journal] 3 (1): 24–42.

Heraclides, A. (2003), *Yunanistan ve 'Doğu'dan gelen Tehlike' Türkiye Türk-Yunan İlişkilerinde Çikmazlar ve Çözüm Yollari* [Greece and Turkey in the Context of the 'Dangerous Coming from the East' – Dilemmas and Solutions in Turkish–Greek Relations], trans. Mihalis Vasilyadis-Herkül Millas, 2nd edn, İstanbul: İletişim.

Kalelioğlu, O. (2008), 'Türk-Yunan İlişkileri ve "Megali Idea"' [Turkish–Greek Relations and the 'Megali Idea'], *Ankara Üniversitesi Türk İnkilap Tarihi Enstitüsü Atatürk Yolu Dergisi* [Ankara University Institute of Turkish Revolution History Journal of Atatürk's Road] 4: 105–23.

Karpat, K. H. (2004), *Balkanlar'da Osmanli Mirasi ve Ulusçuluk* [Ottoman Heritage and Nationalism in the Balkans], Ankara: İmge.

Komisyon [Commission] (2014), *Ortaöğretim Türkiye Cumhuriyeti İnkılap Tarihi ve Atatürkçülük* [The History of the Republic of Turkey – The Revolution and Atatürkism in Secodary Education] (2014), 3rd edn, Ankara: MEB.

Lerner, G. (1979), *The Majority Finds Its Past: Placing Women in History*, New York: Oxford University Press.

Λούβη, Ε. & Ξιφαράς, Δ. Χρ. (2007), *Νεότερη και Σύγχρονη Ιστορία. Γ΄ Γυμνασίου*. Αθήνα: Οργανισμός Εκδόσεως Διδακτικών Βιβλίων [Louvi, E. and Xifaras, D. C. (2007), *Recent and Contemporary History: Third Grade Junior High School*, Athens: OEDV.]

Μαργαρίτης, Γ., Αζέλης, Α., Ανδριώτης, Ν. & Δετοράκης, Θ. (1999), *Θέματα νεοελληνικής ιστορίας. Γ΄ Λυκείου, Θεωρητική Κατεύθυνση*. Αθήνα: Οργανισμός Εκδόσεως Διδακτικών Βιβλίων. [Margaritis, G., Azelis, A., Andriotis, N. and Detorakis, T. (1999), *Greek Contemporary History Issues: Third Grade High School*. Athens: OEDV.]

Meydan, S. B. (2012), 'Mübadillerin Gözünden [From The Eyes of the Refugees]', in H. Köksal (ed.), *Yenilikçi Tarih Öğretimi Etkinlik Örnekleri* [Innovative History Teaching Activity Examples], 13–20, Ankara: Harf.

Millas, H. (2004), *Geçmişten Bugüne Yunanlilar* [The Greeks from Past to Present], 2nd edn, İstanbul: İletişim.

Millas, H. (2006), *Yunan Ulusunun Doğuşu* [The Emerging of the Greek Nation], 3rd edn, İstanbul: İletişim.

Millas, H. (2011), 'Cumhuriyet Türkiyesi Tarihyaziminda Gayrimüslim Azinliklar: Yunan Örneği [Non-Muslim Minorities in Turkish Republic Historiography: The Example of the Greeks]', in F. Adanir and S. Faroqhi (eds), *Osmanli ve Balkanlar* [Ottomans and Balkans], İstanbul: İletişim.

Neyzi, L. (2013), *Ben Kimim? Türkiye'de Sözlü Tarih, Kimlik ve Öznellik* [Who Am I? Oral History, Identity and Subjectivity in Turkey], 5th edn, İstanbul: İletişim.

Önder, B. (2014), *Ortaöğretim Tarih 9 Ders Kitabi* [Secondary Education History Year 9 Textbook], Ankara: Biryay.

Özkırımlı, U. and Sofos, S. A. (2013), *Tarihin Cenderesinde Yunanistan ve Türkiye'de Milliyetçilik* [Nationalism in Greece and Turkey in History's Mangle], trans. Sezin Tekin Özsakinç and Özlem Bülbül, İstanbul: İstanbul Bilgi Üniversitesi.

Öztan, G. G. (2014), 'Fetih'in Cazibesi: Çocuk Edebiyatinda İstanbul'un Fethi ve Çağriştirdiklari. [Conquest's Charm: The Conquest of İstanbul in Children's Literature and its Evocation]', in I. O. Kerestecioğlu and G.G. Öztan (eds), *Türk Sağı, Mitler, Fetişler, Düşman İmgeleri* [Turkish Right Wing Myths, Fetishes, Enemy Images], 2nd edn, 345–75, İstanbul: İletişim.

Saigol, R. (2004), 'Militarizasyon, Ulus ve Toplumsal Cinsiyet: Şiddetli Çatişma Alanlari Olarak Kadin Bedenleri [Militarization, Nation and Gender: Women's Bodies as Arenas of Violent Conflict]', in A. Gül Altinay (ed.), *Vatan Millet Kadinlar* [Homeland Nations Women], 227–59, İstanbul: İletişim.

Saray, Ş. (2005), 'İnkılap Tarihi Dersi Okullarda Nasil İşlenmeli ve Uygulanmali? [How Should the Revolution History Course be Taught in Schools?]', in M. Saray and H. Tosun (eds), *İlk ve Ortaöğretim Kurumlarinda Türkiye Cumhuriyeti İnkılap Tarihi ve Atatürkçülük Konularinin Öğretimi: Mevcut Durum ve Çözüm Önerileri* [Teaching the History of the Republic of Turkey – The Revolution and Atatürkism in Primary and Secondary Education: The Current Situation and Solutions], 101–8, Ankara: Atatürk Araştirma Merkezi.

Seyitdanlioğlu, M. (2004), 'Yunan İhtilali ve II. Mahmud'un Politikalari [Greek Revolution and the Politics of Mahmud II]', *Manas Journal of Social Studies* 6 (12): 49–56. Available online: http://journals.manas.edu.kg/mjsr/oldarchives/Vol06_Issue12_2004/396.pdf (accessed 23 February 2015).

Σκουλάτου, Β., Δημακοπούλου, Ν. & Κόνδη, Σ. (1995), *Ιστορία νεότερη και σύγχρονη. Α' Λυκείου, Τεύχος Α'*. Αθήνα: Οργανισμός Εκδόσεως Διδακτικών Βιβλίων. [Skoulatou, V., Dimakopoulou, N. and Kondi, S. (1995), *History, Recent and Contemporary: First Grade High School, Volume 1*, Athens: OEDB].

Stathis, P. (2013), 'Yunan [Ve Türk] Tarih Ders Kitaplarinda "Ben" ve "Öteki" İmgeleri [Images of "Us" and the "Other" in Greek and Turkish History Textbooks]', in A. Berktay and H. C. Tuncer (eds), *Tarih Eğitimi ve Tarihte Öteki Sorunu* [History Teaching and the Issue of 'Other' in History], 2nd edn, 125–33, İstanbul: Tarih Vakfi Yurt Yayinlari [History Foundation Dormitory Publications].

Tılıç, İ. D (2010), 'Türk Medyasinda Yunanistan: Resmi Politikalarin İzdüşümünde "Ötekilikten 'Biz'e" [Greece in Turkish Media: From "Otherness" to "Us" in the Projection of Official Politics]', *Sözde Masum Milliyetçilik* [Nationalism So-Called Innocent], 201–20, İstanbul: Kitap.

Turan, V., Genç, İ., Çelik, M., Genç, C. and Türedi, Ş. (2014), *Ortaöğretim Tarih 10 Ders Kitabi* [Secondary Education History Year 10 Textbook], 6th edn, Ankara: MEB.

Ünay, B. (2007), 'Türk-Yunan İlişkilerinde Temel Sorunlar Ve 1999 Sonrasi Yumuşama Dönemi [Main Issues in Turkish-Greek Relations and the Detente Era After 1999]', Yayimlanmamiş Yüksek Lisans Tezi [unpublished Master's thesis], Ankara: Atilim.

Yuval-Davis, N. (2003), *Cinsiyet ve Millet* [Gender and Nation], trans. Ayşin Bektaş, İstanbul: İletişim.

5

South Africa and Rwanda: Remembering or Forgetting?

Gail Weldon

Introduction

On 27 April 1994 South Africans went to the polls in what were regarded internationally as miracle elections, ending over forty years of formal apartheid. Against the expectations of many, the elections were peaceful and generated enormous goodwill between South Africans. However, it had not been a miracle, but the result of tough negotiation processes. After the 1994 elections, South Africa entered a period of compromise and reconciliation under a Government of National Unity and its first democratically elected president, Nelson Mandela.

On 27 April 1994, with the international media focused on South Africa, Rwanda was three weeks into a swift and brutal genocide that shocked the world. By the time the genocide had ended with military victory by the invading Rwandan Patriotic Front (RPF) under the command of Paul Kagame, some 800,000 to a million Tutsi and Hutu were dead. In July 1994 an interim Government of National Unity was set up in Kigali. Kagame became vice president and minister of defence and was regarded as the de facto leader of Rwanda. In 2000 he became president. The military victory left the new government in Rwanda with the widest discretion to decide how to reconstruct Rwandan society and how to engage with the divided past.

Two critical issues face societies emerging from identity-based violent conflict: how to build a democratic society in contrast to the old; and what should be done with the traumatic knowledge of the past. The choices are complicated when the post-conflict society is one in which victims and perpetrators have to find a way of making sense of the past together in a fragile political context. The political choices made for the future in relation to the past are, at the same time, educational choices.

This chapter engages with remembering and forgetting in South Africa and Rwanda within the school curriculum; with the creation of an appropriate history curriculum in an emerging democracy; and with effective teacher professional development in a society in transition from conflict.

Literature review

Since 1989 there has been increasing interest in the link between education and conflict, and rebuilding education after conflict. In that year the fall of the Berlin Wall and the subsequent collapse of communism opened up new avenues for re-examining the past of societies involved in identity-based conflict (Bush and Saltarelli 2000; Smith and Vaux 2003; Tawil 1997; Tawil and Harley 2004). However, there is a gap in the research as few studies frame education policy and history curriculum revision within the political context and legacies of trauma in countries in transition from conflict.

Research into Germany after the Second World War provides insight into when and why countries develop a culture of remembering or forgetting. In the 1950s and 1960s Germany was silent about the extent of popular participation in the Holocaust. This changed after the 1950s when the politics of memory became more intense (Herf 1997; Jarausch and Geyer 2003). There has also been groundbreaking research in Germany on inter-generational transmission of memory of both perpetrators and victims (Mitscherlich and Mitscherlich 1975; Sichrovsky 1988; Bar-On 1989; Hoffman 2004).

The major focus of the research in Eastern Europe has been on the re-evaluation of national narratives in history curricula and reconciling histories within school textbooks after the collapse of the Soviet Union (Kujawska and Skórzynska 2000; Kissane 2005; Janmaat 2007; Zajda 2007; Torsti 2007). None of the studies engages with traumatic legacies of conflict and the way in which they might impact the construction of post-conflict narratives and history education.

Northern Ireland and Israel provide fascinating examples of countries still divided and still within a situation of conflict if defined in its broadest sense, revealing how deep the barriers to teaching a common history can be (Gallagher 2005; Barton and McCully 2005; Naveh 2005). More recently research has focused on post-conflict education and transitional justice in South America (for example Guatemala and Colombia), Asia (Cambodia) and Africa (Sierra Leone and Liberia).

While some studies situate the research within the political processes in countries in transition, none engage with the legacies of trauma, including inter-generational transmission of particularly historic trauma. This is concerning given the rich research in the field of psychology and psychoanalysis on the inter-generational transfer of traumatic knowledge. Key researchers in the field include Volkan (2006a; 2006b), Lindner (2004, 2006, 2008), Staub (2003) and Staub et al. (2005).

Approach, design and methods

My training as an academic historian is central to my approach to comparative education research, providing a depth beyond that of theoretical approaches that might not recognize historical subtleties (Martin 2003: 105–17). In examining the national processes that contributed to curriculum change in South Africa, I drew on my personal experience as a participant researcher of curriculum development within South Africa. I was part of the writing teams for *History in Social Sciences for the National Curriculum Statements (NCS) (Grades 1–12)* (Grades R–9 2002; Grades 10–

12 2003) on which this research is based. I was also a co-founder of the *Facing the Past* (FtP) programme and have co-facilitated teacher development workshops since 2003.

Comparisons between South Africa and Rwanda were possible on a number of levels. I examined official political and educational policy documents in both countries, analysing ideology and pedagogy in the documents. The historical analysis of the context in which the documents were produced was critical to the understanding of the language and symbols of the education documents in both countries.

In both countries, similar professional development workshops had been developed: FtP (in partnership with *Facing History and Ourselves* (FHAO), Boston, USA) in South Africa; workshops conducted by FHAO in Rwanda, which I attended. This made data gathering from the workshops and comparison possible. During and after each workshop, teachers completed evaluations which asked questions about personal and professional development. From 2011 to 2014 I conducted a longitudinal study in South Africa, interviewing a *Facing the Past* teacher working group, conducting group interviews with pupils from two very diverse schools, and individual interviews with a group of pupils from a third school. This was part of an international research project, Development of Ethical Civic Actors in the Face of Identity-Group Conflicts (DECIDES). *Facing the Past* teachers taught all pupils interviewed.

Data in the initial research were coded using open coding (for Rwanda and South Africa) as well as the Atlas data-coding programme for the most recent longitudinal South African data, looking for: expressions of teacher and pupil identity and the legacy of apartheid; understanding of democracy; evidence of ethical civic thinking and action; and evidence of 'border crossing'.[1] In Rwanda I looked for the correlation between the teachers' discourse about the past and the official narrative, for what was said or intimated about Rwandan identity in the past and the present and the tensions that emerged around what should be taught as official history and the way in which it should be taught. The use of multiple sources of data, such as documents, workshop observation and individual and group interviews, helped to triangulate the findings.

Country contexts

The history and nature of the conflict and the way in which the conflict ends has particular implications for an emerging curriculum. In both South Africa and Rwanda the conflicts were identity-based, but with significant differences.

South Africa

South Africa was a society based on over three hundred years of slavery, conflict, segregation and apartheid. The aim of the National Party after their 1948 election victory was to entrench 'the protection of Afrikanerdom, white power and the white race' (Beinart 1994: 141). A series of laws put in place between 1949 and 1954 formalized segregation within the legal system, and in 1952 the introduction of what became known as the 'Pass Law' aimed at controlling the movement of black South Africans. The Population Registration Act (Republic of South Africa [RSA], 1950) classified people as belonging to different 'races'; the Prohibition of Mixed Marriages Act (RSA, 1949) banned marriages across the racial divides; the Group Areas Act (RSA, 1950) identified separate residential areas; and the Separate Amenities Act (RSA, 1954), in theory, provided equal separate amenities such as park benches, beaches and toilets for the different 'races'.

The implementation of apartheid laws resulted in large-scale social engineering as people were forcibly removed and resettled, creating a racialized geographic settlement pattern. For the vast majority of South Africans contact between 'racial' groups was a master/servant or boss/manual labourer relationship. The policing of free movement of black South Africans under the pass law system criminalized millions of ordinary men and women arrested for contravening these laws. Resistance to apartheid was brutally suppressed. The scale of repression, including states of emergency, banning, house arrest, detention without trial, imprisonment, torture, abduction and murder, increased with the increasing scale of resistance from the 1950s to the end of the 1980s.

Education during apartheid was an instrument of division and oppression, which reinforced inequality and entrenched notions of white superiority and black inferiority. History education was manipulated to legitimize National Party rule and the right of white Afrikaners to hold a dominant position in society. In 1953 the Bantu Education Act formalized the system of unequal education for black South Africans, who were to be educated to the level of manual labour. From the 1950s Bantu Education became the focus of resistance and from the Soweto uprisings in 1976 schools became sites of struggle. This intensified in the mid-1980s.

In South Africa the formal conflict ended through negotiation and compromise. During the negotiation process the apartheid government and the liberation movements, particularly the African National Congress (ANC) as the largest of those movements, made significant compromises in the interests of the peaceful transfer of political power. In 1994 the Government of National Unity was inaugurated and Nelson Mandela was sworn in as South Africa's first democratically elected president.

Rwanda

Rwanda experienced some seventy years of colonialism, which entrenched ethnic identities between the Hutu majority and Tutsi minority. It was first a German sphere of interest from 1890, and after the First World War was taken over as a mandate by Belgium. There is debate among historians about the extent to which ethnic identities in Rwanda had been formed before colonial rule (Longman and Rutagengwa 2004: 162–82) but what is accepted is that colonial rule entrenched ethnic identities that were already forming. Colonial rulers drew on pseudoscientific ideas, common in the late nineteenth century, of the hierarchy of races. Applying this to Rwanda, they ranked the 'Hamitic' Tutsi, supposedly later immigrants to the region, above the 'indigenous' Hutu. The 'Hamitic' people were said to be biologically and culturally superior to Indigenous Africans.

In the late 1950s, PARMEHUTU (Party for the Emancipation of the Hutus), formed in 1957, rebelled against the Belgian colonial power and in 1962 Rwanda became independent. Under the Hutu-led government the colonial narrative of Tutsi superiority was manipulated within history education to demonstrate Tutsi abuse of power (Mamdani 2001: 23). Tutsi were cast as foreign invaders to be sent back to where they came from. As such, Tutsi were denied Rwandan identity, which conferred legitimacy – and acceptance as citizens – with associated legal, political, social, cultural and economic rights. In the 1960s and 1970s there were Hutu-led massacres of Tutsi in Rwanda. Many fled to Uganda where by 1990 the Rwandan Patriotic Front (RPF) had been formed. In October 1990, RPF guerrillas began an invasion of Rwanda from Uganda. In the years that followed, intensifying in the weeks just before the genocide, the Rwandan state media used the narrative of Tutsi 'foreigners' – nomads and invaders – to fuel the hate speech that contributed to the mass slaughter of April 1994.

There is general agreement that the precipitating factor which unleashed the genocide was the direct hit on the plane carrying the President of Rwanda, Juvénal Habyarimana, by a surface-to-air missile as it was about to land in Kigali on the night of 6 April 1994. However, as far as the causes of the genocide and its course are concerned, there 'are few parallels for the sheer depth of the discords and disagreements the 1994 genocide has generated among observers, survivors and perpetrators' (Lemarchand 2007). This is important when set against the dominant RPF genocide narrative that has emerged since 1994. By the time the genocide had run its course, between 800,000 and a million people had been murdered. In Rwanda the conflict was ended by a RPF military victory under the leadership of Paul Kagame, now President of Rwanda.

The different ways that formal conflicts are ended have implications for the way in which education policies are created in the transition period. The formulation of education policy after a negotiated settlement is more likely to be contested and result in compromise than after a conflict that ends with a military victory. The kind of history curriculum that emerges from negotiation will in all likelihood be less exclusive in terms of its content than one that is written by the victors. This has particular implications for reconciliation and the construction of democracy. Victory presupposes the right to impose a new vision of national identity and a linked new national narrative on those who have been defeated. However, the implications of this include the danger of unfinished business when the past is not dealt with in a way that enables both victors and defeated to engage in the traumatic legacy of that past together. The new ruling elite may construct a single, politically acceptable, new dominant narrative that can become a new truth, equally as oppressive as that of the previous regime. The extent to which this holds true for South Africa and Rwanda is engaged with in the next part of this chapter.

Confronting traumatic knowledge

South Africa

In 1994, the Government of National Unity in South Africa inherited a traumatized country of racial inequality and racialized identities; a country in which privilege and power had been racialized (Mamdani 2000). The education system was fragmented and unequal, with nineteen different education departments. In 1995 the White Paper on Education and Training outlined the vision for post-apartheid education: to promote democracy and a free, equal, just and peaceful society with well-informed and critical citizens (DoE 1995). Work on a new curriculum began in 1996 – the year of the first Truth and Reconciliation Commission (TRC) hearings. This very public acknowledgement of the gross human rights abuses of the apartheid state may well have had some influence on the decision made by the new policymakers about the position of history within the curriculum – to 'forget' rather than to 'remember' the past. The first post-apartheid curriculum, Curriculum 2005, was launched in 1997. Although clearly positioning itself in relation to the past, the vision for the future was economic: to create a 'prosperous, truly united, democratic and internationally competitive country with literate, creative and critical citizens leading productive, self-fulfilled lives in a country free of violence, discrimination and prejudice' (DoE 1997: 1)

The emphasis in the document was on economic development and the need to situate South Africa within the global economy. Subjects were replaced with Learning Areas, none of which included history. Forgetting the past is not unusual in countries emerging from conflict – Germany did this to a large extent in the 1950s and 1960s. However, while this may have been understandable in post-Nazi Germany, in which there were few victims to demand remembrance, it was less understandable in South Africa where the victims, living side by side with former perpetrators, were in fact in the majority, not only in society but also in the new government. Possible explanations may be that this was a period of compromise, and the TRC hearings, by opening up the depth of trauma experienced under apartheid, meant that the past might have been too contentious, too emotionally charged, to grapple with so soon. On another level school history was widely regarded as having contributed significantly to divisions in the past – so could not in the view of many key policymakers contribute to unity. Lastly, within the stated economic aims of the new curriculum, it was probably not clear how history could contribute to these aims. While history was no longer part of a school curriculum, the TRC narratives were shaping a new official memory and history, with the possibility of this becoming the new 'truth' about the apartheid past.

In 1999 the second democratic elections returned an ANC government with a substantial majority, ending the period of compromise. The new Minister of Education, Professor Kader Asmal, reversed the collective amnesia when he launched a curriculum revision in 2000. For Asmal, education was more than a strategy for economic growth and poverty reduction: it was intrinsic to the development and support of democracy. To him, ethical remembrance within history education was a critical part of building democracy (Asmal 1998). *The Revised National Curriculum Statements (RNCS)*, which emerged in 2002, were infused with issues of human rights and social and environmental justice. There were firmer subject structures within Learning Areas, and during the writing process particular attention was paid to the emerging history curriculum because of the central role it was intended to play as a vehicle for human rights.

The history curriculum launched in 2002 did not, as in so many other post-conflict societies, replace one national narrative with another. What was created was an official history which aimed 'at permitting the unofficial, the hidden, to become visible' (Chisholm 2004: 188). It aimed to contribute to the emergence of a society in which diversity was seen as a source of strength, through providing for diverse memories within the new national narrative. This would hopefully provide opportunities for young people, in Giroux's terms, to become border crossers. According to Giroux's concept of border pedagogy, young people need to be provided with opportunities to engage with texts that both affirm and interrogate the complexity of their histories. They should not be seen as a cohesive group, but young people whose 'multilayered and often contradictory voices and experiences, intermingle with the weight of particular histories that will not fit easily into the master narrative' (Giroux 1992: 34). Within the new curriculum, there was, therefore, no attempt to delineate a 'true' history. Rather the new 'official history', through a commitment to the idea that historical 'truth' can be subjected to rigorous analysis by entering conversations structured by the 'disciplinary traditions' and that there are complex histories within the South African experience, became an 'open' rather than a 'closed' text (Weldon 2009: 180).

Three things need to be in place if history education in a post-conflict society is to contribute to strengthening democracy: the political will, an enabling curriculum and a cohort of teachers able to facilitate 'border crossings' in their history classrooms. In 2002 the first two were in place. However, little attention had been paid to appropriate teacher development in support of the new curriculum.

If the curriculum provides opportunities for border crossings, this has to be facilitated by the teachers within a democratic space. However, South Africa has a tradition of authoritarian education structures, and the power relations within the majority of South African schools and classrooms in 2002 continued to be authoritarian. Furthermore, policymakers and education officials failed to engage with what it might mean for teachers, shaped by the apartheid conflict and grappling with traumatic legacies, to have to teach a new curriculum that was infused with a human rights perspective. One teacher at a FtP workshop put it this way:

> We are not admitting enough about how messed up we are . . . We have to work things out ourselves first . . . we have to get rid of our stereotypes before we can help learners.
>
> FtP Teacher, 2008

The new curriculum included the history of the apartheid conflict, the work of the TRC and the transition to democracy. Neither the curriculum writers nor the officials setting up training programmes paid any attention to the possible re-traumatization of teachers. In an email after a FtP workshop session on teaching the TRC, one teacher wrote to the facilitator:

> I have been thinking about the TRC and our response to it – and the difficulties I find in dealing with our past. I must admit, I didn't sleep so well last night . . . I realized that what we are attempting to do is to teach our own nation's trauma while still in a period of mourning – especially for those of us who experienced apartheid.
>
> email, 28 August 2008

Personal change in societies emerging from identity-based conflict has a very specific context – that of confronting individual traumatic legacies and the stereotypes of 'the other' shaped during the conflict. In response to the lack of appropriate official training, a partnership programme with FHAO, *Facing the Past – Transforming our Future* (FtP), was set up in Cape Town. The first workshop was held in 2003. It became clear from the first that the programme would have to provide teachers with the support needed to examine the ways in which the apartheid past had affected them as individuals and as teachers. It was hoped that this, in turn, would help them to mediate difficult conversations about the apartheid past with pupils, in a way that would contribute to a democratic future.

The concept of 'moral imagination' developed by peace educator, John Paul Lederach, was valuable for conceptualizing the FtP approach in teacher workshops (Lederach 2004); in particular, providing a community of practice in which teachers develop the capacity to 'imagine themselves in a web of relationships even with their enemies' (Lederach 2004: 4–5), desiring to understand our enemies from their point of view (Lederach 2005). Lederach emphasizes the importance of understanding the past in order to comprehend cycles of violent conflict with shared narratives helping to find the place, voice and story of individuals within the group (ibid.). For teachers engaging with the legacy of identity-based conflict, this provides a context not only for personal change but also for engaging in difficult conversations about the past and present with their pupils. A key moment for teachers in the workshops is engaging in 'silent conversation' within groups with a variety of personal narratives of apartheid experiences that echo their own experiences. The debriefing in a large-group context has led to many teachers voicing their own trauma for the first time in the presence of the historical 'other'. As a participant wrote at the end of a FtP workshop:

> The fact that I was willing to share my deepest emotions with people I did not know four days ago, actually set me free. I realized I can talk about stuff without the fear of being labelled a racist or a privileged white man.
>
> [white male], *Facing the Past* workshop, 2008

Personal change is a complex and long process, and the FtP workshops are only the beginning of that journey. Many of those who were part of the first group of teachers in 2003 have continued to come to events and workshops. The self-exploration and conversations deepen with each group contact, and members of the group become part of the crucial support structures for one another.

The FtP pupils who were part of the longitudinal research project are second-generation survivors of apartheid. They are the so-called 'born frees', born after 1994. However, they all carry within them the inherited knowledge of apartheid transmitted to them by family and the communities in which they find themselves. Eva Hoffmann, writing about her experience as a second-generation Holocaust survivor, calls the inter-generational transfer of traumatic memory and knowledge the 'paradox of indirect knowledge' (2004: 25). In South Africa the indirect knowledge passed on to the second generation by white and black survivors of apartheid both consciously and unconsciously is not only a narrative knowledge of the past, 'but [also] a terrible legacy which, rather than breed consciousness and responsibility, has drawn out the worst racial stereotypes, prejudices and aggression among [university] students' (Jansen 2004).

The evidence from the preliminary analysis of the DECIDES data indicates that the FtP teachers are mitigating the 'terrible legacy'. South African pupils emerged as possessing the greatest historical awareness and civic efficacy among the countries of the study. Most of the pupils interviewed engaged with the apartheid past in a thoughtful and critical way. This included evidence that many pupils were aware of the traumatic legacies within family and community and were themselves seeking to interrupt the inter-generational transfer of trauma. The data was further analysed for evidence of border crossing. Many pupils understood that twenty years was not long enough for apartheid to disappear in hearts and minds:

> The more we say apartheid is over, apartheid is over, it's not really, it's just the opposite. I think apartheid is not really over . . .
>
> Grade 9, FG_SA_Southern Suburbs High_110622

Virtually all at one time or another referenced the apartheid past in relation to the present. In commenting on the shooting by police of thirty-four striking miners at the platinum mine in Marikana, in the North West Province, on 13 August 2012, one pupil for example noted:

> When I first heard I realized immediately . . . that it's one of the hugest atrocities in South Africa since the apartheid regime . . . I couldn't comprehend that because in my lifetime I've never witnessed anything so extreme in South Africa. I was fortunate enough to be one of the born frees . . . and the first thing I thought was have they not learned from their past mistakes? This is history repeating itself . . .
>
> Grade 10, CS_SA_SIN_Northern Suburbs High_121126

One pupil felt deeply for her father, who was caught up in apartheid's legacy, and understood where she needed to be in relation to her father's experiences – interrupting transfer of trauma:

> I just felt for him as a father coz it's like he's still blaming the white people for the circumstances he had to grow up in . . . not being able to achieve all those things you could because of your race . . . I told him, 'Daddy look, OK, yes. The past is bad. I'm not gonna say I know how it is because I didn't grow up in that world. But if you look at yourself now you are a successful entrepreneur. You have two cars, you have a house you have a family you have health . . . that is more than most people have.'
>
> Grade 11, CS_SA_SIN_Northern Suburbs High 131110

There was evidence of being able to step into the shoes of others – of border crossing. In doing community service at an old age home, this pupil understood how difficult it is for elderly white South Africans to adapt to a new society:

> We have our generation born two years into democracy . . . we've never felt that oppression . . . we are basically taking our freedom for granted . . . just speaking to

> the elderly people and listening to these stories . . . it clicked with me that this really happened, it's not just something they're making me study for no reason . . . I particularly spoke to the coloured people because the white people weren't all that – not to be racist – but they were quite reluctant to speak to me and what the nurses said, they said that a lot of the people were there because of how old they were they were still stuck in the apartheid regime and I immediately understood that and instead of intervening or anything I just took a step back. I didn't want to create any unnecessary tension.
>
> Grade 11, CS_SA_SIN_Northern Suburbs High_131107.
> The pupil is a South African of Indian descent.

South Africa continues to grapple with legacies of deep economic disparities. The pupils of Township High, living in one of Cape Town's oldest black townships, are in many ways defined by their poverty, which frames their understanding of what democracy means. Two major issues for the poor in South Africa are lack of service delivery and government corruption:

> For me – democracy – the people elect the government – the leaders . . . must lead by example – and the government must know what the peoples' needs are so that they can provide for them. We also need people who care about their country and not run it to the ground – and protection from corruption . . . what's good about South Africa's democracy is that people know their rights . . . and the bad side is that . . . there is a lot of corruption and government is slow in getting services to people, especially in the rural areas – people don't have services such as electricity and housing.
>
> Grade 10, FG_SA_Township High_120613

What has clearly emerged is that how the past is taught and engaged with in the FtP classrooms enables pupils to demonstrate some of the kinds of skills and behaviours and dispositions that countries would want citizens to have. It is critical for the health of a fragile democracy to have young people who are able to reference the past as they engage with the legacies, who understand identity and bias, and the ways in which these can be used for evil, who engage in civic thinking and who understand and act upon threats to our democracy in their daily lives. This contrasts sharply with Rwanda.

Rwanda

After four years of civil war and genocide, Rwanda was a wasteland of death and destruction. Mutilated bodies were piled up in the streets, the churches, the schools and the fields. Schools had been sites of massacres and many schools and school grounds had been 'turned into stinking stores of human bodies' (Mamdani 2001: 271). The genocide was accompanied by wide-scale rape and infection with the HIV virus. Thousands of traumatized survivors were pregnant with unwanted babies, the *enfants de mauvais souvenirs* (children of bad memories) (OAU 2000: 6: 17; Crawley and Simic 2012) that were born in early 1995. While the RPF were able to take control of the country and form the new government, the problem is that this was a victory of a minority over the majority and it had been accompanied by gross human rights abuses carried out by the RPF army (Longman and Rutagengwa 2004: 176; Nyirubugara 2013: 48).

The Government of National Unity set up in July 1994 was dominated by the RPF and in particular by a group of returned Ugandan exiles, led by Vice President Paul Kagame (Prunier 1995: 329ff.). The founding ideology of the new RPF-led state was the memory of the genocide and the moral compulsion never to let it happen again (Reyntjens 2004: 177–210). This is understandable, but what is questionable is the way in which the RPF government is going about this.

While South Africa had inherited a severely fragmented education system, which had to be reorganized, Rwanda had to rebuild an entire infrastructure and system that had been shattered during the genocide. There had been an erosion of faith in the education system which had been divisive. Thousands of teachers had been massacred or had fled. School buildings had been demolished, burned, looted and pillaged, the furniture smashed and removed and documents destroyed, stolen and scattered. Three-quarters of all primary schools had been damaged. The Ministry of Education could not operate. Ministerial staff had fled and many had been massacred (Obura 2003: 46–9). Rebuilding infrastructure and getting schools up and running took immediate priority over curriculum issues.

In 2000 President Kagame launched Rwanda Vision 2020, setting out the vision and goals for the country and for education. Vision 2020 situates the new state within the context of the genocide:

> Rwanda is rising from its ashes, healing its wounds and rifts, thinks of its future and formulates its aspirations . . .
>
> Republic of Rwanda 2002: Introduction

The values signalling the new society are those said to be the positive values of the pre-colonial Rwandan culture, which had been destroyed by colonialism:

> courage, humanism, patriotism, dynamism, dignity, integrity (*kwanga umugayo*), sense of honour and solidarity, self-abnegation, denial of selfish and partisan interests (*kudashyira inda imbere*, etc.)
>
> Ibid.: 50

Like South Africa, post-genocide Rwanda was concerned to focus on economic development, with education regarded as a major instrument of national development, 'providing human capital necessary for poverty reduction' (Rutayisire 2004). Education was also intended to combat prejudice, foster common citizenship and achieve national reconciliation. This was not to be through history education: a moratorium was placed on the teaching of Rwandan history in schools. It was said that, before it could be re-introduced, Rwanda would first have to reach a consensus on how to interpret the events before and after the 1994 genocide and to determine how to look forward to the future (Rutayisire 2004: 11). History could be re-introduced into the schools once

Rwandan historians had 'scientifically' reviewed the 'depiction of the history of Rwanda' and the 'true' history had been written (Obura 2003: 11).

In April 2006, the *Education Sector Strategic Plan 2006–2010* noted that education at all levels is an important means of addressing issues of peace and reconciliation; and that the values of peace, harmony and reconciliation would infuse a revision of history and civic education by the National Curriculum Development Centre (Ministry of Education (MINEDUC) 2006: 19). By 2008 a new history curriculum had been completed, but would not be released until the teachers' manual was ready (MINEDUC 2008). In 2011 a French language textbook produced in cooperation with the National University of Rwanda (NUR), *Histoire du Rwanda: des origins à la fin du xxe siècle* was published for use in schools. It is critical of 'western' interpretations of Rwandan history, 'ensuring that the history curriculum in public schools is dominated by the only official version of history available, that of the RPF' (Melvin 2013: 21). It faithfully repeats the narrative used by the National Unity and Reconciliation Commission (NURC), creating a closed rather than an open text. In 2014 Rwanda's school curriculum was undergoing revision and is due to be re-launched at the beginning of 2016.

The lack of Rwandan history in the school curriculum did not mean that Rwanda was forgetting the past. An exclusionary RPF narrative of the genocide was being constructed in a variety of public spaces: genocide memorial sites, government websites, political speeches, the media, and the NURC through their *ingando* 're-education' camps, *gacaca* courts and official public commemorations of the genocide.

The narrative firstly emphasizes the unity of all Rwandans before colonial times. This was expressed by a Rwandan facilitator from the NUR at a FHAO workshop in Butare. He subsequently contributed to the new French-language history textbook:

> Identity – Hutu, Tutsi, Twa ... In ancient times there was no Hutu, Tutsi, Twa, but clans. You could all belong to the same clan – you didn't know you were Hutu/Tutsi; you were part of a clan. The Belgians are responsible for ethnicity ... This was used for division ...
>
> FHAO workshop, 2006

It secondly claims that ethnicity was created by the Belgians during colonial times by applying the contemporary European racist theories to the Rwandan society. Through this they deeply divided the Rwandan people on an ethnic basis (Republic of Rwanda 2002). Thirdly the narrative is of a 'Tutsi genocide' – with Hutu perpetrators and Tutsi victims – apportioning collective guilt to the Hutu. A million Tutsi are said to have been killed. It plays down the deaths of thousands of Hutu during the hundred days of the genocide. Fourthly, the Kagame regime denies the crimes against humanity carried out by the RPF in 1994 and the mass killings carried out in neighbouring DRC since 1994: 'they keep saying that the RPF, too, killed people? Whom did they kill? ... The RPF does praiseworthy things only' (Kagame 2013). The narrative is reinforced by the current public political discourse of the unity of all Rwandans: one nation, one language, one culture – 'now, we are one family and country in districts' (NUR facilitator, FHAO workshop) – and is driving Hutu memory underground. Those who talk publicly of ethnicity, of Hutu, Tutsi and Twa, face being accused of divisionism and genocide ideology and are liable to be arrested (Freedman et al. 2008; Reyntjens 2004).

This narrative is being widely disseminated in policy documents, the media, the university and the NURC 'solidarity' or *ingando* re-education camps – the last of these are where the most aggressive dissemination occurs. The Civic Education department of the NURC developed the *ingando* camps as a tool to build co-existence within communities. One of its first functions was the social reintegration of ex-prisoners and those released from prison, the education of youth and the provision of military training (Melvin 2013). The programme now includes school-going youth and students at secondary and tertiary levels. While social reintegration may be the stated aim, the *ingando* camps disseminate pro-RPF ideology through political indoctrination (Mgbako 2005). The official RPF version of the past forms the core of the *ingando* course on 'the history of Rwanda'. Re-education regarding ethnicity in Rwanda is at the heart of the *ingando* programme for students and pupils. They learn about the united Rwandan 'nation' before colonialism, and the damaging effects of colonialism, which created difference in Rwanda. In terms of the genocide, the contents of the course are silent on the Hutu who resisted participating in the genocide and on those who rescued Tutsi from the killers. The *ingando* camps support the government's image as the 'sole purveyor of *accurate* history' and ensure that they function as a 'government-sponsored indoctrination camp' disseminating a single narrative (Melvin 2013: 14). Commemorative events refuse to recognize Hutu survivors, causing resentment among Hutu, some of whom express anger and frustration over the one-sided nature of commemoration that focuses on the suffering of the Tutsi while ignoring the suffering of the Hutu (Longman and Rutagengwa 2004: 175). The anger is exacerbated by the refusal of the authorities to allow Hutu to bring human rights abuses carried out by the invading RPF army in 1994 to the *gacaca* courts.

This has resulted in two forms of remembering in Rwanda today: the public acts of remembrance and remembering internally without any external manifestation of the act of remembering (Nyirubugara 2013: 47). For the majority, remembrance is fraught with danger, with the legal system being used to intimidate and prosecute those who want to publicly remember other past experiences than those defined by the government (ibid.). The Kagame government is 'forcing part of the population to forget, to purge their memories, or to remember events in a different way from how they took place' (ibid.: 49).

Accusations of divisionism and genocide ideology are being used as vigorous mechanisms to silence any opposition to and critique of the government (Buckley-Zistel 2006: 110–12). In 2008 fifty school principals and teachers were suspended on suspicion of disseminating the 'ideology of genocide' (News24 2008). There is widespread political coercion and intimidation and these accusations are used to disqualify political opposition and secure election victory for the RPF. Many critics of the government have gone into exile (ICG 2002: 11). Kagame has won all elections since 1994 with over 90 per cent of the votes – a political impossibility in a healthy democracy.

Twenty years after the genocide the hegemonic RPF narrative is psychologically explosive. Psychologists warn of the dangers of an unprocessed past of collective historical trauma, which could lead to ongoing cycles of violence (Volkan 2006a). Volkan refers to this as 'chosen trauma', which is transmitted to successive generations. The impact of the trauma is exacerbated when the original population experiences 'disenfranchised grief'. This is grief as the result of historical trauma when loss cannot be voiced publicly, or loss is not openly acknowledged by the public (Johnson n.d; SAMHSA n.d.). There is a lack of recognition of their right to grieve over the collective experiences. This can result in 'perennial mourning' within the society, whether actively experienced or 'hidden'. The trauma suppressed by political oppression can resurface decades even centuries later (Šuber 2006), as was demonstrated by Slobodan Milošević's re-traumatization of Serbians in the 1990s through narratives connected to the battle of Kosovo in 1389. This resulted in ethnic cleansing and genocide of Bosnian Muslims during the war of 1992–5 and massacre of Bosniaks at Srebrenica in 1995. What is significant is that the narratives survived Tito's politics of anti-nationalism and 'forced amnesia' in the then Yugoslavia (Šuber 2006). There is no reason to think that this might not happen in Rwanda in the future if the Hutu narratives of trauma continue to be forced underground.

Conclusion

There are clear similarities as well as major differences in the way in which the 'traumatic knowledge' of the past has been engaged in Rwanda and South Africa. While both responded in the immediate aftermath of conflict with 'forgetting', South Africa's path away from that point diverged sharply from the path taken by Rwanda. The NURC/RPF 'truth' about the Rwandan past contrasts with South Africa's rigorous interrogation of historical 'truth'. Mamdani has argued that it is not possible to think of reconciliation between Hutu and Tutsi in Rwanda without a prior reconciliation with history (Mamdani 2001: 267), but this requires understanding the nature of the construction of narratives of the past, of the political nature of collective memory, and the recognition of Hutu trauma.

The legacy of trauma has not been addressed in Rwanda in a manner that could lead to deep reconciliation. Quite the contrary, the exclusion of Hutu in the processes of mourning is dangerous both on an individual as well as on a societal level. Several studies in Germany have confirmed a relationship between personal problems, even mental disturbances, among post-war Germans and the emotional burdens of an unprocessed Nazi past (Neumann 2002: 6). On a societal level psychologists and political scientists agree that reconciliation between victims and perpetrators is a crucial element of the ability to move forward after internecine violence. Unprocessed, the traumatic memories of the past are not forgotten but remain in the present.

What role, then, should history education play in remembering and forgetting? What has become evident in South Africa is that forgetting should not be an option. However, it is not only what is remembered, but also how it is taught that is essential to ethical remembrance that contributes to reconciliation. South Africa has begun this journey but still has some way to go. Rwanda needs to begin it, bringing Hutu victims into the pedagogy of remembrance accorded at the moment only to Tutsi victims.

Notes

1 Henry Giroux (1992) writes about this concept, as is discussed later.
2 Ingando courts are a traditional Rwandan system of 'grassroots' justice, administered locally; they were actively re-introduced on a wider scale after the genocide to speed up the processing of cases.

References

Asmal, K. (1998), Minister of Education, Address in the Debate on the Truth and Reconciliation Report, National Assembly, Cape Town.

Bar-On, D. (1989), *Legacy of Silence: Encounters with Children of the Third Reich*, Cambridge, MA: Harvard University Press.

Barton, K. and McCully, A. (2005), 'History, Identity, and the School Curriculum in Northern Ireland: An Empirical Study of Secondary School Students' Ideas and Perspectives', *Journal of Curriculum Studies* 37 (1): 85–116.

Beinart, W. (1994), *Twentieth-Century South Africa*, Oxford: Oxford University Press.

Buckley-Zistel, S. (2006), 'Dividing and Uniting. The Use of "Citizenship" Discourses in Conflict and Reconciliation in Rwanda', *Global Society* 20 (1): 101–13.

Bush, K. and Saltarelli, D. (2000), *The Two Faces of Education in Ethnic Conflict: Towards a Peace-building Approach to Education*, UNICEF Innocenti Centre.

Chisholm, L. (2004), 'The History Curriculum in the (Revised) National Curriculum Statement: An Introduction', in S. Jeppie (ed.), *Toward New Histories for South Africa*, Cape Town: Juta Gariep.

Crawley, K. and Simic, O. (2012), 'Unintended Consequences: Representations of Rwandan Women and their Children Born from Rape', *The Australian Feminist Law Journal* 36: 87–106. Available online: http://www.academia.edu/2064355/Unintended_Consequences_Representations_of_Rwandan_Women_and_their_Children_Born_from_Rape (accessed 15 February 2015).

Freedman, S. W., Weinstein, H. M., Murphy, K. and Longman, T. (2008), 'Teaching History after Identity-based Conflicts: The Rwanda Experience', *Comparative Education Review* 52 (4): 663–90.

Gallagher, T. (2005), 'Teaching History in Northern Ireland: A Consideration of Patterns and Problems', a paper presented at *Unite or Divide? The Challenges of Teaching History in Societies Emerging from Violent Conflict*, an international, inter-professional conference organised by the Carnegie Council on Ethics and International Affairs and the United States Institute of Peace, November 2005.

Giroux, H. A. (1992), *Border Crossings: Cultural Workers and the Politics of Education*, London: Routledge.

Herf, J. (1997), *Divided Memory: The Nazi Past in the Two Germanys*, Cambridge, MA: Harvard University Press.

Hoffman, E. (2004), *After Such Knowledge: Memory, History and the Legacy of the Holocaust*, London: Secker & Warburg.

International Crisis Group (ICG) (2002), *Rwanda at the End of the Transition: A Necessary Political Liberalisation*, Nairobi/Brussels: ICG.

Janmaat, J. G. (2007), 'The Ethnic "other" in Ukrainian History Textbooks: The Case of Russia and the Russians', *Compare* 37 (3): 307–24.

Jansen, J. (2004), 'Race and Education after Ten Years', *Perspectives in Education* 22 (4): 117–28.
Jarausch, K. H. and Geyer, M. (2003), *Shattered Past: Reconstructing German Histories*, Princeton, NJ: Princeton University Press.
Johnson, J. (n.d.), *This is Indian Country*, available online from the University of Idaho American Indian Studies 484 course website: http://www.class.uidaho.edu/engl484jj/Historical_Trauma.htm (accessed 15 January 2015).
Kagame, P. (2013), Speech in Murambi, Southern Province, 2007, cited in O. Nyirubugara, *Complexities and Dangers of Remembering and Forgetting in Rwanda*, Leiden: Sidestone Press.
Kissane, C. (2005), 'History Education in Transit: Where to for Kazakhstan?', *Comparative Education* 41 (1): 45–69.
Kujawska, M. and Skórzynska, I. (2000), 'Truth – Memory – Reconciliation : On the Cultural Context of the Activities of the Polish-Eastern-Central Europe Secondary School Textbook Commissions', a paper presented at a conference, *Memory and History: Remembering, Forgetting and Forgiving in the Life of the Nation and the Community*, Cape Town, 9–11 August 2000.
Lederach, J. P. (2004), 'The Moral Imagination: The Art and Soul of Building Peace', keynote address to the Association of Conflict Resolution Annual Conference, Sacramento, 30 September 2004. Available online: www.acrnet.org/conferences/ac04/lederachspeech.htm (accessed 14 June 2007).
Lederach, J. P. (2005), *The Moral Imagination: The Art and Soul of Building Peace*, Oxford: Oxford University Press.
Lemarchand, R. (2007), '[Scholarly Review] Rwanda: The State of Research', *The Online Encyclopaedia of Mass Violence*, 2007. Available online: http://www.massviolence.org/RWANDA-THE-STATE-OF-RESEARCH,742 (accessed 14 February 2015).
Lindner, E. (2004), 'The Psychology of Humiliation: Somalia, Rwanda/Burundi, and Hitler's Germany', unpublished PhD Thesis, University of Oslo.
Lindner, E. (2006), *Making Enemies: Humiliation and International Conflict*, Westport, CN: Praeger.
Lindner, E. (2008), 'The Educational Environment as a Place for Humiliating Indoctrination or Dignifying Empowerment', in D. R. Ganesan, D. Raja and P. Brown (eds), *Humiliation in the Academic Setting: A Special Symposium Issue of 'Experiments in Education'*, 36 (3): 61–70, New Delhi: SITU Council of Educational Research.
Longman, T. and Rutagengwa, T. (2004), 'Memory, Identity, and Community in Rwanda', in E. Stover and H. M. Weinstein (eds), *My Neighbor, My Enemy*, 162–82, Cambridge: Cambridge University Press.
Mamdani, M. (2000), 'In Their Own Voices: Truth and Reconciliation in South Africa', in L. Huntley (Dir.), *Beyond Racism: Embracing an Interdependent Future*, 18–19, Atlanta: The Southern Education Foundation. Available online: http://www.beyondracism.org/Voices/InTheirOwnVoices.pdf (accessed 14 February 2015).
Mamdani, M. (2001), *When Victims Become Killers: Colonialism, Nativism, and the Genocide in Rwanda*, Princeton: Princeton University Press and Cape Town: David Philip.
Martin, T. J. (2003), 'Divergent Ontologies with Converging Conclusions: A Case Study Comparison of Comparative Methodologies', *Comparative Education* 39 (1):105–17.
Melvin, J. (2013), 'Correcting History: Mandatory Education in Rwanda', *Journal of Human Rights in the Commonwealth* 2 (Autumn): 14–22. Available online: http://sas-space.sas.ac.uk/5215/1/1715-2295-1-SM.pdf (accessed 16 February 2015).

Mgbako, C. (2005), 'Ingando Solidarity Camps: Reconciliation and Political Indoctrination in Post-Genocide Rwanda (Note)', *Harvard Human Rights Journal* 18: 201–24. Available online: http://ir.lawnet.fordham.edu/faculty_scholarship/377 (accessed 13 January 2015).

Mitscherlich, A. and Mitscherlich, M. (1975), *The Inability to Mourn*, New York: Grove Press.

Naveh, E. (2005), 'What is Your Story? Learning Each Other's Historical Narrative in an Israeli–Palestinian Textbook', paper presented at a conference, *Unite or Divide? The Challenges of Teaching History in Societies Emerging from Violent Conflict: An International, Inter-Professional Conference*, Carnegie Council on Ethics and International Affairs and the United States Institute of Peace.

Neumann, W. (2002), 'The Presence of the Past: Using Memory Work to Search for Psychological Traces of the Nazi Past in Contemporary Germans', *British Journal of Guidance & Counselling* 30 (1): 5–16.

News24 [Archives] (2008), *'Genocide' Teachers Suspended*, Kigali, Rwanda, 21 January. Available online: http://www.news24.com/Africa/News/Genocide-teachers-suspended-20080120 (accessed 14 February 2015).

Nyirubugara, O. (2013), *Complexities and Dangers of Remembering and Forgetting in Rwanda*, Leiden: Sidestone Press.

Organisation of African Unity (OAU) (2000), *Rwanda: The Preventable Genocide*, Organisation of African Unity.

Obura, A. (2003), *Never Again: Educational Reconstruction in Rwanda*, Paris: IIEP/UNESCO. Available online: http://unesdoc.unesco.org/images/0013/001330/133051e.pdf (accessed 15 January 2015).

Prunier, G. (1995), *The Rwanda Crisis: History of a Genocide*, London: Hurst and Co.

Reyntjens, F. (2004), 'Rwanda, Ten Years On: From Genocide to Dictatorship', *African Affairs* 103: 177–210.

Rutayisire, J. (2004), 'Education for Social and Political Reconstruction: The Rwandan Experience from 1994–2004', a paper presented at the BAICE [British Association for International and Comparative Education] Conference, University of Sussex, September 2004.

Sichrovsky, P. (1988), *Born Guilty: The Children of the Nazis*, London: I.B. Tauris.

Smith, A. and Vaux, T. (2003), *Education, Conflict and International Development*. London: Department for International Development [DfID].

Staub, E. (2003), 'Preventing Violence and Generating Human Values: Healing and Reconciliation in Rwanda', *International Review of the Red Cross* 85 (852): 791–806. Available online: https://www.icrc.org/eng/assets/files/other/irrc_852_staub.pdf (accessed 15 January 2015).

Staub, E., Pearlman, L.A., Gubin, A. and Hagengimana, A. (2005), 'Healing, Reconciliation, Forgiving and the Prevention of Violence after Genocide or Mass Killing: An Intervention and its Experimental Evaluation in Rwanda', *Journal of Social and Clinical Psychology* 24 (3): 297–334.

Šuber, D. (2006), 'Myth, Collective Trauma and War in Serbia: A Cultural-Hermeneutical Appraisal', *Anthropology Matters* 8 (1). Available online: http://www.anthropologymatters.com/index.php/anth_matters/article/view/74/144 (accessed 14 February 2015).

Substance Abuse and Mental Health Services Administration (SAMHSA) (n.d.), *Fact Sheet: Historical Trauma*, Delmar, NY: SAMHSA'S GAINS Center for Behavioral Health and Justice Transformation. Available online: http://gainscenter.samhsa.gov/

cms-assets/documents/93078-842830.historical-trauma.pdf (accessed 1 January 2015).
Tawil, S. (ed.) (1997), *Educational Destruction and Reconstruction in Disrupted Societies*, final report of meeting, Geneva, 5–6 May, Geneva: International Bureau of Education.
Tawil, S. and Harley, A. (eds) (2004), *Education, Conflict and Social Cohesion*, Geneva: International Bureau of Education.
Torsti, P. (2007), 'How to Deal With a Difficult Past? History Textbooks Supporting Enemy Images in Post-War Bosnia and Herzegovina', *Journal of Curriculum Studies* 39 (1): 77–96.
Volkan, V. D. (2006a), 'Trauma, Mourning, Memorials and Forgiveness', keynote address, *Memory, Narrative and Forgiveness: Reflecting on Ten Years of South Africa's Truth and Reconciliation Commission* conference, University of Cape Town, 23–27 November.
Volkan, V. D. (2006b), 'Large-Group Identity and Chosen Trauma', *Psychoanalysis Downunder* 6: 1–14. Available online: http://www.psychoanalysisdownunder.com.au/issues/6/papers/81 (accessed 16 February 2015).
Weldon, G. (2009), 'A Comparative Study of the Construction of Memory and Identity in Curriculum in Societies Emerging from Conflict: Rwanda and South Africa', unpublished PhD thesis, University of Pretoria, 2009. Available online: http://repository.up.ac.za/bitstream/handle/2263/28159/Complete.pdf?sequence=8 (accessed 16 March 2015).
Zajda, J. (2007), 'The New History School Textbooks in the Russian Federation: 1992–2004', *Compare* 37 (3): 291–306.

Documents and reports

International

Freedman, S. (n.d.), 'The Development of Ethical Civic Actors in the Face of Identity-Group Conflicts (DECIDES): Inside Secondary Schools in the United States, South Africa, and Northern Ireland'. Available online: http://www.spencer.org/development-ethical-civic-actors-face-identity-group-conflicts-inside-secondary-schools-united (accessed 1 August 2015).

South Africa

Department of Education (DoE) (1995), *White Paper on Education and Training, Notice 196*, Pretoria: DoE.
Department of Education (DoE) (1997), *Intermediate Phase Policy Document*, Pretoria: DoE.
Department of Education (DoE) (2002), *Revised National Curriculum Statement for Grades R-9 (Schools) Policy: Social Sciences*, Pretoria: DoE. Available online: http://wced.pgwc.gov.za/ncs/lg.html#rncs.pdf*info_ncs.html [Introduction]; http://wced.pgwc.gov.za/ncs/ss1_grade.html [Social Sciences (History) all grades R-9] (accessed 14 February 2015).
Department of Education (DoE) (2003), *National Curriculum Statement Grades 10–12 (General): History*, Pretoria: DoE. Available online: http://www.education.gov.za/LinkClick.aspx?fileticket=KU/EDBh6z6Y=> (accessed 14 February 2015).

Rwanda

Ministry of Education (MINEDUC) (2003), *Education Sector Policy*, Kigali: Ministry of Education. Available online: http://www.mineduc.gov.rw/fileadmin/user_upload/EDUCATION_POLICY.pdf (accessed 1 August 2015).

Ministry of Education (MINEDUC) (2006), *Education Sector Strategic Plan 2006–2010*. Available online: http://planipolis.iiep.unesco.org/upload/Rwanda/Rwanda%20Education%20Sector%20Plan%202006%202010.pdf (accessed 26 February 2015).

Ministry of Education (MINEDUC) (2008) *Education Sector Strategic Plan 2008–2012*. Available online: lanipolis.iiep.unesco.org/upload/Rwanda/Rwanda_ESSP_2008-2012.pdf (accessed 26 February 2015).

National University of Rwanda (NUR)/Université Nationale du Rwanda (UNR) (2011) *Histoire du Rwanda: des origins à la fin du xxe siècle* [History of Rwanda: From its Origins to the End of the 20th Century], National Unity and Reconciliation Commission (NURC)/Commission Nationale pour l'Unité et la Réconciliation (CNUR), Université Nationale du Rwanda (UNR). Available online: http://www.nurc.gov.rw/uploads/media/Histoire_du_Rwanda_version_Francaise.pdf (accessed 16 February 2011).

Republic of Rwanda, Ministry of Finance and Economic Planning (2002), *2020 Vision, Draft 3* (English Version), Kigali: Republic of Rwanda, November.

6

Discussant on Part 1 – Shared Histories in Transnational and Intranational Post-Conflict Settings

Robert Guyver

One factor that an editor can note across these chapters is that theoretical perspectives appropriated to one transnational situation can also be applied to others. Coming to terms with traumatic memory was a feature in post-conflict situations in South Africa and Rwanda, but could equally be applied not only to Palestine–Israel but also to Northern Ireland and the Republic of Ireland, as well as to both Russia–Ukraine and Turkey–Greece. The relationship between history education and citizenship and the perspectives of Davies (2001), Lee and Shemilt (2007) and Barton and Levstik (2004) referred to by Waldron and McCully in the context of both jurisdictions in Ireland also have an element of universality, not to mention the principles of subverting official and overtly nationalist narratives that can be found in the chapter on Turkey–Greece.

Within these five chapters there are two sets of jurisdictions where 'post-conflict' is hardly a correct description as conflict is still going on, and those two chapters are the ones on Russia–Ukraine and Israel–Palestine. Clearly there are elements in common between these two particular chapters, and the relationship between politics, citizenship, identity, memory and history education must be unpacked to have a deeper sense of dynamic similarity. The intervention of external bodies in these situations has been both appreciated and regarded with suspicion in equal measure. The setting up of the Israel–Palestine Centre for Research and Information (IPCRI) in 1988 after the first Intifada of 1987 was an initiative that continued after the Oslo Accords of 1993 and 1995, involving Israel, the Palestinian Authority, the USA and Norway, but has proved to have many shortcomings, especially in the way that the need for an Israeli response to the Palestinian narrative was neglected, and indeed in the way that this unsatisfactory reaction was accepted.

The rise of a new and aggressive form of nationalism in the Russian Federation has meant that the future of further Western European initiatives within Russia, such as EUROCLIO's past joint involvement with MATRA 'social transformation' projects (for example 'Uroki Clio' and 'Mosaics of Culture') funded by the Dutch government, are in doubt. Pressure put on those pursuing the profession of history teaching is very politically motivated, and history teachers are expected to carry out political demands at odds with their professional honour and connected with demonstrations and elections; the integrity of history teaching is undermined by the possibility of students purchasing examination answers on the black market. However, the setting up and continued existence of history teaching associations are parallel developments in Ukraine and the Russian Federation where cross-border collegiality is still operating even while conflict is taking place, and this can be seen in the chapter itself as an example of professional dialogue. The fact that an association was established in Khabarovsk, some 8,500 kilometres to the east of Moscow, is reassuring. The EUROCLIO website gives details of further 'mosaics of culture' seminars organized by Tamara Eidelman in Vladivostok, Rostov, Vladikavkaz, Moscow and Kazan.

The existence in Ukraine of problematic historical memories, especially those associated with the Second World War, has shown that any attempt, for example, by a pro-Russian government in Ukraine to 'collectivize' this memory under a received official Russian narrative about the Great Patriotic War would be bound to fail. Such a government was forced to retreat after the large-scale public demonstrations in Ukraine in February 2014, but not without considerable violence. In the east of Ukraine, which has a large ethnic Russian population, a different kind of war broke out, a 'hybrid' war, with unofficial infiltration by Russian forces, and the annexation of Crimea by Russia in March 2014. Ukraine itself has to come to terms with its own kind of nationalism, and 'responsible action' among its youth, as well as a need to move away from too much 'self-identity' to a more favourable stance towards outsiders, are aims of both citizenship and history education.

Palestine is both an invented jurisdiction and a place in memory – with Haifa, for example, being regarded by Palestinians as a predominantly Palestinian city, even today; this belief about Palestine being wherever – even in Israel – Palestinians live is widespread. The Israeli unwillingness to recognize the Palestinian narrative about the Nakba (in Arabic, 'the catastrophe'), referring to the 1948 appropriation of Palestinian land by Israel and the associated human cost in displacement and lives lost, is linked to Israel's belief in the legitimacy of the State of Israel itself and a sense that an incorporation of the Nakba narrative would undermine this legitimacy. However, the memory of the Nakba will not go away, and the events and subsequent developments themselves are now being seen by Nadia Naser-Najjab and Ilan Pappé as evidence of a once started and continuing 'settler colonialism'. In addition, there are 'facts on the ground' which add present experience to a traumatic memory. These are the Separation Wall, difficulties in getting through checkpoints, psychological damage to school-age children and physical damage to houses and schools, as in the most recent example of conflict in Gaza in 2014.

The way a history curriculum is managed officially is a reflection of the nature of the political situation under which this happens, and Gail Weldon in her chapter on South Africa and Rwanda has shown that there are critical tools for analysing the managing of memory for both political and curriculum purposes. These critical tools draw on research in the field of psychology and psychoanalysis about the inter-generational transfer of traumatic knowledge. The kind of polity a nation aspires to is reflected in its official curriculum documents, and the co-existence within nations of two or more ethnic groups with distinctive identities and memories ideally requires a political framework which allows a particular set of bridging negotiations with regard to curriculum. Sometimes these work well; at other times one party has an unfair weighting with insufficient empathy for the other party and too much self-identity for its own. This has happened also with the IPCRI negotiations.

Gail Weldon regards the South African history curriculum as an example of curriculum success based on 'remembering' whereas Rwanda's efforts in this direction are seen as 'work in progress' in their coming to terms with the possible negative effects of an official policy of 'forgetting'. Also, she recognizes the positive significance in South Africa after the elections of 1999 of Education Minister Kader Asmal's policy of 'ethical remembrance' within history education, which he saw as a critical part of building a democracy. The emerging history curriculum did not just replace one official national narrative with another. To use the words of Linda Chisholm (2004: 188) this was an official history which aimed 'at permitting the unofficial, the hidden, to become visible'. This contrasts with the Rwandan Patriotic Front (RPF) official policy on remembering which is in effect driving Hutu memory underground. This failure to address the traumatic memory of a large portion of the population can lead to further cycles of violence, possibly arising from, in Volkan's words, 'disenfranchised grief' (Volkan 2006a; 2006b).

Nadia Naser-Najjab and Ilan Pappé in their chapter on Palestine draw on critical tools that include Foucault's interpretation of knowledge as control (and even as, in some circumstances, a form of discipline or punishment). They also refer to Gramsci's theory of cultural hegemony and Gadamer's notion of the fusion of horizons in order to highlight both what was happening and what was not happening. They make a significant point that, although politics can try to control education, when memory is so powerful and where there are identifiable fault lines in the political–educational relationship, education itself makes demands that the wider society itself should change in order for justice in the educational realm to happen. The continuation of the Israeli–Palestinian conflict itself is about an inability to come to an agreement about each other's narratives.

> The gap between historical framing and narrative has been ignored by peace brokers ever since 1967 and depicted as an obstacle for peace. In fact what the issue at hand proves is that this very gap is the reason for the conflict, and if it cannot be breached between the most moderate Palestinians and liberal Zionists, we need a new framing, which to our mind only the settler colonialist paradigm offers.
>
> Naser-Najjab and Pappé, this volume, p. 27

This requires a raising of levels of honesty in how self-awareness (or 'moral imagination', to draw a phrase from Paul Lederach in Gail Weldon's chapter) is reached in relation to 'the other'. This can be attempted by 'providing a community of practice in which teachers develop the capacity to "imagine themselves in a web of relationships even with their enemies" desiring to understand our enemies from their point of view' (Lederach 2005: 4–5; see also Lederach 2004). Education is just one arena where the need to accommodate the kinds of changes in society which would allow such relationships to happen has consequences for whether the conflict will either continue or end.

It is possible to adapt what Weldon has said about Rwanda to the situation in Palestine, and by drawing on Mamdani's argument that 'it is not possible to think of reconciliation between Hutu and Tutsi in Rwanda without a prior reconciliation with history' (Mamdani 2001: 267). The same would be true and could be applied to Arab Palestinians and Jewish Israelis, but indeed, as Weldon says, 'this requires understanding the nature of the construction of narratives of the past, of the political nature of collective memory, and the recognition of ... trauma' (p. 108) when applied to significant, large population groups. It also requires a partnership between politics and education, especially in a political empowerment of educational agencies to permit this to happen, and establishing a political climate in which a public discourse about these matters can be sustained using 'moral imagination' without a constant resorting to polarization, and the role of history teacher associations that cross cultural borders could be crucial in this process.

It might, however, be possible to draw up a template of criteria for constructing a history curriculum for societies locked in conflict to unlock their fraught situations, and the five chapters in this first part of the book provide many clues. The relationship between Turkey and Greece as described by Gülçin Dilek and Eleni Filippidou shows a great deal of overlap in the narrative arc of the various empires to which both Greece and Turkey at various times belonged, especially the Byzantine and Ottoman empires, and how a certain area of İstanbul was actually where the Patriarchate of the (Greek) Orthodox Church was based. The concept of the *Megali Idea* or Great (as in Great*er*) Greece is seen in the fact that there were Greek populations living in northern Anatolia and on the western Anatolian coastline for hundreds, and in some cases thousands of years, and it was in response to the strident calls for nationalism that both Turkish and Greek populations were placed under pressure and in the end exchanged. The process during a time of war and inter-ethnic conflict often had fatal consequences, caused either deliberately or by deliberate neglect, with Western powers also culpable in a callous interpretation of their own neutrality, especially in the Smyrna/İzmir situation.

Gülçin Dilek and Eleni Filippidou, however, hit on a set of principles that could enable an increased level of dialogue to be sustained even in the most fraught of situations. They recognize that the past can be re-interpreted to fit the demands of current policy, for example in efforts to find in Ottoman history evidence of early examples of human rights awareness, but also they see that official histories, as sometimes – indeed often – found in textbooks, tend to neglect the subtle layers which make history more complex by the inclusion of individual micro-histories. Also, and powerfully, they recommend that some traumatic events like sexual violence against women and even massacres during war be seen not just through a nationalist interpretation, but also as examples of a universally experienced wartime problem. They also find examples of historians (like Karpat 2004 and Millas 2006; Millas also being a textbook author) whose own researches show that official narratives demonstrate an over-simplicity which can feed back into an unhelpfully nationalistic or monolithic stance.

If these principles were transferred, for example, to the Israel–Palestine situation an objective approach, although still no doubt fraught with difficulties, would be to take specific examples of forced population expulsion (in Palestine–Israel and in Europe or even South Asia) and compare oral histories associated with them. The dynamic driving this would be a comparison of human suffering at a micro-historical level rather than a confirmation or denial of a national (or nationalist) principle. It would work both ways because in the end it could involve both a Palestinian appreciation of the human cost of the European Holocaust *and* an Israeli realization of the effect on individuals of being removed from what they believed were, and what they had indeed known as, their lands and their homes. An exchange of empathy at a level where the concerns about the legitimacy of nationhood were temporarily put to one side could do nothing but good. There are obvious political barriers to this approach, especially in the wake of Israel's law of 2011 which makes it illegal to commemorate Independence Day (15 May) or the day of the establishment of the state as a day of mourning (which the very word 'Nakba' implies) (Amendment no. 40 (2011) to the 'Budgets Foundations Law (1985) – Reducing Budgetary Support due to Activity that is Contrary to the Principles of the State').

The three sets of theoretical perspectives identified by Fionnuala Waldron and Alan McCully in the context of the Republic of Ireland and Northern Ireland could also be applied when critically analysing the same factors in other situations. All sets examine the relationship between history education and citizenship education. For Davies (2001) the three linked outcomes of history *and* citizenship education should be the knowledge dimension, the development of skills of enquiry and communication, and skills of participation and responsible action. This is clearly reflected in the dialogue between Tamara Eidelman, Polina Verbytska and Jonathan Even-Zohar about youths in both Russia and Ukraine. For Lee and Shemilt (2007) there are three models of citizenship – the cornucopian, the carrier and the complementary – of which the preferred model is the complementary where history education is informing the kind of historical consciousness needed for decision-making in a democracy. Beyond this, Barton and Levstik (2004: 36–40) believe that education for democratic citizenship requires the development of 'reasoned judgement about human affairs', 'an expanded view of humanity' and 'deliberation over the common good'. The need for all three of these last points can be found across all five of these chapters.

Waldron and McCully echo some of the points made by Dilek and Filippidou when they reflect on some of the limitations of using the local dimension to illustrate or problematize the historical perspectives associated with identity. 'Big picture' history can play a role too in refocusing attention away from the narrower concerns of immediate community tension, and this can include asking questions about bigger political and economic concerns, including the imbalance between the North and the South and the role of large multinationals. They also call for more attention to be given to ways in which citizenship education and history might be jointly re-structured to draw strength from each other, but also to utilize 'big picture' dimensions to contextualize ideas that may apply to the nation or the locality but can only be fully understood if studied across a wider, global stage.

References

(TT) indicates that the original text was in Turkish

Barton, K. C. and Levstik, L. S. (2004), *Teaching History for the Common Good*, London: Lawrence Erlbaum Associates.
Chisholm, L. (2004), 'The History Curriculum in the (Revised) National Curriculum Statement: An Introduction', in S. Jeppie (ed.), *Toward New Histories for South Africa*, Cape Town: Juta Gariep.
Davies, I. (2001), 'Citizenship Education and the Teaching and Learning of History', in J. Arthur, I. Davies, A. Wrenn, T. Haydn and D. Kerr, *Citizenship through Secondary History*, 29–43, London: Routledge-Falmer.
Karpat, K. H. (2004), *Heritage and Nationalism in the Balkans*, Ankara: İmge (TT).
Lederach, J. P. (2004), 'The Moral Imagination: The Art and Soul of Building Peace', keynote address to the Association of Conflict Resolution Annual Conference, Sacramento, 30 September 2004. Available online: www.acrnet.org/conferences/ac04/lederachspeech.htm (accessed 14 June 2007).
Lederach, J. P. (2005), *The Moral Imagination: The Art and Soul of Building Peace*, Oxford: Oxford University Press.
Lee, P. and Shemilt, D. (2007), 'New Alchemy or Fatal Attraction? History and Citizenship', *Teaching History* 129: 14–19.
Mamdani, M. (2001), *When Victims Become Killers: Colonialism, Nativism, and the Genocide in Rwanda*, Princeton: Princeton University Press and Cape Town: David Philip.
Millas, H. (2006), *The Emerging of the Greek Nation*, 3rd edn, İstanbul: İletişim (TT).
Volkan, V. D. (2006a), 'Trauma, Mourning, Memorials and Forgiveness', keynote address, *Memory, Narrative and Forgiveness: Reflecting on Ten Years of South Africa's Truth and Reconciliation Commission* conference, University of Cape Town, 23–27 November 2006.
Volkan, V. D. (2006b), 'Large-Group Identity and Chosen Trauma', *Psychoanalysis Downunder* 6: 1–14. Available online: http://www.psychoanalysisdownunder.com.au/issues/6/papers/81 (accessed 16 February 2015).

Part 2

Shared Histories in Post-Colonial Settings

7

Portugal and Brazil: How Much of 'Our' Past Is 'Theirs' Too?

Marlene Cainelli, Helena Pinto and Glória Solé

The nation – politics and transnational dimensions

Political and cultural changes at both a national and worldwide level during and since the 1980s have had deep effects on the Portuguese and Brazilian educational systems, and these changes have consequently influenced history education.

In Portugal, the national curriculum is compulsory. The Portuguese educational system is governed by the constitution of 1976. In addition to the constitution, Portuguese education is governed by decree laws promulgated by the executive branch. The General Law of Education that presently regulates the educational system was passed in 1986 and sets the main goals of the educational system in cycles of schooling (Pires 1987). Thus the Portuguese educational system is highly centralized. Despite some efforts at decentralization, the Ministry of Education in Lisbon sets education policy for all public and private schools.

After the Portuguese revolution of 1974 and a transitional period, the Education System Law was designed and implemented (Law no. 46/86, later amended by Law no. 115/97, Law no. 49/2005 and Law no. 85/2009). Since 1986, elementary education (*Ensino Básico*) – universal, compulsory and free – extends for nine years, comprising three cycles – the first cycle, from the first to the fourth grade (six to nine years old), the second cycle, corresponding to the fifth and sixth grades (ten and eleven years old), and the third cycle, from the seventh to the ninth grade (twelve to fourteen years old). By Decree-Law no. 286/89, 29 August, a curriculum reform for primary and secondary schools was established, and has been implemented since 1991, when the Portuguese Ministry of Education (ME) defined primary and secondary curricula. There was a short consultation period involving teachers' associations. These statutory requirements are still in place, and include the subject of history. The first cycle of elementary education had a new curriculum arrangement by Decree-Law no. 91/2013, 10 July, but with regard to the area of Environmental Studies the curriculum as defined in 1991 still applies. Environmental Studies covers a combination of content areas, concepts and methods from various subjects including history, geography, natural sciences and ethnography, among others, and seeks a progressive understanding of the interrelationships between nature and society (ME 1998: 104). In the second cycle of elementary education, the subject of History and Geography of Portugal – thus integrating the two components, history and geography – is embedded in the area of languages and social sciences, complementing the first cycle of Environmental Studies. Its curriculum includes the content areas, concepts and goals as proposed by the curriculum reform (ME 1991a, 1991b). In the Portuguese curriculum system, history and geography are mandatory and autonomous subjects only in the third cycle of elementary education.

The process of curriculum reorganization of elementary education entered into a new stage with the passing of Decree-Law no. 6/2001, 18 January, which set out the National Curriculum of Basic Education. The Ministry of Education and the Parliament approved a curricular reorganization of 'basic' school (involving students from six to fourteen years old) that had been tested since the beginning of the 1990s. This document assumed a comprehensive notion of competence, which included knowledge, skills and attitudes. The overall culture that everyone should have developed at the end of elementary education included the appropriation of a set of fundamental concepts and procedures, but not a simple memorized knowledge of facts and 'simple' procedures, lacking the elements of understanding, interpretation and problem solving. This curriculum reorganization did not focus on changes to programmes, considering that competences and learning experiences should be points of reference to interpret programmes.

If history programmes have not changed since the 1990s, deep changes have been introduced in methodological and teaching practices. These changes related to a new perspective towards history teaching that originated in the 2001 National Curriculum of Basic Education document, embodied in a constructivist teaching approach. The logic of teaching now focused on the achievement of a 'knowledge in action or in use', by promoting specific and general competences (Roldão 2010). In order to put these proposals into action, the guiding document 'Learning Outcomes' was developed in 2010. The learning outcomes of history, produced by the team coordinated by Isabel Barca, were grounded in research results and empirical studies in history education, applied in school settings with Portuguese students. According to Barca and Solé (2012) these studies 'rely on recent epistemological perspectives on this area of knowledge, giving relevance to the construction of notions of change, evidence, empathy and explanation in history' (p. 92). However, this process of curricular reorganization was not enforced, due to governmental changes and a new political agenda, as in late 2011 the National Curriculum of Basic Education was revoked by Order no. 17.169/2011, 23 December, and official documents of the Ministry of Education and Science, such as programmes and examinations, stopped making reference to its learning guidelines.

In the last two years, the Portuguese Ministry of Education and Science (MEC) has been establishing an agenda of curricular reorganization, implementing a new regulatory document, the 'Curricular Outcomes', for different subjects, but programmes created after 1991 are still a point of reference. The 'Curricular Outcomes', which identify essential learning for students, are organized by domains (for example, corresponding to the themes of the Geography Curriculum Guidelines and History Programme) and these are divided into sub-domains which are organized into general objectives, and afterwards specified in descriptors. These curricular outcomes, which have been subordinated to existing programmes since 1991, have been strengthening the role of content that students should learn, and reflect a more conservative political approach. So far they have been published for History and Geography in the second and third cycles of elementary education; but in the first cycle, however, these are only compulsory for the Portuguese language and Mathematics, leaving a huge gap in Environmental Studies, a less valued area in the current education system.

The Curricular Outcomes of History and Geography of Portugal for the second cycle of Basic Education (MEC 2013) identify the essential learning that must be undertaken by fifth- and sixth-graders, based on the content and guidelines of the existing History and Geography of Portugal Programme (ME 1991a, 1991b). This seeks to provide students with an introduction to specific tools and concepts, bearing in mind that they are required for the transmission and use of knowledge – dealing with time and space, the actions of people and their decisions in specific contexts, the comparison between different temporal contexts, and the communication and transmission of historical and geographic knowledge.

Finally, the Curricular Outcomes of History for the third cycle of Basic Education (MEC 2013) identify the essential learning that must be undertaken by seventh-, eighth- and ninth-graders. Based on the existing History Programme (ME 1991a, 1991b) the document defines core content that should be taught to students, shaping the teaching of this subject. To achieve the goals implies following procedures related not only to the acquisition of information (knowing) but also to the integration and elaboration of that information (understanding).

In Brazil, which is a federal country with twenty-six states (and each one of these has considerable autonomy), the Ministry of Education does not establish nationwide educational programmes, in contrast to what happens in Portugal, but defines by legal instruments the guiding principles for the organization of such programmes. For obligatory education (*Ensino Fundamental*), the Federal Educational Council determines which subjects are compulsory for the national common core, defining their objectives and scope. The Federal Council in each state lists the subjects contained in the diversified part of school curricula, for the area under its jurisdiction.

Brazilian political open-mindedness in the 1990s allowed a curricular flexibility under the supervision of National Curricula Parameters (SEF 1998) considering that primary and secondary curricula should have a common basis which would be complemented in each Brazilian state according to regional and local aims and features.

In Brazilian elementary education, the discussion of cultural, racial, social and economic diversity has been included in school curricula since the end of the twentieth century. The first document that brought to light these discussions, the National Curricular Parameters of 1998, mentioned the possibility of working crosswise with different issues.

Whereas in the last decades in Brazil the debate on cultural pluralism and multiculturalism has gained momentum both in academic and in educational fields, several changes have been proposed, including those covered by the law that made mandatory first the study of Afro-Brazilian and African culture (Law no. 10.639/03), and second Indigenous culture (Law no. 11.645/08). However, working with these issues involves a recognition that there are struggles over changes which can be seen in a move away from teaching history to create a consolidated identity, traditionally connected to the idea of nationalism and the construction of a single, homogenous and Eurocentric past, to a position which makes it possible to work diversity and difference into the construction of Brazilian identity. This is in some ways an approach that corresponds with a recommendation by Jonker, who writes that there should be a refraining from identity politics, a doing away with grand narratives and instead a teaching of 'little histories in an open framework'. Drawing on a recommendation by Peter Seixas (Seixas 1993: 301–27), Jonker suggests that teachers should:

> [m]ake room for personal histories that colour, flavour, and contradict the larger stories, thus making critical interpretations of the grand narratives possible. To accomplish this, a certain 'provincialism', in the sense of a lack of centralized curricular power, may contribute to the freedom needed to challenge identities and canons.
>
> Jonker 2007: 106

In historical narratives the 'other' is often seen as different, diverse, exotic and strange when compared to the dominant, Western, white, European, civilized, Christian culture. Qualified this way, the culture of the 'other' turns out to be identified as primitive, ethnic, inferior and archaic. Alternatively this can be understood as essentialist, i.e. pure, static, unchanging and stable, thus ahistorical. Ultimately, depending on the approach, the relation identity/difference can be seen as a process of controlling the 'other' as a victim or a submissive person, stealing or diminishing the diversity of their life experiences (Fernandes 2014). For a long time in Brazil, history teaching approaches to Indigenous people were generally characterized by reducing them to the category of Indians, belonging to a single ethnic group sharing the same culture. This can be seen in the textbook pictures and texts representing Indigenous people that were used in Brazilian schools until the late twentieth century.

Despite several changes occurring in history teaching due to textbook evaluations, recent research on history teaching and curricula has revealed that some history textbooks and teachers are still working with a historiographical conception that approaches national history through an identity reconstruction linked to the great deeds of so-called 'national heroes', usually white Portuguese, hiding the participation of other social segments in the historical process of the country. Most of the textbooks had neglected the participation of ethnic minorities, especially Indigenous and Afro-descendants.

There are two types of approaches to Indigenous history in Brazilian schools. The first inserts Indigenous people within a setting of Brazilian prehistory. Their story is focused on their ethnic structure and organization. The second addresses Indigenous history starting from the contact with Portuguese colonizers. In these two approaches the Indigenous appear as inferior to white people, in both their way of life and their social structure. Another important factor is the temporal existence of the Indigenous, which is always placed in the past. When Indigenous history refers to the present it is always relegated to an inferior position to the triumphant story of the whites.

Landmarks with questions

Brazil was a Portuguese colony from the beginning of the sixteenth century until the beginning of the nineteenth century. For three hundred years the colony's economy was based on sugar plantations, linked to slave traffic from Africa, and on gold mining. The independence of Brazil in 1822 followed the Portuguese Liberal Revolution of 1820 and accompanied other independence movements in South America, following the example of the United States. After independence, immigration of many European peoples (especially Italians, Poles and Germans, beside Portuguese) added complexity to the social, economic and demographic structure of Brazil, especially after the abolition of slavery in 1888.

In a brief diachronic view of history teaching in Portugal, based on Torgal (1996), we will focus on history teaching in primary education. The teaching of history in Portugal appeared in the context of the liberalism associated with public education reform in 1830. This affected both primary schools and secondary schools and was part of an educational project which would prevail until the beginning of the Republic in 1910.

During the New State (the period of dictatorship in Portugal, from 1933 to 1974) there were not any structural changes in the historical content taught in primary schools, which focused on the third and fourth grades, but changes were rather in the ideological orientation of the content, privileging certain periods of the history of Portugal, such as the foundation of nationality and the 'discoveries', golden eras in the history of the nation, thus ignoring or devaluing other periods such as the Spanish domination from 1580 to 1640, and sometimes taking critical positions against certain events and periods, such as the Liberal Revolution (1820–34) and the Republic (1910–26). The New State emerges as a corollary period during which the nation's problems were solved, a situation widely exalted in the primary education textbooks of the time. Nevertheless, during the 1960s, programmes were modified and textbooks reduced their nationalist ideological burden, which had focused on memorizing facts, events, dates and names of national heroes. However, according to Freitas (2005) some textbook authors during this period reflected 'a concern to integrate somehow a story of everyday life' (p. 2139). This movement was reinforced after the Democratic Revolution of 25 April 1974, which retrieved the liberal-republican paradigm, banishing the 'reactionary' ideological principles of the New State[1] and enhancing local history, enabling it to be integrated in the national context.

The analysis of Portuguese primary education programmes reveals that their history content had been shrinking since the 1970s. During the 1980s programmes included a rubric called 'Historical Perspective', which focused on great moments in the history of Portugal: foundation of nationality; 'discoveries' of the fifteenth and sixteenth centuries; and political developments of the nineteenth century. In the 1990s, the Environmental Studies programmes reduced the study of the past to the personal and family past, to references about events related to local or regional heritage, and to the knowledge of historical facts linked to national holidays, according to a spiral approach, albeit with a narrow view of Bruner's 'spiral curriculum' (Bruner 1960). Beginning with the hypothesis that 'any subject can be taught effectively in some intellectually honest form to any child at any stage of development', Bruner (1960: 33) explained that this involved information being structured so that complex ideas can be taught at a simplified level first, and then revisited at more complex levels later on. Therefore, subjects would be taught at levels of gradually increasing difficulty. In this type of Environmental Studies teaching structure a child starts from the 'nearby' and moves to the 'distant', and from what is 'known' to the 'unknown' (Roldão 1995: 14–15). Within this curriculum structure the child is seen as being active in the learning process, and their life experience knowledge must be valued as the starting point for learning, so the subject content should be adjusted to the different years of schooling levels. These theoretical principles held by Dewey and Piaget had implications for the practice of teaching, and drew on the conception of the curriculum structure called 'expanding horizons' associated with a 'progressive perspective' of moving spatially outwards and chronologically backwards from the child's immediate experience. This could be seen mostly in Social Studies, both in the Anglo-Saxon world (Egan 1986) and also in Portugal (Roldão 1995).

Thus the study of the personal and family past is addressed mainly in the first and second grades of the first cycle of Basic Education. In the third grade particular emphasis is given to the local past, and deepened in the fourth grade with an investigative strand. Also in the fourth grade it is aimed to approach the topic of multiculturalism within the units 'knowing the customs and traditions of other people' and 'other cultures of their community'. The national symbols (flag and hymn) of Portugal and the autonomous regions of Madeira and Azores, related to the identity of the nation and the Portuguese people, are explored in this grade too. The study of history is now extended to the nation (*History of Portugal*), valuing historical facts linked to national holidays (the dates that are commemorated: the restoration of independence, 1 December 1640; the launch of the Republic, 5 October 1910; and the Democratic Revolution of 25 April 1974), personalities and important events of national history, such as the foundation of nationality, 'discoveries', colonization and decolonization, the New State and the key event of 25 April 1974, valuing the essence of political history, but also revealing aspects of daily life in the past, though with less emphasis.

In the second cycle of Basic Education (fifth and sixth grades) the subject of the History and Geography of Portugal involves two components in which the programme is organized in three key topics. The first one, *Place of Passage and Residence, Portugal in the Past and Today*, focuses on the Iberian Peninsula in terms of natural resources and people who had inhabited the area before the foundation of Portugal (Indo-European, Pre-Celtic, Celtic and Iberians, Greeks, Carthaginians, Romans, Visigoths and Muslims).

The second topic, *Portugal in the Past*, includes the key episodes of Portugal's history, from the foundation of Portugal (twelfth century) to nowadays, in a long-term overview or diachronic perspective emphasizing the dynamics of change. The role of personalities of the history of Portugal who represent different epochs is contextualized so as to help students understand that historical events cannot be explained only by individual actions, but also by valuing the social components and everyday life. Also here there is an element of 'high politics' encountering 'history from below' because ordinary people have always had to live with the consequences of the actions of the 'great and the good', including politicians.

Within this second topic, one of the most extended issues in the fifth grade is *Portugal in the Fifteenth and Sixteenth Centuries*, which corresponds with the maritime expansion period (from the conquest of Ceuta in northern Africa to the 'discovery' of Brazil). The Portuguese diaspora is explored, and economic, political, religious and cultural factors are examined. Acculturation and miscegenation are part of the expansionist movement of Portuguese people, as well as concepts such as (religious) mission; colonization; and ethnic, Indigenous and cultural diversity. The relationship between Portugal and Brazil arises in various issues which begin with the arrival in Brazil (Land of Vera Cruz) of the Portuguese navy commanded by Cabral in 1500; being of relatively little interest if compared with the Cape Route and its rich spice trade, the former exploration focused on natural resources (dye plants and exotic birds). After the restoration of independence in 1640, and the spice trade crisis in the late sixteenth century, the Portuguese Crown's interests turned to Brazil and its economic potential, associating sugar or tobacco plantations with the slave trade, and later focused on gold, coffee and cotton. This triangular relationship between Europe, Africa and America (Brazil) was mirrored in the exchange of different cultures that crossed over several generations and manifested not only in the ethnic crossroads (miscegenation) but also in the cultural intersection (acculturation, assimilation, interculturality), depending on the perspective of colonizer or colonized. Brazil is once again a content area within this diachronic approach, especially when studying the period of the French invasions which led to the moving of the entire Portuguese court to Brazil in 1808 and to a change in Brazil's status, then considered as a kingdom joined to Portugal.

After the American and French revolutions fostered the desire for independence of Brazil in 1822, there followed the rise of the liberal movement. The study of the decolonization of Brazil or other events of its history as a country is not part of any history programme in the three cycles of Basic Education (even in secondary education), with the sole exception of the reference to the European emigration movement to Brazil in the late nineteenth century. The third topic that students of the second cycle are taught is *Portugal Today*, and here it is intended that students should be given opportunities to understand their current society, focusing on economic, political and social matters.

Regarding the third cycle of Basic Education in Portugal, the organizational concept of history curricula that is used is a spiral, involving the revisiting of almost the same topics as in the second cycle, namely in the fourth grade, but within a broader scope (mostly European) and a deeper exploration of sources and knowledge of contents.

As for Brazil, the study of Africa and Afro-descendant people became mandatory in Brazilian schools and in universities with Law no. 10.639/03, mainly because until then the bulk of the work in schools was limited to the substantive content of 'Brazilian Slavery'. African and Afro-Brazilian descendants were thus only fitted into Brazilian history in the condition of slaves. Once slavery ended they either disappeared as historical individuals, or if they did not disappear completely they were seen in contemporary images connected to misery and poverty.

Along with the new law teachers were required to emphasize in the classroom the role of Afro-Brazilian culture in founding and constituting a renewed vision of Brazilian society in which black people are perceived as historical individuals. In this enterprise black personalities of Brazil are valued, and respect is given to the different dimensions of the Afro-Brazilian world, its intellectual and cultural achievements, including the realms of religion, music, cuisine and dance.

The way students of both countries conceive the 'discovery' and colonial periods in terms of historical significance is one of the goals of this study. Indeed, for them to understand the role of the Portuguese in Brazil, the tropes of 'discovery' and colonization are central questions.

Pedagogy, democracy and dialogue

As regards history, regulatory documents in both Portugal and Brazil recommend teachers to approach topics such as citizenship, memory, heritage and social identity with the purpose of developing students' sense of belonging to a group, a place, a nation, the world, analysing differences and similarities, continuity and change, with the aim of improving and making more inclusive the old perception of the 'us' and the 'others', making it possible to go beyond a standardized view and a traditional perspective of history teaching that used to overvalue heroes and narratives of conquerors and colonizers. As in other countries, for example Australia, there seems to be a growing acceptance of a need to go 'beyond the canon', to have a combination of a disciplinary approach with an element of collective memory, but a collective memory informed by inclusion and diversity.

Within this framework, we unveil some results of several qualitative research studies carried out in the last five years in the north of Portugal and in the state of Paraná, Brazil, with students from eight to sixteen years old taking part in history-learning activities. Underpinned by the theoretical scaffold of Jörn Rüsen, Peter Lee and Peter Seixas, among other authors, the studies reported here have focused on historical consciousness, aiming to understand students' ideas on significance and historical empathy as regards people in the past, namely in the 'discoveries' epoch.

The concept of significance can be considered at a basic level related to historical facts and the intrinsic importance they assume in the past or in the present, and at a broader level connected to the notion of historical interpretation. In this second idea, significance is generally relative because it acknowledges an underlying relationship between events, which depends on the historian's perspective, on the 'historiographical' line-up and on the context as well as the attention given to evidence (Pinto 2011).

Lee and Ashby (2001) state that in the UK 'empathy' tends to be used to mean the explanation of the action itself or the ideas, beliefs and values that lie behind the actions and social institutions. The complexity of this 'second order' concept has been the subject of debate and research since the 1980s, which has required a progressive clarification – since the term has a broad scope not only within the diverse areas of social sciences, but also a specific sense in the area of historical cognition. Empathy allows students to understand social actions and practices, thus to be able to consider (but not necessarily accept or share) the connections between circumstances and actions (Lee 2003). Besides knowing that people in the past had a certain historical perspective towards the world, students should be able to see how this perspective will have affected certain actions in specific circumstances. According to Lee (2005) the central idea in historical empathy is that people in the past did not share the way we see the world. It implies an understanding of institutions, social practices and past actions, making sense of them in the light of circumstances and contexts in which those people lived – without the distortions of anachronism or retrospective teleology.

Understanding how students, teachers and people in general 'use' the past in terms of temporal orientation is also a core research problem in the field of history education, as it shapes formal history teaching and learning practices (Pinto 2011, 2013). The need to make individual historical meanings usable in personal everyday life has been emphasized under the notion of historical consciousness, which has implications for history education. Historical consciousness functions as a key temporal orientation, providing a temporal matrix to practical life (Rüsen 2004), evoking the past as a mirror of experience within which contemporary life is reflected and its temporal features are revealed.

Rüsen (2007) considers that historical consciousness is a specific form of historical memory: it is rooted in it and, to a great extent, even identical with it, but it is also different in some important aspects. The specificity of historical consciousness lies in the fact that 'the temporal perspective, in which the past is related to the present and through the present to the future, is designed in a more complex and elaborate way' (Rüsen 2007: 175). Lowenthal (1999) also states the distinctiveness of memory and history, considering that both history and memory engender new knowledge, but only history intentionally sets out to do so: 'We accept memory as a premise of knowledge; we infer history from evidence that includes other people's memories' (Lowenthal 1999: 213).

Historical memory and historical thinking have an important cultural function: they form and express identity in a temporal perspective. Therefore, a crucial dimension of the study of historical consciousness involves how cultural practices and tools for understanding the past are handed down to the next generation (Pinto 2013), possibly contributing to or even challenging notions of 'collective memory' (Seixas 2000). Applying these ideas of historical consciousness to history education, Lee (2004a) suggests that we might ask questions about the cultural tools which are available to the students in relating themselves to the past, their content, the social action they inhibit, and the ways these tools affect students' conceptions of the past and of history. Lee (2004b) states that the kind of past that students work with helps determine the kind of orientation available to them. Although children and adolescents have ideas about the past that merit serious consideration, they construct those ideas not just from what they learn at school but from the historical information they encounter in their families, their local and national communities and the media. Research on these ideas and their social contexts can help us to understand better how students make sense of the nature and purpose of history (Barton and Levstik 2004), and this can support developing meaningful programmes of history education.

Most school lessons underline the episodes and processes of national history to strengthen national identity and pride while ignoring the wider dimensions, whether they are European, trans-American, transatlantic or international (Pinto 2011). However, students will understand history better when they perceive the linkage between local and international events and trends and find out about differences and similarities in local and a more international history. In this case, of course, with the natural link between Portugal and its former colonies or empire, and the commonalities of language across these boundaries, Brazil and Portugal can form genuine transnational links.

Shared histories, shared commemorations and re-evaluating past denials

Albeit that each country has a lot of particularities, namely the teaching history topics involving African–Brazilian history and Indigenous history in Brazil, and the contribution of different people to Portuguese culture and history, there are several political similarities and shared cultural features.

The historical paths of Portugal and Brazil since the nineteenth century have several similarities, but the most significant parallels are the political change from monarchy/empire to a republic (Brazil in 1889 and Portugal in 1910) and the periods of dictatorship (Portugal from 1926 to 1974; Brazil between 1937 and 1945, and from 1964 to 1985).

There are several common topics in both school history curricula concerning the period of colonization of Brazil, namely those concerning features of the administration and the commemoration of historical events. On the other hand, features related to acculturation, miscegenation and slave traffic are treated in a 'softer' way within the Portuguese curriculum than in Brazilian ones.

Brazilian Federal Law no. 11.465/08 has defined the inclusion of Afro-Brazilian issues in all elementary and secondary school curricula (implemented since 2003), and also the teaching of Indigenous history and contribution to Brazilian culture in the subjects of History, Geography and Literature.

Traditionally work with substantive content dominates the subject of History in Brazilian elementary education. Generally there is no place for students to engage in dialogue, to share their ideas, to decide or to hypothesize. Students are used to repeating what they have been taught and to reproducing the contents of the textbooks.

Based on Collingwood's (1978)[2] statement that historical thinking is an intellectual activity involving recreating the past grounded in the interpretation of existing sources as evidence, a questionnaire was given to Portuguese and Brazilian students, asking them several questions related to events discussed in history teaching about the 'discovery' of Brazil (Cainelli and Barca 2013). As to the method, this was a descriptive study (with both qualitative and quantitative approaches) whose guidelines belong to the field of history education. The research focused on questions related to historical cognition. The sample included 450 students from the sixth and ninth grades in two schools of Londrina (Paraná, Brazil) and two other schools in northern Portugal. It was intended to analyse how Portuguese and Brazilian students from twelve to fifteen years old constructed their historical thinking when approaching facts related to national history in both countries, such as the topic referred to above. Thus, one of the questions students were asked to answer admitted the possibility that Portuguese were not the 'discoverers' of Brazilian lands in 1500, and they were challenged to think about the history of Brazil without the Portuguese presence:

> If the Portuguese had not arrived in Brazil in 1500 how would it be for the history of the country? What would be different and what would remain in the history of Brazil?

Analysis of students' answers revealed two categories regarding substantive content and two meta-historic possibilities as to second-order concepts.

Within the first category Brazilian students referred to the maintenance of Brazil's Indigenous population and its untouched state of nature, the absence of technology (mostly sixth-grade students) and a change in the way of teaching history. It showed that some nineteenth-century romantic myths seemed to persist as well as the influence of a mass-media version of historical culture:

> Yes, it would be different, because if Portuguese had not arrived here, we would be living with thongs and in the woods. Gold and silver could be found easily and we would know how to deal with the most common diseases in Brazil. Wars between tribes would remain.

> It's hard to find something that has not changed. Possibly our fauna and flora, there would be more trees and plants, and the extinct animals, but none of us would be born. In short, if Pedro Álvares Cabral had not mistaken his trip, maybe Brazil would be a big jungle.

> It would not be the same because there would be many trees, Indigenous people, and if nobody had discovered it yet, it would be a greener (natural) country.

> If the Portuguese had not come to Brazil we would not be white, we would be living in the forest instead of the houses, and the air would be a bit cleaner.

Portuguese students also stated the maintenance of Brazil as it had been before the Portuguese arrival, and some of them focused on what would have happened to Portugal (mostly sixth-grade students) with regards to wealth and colonial exploitation:

> If Portuguese had not arrived in Brazil, Portugal would not have known the gold, the Indians and many other things. And if Portugal had not known Brazil the king would not have had the possibility to move there [during French invasions] to protect himself, and maybe Portugal could be a French country.
>
> Sixth-grade student, northern Portugal

Some Portuguese students mentioned that other countries could have discovered Brazil, or the absence of Brazil on the map, or the cultural development and current influences:

> It would remain the same, i.e. Indigenous.
>
> It would stay the same way – animals and plants, and people would be darker because they were Indians.
>
> It would remain as at the beginning, there would be even more Indians because they would not have been so brutally exploited.

Students' answers show an idea of permanence, even an idea of no change in the case of absence of the event of Pedro Álvares Cabral's arrival in Brazil (Cainelli and Barca 2013). There is a break in the history of Brazil, in the untouched time of the nature. The idea of a 'non-event' caused perplexity in attempts to reach historical conclusions and left students a bit lost without their textbooks or teachers' indications about the historical possibilities of a change in events.

The way history teaching has been constructed is one of the reasons for the core messages of Portuguese and Brazilian students, somehow still facing the formation of a national identity as in the nineteenth century (Cainelli and Barca 2013). What we can infer is the idea of a foundation myth expressed in the Portuguese arrival in Brazil. It is a myth that is always gaining new ways of expression, new forms of language, but it is a repetition of itself (Chauí 2000). School history in Brazil continues to remake this myth every year all over the country. This and other topics that conform to and confirm this version of a mythic past of the nation resist the critics and continue to reproduce themselves in Brazilian textbooks and classrooms.

The second study referred to here is part of research for a PhD thesis (Solé 2009, 2013) with Portuguese children, which allowed students (twenty-five fourth-graders) to understand concepts of historical empathy and historical consciousness. We have analysed students' ideas regarding the 'other' when studying the topic 'overseas expansion', based on the exploration of several sources: a comic about Portuguese discoveries, written documents and iconographic sources (images and maps). When exploring comics and discussing their ideas, students revealed different levels of historical empathy in their arguments, according to the category model in terms of the progression of ideas proposed by Ashby and Lee (1987), which seem to match with the categorization proposed by Shemilt (1984). Ashby and Lee (1987) based their classification on their studies with students from eleven to eighteen years old, and on the studies of Dickinson and Lee (1978), but mainly on Shemilt (1984) and have revealed a categorization of students' ideas on historical empathy which included five progression levels: (1) 'the "divi" past'; (2) 'generalized stereotypes'; (3) 'everyday empathy'; (4) 'restricted historical empathy'; and (5) 'contextual historical empathy'. In the first stage, 'the "divi" past', students perceived the past as unintelligible and people in the past as 'not as clever as us'. In the second stage, 'generalized stereotypes', they provided a stereotypical account of people's roles and actions. In stage three, 'everyday empathy', students understood the past with reference to the present and were thus unable to see the differences between the past and present. In stage four, 'restricted historical empathy', students were able to understand the past with specific reference to the situation in which people found themselves, noting that these situations must be different from similar ones in the present. In stage five, 'contextual historical empathy', children were able to apply the fourth concept to a wider picture, indicating that if a particular situation in the past differs from a similar one in the present people's lives in general must have differed in the past (Ashby and Lee 1987).

While exploring various sources and focusing on comics, students recognized the diversity of people with whom the Portuguese had contact (Muslims, Africans, Indians, Chinese, Brazilian Indians), identifying physical, cultural and civilizational differences, which led them to conclude the co-existence of different degrees of civilizational development as stated in their comments: 'blacks wore a cloth around the waist, were very poor, accepted all from the Portuguese, and did not defend themselves' (Isidro); 'Brazilians [Indians] stayed naked and had plumages on their hair' (Tiago) – also making inferences from the map by Lopo Homem that had been previously explored; 'They used necklets and shaved [their] hair' (Roberto Manuel); 'Brazilians were much more peaceful' (Ricardo Manuel). These comments seem to express a stereotypical view of blacks as being peaceful and slow workers and Brazilian Indians as friendly and serene. They can be included, in terms of historical empathy, in the generalized stereotypes level of the category model proposed by Ashby and Lee (1987). Anabela's comment seems to be at a more sophisticated level: 'Those from India were more developed as regards clothing, Brazilian Indians stayed naked and the others have clothes, and one can see an umbrella'; comparing the two people in terms of development, she already reveals a restricted historical empathy, by showing some understanding of the past and the existence of multiple contexts to justify differences between people.

Students often denote in their comments what people had or did not have in terms of material progress referring to change markers in material culture: 'They [in India] had more buildings' (Marco Angelo); 'In Brazil they only had wood shelters' (Tiago). They recognized the co-existence of people with different civilization levels of development, as stated by Anabela: 'There are people who are more developed than others'; and Isidro invokes this same idea with regard to the present: 'Nowadays not everyone lives as we do.' These two comments reveal more sophisticated ideas of historical empathy close to a level of contextual historical empathy as proposed in Ashby and Lee's (1987) model of categorization, as these students recognize civilizational differences between people in the past in cultural, technological and other dimensions, placing them in context.

In another task of this didactic experience students explored an iconographic source, an engraving of India of 1619, and a discussion took place about the people represented. Initially it appeared them to be an image of Brazil, focusing on fruit trees and skin colour: 'they do not seem to be black, blacks are dark and these are more like brunette' (Roberto Manuel). Anabela claims: 'This cannot be in Brazil because these men do not have long hair', expressing a conception that the Brazilian Indigenous people have long, black and straight hair. Roberto replies: 'But this may be more modern than what we saw about Brazil', recalling the Lopo Homem map ('Terra Brasilis' – Miller Atlas, 1519) they had explored before, representing part of the Brazilian coast and illustrations of the Indigenous population. Another student, Isidro, argues the relevance of the source as witness of an epoch, recognizing that there may have been different representations of the 'other', for example the Indigenous, according to the context in which one of them was living, which may not correspond to the traditional image of the Brazilian Indian. Thus, when one student exclaimed: 'It seems to be in India', Anabela agreed and concluded: 'In India there are people with dark skin but not as black as those in Africa'.

These types of tasks allow us to analyse students' historical thinking and reasoning, with special focus on historical empathy and historical consciousness as evinced above, and revealing very different levels of historical thinking, from a less elaborate level to a more complex and sophisticated one.

History teaching and learning activities focusing on a thematic and historical period, such as 'Portuguese Discoveries', can be implemented from the early years of primary school. The exploration of diverse sources such as history comics, historical pictures, maps, timelines and historiographical documents, when combined and systematically interpreted by students, may enhance historical understanding, helping them to make sense of the past – especially with regards to dealing with historical empathy and significance – and to orientate themselves in time, since historical consciousness implies an interconnection between past and present, and eventually the future.

Conclusions

The learning and teaching of history covers subject matter as well as skills and concepts. Even though the content of history is important, isolated recall of facts and events makes little sense as a skill to serve young people in becoming active citizens in the increasingly globalized world.

History education is an important bridge in understanding how different groups have interacted over time, and in promoting mutual respect, tolerance and social justice. In the classroom history educators have to find ways to explore sensitive and uncomfortable issues in national and international history. It is important that those aspects of the past are not ignored or hidden. If we are to encourage young people to become active participants in democratic society, history teaching has much to contribute to this process, strengthening critical thinking, multi-perspectivity and inclusion.

With regard to power relations, systematic research is essential to analyse how students understand these interactions and examine what is common to all social spaces. It is also necessary to understand how they identify and locate spaces and historical processes that in the past affected those relations and decision-making. As to cultural relations, it is important that students were able to recognize themselves and others as builders of a common culture, considering the specificities of each social group and the relationships between them. Thus they understand how they realize the constitution of diverse cultural experiences over time, and the continuity and change in different community traditions or societies.

Notes

1 The New State had many similarities to the Italian Fascism of Mussolini, including its youth movements.
2 R. G. Collingwood's *The Idea of History* was first published in 1946.

References

Ashby, R., and Lee, P. (1987), 'Children's Concepts of Empathy and Understanding in History', in C. Portal (ed.), *The History Curriculum for Teachers*, 62–88, London: Falmer.

Barca, I. and Solé, M. G. (2012), 'Educación histórica en Portugal: metas de aprendizaje en los primeiros anos de escolaridade [History Education in Portugal: Learning Outcomes of First Years of Primary School]', *Revista Electrónica Interuniversitaria de Formación del Profesorado* [Inter-University Electronic Journal of Teacher Education] [REIFOP] 15 (1): 91–100. Available online: www.aufop.com (accessed 30 January 2014).

Barton, K. and Levstik, L. (2004), *Teaching History for the Common Good*, Mahwah, NJ: Lawrence Erlbaum.

Bruner, J. (1960), *The Process of Education*, Cambridge, MA: Harvard University Press.

Cainelli, M. and Barca, I. (2013), 'A constituição do pensamento histórico de jovens estudantes no Brasil e Portugal: a construção de explicações sobre o passado a partir da tomada de decisões sobre questões históricas [The Construction of Brazilian and Portuguesese Young Students' Historical Thinking]', in J. Prats, I. Barca and R. Facal (eds), *Historia e identidades culturales. Atas do V Simposio Internacional de Didáctica de las Ciencias Sociales en el Ámbito Iberoamericano & Congresso Internacional das XIII Jornadas de Educação Histórica*, 1081–92, Braga: CIEd, Universidade do Minho. Available online: http://webs.ie.uminho.pt/conscienciahistorica/Historia_Identidades_culturales.pdf (accessed 30 January 2014).

Chauí, M. (2000), *Brasil: Mito Fundador e Sociedade Autoritária* [Brazil: Foundation Myth and Authoritarian Society], São Paulo: Editora Fundação Perseu Abramo.

Collingwood, R. G. (1978), *A ideia da História* [The Idea of History], Lisboa: Editorial Presença.

Dickinson, A. and Lee, P. (1978), 'Understanding and Research', in A. Dickinson and P. Lee (eds), *History Teaching and Historical Understanding*, 94–120, London: Heinemann.

Egan, K. (1986), *Teaching as Story Telling*, London, ON: University of Western Ontario.

Fernandes, A. (2014), *Ensino de História, Identidade e Diferença: Indígenas e Afrodescendentes na História e no Ensino de História* [History Teaching, Identity and Difference: Indigenous and Afro-Descendants in History and History Teaching], São Paulo: Simpósio Temático, Anpuh/SP.

Freitas, M. L. (2005), 'História de Portugal no 1.° ciclo do Ensino Básico: Os programas, os manuais e as vozes dos alunos [History of Portugal in the 1st Cycle of Basic Education: Curricula, Textbooks and Students' Voices]', in B. Silva and L. Almeida (coord.), *Actas do 8.° Congresso Galaico-Português de Psicopedagogia*, 2135–49, Braga: Centro de Investigação em Educação, Instituto de Educação e Psicologia da Universidade do Minho [CD-ROM].

Jonker, E. (2007), 'Citizenship, the Canon and the Crisis of the Humanities', in M. Grever and S. Stuurman (eds), *Beyond the Canon: History for the Twenty-First Century*, 94–109, Basingstoke: Palgrave Macmillan.

Lee, P. (2003), 'Nós fabricamos carros e eles tinham que andar a pé: compreensão da vida no passado [We Make Cars and They Had to Walk: Understanding Life in the Past]', in I. Barca (ed.), *Educação Histórica e Museus. Actas das Segundas Jornadas Internacionais de Educação Histórica* [History Education and Museums. Proceedings of the Second International Workshop of History Education], 19–36, Braga: CIEd, Universidade do Minho.

Lee, P. (2004a), 'Understanding History', in P. Seixas (ed.), *Theorizing Historical Consciousness*, 129–64, Toronto: University Press of Toronto.

Lee, P. (2004b), '"Walking Backwards into Tomorrow": Historical Consciousness and Understanding History', *International Journal of Historical Learning Teaching and Research* 4 (1). Available online: http://centres.exeter.ac.uk/historyresource/journal7/7contents.htm (accessed 3 October 2011).
Lee, P. (2005), 'Putting Principles into Practice: Understanding History', in M. S. Donovan and J. D. Bransford (eds), *How Students Learn: History in the Classroom*, 31–77, Washington, DC: The National Academies Press.
Lee, P. and Ashby, R. (2001), 'Empathy, Perspective Taking, and Rational Understanding', in O. L. Davis, E. Yeager and S. Foster (eds), *Historical Empathy and Perspective Taking in the Social Studies*, 21–50, Oxford: Rowman & Littlefield.
Lowenthal, D. (1999), *The Past is a Foreign Country*, Cambridge: Cambridge University Press.
Ministério da Educação (ME) (1991a), *Programa de História e Geografia de Portugal do Ensino Básico – 2.° Ciclo* [Curriculum of History and Geography of Portugal. 2nd Cycle of Basic Education], Ministério da Educação, Portugal. Available onlie: http://dge.mec.pt/metascurriculares/index.php?s=directorio&pid=18 (accessed 3 March 2014).
Ministério da Educação (ME) (1991b), *Programa de História do Ensino Básico – 3.° Ciclo* [Curriculum of History – 3rd Cycle of Basic Education], Ministério da Educação, Portugal. Available online: http://dge.mec.pt/metascurriculares/index.php?s=directorio&pid=19 (accessed 3 March 2014).
Ministério da Educação (ME) (1998), *Programa de Estudo do Meio – 1.° ciclo do Ensino Básico* [Curriculum of Environmental Studies – 1st Cycle of Basic Education], Ministério da Educação, Portugal. Available online: http://dge.mec.pt/metascurriculares/index.php?s=directorio&pid=48 (accessed 3 March 2014).
Ministério da Educação (ME) (2001), *Currículo Nacional do Ensino Básico: Competências Essenciais* [National Curriculum of Basic Education: Essential Competences], Lisbon: Ministério da Educação, Departamento da Educação Básica.
Ministério da Educação (ME) (2002), *Geografia – Orientações curriculares, 3.° Ciclo* [Geography – Curricular Orientations, 3rd Cycle of Basic Education], Ministério da Educação, Portugal. Available online: http://dge.mec.pt/metascurriculares/index.php?s=directorio&pid=20 (accessed 3 March 2014).
Ministério da Educação e Ciência (MEC) (2013), *Metas Curriculares* [Curricular Outcomes], Ministério da Educação e Ciência, Portugal. Available online: http://dge.mec.pt/metascurriculares/index.php?s=directorio&pid=2 (accessed 9 June 2014).
Pinto, H. (2011), 'Educação histórica e patrimonial: conceções de alunos e professores sobre o passado em espaços do presente [History and Heritage Education: How the Past is Read Through Present Sites by Students and Teachers]', PhD thesis in Education in History and Social Sciences, University of Minho, Portugal. Available online: http://repositorium.sdum.uminho.pt/handle/1822/19745 (accessed 6 October 2012).
Pinto, H. (2013), 'Challenging Students' Ideas on Historical Evidence by Using Heritage Remains in Field Activities', *International Journal of Historical Teaching, Learning and Research* 12 (1): 121–36. Available online: http://www.history.org.uk/resources/secondary_resource_7132.html (accessed 18 February 2014).
Pires, E. (1987), *Lei de Bases do Sistema Educativo: apresentação e comentários* [Law of the Education System: Introduction and Comments], Porto: Edições Asa.
Roldão, M. C. (1995), *O Estudo do Meio no 1.° ciclo: Fundamentos e estratégias* [Environmental Studies in the 1st Cycle: Basis and Strategies], Lisboa: Texto Editora.
Roldão, M. C. (2010), *Estratégias de Ensino* [Teaching Strategies], Vila Nova de Gaia: Fundação Manuel Leão.

Rüsen, J. (2004), 'Historical Consciousness: Narrative Structure, Moral Function, and Ontogenetic Development', in P. Seixas (ed.), *Theorizing Historical Consciousness*, 63–85, Toronto: University of Toronto Press.

Rüsen, J. (2007), 'How to Make Sense of the Past: Salient Issues of Metahistory', *The Journal for Transdisciplinary Research in Southern Africa* 3 (1): 169–221.

Secretaria de Educação Fundamental (SEF) (1998), *Parâmetros Curriculares Nacionais – História* [National Curricular Parameters History], Brasília: Secretaria de Educação Fundamental, MEC/SEF. Available online: http://portal.mec.gov.br/seb/arquivos/pdf/pcn_5a8_historia.pdf (accessed 3 March 2014).

Seixas, P. (1993), 'Historical Understanding Among Adolescents in a Multicultural Setting', *Curriculum Inquiry* 23: 301–27.

Seixas, P. (2000), 'Schweigen! Die Kinder! or, Does Postmodern History Have a Place in Schools?', in P. Stearns, P. Seixas and S. Wineburg (eds), *Knowing, Teaching and Learning History: National and International Perspectives*, 19–37, New York: New York University Press.

Shemilt, D. (1984), 'Beauty and the Philosopher: Empathy in History and the Classroom', in A. Dickinson, P. Lee and P. J. Rogers (eds), *Learning History*, 39–61, London: Heinemann.

Solé, M. G. (2009), 'A História no 1.° Ciclo do Ensino Básico: a concepção do tempo e acompreensão histórica das crianças e os contextos para o seu desenvolvimento [History in the 1st Cycle of Basic Education: Children's Conceptions of Time and Historical Understanding, and Contexts for Their Development]', PhD thesis, Braga: Universidade do Minho, Instituto de Estudos da Criança. Available online: http://hdl.handle.net/1822/10153 (accessed 3 March 2014).

Solé, M. G. (2013), 'Promoting Creativity, Empathy and Historical Imagination: Early Years' Students Learning the Topic Portuguese Discoveries', *Primary History* 63: 24–6.

Torgal, L. R. (1996), 'Ensino da História' [The Teaching of History], in L. R. Torgal, J. A. Mendes and F. Catroga, *História da História em Portugal – Séc. XIX–XX*, 430–89, Lisboa: Círculo de Leitores.

8

The United States: Learning about Native American History

Cyndi Mottola Poole

Native American history: a brief overview

While a comprehensive treatment of Native American[1] history is well beyond the scope of this chapter, it is important to highlight a few key events to frame later discussion. Furthermore, it is important to note that there is still much debate amongst historians regarding the exact origins and lifestyles of, as well as the interactions between, the many peoples who inhabited the Americas before 1492. The largely accepted origin theory most frequently taught in American history classes is that the peoples travelled on foot across the Bering Strait land bridge (sometimes called 'Beringia') from Siberia into modern-day Alaska sometime between 10,000 and 70,000 years ago, and from there spread out across the continents over succeeding generations, discovering farming around 9,000 years ago and from there building permanent settlements throughout the continent (Foner 2014; Loewen 2007; Nicholas 2014).

Europeans arriving from the fifteenth through the seventeenth centuries would have encountered an extraordinary diversity of cultures, beliefs, languages and economic and political systems created by thousands of distinct Native American communities. Rather than virgin wilderness, they would have seen cities with complex political systems, trade networks, roads and irrigation systems. Throughout the Midwest, the 'Mississippian' societies built complex settlements that included platform burial mounds, temples and residential villages. Archaeological evidence seems to indicate a significant distinction between the elite and common peoples, which can be seen in the foods they consumed, the extent of manual labour they performed, the types of homes in which they lived, and even in their grave sites. Similarly, the Anasazi peoples of the Southwest also created planned towns with large multiple-family dwellings, an impressive dam and canal system to manage scarce water resources, and extensive trade networks. Eastern Native Americans farmed corn, squash and beans and hunted deer and turkeys. Individual communities created regional confederacies for trade and mutual defence (Foner 2014; Salisbury 2007). While historians' estimates vary wildly, it is possible that close to 45 million people inhabited North America in the early fifteenth century (Loewen 2007).

Everything changed on a fall day in 1492, when the Arawaks spotted three mysterious ships approaching off the coast of the Bahamas. The Arawaks initially greeted the strange visitors with wonder and gifts, unsuspecting that Columbus and his men had less than beneficent intentions. The Europeans viewed the natives as childlike, ignorant and uncivilized; and from the beginning their intent was conquest (Zinn 2005). Columbus' oft-quoted journal described the Arawaks as generous with their belongings and physically strong and attractive, but simultaneously concluded that 'they would make fine servants', and, due to their lack of metal weaponry, conjectured that 'with fifty men we could subjugate them all and make them do whatever we want' (quoted in Zinn 2005: 1). This inauspicious beginning became a hallmark of Native/European relations: in most circumstances, Natives were enslaved, slaughtered or died from European diseases.[2] Within two years of this initial contact, half of the 250,000 Indians were dead, and by 1650 no Arawaks were left alive (Zinn 2005).

When the first English settled permanently in Jamestown in 1607, similar events occurred. Despite evidence that the local Powhatan people assisted the colonists in hunting and farming, and brought provisions to sustain them during the famed 'starving time', English intentions were clear: to take over Native lands for tobacco production and to kill any Natives who got in the way. Likewise, early colonists in Plimoth eagerly took over Native lands when tribes were decimated by European illnesses, and viewed the virtual extinction of some peoples as an endorsement of colonization by their Christian God (Takaki 2008). Warfare and removal from ancestral lands continued throughout the early years of the United States as well. While historians' estimates vary, it is possible that in the four hundred years between 1492 and 1900 the Native population of North America declined by as much as 98 per cent (Loewen 2007).

Despite the devastating effects of European colonization and continual expansion, Native Americans fought to keep their civilizations and cultures alive. A series of rebellions far too numerous to discuss here, but including such diverse battles as King Philip's War (1675–6), the Pueblo Revolt (1680), the Northwest Indian War (1785–95) and the first (1817–18) and second (1835–42) Seminole Wars, relatively continuous from the seventeenth through the nineteenth centuries, have come to be seen by some historians as constituting an 'Indians' Revolution' (Nicholas 2014). Resistance to forced assimilation and 'civilization' continued through the nineteenth and early twentieth centuries, and even to the modern day, through resistance to deculturalizing boarding schools, organizations such as the American Indian Movement, and recent court battles to force the United States to recognize previously unenforced treaties and remunerate nations for stolen lands.

The legacy of colonialism and past atrocities continues into the present day, both in the United States and elsewhere. According to the US Census, there are approximately 4.5 million Americans who identify themselves as having Native American or Native Hawaiian ancestry (NIEA 2008). Despite the 2007 United Nations Declaration on the Rights of Indigenous Peoples' assertion that Indigenous peoples had the right to control their own children's education (United Nations 2007), approximately 93 per cent of Native American children attend public schools, constituting about 624,000 children

(NIEA 2008). Only about 49 per cent of American Indian students graduate from high school, while about 76 per cent of white students do. American Indian students are more likely to receive disability services than children of any other ethnic group (NIEA 2008). In the United States today, Native Americans have the highest unemployment rate and second lowest rate of college completion of any ethnic group (NIEA 2008). Low perceived social status and high incidents of classism lead many Native American students to have a low college outcome expectation (Thompson 2013). Hoffman, Jackson and Smith (2005) found that common reasons for low college graduation rates amongst Native Americans were family pressure to stay on reservations, academic under-preparedness, lack of money to pay for college, and a feeling of low prospects for employment after graduation.

Unfortunately, many post-colonial societies share a similar legacy for their native peoples. A recent Canadian study found a diminished sense of self-worth, a comparatively low life expectancy and higher crime rates amongst Canadian native peoples, and found most of them living at the low end of the socio-economic strata, therefore concluding that they were the most disadvantaged group in Canadian society (Nguyen 2011). Likewise, the odds of the Indigenous Australian youth (when adjusted for socio-economic disadvantage) having had involvement with the youth justice authorities was found to be 2.51 times that of their non-Indigenous peers (Doolan et al. 2013); and Aboriginal and Torres Strait Islander young people are at a much higher risk than Caucasian peers of progressing to adult correction centres (Lynch, Buckman and Krenske 2003). Moreover, other researchers have cited a marked increase in political violence against Indigenous people in Peru (Huaman and Valdiviezo 2014).

Literature review

The state of Native American history instruction

Despite the irrefutable facts of Native American subjugation in American history, it has frequently been the case that classroom and textbook narratives have told a very different story. Most research available on the teaching of American history has discovered that European views of historical interactions and events dominate instruction, and that the 'inconvenient history' of European atrocities is minimized (Zinn 2005).

> To emphasize the heroism of Columbus and his successors as navigators and discoverers, and to deemphasize their genocide, is not a technical necessity but an ideological choice. It serves – unwittingly – to justify what was done.
>
> Zinn 2005: 9

Another oft-cited concern is that Native American history frequently disappears from our curricula after the settlement of the West. Pervasive stereotypes of Natives only living in the past and in traditional homes and clothing serve to marginalize

Natives as an extinct species (Meyer 2011). Traditional teaching about Native Americans reinforces stereotypes that students may already have and minimizes the impact Native communities had on the construction of the country (Chandler 2010).

This has not been a problem unique to the United States. One Canadian researcher noted 'teachers' resistances to affording room for Aboriginal perspectives, and a general absence of engagements with these perspectives in the classroom' (Scott 2013). Similarly, Tupper and Cappello (2008) found that the Canadian middle and high school students in their sample knew little to nothing about the treaties that made up the basis of British–Native historical relations in their province. Still other researchers insist that non-Indigenous people in Canada exhibit a lack of awareness of and misinformation about Indigenous worldviews and lived experiences which can be directly attributed to their systematic exclusion from educational curricula (Castleden et al. 2013). Australian researchers have also found a narrative of Australian history as generally positive and stereotyping of Indigenous peoples in their primary social studies curriculum, positioning Indigenous peoples as the 'exotic other' (Sharp 2012).

Contributing factors

There are many reasons cited in the literature for this apparent lack of accurate and fair education about Native American history in modern American schools. The most obvious place to start is to look at the teachers, because teachers in most school districts possess a considerable amount of autonomy over instructional decision-making (Barton 2012). Thornton (1991) described the teacher's role as that of a curricular-instructional gatekeeper, responsible at the individual classroom level for choosing the exact content to be covered and the pedagogical strategies employed. Thus, the extent to which Native American history and perspectives are integrated into the classroom rests to a considerable extent on teacher decision-making. Taylor (1969) summarized this concept eloquently: 'education is only as good or as bad as the teachers who plan it and carry it on' (p. viii). Therefore, '[i]t is the educator's responsibility to expand his or her knowledge base, an endeavour that will help uncover distortions, stereotypes, and misconceptions' (Sanchez 2007: 316). Mason and Ernst-Slavit (2010) found that, when teaching about Native Americans, fourth- and fifth-grade teachers used language that perpetuated stereotypes and biased perceptions.

Some researchers have discovered that teachers may shy away from controversial topics or those that they fear may cast the United States in a negative light. Race may be one topic that American public school teachers, who are predominately Caucasian, may be reluctant to discuss. Chandler (2010) argued that Critical Race Theory must be extended to begin with the experiences of the Indigenous people of North America since that is where and when racism as a defining feature of our country began. 'It would seem that the power that race has played in the unfolding of the American nation state could, and maybe should be a focal point of the social studies or history curricula in American schools. [Racism] represents the central theme in American history' (Chandler 2010: 29). The negative effects of avoiding critical discussions of race in the classroom may lead to what King (1991) called 'dysconscious racism', an 'uncritical habit of mind that justifies inequity and exploitation by accepting the existing order of things as given' (p. 135), which then subconsciously discourages individuals to take active steps to change society.

Another crucial concern is the lack of readily available, high-quality resources for teachers who do want to portray Native American history in a fair and responsible way. The primary resource used in most history classes in the United States is the textbook, and many studies suggest that high school history textbooks 'unapologetically present Native Americans through white eyes' (Loewen 2007: 93). Much of the language used by textbooks to describe contact between European-Americans and Native Americans, including 'settlers', 'discovery', 'frontier', 'exploration' and 'civilization', shows evidence of this bias (Chandler 2010; Loewen 2007). 'When we read the history books given to children in the United States it all starts with a heroic adventure – there is no bloodshed – and Columbus Day is a celebration' (Zinn 2005: 7). Furthermore, textbooks frequently minimize or entirely leave out 'inconvenient' events and issues, including the sheer brutality of the first Europeans in North America, the true toll of European illnesses on Native societies, and the extent of Native American slavery (Loewen 2007). Native American contributions to modern American society may also be minimized. The ways in which Europeans benefited from native knowledge and inventions through the Columbian exchange may be omitted (Loewen 2007). Similarly, the fact that Native ideas about government and politics had a profound impact on the creation of our own democracy is completely missing from our textbooks and public consciousness (Chandler 2010).

In a 2012 study of North Carolina state history textbooks, Hillburn and Fitchett found that the treatment of Native Americans has changed over time. Textbooks written before 1969 tended to promote a dichotomy of Native American tribes as either friendly or hostile, and only discussed Native Americans in the context of their interactions with European settlers. While more recent texts investigated in the study included more information about pre-Columbian Native American culture, they tended to portray Native Americans as 'victims of European-American aggression' (Hillburn and Fitchett 2012: 54). Additionally, the texts concentrated on the colonial period, with little or no information provided about more recent Native American history. Several other studies have also indicated that few US history textbooks include any recent Native American history (Hawkins 2005).

Due to the lack of reliable and fair information in many history textbooks, teachers frequently attempt to supplement the textbook with other sources. However, many school libraries are full of outdated or inaccurate texts. While it is crucial to include texts that are written from a tribal perspective, it is uncommon to find many of these included in the out-of-class resources available to students and teachers (Meyer 2011). Teachers may also attempt to incorporate primary sources to foster more equitable Native history instruction. However, despite the great possibilities for democratic education that the frequent and skilled use of primary sources hold for the history classroom (Mason and Ernst-Slavit 2010), very often the actual instruction falls short. '[C]urricular resources that include Native primary sources do not necessarily provide adequate contextual information to accurately and responsively represent those accounts. Little attention is given to the broader historical or contemporary political context' (Stanton 2012: 361).

Yet another frequently cited barrier to the integration of more accurate Native American history is state content standards, which guide the instruction of all teachers in the United States. While some literature suggests that certain states do include multiple standards that require teachers to address Native American history in more detail, particularly those in the Pacific Northwest (Meyer 2011), the vast majority of state standard systems relegate Native American history to a backseat behind the master American narrative. Additionally, the number of standards that the typical US history teacher is expected to cover is so vast that they are essentially forced to cover every topic minimally, with no time for extended reflection on any individual event (Loewen 2009).

Recommendations for improvement

Suggestions from the literature for improving instruction in Native American history include:

1. being aware of our instructional language – unconscious 'othering' (Mason and Ernst-Slavit 2010);
2. using primary sources to allow students to analyse and draw their own conclusions (Chandler 2010; Mason and Ernst-Slavit 2010). Primary sources created by Native Americans themselves may be particularly useful (Sanchez 2007);
3. inviting community members or family members of class to participate in oral history (Mason and Ernst-Slavit 2010);
4. spending considerable class time on pre-Columbian civilizations (Mason and Ernst-Slavit 2010);
5. providing students with materials that challenge the master narrative and allow them to see diverse perspectives on an issue (Mason and Ernst-Slavit 2010);
6. bringing Native American history into the present day to avoid the notion that they are extinct (Mason and Ernst-Slavit 2010);
7. training pre-service teachers to detect bias in curricular materials (Meyer 2011);
8. explicitly discussing race and racism as a central theme in American history (Chandler 2010).

Methods

Participants

The participants in this study were all middle school history teachers currently employed by public school districts across the United States. Potential participants were selected through a multi-stage random sampling method (Fraenkel and Wallen 2006). First, the United States was divided into five regions: Northeast, Southeast, Midwest, Southwest and West. Two states from each region were then selected using a random number generator. A list of public school districts in each selected state was accessed through the NCES (National Center for Education Statistics) database. A random number generator was used to select five public school districts from each state. The Internet was used to access the middle or junior high school information for each district. All American history teachers from the selected schools were invited via email to participate in this study.

Sixty-four middle and junior high school American history teachers agreed to participate in the study. Eighty-eight per cent of participants were Caucasian, 3 per cent were Asian or Pacific Islander, 3 per cent were of multiple ethnicities, and 5 per cent chose not to indicate their race. No African-American or Native American teachers chose to participate. Participants were 52 per cent female and 48 per cent male. Two per cent of respondents indicated that they were 24 years of age or younger, 29 per cent were between 25 and 34, 28 per cent were between 35 and 44, and 42 per cent were age 45 or older. Thirty-two per cent indicated that they had a Bachelor's Degree, while 66 per cent had a Master's Degree. Only one respondent had a doctoral degree. Thirty per cent of teachers had been teaching five years or fewer, 30 per cent had six to ten years of experience, and 40 per cent had more than ten years of teaching experience.

Data collection and analysis

All teacher-participants in this study completed a qualitative questionnaire about their beliefs and experiences using researcher-created semi-structured questions. In addition, twelve participants also agreed to participate in follow-up interviews, where semi-structured interview questions and clarification questions were asked by the researcher. Collected data from all questionnaires and follow-up interviews were aggregated and anonymized. Data analysis of the compiled data was conducted utilizing structured codes based on the original questionnaire and interview questions and themes from the literature (Saldana 2011). Five themes were identified using this process.

Limitations

The main limitation of this study is that it relied on self-reported data only, which may be skewed by the perceptions of the participants, participant concerns about the social desirability of their answers or a desire to please the researcher. Due to the limited sample size, the results of this study are not intended to be generalized to all middle or junior high school American history teachers, but instead are intended to represent the experiences and beliefs of a select group of teachers.

Findings

As the data were analysed, five themes emerged that explained the attitudes and experiences of participants regarding the teaching of Native American history in their middle or junior high school American history classes. These themes were:

1. Importance of Native American history
2. Lack of teacher autonomy
3. Insufficiency of available resources
4. Issues of patriotism and democratic education
5. Social justice issues and critical pedagogy

Importance of Native American history

All but one study participant emphasized the importance of including Native American history and perspectives in middle and junior high school American history classes. One common belief was that American history should include not just the history of the country of the United States, but pre-Columbian civilizations as well. One teacher explained: 'I consider my history class to include American Indian history.' Despite this conviction, however, many teachers indicated that they did not or could not include much pre-Columbian history in their courses due to curricular constraints which will be discussed later in this chapter.

Most teachers also expressed a strong conviction that Native American history and perspectives be included throughout the history of the United States. One teacher insisted that 'students cannot get a truly rich and accurate appreciation of who we are as a nation without this facet'. Another explained that '[i]t's an important topic and very complex'. Many teachers felt that an effort should be made to include as much non-dominant history as possible, complaining that, '[w]e get plenty of European-American viewpoints, but not enough of the rest of the world's.' Another participant posited that 'their [Native American] history deserves to be taught just as much as [that of other ethnic groups]'.

Only one participant expressed disdain for the inclusion of Native American viewpoints. He rejected the notion of including minority histories into the dominant American narrative: 'We obviously do not cover in detail Native American issues nor do we have the time to single out any ethnic group . . . If Native American history is that important offer a specific class . . . [and] do not try and push an agenda [into standard American history classes]'. While this statement represents the beliefs of only one teacher in the study, it is important to acknowledge that his statements may reflect the beliefs of a segment of American history teachers.

Despite the fact that all but one teacher in the study clearly expressed their belief in the importance of frequently including Native American history and perspectives in American history classes, few were actually able to do so. Forty-nine per cent of participants stated that they spend less than 10 per cent of their total class time discussing Native American topics. Additionally, nearly half (40 per cent) of the teachers interviewed in this study indicated that they spent either very little or no instructional time covering pre-Columbian civilizations. The next theme explains one of the main reasons cited by teachers for this apparent contradiction.

Lack of autonomy

While all of the teachers in this sample had strong feelings about what should and should not be included in the curriculum, they also all felt limited autonomy to make curricular decisions. The most commonly cited reason for not including more Native American topics and viewpoints into classes was state standards, with 29 per cent of participants indicating that these restricted their instructional autonomy. An additional 22 per cent cited district-created curriculum or pacing guides as a significant limiting factor. One teacher explained that '[c]urrent state standards include very little Native American topics except for major events such as [the] Indian Removal Act [1830], [the] French and Indian War [1754–1763, part of the Seven Years' War], and Indian conflicts with American settlers'. Another teacher admitted, 'I know I am lacking in covering Native American culture and heritage. I relate this to the fact that Native American culture is not covered in our curriculum.' Even most teachers who indicated they included a lot of Native American topics in their courses pointed to state or district-mandated standards, with such explanations as 'it's in the standards' and '[w]e have a good set of state standards in my state for Native American history, in my opinion'.

While state standards are undoubtedly intended to provide a basis for the minimum requirements rather than to limit teachers who desire to exceed them, many teachers felt that the sheer amount of required material made surpassing them impossible. A typical statement was 'I teach mainly what the standards are asking to teach due to the lack of time for instruction.' Similarly, another teacher explained, 'I have to treat my class as a survey class at times.' The feeling of being overwhelmed by required content was shared by many. 'In my class we have soooo [*sic*] much history to cover that sometimes some topics (even though I hate it) do not get as much coverage.' A full 25 per cent of participants indicated that they could not find the instructional time to exceed the state standards and/or district curriculum guide, while another 4 per cent admitted that they frequently failed to even meet the required standards.

The data collected in this study seem to indicate that standardized testing pressures are less of a concern for social studies teachers than for teachers in many other fields. While one teacher did explicitly mention that 'it is hard to get everything in before State testing in the spring', this was an expressed concern for only two participants. The main reason for this may be that middle school social studies is not tested in most states.

Many teachers also felt that they lacked sufficient autonomy in the selection of instructional methods. One participant specifically cited the Common Core standards[3] recently adopted in many states as influencing instructional practices, stating that '[t]hese [instructional activities] are ways we are required to use with Common Core English Language Arts, but also ways that are appropriate I feel to teach History'. Other participants pointed towards district instructional guidelines, explaining their pedagogical decisions as 'the methods used from the district curriculum' and 'the methods that best fit the needs of my students and are expected by my county standards'.

If state standards and district mandates are seen by teachers as limiting their ability to teach certain topics or utilize certain methods, they are also seen as the potential answer to the problem. Many teachers who wanted to increase their teaching of Native American topics felt a change in standards and curriculum guides was necessary and desirable. One participant shared, 'I believe that more standards need to be implemented by states to cover Native American history.' Another teacher hoped to influence the district curriculum guide in this way, stating, 'I am writing and developing our curriculum this year and plan to incorporate much more Native Americans in American history'.

Insufficiency of available resources

This research discovered that many teachers feel that their own knowledge base on Native Americans is insufficient to cover topics thoroughly without assistive resources. Seven per cent of participants recalled taking no courses in college that covered any Native American topics, while another 11 per cent recalled taking only one college course that did so. One teacher admitted this unpreparedness in this way: 'there were some events [we discussed] that I have never even heard of – and I was a History major'.[4] Similarly, another teacher felt that the district and state should help fill in the gaps, explaining, 'I would love to have more information on ways to teach this area with more knowledge.' A different participant admitted limiting the topics she covered due to her lack of knowledge, stating, 'I do not [cover these topics] because I am worried to speak inaccurately and offending students because I feel I don't know enough about the situation currently.'

The most common resource in any American classroom is the textbook, which in most cases individual teachers have no or little influence in selecting (Loewen 2007). Only 4 per cent of study participants responded that they felt their textbook treated Native American history fairly and/or accurately. One teacher felt so strongly about the inadequacy of her textbook that she exclaimed, 'Our text is lame! It is so watered-down, that often Native American issues are not even addressed.' Another participant expressed concern that 'our textbooks might mention/or refer to Native Americans with disrespect', while another mentioned several 'inaccuracies in the textbook'. Other teachers seemed to believe that the textbooks were trying to improve their coverage, despite some serious flaws. 'This textbook aims to provide us multiple stories into our history, but most of them are from an Anglo male's perspective.' In a similar vein, another teacher insisted that 'the textbook alone cannot convey the truth of what has happened in history, especially in regards to the history of Native Americans'. Despite the overwhelming consensus that the textbooks were seriously flawed in their coverage of Native American issues, 69 per cent of the teachers in this study still admitted using textbook reading as a primary means of teaching Native American history.

One specific topic that many teachers mentioned as having a lack of resources for teaching was pre-Columbian Native life. One teacher explained, 'we have very little resources that would help us teach about early Native American before the "age of exploration". My curriculum mentions briefly about Native Americans before in basically one paragraph.' In fact, fewer than half of the teacher-participants indicated they taught pre-Columbian history in any detail, and a lack of resources to support doing so was the primary reason given.

Many teachers mentioned at least one alternative resource they used to learn about Native American history on their own, or even used in class in some cases. These resources included Howard Zinn's books and the Zinn Educational Project website; James Loewen's books; *American Progress*, a painting by John Gast (1872); and Gary Nash's *Red, White, and Black* (Nash 2014). Some participants indicated that these were books they were asked to read in college, while others received recommendations from colleagues, and some had found these sources as the result of a personal search.

The vast majority of teachers in this study expressed a need for supplemental instructional resources to assist them in creating more appropriate lessons on Native American topics. Limited planning time was a huge consideration for many. 'Honestly, I have always wanted to do more, but as a young teacher starting and developing an understanding [of] the curriculum as a whole, it was difficult.' Another teacher concurred, affirming, 'In my case, the biggest hindrance is lack of time!' Multiple teachers felt that high-quality supplemental resources would enable them to plan appropriate lessons despite these constraints. '[I]t takes a long time to pull together materials and make it accessible for my students. Sometimes I wish that there were more units about Native Americans that I could apply to my 8th graders.' Another teacher commented, 'I am guilty [of not teaching much about this topic] ... because of lack of resources/professional development in this area.' Several teachers even requested supplementary resources from the researcher with comments like, '[I'd] love to have some activities and resources for incorporating more Native American history in my class.'

Patriotism and democratic education

It has been posited in the literature that teachers may avoid controversial or inconvenient histories in their classes due to concerns about portraying their nation in a negative light (Loewen 2007). Only one participant in this study admitted to feeling a contradiction between teaching the truth of our history and his intense patriotism, insisting that the United States is 'the greatest, fairest and most opportunity-based country I know of'. He was the only participant who indicated that encouraging patriotism was a reason to limit instruction about Native American history.

In contrast, multiple other participants indicated that true patriotism required efforts to develop democratic citizens, an oft-cited goal of social studies education (Campaign for the Civic Mission of Schools 2003; National Council for the Social Studies 2013; Ochoa-Becker 2007). In fact, one teacher observed that 'I have found sincere patriotism in our community and amongst my students so we honor that [in my classes].' One manifestation of this effort on the part of teachers, which can be classified under the Campaign for the Civic Mission of Schools' (2003) first component of democratic education, classroom instruction, is telling the truth about the events that occurred, even if they were unpleasant. One teacher explained, 'I teach American History, the good, the bad and the ugly.' Another teacher explained his inclusion of controversial topics by saying, 'while new information occasionally startles [my students], we never breeze over these topics. We take the time we need to discuss these events: slavery of indigenous peoples, land rights, eradication of indigenous peoples, etc.' A similar orientation was described by another teacher who stated, 'I feel it is important to teach all parts of History, even the parts that are not pretty ... we will not leave out parts of history just because they are hard to hear about.' One teacher in this study even used the term 'American Holocaust' in his classes, because he felt '[t]hat phrase seems to be the deciding factor in opening kids' eyes to what has really happened the past 400 years'.

However, despite teachers' frequent claims of covering controversial or potentially difficult topics in class, the actual Native American topics they claim to emphasize tell a slightly different tale. Only about half of the teachers in this sample confirmed that they typically discussed Native American slavery with their classes. Only about one-third typically teach the 1887 Dawes Severalty Act, which delegitimized Native tribes and stripped Native Americans of nearly one hundred million acres of tribal lands. The number of specific Native–European military conflicts taught by these teachers was also very low, with King Philip's War (1675–6), the Pueblo Revolt (1680), the Sand Creek Massacre (29 November 1864) and the Nez Perce War (1877) all being taught by less than one-third of teachers. Similarly, fewer than one-third of teachers in this study covered the forced assimilation of Native American children through boarding schools.

A second component of democratic education embraced by the majority of the teachers in this study was open discussion of issues. In fact, 92 per cent of the teachers in this study indicated that class discussion was a primary method they used to uncover Native American issues. One teacher emphasized the importance of class discussion by stating, 'We have class discussions daily over the materials in our class textbook and I use these as teachable moments.' In these types of discussions, acceptance of multiple perspectives is of key importance. One teacher explained, 'My students and I are committed to analyzing primary sources and exploring multiple voices in history class.' Similarly, another teacher described how '[w]e analyze primary sources from all subgroups of people and seek to understand the whole picture, not just that of the "old, dead, white guy"'. The purpose of democratic discussion was made clear by one participant who said that she introduced 'multiple perspectives to reduce bias and eliminate stereotypes'.

Incorporating authentic Native voices was also a priority to many teachers in this study. Several teachers were able to arrange guest speakers from local Native nations. One teacher boasted, 'I have access to Elders and others willing to come in and talk to the class.' Another teacher hoped to promote admiration for Natives through classroom guests: 'I also seek out Native American role models that show how . . . advanced their thinking was and make sure these people are introduced to my students.' Other teachers were able to encourage Native American students in their classes to express their viewpoints, with one teacher indicating that nearly 25 per cent of his class had Native American ancestry. Even teachers who did not have access to Native American speakers tried to incorporate Native voices through primary source readings.

One teacher asserted, 'I try to bring in clips and articles from Native American perspectives', while another explained, 'I regularly select texts that include multiple perspectives of our historical topics, and locate primary sources (speeches, sketches, photographs, interviews, etc.) that were created by indigenous peoples.' Only one teacher thought incorporating native voices could potentially have unintended negative consequences, and she stated, 'I would like to [include Native voices] but I think that stereotypical ideas would influence my students.'

Critical literacy was also emphasized by many participants. One teacher described this imperative by stating, 'I also caution my students to never just believe everything they hear or read. They always need to think critically about the things they read and hear no matter what the source is.' Another teacher explained, 'I have tried to gear my teaching toward being able to read anything with an understanding that almost everything in History that you read was written by one side and that we need to be aware there is always another side to the story.' Encouraging students to consider all sides was also important to many teachers, as one stated: 'I also encourage students to consider every side of a topic before rushing to judgment.' Many teachers felt that teaching critical literacy to their classes would give students a skill they could transfer to their out-of-class life; a typical response was: 'I am hoping the students can carry that skill to other classes and use it in their lives.'

Social justice and critical pedagogy

Many teachers in this study indicated that one of their intentions in teaching Native American history in their classes was to encourage their students to challenge the master narrative provided in the textbook or encouraged by societal norms and take a critical stance on past events. One teacher clarified, 'we discuss how the Indians/Native Americans are portrayed. Is it accurate? Is it prejudiced in favor of the settlers?' Another teacher encouraged his students to 'make decisions about who was right and wrong'. The controversy surrounding the celebration of Columbus Day was one topic mentioned by several participants about which they frequently held class discussions and debates.

Many teachers expressed a desire for their students to feel empathy towards modern Native Americans. One participant emphasized his commitment 'to connect student consciousness with current Native American issues', while another desired to 'raise consciousness of [the] diversity of [our] nation'. Some teachers who wanted to connect history to modern circumstances felt it was not within their power to do so, stating, 'it seems almost taboo to talk about N.A. life after [Western expansion].' Another participant concurred: 'There is no mention of life for Native Americans after the Western expansion period. I feel this might be one reason my students feel a disconnect with current Native Americans.'

Empowering students to use their knowledge to make a difference in the modern world was a theme embraced by many teachers. 'We discuss how citizenship is important, as well as the participation of government at every level, as citizens.' Another teacher described her purpose by explaining, 'I make sure they leave my classroom feeling empowered to interact in our society today, to prevent the issues from ever reoccurring.' A different participant described the general motivation of teachers in the History department at her school: 'We work to preserve the [sic] [their] natural patriotism and foster interest in participation in their government. Self-advocacy is a priority'.

Despite the suggestion from the literature that race should be taught as the fundamental theme of US history (Chandler 2010), most teachers expressed discomfort with this notion. One main concern was that the teacher's intentions would be misunderstood, and they would themselves be perceived as racist. One teacher explained her hesitation this way: 'I myself would be concerned to [explicitly discuss race] because no matter how presented students will still have their own views on how they think it was being taught and can misunderstand a teacher.' One teacher provided an example of a time when she was actually accused of making a racist comment to a student, which she denied. Another common reason given by the teacher-participants was that because they were Caucasian, they could not thoroughly comprehend racism. One participant, however, did endorse the importance of teaching these topics, explaining, 'it is really important to have open discussions about racism in class, as well as racial tension, because it exists. It has shaped our society and world.' She later went on to clarify, 'I will do this in a tone of voice that does not indicate apology for my being white.'

Conclusion

The data collected in this study indicated that most of the teacher-participants felt that discussing Native American history was a pedagogical imperative for middle and junior high school American history classes. Most teachers claimed to go beyond the curricular mandates and textbook accounts to incorporate a more thorough and authentic coverage of Native American topics. In order to help students to develop a critical knowledge base, many teachers incorporated primary source documents, multiple perspectives and collaborative discussions into their instruction. Some teachers strove to include authentic Native voices, as well. It is encouraging that many teachers specifically mentioned critical literacy, democratic education and social justice goals in their pedagogical approaches.

However, there are still many ways in which Native American history education in US history courses could be improved. Many teachers expressed regret that they were not able to include more Native American instruction due to such circumstances as lack of personal knowledge, inaccessibility of fair and accurate resources, lack of planning time and stringent state and/or district curriculum requirements. Few teachers felt they could incorporate much pre-Columbian history or modern-day events into their classes. Additionally, despite most teacher-participants' insistence that they did not shy away from controversial or 'inconvenient' history, the data they provided about the topics they typically taught suggests otherwise. Several teachers also felt uncomfortable explicitly discussing race and racism in their classes. These may be some areas of need which can be more fully integrated into teacher-education programmes in order to better prepare future American history teachers to tackle these tough, yet crucial, topics.

Notes

1 The proper terminology to refer to the first known inhabitants of North America is still in debate. Within the United States, the terms 'Native Americans' and 'American Indians' are common. Other nations may use the phrases 'First Peoples' or 'First Nations'.

2 Historians estimate that between 75 to 90 per cent of the Native Americans who died in the century following initial contact with Europeans succumbed to European diseases such as smallpox and influenza, to which they had developed no immunity (Loewen 2007).
3 While the creation of public education standards is a responsibility of each individual state, the Common Core standards are a set of national standards created by representatives of many states to ensure college and career readiness for all American high school graduates. They have been adopted by forty-three states.
4 In the United States, most social studies teacher candidates major in Education rather than History in college. Presumably, a History major would have taken more history courses than the average teacher.

References

Barton, K. (2012), 'Wars and Rumors of War: The Rhetoric and Reality of History Education in the United States', in T. Taylor and R. Guyver (eds), *History Wars and the Classroom: Global Perspectives*, 187–202, Charlotte, NC: Information Age Publishing.

Campaign for the Civic Mission of Schools (2003), 'Guardian of Democracy: The Civic Mission of Schools', Silver Spring, MD: Campaign for the Civic Mission of Schools. Available online: http://www.civicmissionofschools.org/the-campaign/guardian-of-democracy-report (accessed 28 February 2015).

Castleden, H., Daley, K., Morgan, V. S. and Sylvestre, P. (2013), 'Settlers Unsettled: Using Field Schools and Digital Stories to Transform Geographies of Ignorance about Indigenous Peoples in Canada', *Journal of Geography in Higher Education* 37 (4): 487–499.

Chandler, P. T. (2010), 'Critical Race Theory and Social Studies: Centering the Native American Experience', *Journal of Social Studies Research* 34 (1): 29–58.

Doolan, I., Najman, J. M., Mills, R., Cherney, A. and Strathearn, L. (2013), 'Does Child Abuse and Neglect Explain the Overrepresentation of Aboriginal and Torres Strait Islander Young People in Youth Detention? Findings from a Birth Cohort Study', *Child Abuse & Neglect* 37: 303–9.

Foner, E. (2014), *Give Me Liberty: An American History*, Brief 4th edn, New York: WW Norton.

Fraenkel, J. R. and Wallen, N. E. (2006), *How to Design and Evaluate Research in Education*, New York: McGraw-Hill.

Gast, J. (1872), *American Progress*, painting, Museum of the American West, Griffith Park, LA.

Hawkins, J. (2005), 'Smoke Signals, Sitting Bulls, and Slot Machines: A New Stereotype of Native Americans?', *Multicultural Perspectives* 7 (3): 51–4.

Hillburn, J. and Fitchett, P. G. (2012), 'The New Gateway, and Old Paradox: Immigrants and Involuntary Americans in North Carolina History Texts', *Theory and Research in Social Studies Education* 40 (1): 35–65.

Hoffmann, L., Jackson, A. and Smith, S. (2005), 'Career Barriers among Native American Students Living on Reservations', *Journal of Career Development* 32: 31–45.

Huaman, E. S. and Valdiviezo, L. A. (2014), 'Indigenous Knowledge and Education from the Quechua Community to School: Beyond the Formal/Non-formal Dichotomy', *International Journal of Qualitative Studies in Education* 27 (1): 65–87.

King, J. (1991), 'Dysconscious Racism: Ideology, Identity, and the Miseducation of Teachers', *Journal of Negro Education* 60 (2): 133–46.
Loewen, J. W. (2007), *Lies My Teacher Told Me*, New York: Simon & Schuster.
Loewen, J. W. (2009), *Teaching What Really Happened*, New York: Teachers' College Press.
Lynch, M., Buckman, J. and Krenske, L. (2003), 'Youth Justice: Criminal Trajectories in Crime and Criminal Justice', *Trends and Issues in Crime and Criminal Justice* [Australian Institute of Criminology] 265: 1–6. Available online: http://www.aic.gov.au/media_library/publications/tandi_pdf/tandi265.pdf (accessed 3 August 2015).
Mason, M. R. and Ernst-Slavit, G. (2010), 'Representations of Native Americans in Elementary School Social Studies: A Critical Look at Instructional Language', *Multicultural Education* 18 (1): 10–17.
Meyer, N. (2011), 'Selecting Diverse Resources of Native American Perspective for the Curriculum Center: Children's Literature, Leveled Readers, and the Social Studies Curriculum', *Education Libraries* 34 (1): 23–32.
Nash, G. (2014), *Red, White, and Black*, 7th edn, New York: Pearson.
National Council for the Social Studies (2013), 'Revitalizing Civic Learning in our Schools'. Available online: http://www.socialstudies.org/positions/revitalizing_civic_learning (accessed 28 February 2015).
National Indian Education Association (NIEA) (2008), *Native Education 101: Basic Facts about American Indian, Alaska Native and Native Hawaiian Education*, Washington, DC: National Education Association.
Nguyen, M. (2011), 'Closing the Education Gap: A Case for Aboriginal Early Childhood Education in Canada, A Look at the Aboriginal Head Start Program', *Canadian Journal of Education* 34 (3): 229–48.
Nicholas, M. A. (2014), *Native Voices: Sources in the Native American Past*, New York: Pearson.
Ochoa-Becker, A. (2007), *Democratic Education for Social Studies*, Greenwich, CT: Information Age Publishing.
Saldana, J. (2011), *The Coding Manual for Qualitative Researchers*, Los Angeles: Sage Publications.
Salisbury, N. (2007), 'The Indians' Old World: Native Americans and the Coming of Europeans,' in P. C. Mancall and J. H. Merrell (eds), *American Encounters: Natives and Newcomers from European Contact to Indian Removal, 1500–1850*, 3–24, New York: Routledge.
Sanchez, T. R. (2007), 'The Depiction of Native Americans in Recent (1991–2004) Secondary History Textbooks: How Far Have we Come?', *Excellence and Equity in Education* 40 (4): 311–20.
Scott, D. (2013), 'Teaching Aboriginal Perspectives: An Investigation into Teacher Practices Amidst Curricular Change', *Canadian Social Studies* 46 (1): 31–43.
Sharp, H. (2012), 'Australia's 1988 Bicentennial: National History and Multiculturalism in the Primary School Curriculum', *History of Education* 41 (3): 405–21.
Stanton, C. R. (2012), 'Hearing the Story: Critical Indigenous Curriculum Inquiry and Primary Source Representation in Social Studies Education', *Theory and Research in Social Education* 40 (4): 339–70.
Takaki, R. (2008), *A Different Mirror: A History of Multicultural America*, New York: Back Bay Books.
Taylor, H. (1969), *The World as Teacher*, Garden City, NY: Doubleday.
Thompson, M. N. (2013), 'Career Barriers and Coping Efficacy among Native American Students', *Journal of Career Assessment* 21 (2): 311–25.

Thornton, S. J. (1991), 'Teacher as Curricular-Instructional Gatekeeper in Social Studies', in J. P. Shaver (ed.), *Handbook of Research on Social Studies Teaching and Learning*, 237–48, New York: Macmillan.
Tupper, J. A. and Cappello, M. (2008), 'Teaching Treaties as (Un)usual Narratives: Disrupting the Curricular Commonsense', *Curriculum Inquiry* 38 (5): 559–78.
United Nations General Assembly (2007), *Report of the Human Rights Council: United Nations Declaration on the Rights of Indigenous Peoples*, New York: United Nations.
Zinn, H. (2005), *A People's History of the United States*, New York: HarperCollins.

9

England and the UK: Conflict and Consensus over Curriculum

Robert Guyver

Introduction

The situations described here throw further light on the debate moved forward by Peter Seixas in his seminal chapter, 'Schweigen! die Kinder!' (2000: 19–37). Seixas provided a useful synthesis of the main issues that contribute to 'history wars' debates around the world by offering what he believed to be the three main positions as 'collective memory, disciplinary and postmodern', although he was clearly asking a question about how far the influence of the postmodern approach might go. The debates being examined in this chapter on England and the UK show that collective memory is not a simple category, especially as it has to embrace varieties of internal and external inheritances. A complex understanding of both memory and 'heritage' can be developed through considering different 'theatres of memory' in a hybrid relationship with a disciplinary approach. 'Theatres of memory' is an expression invented by Raphael Samuel in two works, the latter published posthumously (Samuel 1994, 1998).

The years between 1989 and 2014 saw a flourishing of public debate on school history. After 2004 it ran parallel with debates about the nature of 'Britishness' and the relationship between identity and citizenship, where future 'New' Labour Prime Minister Gordon Brown delivered two major speeches, the last to the Fabian Society (Brown 2004, 2006). Brown, especially after the 7 July London Transport bombings in 2005, raised the question of whether it was possible to be Cornish and British, Scottish and British or even Pakistani, Muslim and British. Brown later wrote at length in support of the 'No' campaign against Scottish independence (Brown 2014). Paul Gilroy had attended the Fabian Society Britishness conference at which Brown had spoken, and in his work on the diaspora associated with slavery had used the notion of 'double consciousness' in the context of a transatlantic sense of both displacement and belonging (Gilroy 1993). He had also and perceptively commented that after the Second World War the Empire had in fact come to Britain, in the form of settlers from the Commonwealth (Gilroy 1987). The devolution of powers was well under way in the constituent parts of the UK. The first meeting of the Scottish Parliament took place in 1999, after the Scotland Act, 1998. Wales underwent this process in stages with the Government of Wales Acts, 1998 and 2006, gaining (devolved) independent powers of legislation only after 2011. The Northern Ireland Assembly was set up after the Good Friday Agreement in 1998 alongside the North/South Ministerial Council with the Republic of Ireland, but experienced a period of suspension of the Assembly, from 2002 to 2007.

The 2011 census revealed:

UK total population	63,181,775
England	53,012,456 (83.9%)
Scotland	5,295,000 (8.4%)
Wales	3,063,456 (4.8%)
Northern Ireland	1,810,863 (2.9%)

England's population was thus ten times more than Scotland's. Against the background of the very narrow success of the 'No' vote in the Referendum on Scottish Independence on 18 September 2014 (Yes 44.7%; No 55.3%), the 7 May General Election in 2015 demonstrated a significant increase of support in Scotland for the Scottish National Party (SNP), which ended up with fifty-six parliamentary seats at Westminster (the UK Parliament in London), with Labour losing forty seats in Scotland and the Liberal Democrats losing ten there. Having had a coalition government for five years, the UK was now to be governed by a Conservative majority of twelve seats. England, however, found itself with a continuing identity crisis, caught in an intranational force field within the UK itself, with Scotland pressing even more for independence. The UK, like many places in the world, faced increasing immigration, but was also pulled in different directions by the conflicting, confusing and contrasting magnetisms exerted by Europe and North America, pending further clarification with a referendum vote on continuing membership of the European Union promised by the new Conservative government.

With the increase of 'academies' and 'free schools' in England there was a significant decline in the local control of schools and even less certainty about whether the kind of history education believed to be suitable for future citizens could be guaranteed, as these schools were not obliged to follow the national curriculum. In an age when there were fears about Islamic radicalization, schools themselves were suspected of nurturing unwelcome ideologies, as was the case in the summer of 2014 when the so-called 'Trojan Horse' situation involving some schools in the Midlands came to the fore.

'Four nations' history

It would be difficult to have a pure diet of 'English' history, as the land-space now called England has been affected over the last two thousand years and more by events and developments to the north and west, in Scotland, Wales and Ireland. 'Four nations' history was built into the first national curriculum for history that was deliberated from 1989 and became law in 1991. Three of its proponents, Keith Robbins, Conrad Russell and Raphael Samuel, were external advisors to the government's own History Working Group in 1989 and 1990. It had also been the subject of work by Kearney (1989) and Pocock (1975, 2005). For example, Russell saw the causes of the first Civil War (in the 1640s) as being directly related to how the Scots had reacted to England's religious policy; and, going even earlier, Robbins believed that the English should know about the aspirations of Scottish independence expressed in the Declaration of Arbroath of 1320. Wales too had landmark events. In the House of Lords debate (see below) Lord Morgan mentioned 'the Blue Books controversy of 1847, which is probably unknown to most of my audience and never mentioned in books on British history', as 'perhaps the most important event in nineteenth and twentieth century Welsh history in stimulating a sense of nationality' (Morgan 2011).

Samuel (1998: 26) writes tellingly first of Pocock's work, in which simple ethnic categories prove impossible to define where there were normanized Irish and hibernicized Normans, bilingual Anglo-Welsh, monoglot Welsh and English, tensions between Highland and Lowland Scots in the clan world – with Lowlanders resorting to litigation rather than warfare, Celts who entered a Norse world and Norsemen assimilated to the Celtic pattern, and the expansion of government at the expense of kinship. 'British history' was seen as 'a history of the constant creation, accompanied by the much less constant absorption, of new subcultures and even subnations'. Clearly this process continues to this day. Then he wrote of Kearney's view of three Scotlands in the nineteenth century – the Highlands (including the Hebrides but not, for good reason, the Orkneys and Shetland, a subculture of their own) and two Lowlands, divided between an industrial Clydeside and an Edinburgh-based east. Wales is likewise divided into two cultures, which are then subdivided according to religion and class (Samuel 1998: 27).

This being the case, constructing an English history curriculum that also satisfies additional demands for a plurinational British dimension has been a recurring problem and a particularly difficult task. Wales and Northern Ireland have history curricula that have been developed with similar criteria to the English curricula at the various stages from the early 1990s to the present, but Scotland has an independent education system and does not yet have a national history curriculum per se. England has felt obliged to include the role of the other UK nations in its own narrative for both historiographical and political reasons.

Pedagogy and curriculum design

Pedagogy and curriculum design have often been ignored or reduced to over-simplified categories in debates by politicians and historians about school history. Nevertheless, from the 1970s in England curriculum structures have been affected by pedagogical thinking (e.g. Bruner's 'spiral curriculum', and much later Seixas's six benchmarks of historical thinking). Leading this process was the School History Project (SHP), which translated these ideas into usable forms and frameworks. An outcome of reforms in curriculum thinking was the embedding of enquiry into content, and towards this end there emerged the use of a bundle of syntactic key concepts (chronology, evidence, interpretation, causes and consequences, change and continuity, similarity and difference) to interrogate substantive knowledge. All of these would be fed into the first national curriculum of 1991. In both pre- and post-national curriculum thinking, frameworks or scaffolding for the organization of substantive knowledge were seen as necessary, and such devices as overviews and depth-studies evolved. Her Majesty's Inspectorate (HMI) before the onset of the national curriculum not only recommended as good curriculum practice a balance of national, international and local history but also made a plea for periods studied to be long enough to illustrate the dimension of change (DES 1985).

Michael Gove, a Scot and the Coalition government's Secretary of State for Education from 2010 to 2014, was a believer in 'the democratic intellect', a Scottish concept with two parallel but interrelated strands. One strand was connected with the educational thinking of American E. D. Hirsch, Jnr, who believed in the power of 'core knowledge' to transform the cultural-literary capital (and therefore the life-chances) of lower socio-economic groups. Another strand was preparation for democratic, participatory citizenship which perceived a good education as a defence against oppressive politicians:

> John Knox, the leader of the Reformation in Scotland sought to establish a school in every parish – and a college in every important town. He believed that every child should have access to knowledge – instead of a society built on outdated hierarchies with an unrepresentative clerical elite keeping knowledge and power to themselves, there should be an educated population using its learning to hold the powers to account.
>
> Gove 2010a: 6

This has strange predictive echoes of a piece from Simon Schama's address to teachers at the Hay-on-Wye Literary Festival in May 2013:

> And for Thucydides history is not about self-congratulation and it's not about tracing the pedigree of the wonderfulness of us, nor is it about tracing the pedigree of the reprehensibly awful nature of us either. It is a chastening, disenchanted, honest, tough-minded version of looking critically at ourselves and seeing what we have become and where we came from. Historians, for Thucydides, are meant to keep the powerful awake at night and keep them honest.
>
> Schama 2013a

What would emerge later in the March–June 2013 history curriculum talks was a blending of these two strands involving a different interpretation of the principles highlighted by Hirsch. This would be a recognition of the importance of subjects as forms (as well as bodies) of knowledge, where depth of meaning and awareness of context can be examined within a healthily varied field of study, highlighting the importance of syntactic as well as substantive knowledge to help future citizens to discriminate and adjudicate.

Michael Gove, like Margaret Thatcher, believed that a Britain in decline needed to believe in itself again. He saw school history as having the power of a restorative medicine, but first the apparently poor current state of school history would have to be addressed. Gove had an underlying belief in the virtues of the British political system and was also and self-confessedly thoroughly 'Whig' in his interpretation of history, believing in a narrative of progress leading to the establishment of stable institutions (in English/British history).[1] In his initial efforts to find a historian who would be able to help him he was unwittingly caught up in the same identity crisis being experienced by both England and the UK as a whole. The first but rather tentative invitation went to Niall Ferguson, another Scot, based at Harvard University, USA, after an encounter at the Hay-on-Wye Literary Festival in late May 2010 (Ferguson 2010). However, although Ferguson was himself interested in reforming school history his vision was for a programme which focused on a narrative analysing the success of the West from about 1500 to around 1914. He was undoubtedly also a 'Whig', but a transatlantic Whig, seeing Whig virtues in the development of European history too, across several empires and in North America (Ferguson 2011).

However, during Michael Gove's speech at the Conservative Party Conference on 5 October 2010 it was Simon Schama who was formally invited to give advice on the reform of the history curriculum (Gove 2010b). Unlike Ferguson, Schama had written a full, if by his own admission selective (Schama 2010a), account of British history in a series of BBC television broadcasts between 2000 and 2002, followed by a three-volume book publication (Schama 2000, 2001, 2002). What Michael Gove may not have realized when he 'appointed' Schama was that he was acquiring not a tame curriculum advisor but a public intellectual who would bring the full set of his skills as perceptively amusing raconteur to a self-chosen role as *agent provocateur*, deeply committed to public debate in every possible media outlet. Only a month after Gove's announcement Schama would write a full statement of his own beliefs (and intent) about school history in the *Guardian* (Schama 2010b). This article would itself provoke a hostile response from leading historian Richard J. Evans (2011).[2]

The issue of identity emerged very clearly as a core concern in Schama's article, and he was able to link this with the importance of teaching the history of the British Empire, especially when seeking to explain the presence of such large numbers of settlers in British cities from South Asia and the Caribbean. Evans, however, whom Schama later described as 'the sneering professor',[3] offered a trenchant criticism accusing Schama (and Gove) of playing identity politics by planning to create a curriculum based on a politicized collective memory apparently undisciplined by the critical methods of history. Rather defying such a definition, Schama seemed to see that the debate was not so much about an overarching category of 'collective memory' (as given by Seixas 2000), but about how different kinds or categories of memory might be managed differently almost to undermine the political process. This had obvious links to the 'theatres of memory' approach presented in such a detailed way by Raphael Samuel. There is clearly a tension between the attempts to collectivize and/or harmonize perceptions of majoritarian memory and another set of attempts to preserve difference and variety in individual, family, local or group memories. This tension within curriculum debate is common to most societies.

The House of Lords debate of 20 October 2011

A key piece of evidence of public concern about history curriculum matters was the House of Lords debate in the autumn of 2011 (House of Lords 2011a, 2011b). A number of chosen publications became points of reference for this, and these were alerts prepared in advance by Ian Cruse (Library Clerk (Research) at the House of Lords) in a Library Note which skilfully synthesized a summary of the arguments and developments for those who took part (Cruse 2011). Among the key documents included in this were the Ofsted, *History for All* Report, March 2011.

The issue of identity was addressed by Lord Morgan:

> History gives children a sense of identity – of where they belong and who they are. Other countries are aware of this. In my wife's country, France, people would be astonished that history is not a compulsory part of our curriculum, as it is so powerfully there. History also gives a sense of a many-sided identity. People in this country have many identities.
>
> Morgan 2011

One significant contribution was by Lord Bew (a crossbencher, i.e. politically unaffiliated), who would be further involved as a member of the round table talks which followed the publication of the draft national curriculum in February 2013. Paul Bew (as he was) was firmly in the consensus camp over this debate and, without naming Richard J. Evans, he expressed disapproval of the way it seemed to have been politicized in the pages of the *London Review of Books*. Lord Bew complained about the sterility of having a right/left debate, claiming that there was actually a burgeoning consensus among historians, and that it was absolutely vital that it be acknowledged that 'if there is a patriotic tradition in this country, it is of the left as well as of the right, and of the centre'. There was a need for balance, as we 'cannot have more history about Nelson and Wellington without Peterloo and the Tolpuddle martyrs'. He heartily endorsed everything that was said in the debate by Lord Morgan, about conflict and consensus. He made a plea for a more formalized involvement of historians with school history, as 'what happens on the whole in our schools does not fully reflect the actual quality of work that goes on among British historians and their commitment to knowledge of the past'. Historians could help in the avoidance of sterile polemics and to enable history education in schools to proceed on the basis of understanding and agreement (Bew 2011).

Baroness Walmsley (Liberal Democrat) by contrast supported the views of Richard Evans, and like him praised the existing national curriculum for its variety. Baroness Berridge (Conservative) called for more detail in an appreciation of the English narrative within the broader British story, reminding the House of the negative reactions she had received when calling in 2007 for a commemoration of the bicentenary of the Abolition of the Slave Trade Act of 1807, but added:

> Is it a commemoration? Do we apologise? This lack of national peace over contentious events does little to assist our history teachers who have to teach this without making white children feel bad and black children feel angry. It is not an easy task.

She used a quotation from Simon Schama's statement reported in *The Guardian* (Vasagar and Sparrow 2010): 'Without this renewed sense of our common story – one full of contention not self-congratulation – we will be a poorer and weaker Britain' (Berridge 2011).

Baroness Bakewell (Labour) expressed concern about how postmodern academics had kept the history or culture wars going, to the detriment of the school population.

There were supporters of a more traditional approach to history teaching, namely Lord Cormack (Conservative) and Lord Thomas of Swynnerton (Crossbench). Lord Thomas wanted school pupils to know the story of the struggle for political liberty and have a deeper knowledge of the great politicians of the eighteenth and nineteenth centuries.

> Speaking of those five separate undertakings, I believe that the winning of political liberty in this country is something on which we should dwell. It was not as easy as it must seem. Some of those who challenge it now seem to think that it is not worth talking about. The effort to achieve habeas corpus, constant elections and the rule of law was not an easy undertaking. It took many generations to perfect it. It would be good if in most schools students – pupils – were brought up to understand the golden age of British politics.
>
> Thomas 2011

Politeia

Building up a head of steam behind the scenes in 2012 were three historians writing for the think tank Politeia, a centre-right group describing itself as 'a forum for social and economic thinking', but claiming a stake in establishing good history education across a broad political spectrum. These were David Abulafia, Jonathan Clark and Robert Tombs. Tombs had already been reported in the press defending the publication (Tombs with Waldman and Moule 2012a, 2012b), which included online appendices outlining suggestions for a new secondary history curriculum written by himself and his two colleagues (Abulafia, Clark and Tombs 2012), all implying in their work a critique of current arrangements for history education in England. These appendices would be republished as a separate booklet in April 2013 during the period of consultation following the publication of the draft history curriculum in February 2013 (Abulafia, Clark and Tombs 2013). Tombs was a specialist in French history, and Abulafia was best known for his transnational study of the Mediterranean, *The Great Sea* (2011). Clark had a reputation as a revisionist historian and had developed the idea of 'the long eighteenth century' to describe the period from 1660 to 1832 (see Clark 2014), finding a new interpretation of the American War of Independence as having elements of a war of religion.

Although it might be tempting to see this group (Abulafia, Clark and Tombs) as 'Whiggish', none of these three historians was actually a Whig, but they had in common a dislike for much current historiographical thinking that was postmodern or poststructuralist and which tended, in their view unhelpfully, to separate micro-histories from macro-histories, thereby losing, especially for the school population, an overall sense of chronology in understanding the development of the nation. Clark's 2004 work, *Our Shadowed Present*, gives a fuller explanation of this position. Robert Tombs has since written *The English and their History* (2014). The philosophy behind this and in his support of a stronger curriculum framework for national history was communicated in an email from Tombs to the author on 19 March 2015: 'as we live in a democracy it is desirable for future citizens to be taught the history of the country in whose public life they are expected to participate.' Their names appeared alongside another twelve who expressed support for Michael Gove's draft history curriculum in a letter to *The Times* published on 27 February 2013.

The All Party Parliamentary Group on Archives and History, *History for All?* Report, together with oral evidence, January 2013 (from meetings in May 2012)

In retrospect this seems in many ways to have been a dress rehearsal for the round table talks that took place in the spring and summer of 2013 to resolve the problems of the draft history curriculum, as many of the personnel were the same (House of Commons 2013). Representing the School History Project's Director Michael Riley was Jamie Byrom, himself a Fellow of the SHP. He gave evidence and sought to present the SHP commitment to a 'prescribed diversity' of approach in school history, and this emerges with support from others at the meeting. Colin Jones, the representative of the Royal Historical Society,[4] said:

> As regards the health of the discipline most generally, we agree with what Jamie was saying: diversity is the key. This involves the larger range and the bigger, broader themes, but also the in-depth study, definitely pre-modern as well as late modern; definitely global (by which we mean not just European and American but genuinely global history, in its own terms preferably, rather than a sort of offshoot from British History; different types of History (e.g. intellectual history, political, social)). We like the fact that these things are taught in schools.

The draft curriculum

Michael Gove's draft history curriculum was published as part of the consultation process for the whole national curriculum on 7 February 2013. It prescribed a mainly English focus on British history with eight-to-eleven-year-olds expected to study from ancient times to 1714, and older students from 1714 to the premiership of Margaret Thatcher (1979–90). The draft became a site of some contention. Many events, including military encounters and victories, were listed as having to be learnt. It would attract conflicting responses from two sets of 'elite' networks which Michael Gove would be forced to attempt to reconcile through 'round table' meetings in the period from March to June 2013. These could be categorized as: (a) conservative-traditional with an enthusiasm for national history set in a consecutive chronological framework; and (b) liberal-inclusive with an enthusiasm for contextualizing national history both globally and in a more flexible chronological framework. They could also be seen as having features of 'thesis' and 'antithesis' in response to the Gove canon. Both groups had, in a sense, placed themselves in adversarial positions against what each saw as undesirable curriculum constructs. The fifteen historians who signed *The Times* letter of 27 February 2013 (Abulafia et al. 2013), like Michael Gove himself, saw in present arrangements a lack of curriculum structure and the associated apparent failure to engage with the overall content and narrative of national history as a weakness that could be addressed through legislation. The second group saw the 'canon' itself as a serious obstacle to a democratic approach to the history curriculum. Among its signatories were the President of the Royal Historical Society, the President of the Historical Association, three section chairs of the British Academy and the co-convenor of History UK (D'Avray et al. 2013).

The shortcomings of the intranational and transnational dimensions of the draft would in fact form a major part of the negative evaluations, and approval of the syntactic or disciplinary framework would be accompanied by scepticism about whether a suitably disciplinary approach was being reflected in the chosen arrangement or 'canon' of mainly English events.

The rescue operation

It was not just historians who were involved in the round table meetings that were convened in March and June 2013 during the post-draft consultation period by the Department for Education (DfE) to iron out any remaining history curriculum problems. The Historical Association had already started its own draft curriculum online poll among teachers, which had yielded a number of significant concerns which were shared at the round table meetings (Historical Association 2013). Michael Gove was himself present at both of the main meetings in March and June. These were also attended by representatives of the Historical Association (its Chief Executive, Rebecca Sullivan and its President, Jackie Eales) and the Head of Education at the National Archives (Andrew Payne), who were joined by history teacher educators (Christine Counsell and Sean Lang) and a retired local authority history advisor who was also a freelance consultant (Jamie Byrom). Historians Lord Bew, Jeremy Black and Robert Tombs as well as Arthur Burns, Vice-President of the RHS and Chair of its Education Committee, also attended the meetings. Counsell and Byrom would both write (for the Historical Association) about their original concerns over the draft curriculum, but after the publication of the new curriculum in the late summer Byrom would eventually share his positive reflections on how it could work, particularly how the syntactic or disciplinary structure might interact with the substantive content (Hall and Counsell 2013; Byrom 2013). It was later revealed that Byrom had played a coordinating role in communicating between a sub-group and the main round table.

At the first round table meeting in March 2013 it appears that common ground was established around the importance of developing in young people a coherent, informed and secure chronological framework of the past. This was in keeping with the philosophy of E. D. Hirsch, whose ideas were central to the Secretary of State's core beliefs about the curriculum. Significantly, however, it must also have been agreed at the round table that Michael Gove's detailed curriculum list or 'canon' of events in the February draft would not serve the shared aim of developing a chronologically secure framework. It was decided that the proposals should be revised in ways that gave the curriculum greater range, coherence and clarity of progression as well as breaking out of a requirement that events be taught in a strictly chronological sequence.

The round table meetings were initially surrounded by constraints of confidentiality, with such details as the names of the participants, and the fact that there was a sub-group, only released over a year later after a Freedom of Information request to the DfE (What Do They Know 2014). The identity of other members of the sub-group, however, remains a mystery.

It should be added that Michael Maddison, HMI (Her Majesty's Inspector, and National Lead for History) was an Observer through the whole round table process, but was in a position to offer advice to the Department for Education. Ofsted's own *History for All* (2011) report on the state of school history before 2011 had highlighted both good practice and the need to connect disparate curriculum elements to a stronger overall chronological framework. The ideal emergent curriculum would clearly have to be a workable document which would satisfy both the Department and Ofsted.

What was achieved in effect was a synthesis to bridge the concerns of the two opposing groups (a) and (b) above. A strong chronological spine was retained, but the 'canon' was transformed by removing the lists of 'have-to-know' events and replacing them with beginning and end dates and *examples* of content. Structural adjustments were made to enable the Key Stage 2 (8–11) age group to study a period beyond 1066, and for the Key Stage 3 (12–14) group, a period before 1066. The responses from Key Stage 2 teachers were listened to, particularly their complaints about having too much content (originally ancient Britons to 1714) and about the plans to drop the study of non-British societies. Thus now the 8–11 Key Stage 2 programme included:

> The achievements of the earliest civilizations – an overview of where and when the first civilizations appeared and a depth study of one of the following: Ancient Sumer, The Indus Valley, Ancient Egypt, The Shang Dynasty of Ancient China; Ancient Greece – a study of Greek life and achievements and their influence on the western world; a non-European society that provides contrasts with British history – one study chosen from: early Islamic civilization, including a study of Baghdad c. AD 900; Mayan civilization c. AD 900; Benin (West Africa) c. AD 900–1300.

And the later age group (12–14) as well as studying the nation from 1066 to the present day, also would have access to:

> At least one study of a significant society or issue in world history and its interconnections with other world developments (for example, Mughal India 1526–1857; China's Qing dynasty 1644–1911; Changing Russian empires c.1800–1989; USA in the 20th century).[5]

The Schama address at Hay-on-Wye May 2013 (as a significant event)

It seems in retrospect a dysfunctional way to organize a curriculum review not to involve a key advisor like Schama in leading a team of experts and submitting a report which could have fed into the review. But this did not happen between Michael Gove and Simon Schama, and so the address by Schama at Hay-on-Wye in May 2013 almost has the equivalence of a minority report tendered after the February draft. This event should be seen as part of a corpus of his curriculum advice and critique alongside the *Guardian* article of November 2010, the debates involving him and other historians recorded by the Historical Association, and his brief radio interview with Anne McElvoy in April 2013 (*Nightwaves* 2013).

The Hay lecture was a dialogic process as some of the best parts of Schama's feedback are in the Q&A session after the main address. There are different emphases and priorities to those highlighted by Richard J. Evans, particularly where Schama gives himself and his teachers the permission to 'celebrate' certain features of English/British history:

> [T]here is a glory to British history, but the glory to British history is argument, dissent and the freedom of dispute. It's not an endless massage of self-congratulation (pro-empire versus empire). It's the division, and the celebration of division that is at the heart of the story, beginning with Magna Carta!
>
> Schama 2013b

He juxtaposed Thucydides and Herodotus in a search for a kind of hybrid curriculum historiography and structure that would ensure that a narrative would generate questions and that this story would help classes to understand that history is about other people:

> And for Thucydides history is not about self-congratulation and it's not about tracing the pedigree of the wonderfulness of us, nor is it about tracing the pedigree of the reprehensibly awful nature of us either. It is a chastening, disenchanted, honest, tough-minded version of looking critically at ourselves and seeing what we have become and where we came from.
>
> Schama 2013b

As has been noted, 'historians, for Thucydides', Schama claimed, 'are meant to keep the powerful awake at night and keep them honest':

> I come from a culture where I teach in America and there is a lot of tremendous history being written and being taught! But, if anything, it suffers slightly from a sense of insular self-congratulation. If we take our two Greek founding fathers together: you take Herodotus' aversion to the insularity of history and his attempt to say we cannot understand what makes us Greeks and what makes us come together as a particular cultural force in the world unless we understand Persia, Egypt and Asia Minor. Then you take Thucydides' aversion to history as a chronology of national self-congratulation, you have the glory and honour of western history.
>
> Schama 2013b

He searches the pages of nineteenth-century history to find a group of literary 'tribunes' (Carlyle, Dickens and Ruskin) who were 'most hostile to the ethos of material accumulation', and links the Victorian social conscience to the foundation of the Labour Party.

> You can't not [*sic*] only understand the nature of the Victorian conscience but you can't understand where the Labour Party and trade unionism will eventually come from unless you understand how electrifying, dramatic and powerful the social conscience was in Victorian England. It's something to be proud of, to celebrate – and something for the kids to engage with when they think about our own condition now – and the relationship of the public conscience to private cupidity – and the rip-roaring nature of the economic system.
>
> Schama 2013b

He would criticize the draft for leaving out a significant component of British history – religion. The omission of religion and particularly movements like Puritanism from a study of the seventeenth century was seen by him as a serious shortcoming.

Andrew Marr and *Start the Week*, 30 December 2013

With the history curriculum now finalized and calm settling over these fraught debates, this was an end-of-year discussion between the presenter, Andrew Marr, and his guests Michael Gove, Simon Schama, Margaret MacMillan (another historian) and Tom Holland. Holland was a classicist and ancient historian, and he had just published a translation of Herodotus's *Histories* (2013), beloved of Simon Schama. The programme was remarkable for its mutually tolerant good humour and shared sense of searching for a consensus. It explored some difficult dynamics in the construction of national history curricula like matching the level of what is studied with the age of the children, and the relationship between narrative and enquiry, and indeed between narrative and patriotism. It hit a note already flagged up by Lord Bew in his House of Lords address in 2011, that a pride in the past is not just a possession of the political right, that H. E. Marshall's *Our Island Story* (1905) had a radical subtext, and that one strand in English history (according to Michael Gove himself, citing the example of John Ball[6]) was the subverting of executive power by the people. Gerard Winstanley (1609–76), the Leveller, was included in this category by Tom Holland.

Conclusions

The institutions of England played a role in this account of a strong public debate, Parliament in two forms – first the House of Commons (The All Party Parliamentary Group on Archives and History) and second the House of Lords, and in addition the professional bodies, the Historical Association and the Royal Historical Society. Politicians and the civil servants who work with them had to listen to the concerns of representatives of these institutions and professional bodies, as well as to their own in some cases very outspoken advisors (Simon Schama in particular, although the extent to which he was already or had always been 'disconnected' is perhaps unknowable). The compromise position that was reached achieved a largely acceptable blend of the three knowledge bases that contribute to history curriculum discourse worldwide: a disciplinary approach through a setting out of appropriate elements of syntactic knowledge; a broadly chronological framework for substantive knowledge; and age-related pedagogical devices that allow for a spiralling effect with both the syntactic and substantive knowledge. This extract from the new curriculum was chosen by Jamie Byrom in his HA article (2013: 9) and illustrates the blend of knowledge bases:

> ... gain historical perspective by placing their growing knowledge into different contexts, understanding the connections between local, regional, national and international history; between cultural, economic, military, political, religious and social history; and between short- and long-term timescales.

Perhaps the last words should go to Hannah Arendt, who was quoted by Maria Grever (2007: 41):

> remembrance ... is helpless outside a pre-established framework of reference, and the human mind is only on the rarest occasions capable of retaining something which is altogether unconnected.
>
> Arendt 2006: 5

Notes

1 He admitted this in an interview on *Start the Week* with Andrew Marr, BBC Radio 4, 30 December 2013 (*Start the Week* 2013).
2 Sir Richard J. Evans was Regius Professor of History at the University of Cambridge and is President of Wolfson College, Cambridge.
3 In an interview with Anne McElvoy on BBC Radio 3, 25 April 2013.
4 Professor Colin Jones was President of the Royal Historical Society from 2009 to 2012.
5 This is the new National Curriculum for History (11 September 2013) Key Stages 1 and 2: https://www.gov.uk/government/uploads/system/uploads/attachment_data/file/239035/PRIMARY_national_curriculum_-_History.pdf; and Key Stage 3: https://www.gov.uk/government/uploads/system/uploads/attachment_data/file/239075/SECONDARY_national_curriculum_-_History.pdf. The end date for Key Stage 2 was shifted back from 1714 to 1066, and the beginning date for Key Stage 3 was moved back to 1066.
6 John Ball, c.1338–1381, was a Lollard priest executed after his involvement in the Peasants' Revolt.

References

Abulafia, D. (2011), *The Great Sea: A Human History of the Mediterranean*, London: Allen Lane.

Abulafia, D., Clark, J. and Tombs, R. (2012), 'History in the New Curriculum: Three Proposals', online appendices in R. Tombs with A. Waldman and C. Moule, 'Lessons from History: Freedom, Aspiration and the New Curriculum', in S. Lawlor (ed.), *Curriculum Series*, London: Politeia. Available online: http://www.politeia.co.uk/sites/default/files/files/Final%20Appendix%20to%20Lessons%20from%20History.pdf (accessed 18 February 2015).

Abulafia, D., Clark, J. and Tombs, R. (2013), 'History in the Making: The New Curriculum Right or Wrong?' in S. Lawlor (ed.), *Curriculum Series*, London: Politeia.

Abulafia, D., Beevor, A., Black, J., Burleigh, M., Charmley, J., Clark, J. C. D., Ferguson, N., Foreman, A., Jennings, J., Sebag Montefiore, S., Roberts, A., Skidmore, C., Starkey, D., Thorpe, D. and Tombs, R. (2013), Letter to *The Times*, 27 February.

Arendt, H. (2006), *Between Past and Future: Eight Exercises in Political Thought*, New York: Penguin Books.

Berridge, Baroness (2011), The House of Lords, *Schools: History Debate*, 20 October, Hansard transcript, column 420.

Bew, Lord (2011), The House of Lords, *Schools: History Debate*, 20 October, Hansard transcript, columns 428–9.

Brown, G. (2004), British Council Annual Lecture, 7 July. Available online: http://www.theguardian.com/politics/2004/jul/08/uk.labour1 (part 1) and http://www.theguardian.com/politics/2004/jul/08/uk.labour (part 2) (accessed 19 March 2015).

Brown, G. (2006), 'The Future of Britishness', Fabian Society, 14 January. Available online: http://www.theguardian.com/politics/2007/feb/27/immigrationpolicy.race (accessed 19 March 2015).

Brown, G. (2014), *My Scotland, Our Britain: A Future Worth Sharing*, London: Simon and Schuster.

Byrom, J. (2013), 'Alive . . . and Kicking? Some Personal Reflections on the Revised National Curriculum (2014) and What we Might Do With it', *Teaching History [The Historical Association Curriculum Supplement]*, September: 6–14.

Clark, J. C. D. (2004), *Our Shadowed Present: Modernism, Postmodernism and History*, London: Atlantic Books.

Clark, J. C. D. (2014), *From Restoration to Reform: The British Isles 1660–1832*, London: Vintage.

Cruse, I. (2011), 'Debate on 20 October: Teaching of History in Schools', House of Lords Library Note LLN 2011/030, London: House of Lords, 14 October. Available online: http://www.parliament.uk/business/publications/research/briefing-papers/LLN-2011-030/debate-on-20-october-teaching-of-history-in-schools (accessed 18 February 2015).

D'Avray, D., Eales, J., Fulbrook, M., McLay, K., Mandler, P. and Scott, H. (2013), *Statement on the Draft National Curriculum for History*, London: Royal Historical Society, 12 February. Available online: http://royalhistsoc.org/wp-content/uploads/2014/10/Statement-on-National-Curriculum-12-Feb-13.pdf (accessed 7 March 2015).

Department of Education and Science (DES) (1985), *History in the Primary and Secondary Years: An HMI Report*, London: HMSO.

Evans, R. J. (2011), 'The Wonderfulness of Us (the Tory Interpretation of History)', *London Review of Books* 33 (6), 17 March: 9–12. Available online: http://www.lrb.co.uk/v33/n06/richard-j-evans/the-wonderfulness-of-us (accessed 17 February 2015).

Ferguson, N. (2010), 'Down With Junk History: A Campaign for Real History in Schools', Hay Festival, 30 May. Available online: https://www.hayfestival.com/p-2464-niall-ferguson.aspx (accessed 17 February 2015).

Ferguson, N. (2011), *Civilization: The West and the Rest*, London: Allen Lane.
Gilroy, P. (1987), *There Ain't No Black in the Union Jack*, London: Unwin Hyman.
Gilroy, P. (1993), *The Black Atlantic: Modernity and Double Consciousness*, London: Verso.
Gove, M. (2010a), 'The Democratic Intellect: What do we Need to Succeed in the 21st Century?', Sir John Cass's Foundation Lecture, 2009, London: Sir John Cass's Foundation.
Gove, M. (2010b), 'Michael Gove: All Pupils will Learn our Island Story', Conservative Party Conference, 5 October 2010. Available online: https://toryspeeches.files.wordpress.com/2013/11/michael-gove-all-pupils-will-learn-our-island-story.pdf (accessed 2 August 2015).
Grever, M. (2007), 'Plurality, Narrative and the Historical Canon', in M. Grever and S. Stuurman (eds), *Beyond the Canon: History for the Twenty-First Century*, 31–47, London: Palgrave Macmillan.
Hall, K. and Counsell, C. (2013), 'Silk Purse from a Sow's Ear? Why Knowledge Matters and Why the Draft NC will Not Improve it', *Teaching History* 151: 21–6.
Herodotus (2013), *The Histories*, ed. P. Cartledge, trans. T. Holland, London: Penguin Classics.
Historical Association, The (2013), 'Poll on New History Curriculum Draft Proposal: New Draft Curriculum Online Poll'. Available online: http://www.history.org.uk/resources/resource_view.php?resource_type=secondary&id=6202&subid=6203&cid=8&results=1 (accessed 19 March 2015).
House of Commons, The All Party Parliamentary Group on Archives and History (2013), *History for All?* Report, together with oral evidence, January. Available online: http://www.archives.org.uk/images/documents/news/history%20for%20all%20final%20report.pdf.
House of Lords (2011a), *Schools: History Debate*, 20 October, Hansard transcript. Available online: http://www.publications.parliament.uk/pa/ld201011/ldhansrd/text/111020-0001.htm and http://www.publications.parliament.uk/pa/ld201011/ldhansrd/text/111020-0002.htm (accessed 19 February 2015).
House of Lords (2011b), *Schools: History Debate*, 20 October [video]. Available online: http://www.parliamentlive.tv/Event/Index/062f470f-911a-442b-9938-5727598af432 (accessed 19 February 2015).
Kearney, H. (1989), *The British Isles: A History of Four Nations*, Cambridge: Cambridge University Press.
Marshall, H. E. (1905), *Our Island Story*, London: Nelson.
Morgan, Lord (2011), The House of Lords, *Schools: History Debate*, 20 October, Hansard transcript, column 424.
Nightwaves (Simon Schama's Reflections on Dead Certainties and on Gove's History Curriculum Proposals) (2013), [Radio programme] BBC Radio 3, 25 April, 22.00. Available online: http://www.bbc.co.uk/programmes/b01ryv0x (accessed 20 February 2015).
Office for Standards in Education (Ofsted) (2011), *History for All*, London: OFSTED.
Pocock, J. G. A. (1975), 'British History: A Plea for a New Subject', *Journal of Modern History* 47 (4): 601–21.
Pocock, J. G. A. (2005), *The Discovery of Islands: Essays in British History*, Cambridge: Cambridge University Press.
Samuel, R. (1994), *Theatres of Memory: Volume I – Past and Present in Contemporary Culture*, London: Verso.
Samuel, R. (1998), *Island Stories: Unravelling Britain – Theatres of Memory, Volume II*, ed. A. Light with S. Alexander and G. S. Jones, London: Verso.

Schama, S. (2000), *A History of Britain: Volume 1 – At the Edge of the World? 3000 BC–AD 1603*, London: BBC Worldwide.
Schama, S. (2001), *A History of Britain: Volume 2 – The British Wars 1603–1776*, London: BBC Worldwide.
Schama, S. (2002), *A History of Britain: Volume 3 – The Fate of Empire 1776–2000*, London: BBC Worldwide.
Schama, S. (2010a), *Scribble, Scribble, Scribble*, London: Bodley Head.
Schama, S. (2010b), 'Simon Schama: My Vision for History in Schools', the *Guardian*, 9 November. Available online: www.theguardian.com/education/2010/nov/09/future-history-schools (accessed 17 February 2013).
Schama, S. (2013a), 'Simon Schama and Teachers: Our Children, Our History', Hay Festival Podcast. Available online: http://www.hayfestival.com/p-6108-simon-schama-and-teachers.aspx (accessed 17 February 2015).
Schama, S. (2013b), 'Simon Schama and Teachers', transcript, in Historyworks, *History Curriculum: Gove, Newsprint, & BBC Debates*. Available online: http://historyworks.tv/news/2013/06/04/history_curriculum_debate_updates_new_bbc_r3_night (accessed 17 February 2015).
Seixas, P. (2000), 'Schweigen! die Kinder! or, Does Postmodern History Have a Place in the Schools?', in P. Stearns, P. Seixas and S. Wineburg (eds), *Knowing, Teaching and Learning History: National and International Perspectives*, 19–37, New York and London: New York University Press.
Start the Week (2013), [Radio programme] BBC Radio 4, 30 December, 09.00.
Thomas (of Swynnerton), Lord (2011), The House of Lords, *Schools: History Debate*, 20 October, Hansard transcript, column 409.
Tombs, R. (2014), *The English and their History*, London: Allen Lane.
Tombs, R. with Waldman, A. and Moule, C. (2012a), 'Lessons from History: Freedom, Aspiration and the New Curriculum', in S. Lawlor (ed.), *Curriculum Series*, London: Politeia.
Tombs, R. with Waldman, A. and Moule, C. (2012b), 'Additional Appendix'. Available online: http://www.politeia.co.uk/appendix, found within http://www.politeia.co.uk/sites/default/files/files/Robert%20Tombs%20Second%20Appendix%20Final.pdf (accessed 19 March 2015).
Vasagar, J. and Sparrow, A. (2010), 'Simon Schama to advise ministers on overhaul of history curriculum', The Guardian, 5 October. Available online: http://www.theguardian.com/politics/2010/oct/05/simon-schama-ministers-history-curriculum
What Do They Know (2014), 'History Curriculum Expert Group'. Available online: https://www.whatdotheyknow.com/request/history_curriculum_expert_group (accessed 21 March 2015).

10

Discussant on Part 2 – Shared Histories in Post-Colonial Settings

Robert Guyver

The three or four cases (bearing in mind that one chapter addresses two countries) represented in these chapters are in many ways very different but have in common a background of political change and a recognition that inclusion is an important curriculum principle. There are also some links with previous chapters, especially to the points made in the Palestine chapter about including narratives of displaced people campaigning for nationhood. This was in the final paragraph of Chapter 1 and put into the context of 'settler colonialism' rather than a post-colonial setting. The notion of 'Indigenous people' has recently been brought up even in the context of the UK, with research revealing that there had been much intermarriage between the 'original' British inhabitants and later settlers like the Anglo-Saxons, undermining the whole notion of a distinct and separate Celtic group (Ghosh 2015). However, in the USA the settlement of lands beyond the Appalachians and then beyond the Rockies had a considerable impact on 'Native Americans', especially on their often nomadic lifestyle and their hunting, including of buffalo. The very creation of the USA was dependent on some treaty negotiation whereby these original 'proprietors' might be willing to alienate their lands. In the course of this process of colonization clearly many unfortunate incidents and indeed massacres took place, such as are mentioned by Cyndi Mottola Poole. Genocide refers to the planned extinction of a whole ethnic group, and in the events following the 'discovery' of the Americas by European explorers and the subsequent settlement of these lands, whole tribal groups did indeed disappear, but not necessarily always as a result of deliberate violence. A lack of resistance to European diseases had a fatal impact on the Arawaks, who were the first native peoples to be encountered by Christopher Columbus.

Both Brazil and the USA had been themselves former colonies of European powers, and both had gained independence after a struggle. England and Portugal, however, had themselves been colonial powers, Portugal before England, and Portugal's prowess in shipbuilding and navigation (e.g. caravels and astrolabes) has been taught as part of the curriculum in English (and UK) schools. The search for spices, precious metals, silks and cloths had driven the expansion and had led to the setting up of trading posts, colonies and empires. Both powers had had contact with and later colonies in Africa, India and the Far East. England had of course had contact mostly in North America, whereas Portugal, like its rival Spain, had colonized South America. Both powers had had a strong socio-cultural and indeed religious impact on those parts of the continents with which they traded and in which they settled. Unlike Brazil, some of Portugal's colonies, like Mozambique and Angola, only became independent relatively recently, both of these in 1975, although they experienced protracted civil wars afterwards.

The issue at stake in all three chapters is how history education in these democracies can best incorporate these colonial and post-colonial experiences and dimensions. The chapter by Marlene Cainelli, Helena Pinto and Glória Solé (like the chapter by Cyndi Poole) contains empirical data from students interviewed about how they view these aspects of school history. What emerges is a realization that it is easy to stereotype and indeed patronize Indigenous peoples by generalizations. They can be seen as backward before contact with the West and either poor or invisible afterwards. Cyndi Poole refers to public attitudes to these issues as 'dysconscious racism', but also and more positively includes in her research mention of instances where Indigenous people come into the school and undertake a dialogue with students and teachers. Cainelli, Pinto and Solé investigate in the context of both Portugal and Brazil awareness of the over-simplification of Indigenous perspectives.

Whereas in the last decades in Brazil the debate on cultural pluralism and multiculturalism gained momentum both in academic and in educational fields, several changes have been proposed, including those covered by the law that made mandatory first the study of Afro-Brazilian and African culture (Law no. 10.639/03), and second Indigenous culture (Law no. 11.645/08). However, working with these issues involves a recognition that there are struggles over changes which can be seen in a move away from teaching history to create a consolidated identity, traditionally connected to the idea of nationalism and the construction of a single, homogeneous and Eurocentric past, to a position which makes it possible to work diversity and difference into the construction of Brazilian identity. This is in some ways an approach that corresponds with a recommendation by Jonker, who writes that there should be a refraining from identity politics, a doing away with grand narratives and instead a teaching of 'little histories in an open framework'. Drawing on a recommendation by Peter Seixas (Seixas 1993: 301–27), Jonker suggests that teachers should:

> [m]ake room for personal histories that colour, flavour, and contradict the larger stories, thus making critical interpretations of the grand narratives possible. To accomplish this, a certain 'provincialism', in the sense of a lack of centralized curricular power, may contribute to the freedom needed to challenge identities and canons.
>
> Jonker 2007: 106

This is clearly the same kind of advice that was being given by Gülçin Dilek and Eleni Filippidou in Chapter 4 as a way of avoiding unhelpful generalizations. It has similarities too with the observation by Linda Chisholm noted by Gail Weldon in Chapter 5 about South Africa and Rwanda, that the new South African history curriculum was an official history which aimed 'at permitting the unofficial, the hidden, to become visible' (Chisholm 2004: 188).

After the Restoration of Independence in 1640, and the spice trade crisis in the late sixteenth century, the Portuguese Crown's interests turned to Brazil and its economic potential, associating sugar or tobacco plantations with the slave trade, and later on gold, coffee and cotton. This triangular relationship between Europe, Africa and America (Brazil) was mirrored in the exchange of different cultures that crossed over several generations and was manifested not only in the ethnic crossroads (miscegenation) but also in the cultural intersection (acculturation, assimilation, interculturality), depending on the perspective of colonizer or colonized.

The public debate on the history curriculum which is highlighted in the chapter on England within the UK can be contextualized against a bigger question which is both overt and covert in most of the chapters in this book, and that concerns the kind of history education that is best suited for young people who are being prepared to take part in the social, economic, cultural and political aspects of life in a democracy. The role and indeed nature of knowledge itself has been part of this debate, and this can also be seen in the chapter on Portugal and Brazil, where Bruner and Rüsen are mentioned in sections on method. The notion of a patriotism that can appeal to the left, centre and right in politics was flagged up by historian Lord Bew in his House of Lords debate speech (Bew 2011), but also aligned with a subtler suggestion which links historiography with curriculum, and that is about the relationship between those who exercise executive power and the people affected by it. High politics and subaltern history (history from below) thus interact, and events in a nation's history can be examples of the people subverting or challenging the executive.

The transformation of a traditional national 'canon' of events into a less specific structure which, while allowing the study of history in chronological sequence, also permits some flexibility in the way chronology is handled was a significant development in the curriculum debate in England, but it had not come without lobbying campaigns in the press and the involvement of professional bodies and outspoken public intellectuals such as Simon Schama and Richard J. Evans. The traditionalists, like the Secretary of State himself, had argued for a strong knowledge base as a prerequisite for democratic participation, but in the end it was agreed that such a knowledge base had to go alongside, and indeed match, a set of disciplinary principles. The achievement of this would not have been possible without the involvement of the Historical Association, history teacher educators and professional historians, including members of the Royal Historical Society.

The extent to which the UK can be seen as 'post-colonial' alongside the USA and both Portugal and Brazil is a relevant problem because it concerns the handling of a legacy of guilt and vestigial elements of denial alongside a need to redefine the nation in civic or even constitutional terms that go beyond mere ethnicity to embrace a more inclusive vision of the nation, and in the case of the UK this debate has been about the nature of Britishness. However, set against this are demands for the recognition of old nations or sub-nations as jurisdictions in their own right. Scotland of course is a prime example of this and 'Britishness' in this debate might be seen in Scotland as either negatively hegemonic or as benign, depending on personal attachments or allegiances. But identity will not entirely go away and is not a simple category, especially for the 'third culture' settlers who bring other, and significantly, extra-national allegiances with them (Useem 1999).

Cyndi Poole writes about the process of 'delegitimization'. She points out that the 1887 Dawes Severalty Act which delegitimized Native tribes and stripped Native Americans of nearly one hundred million acres of tribal lands was only studied by one-third of her sample group. Similarly the number of specific Native–European military conflicts taught by this same group of teachers was very low, and she gives examples of these as well as of the forced assimilation of Native American children through boarding schools. Nevertheless, what is more encouraging from her study is that open discussion of Native American issues was embraced by a high proportion of her research group.

References

Bew, Lord (2011), The House of Lords, *Schools: History Debate*, 20 October, Hansard transcript, columns 428–9.

Chisholm, L. (2004), 'The History Curriculum in the (Revised) National Curriculum Statement: An Introduction', in S. Jeppie (ed.), *Toward New Histories for South Africa*, Cape Town: Juta Gariep.

Ghosh, P. (2015), 'DNA Study Shows Celts are not a Unique Genetic Group', *BBC News*, 18 March. Available online: http://www.bbc.co.uk/news/science-environment-31905764 (accessed 1 April 2015).

Jonker, E. (2007), 'Citizenship, the Canon and the Crisis of the Humanities', in M. Grever and S. Stuurman (eds), *Beyond the Canon: History for the Twenty-First Century*, 94–109, London: Palgrave Macmillan.

Seixas, P. (1993), 'Historical Understanding Among Adolescents in a Multicultural Setting', *Curriculum Inquiry* 23: 301–27.

Useem, R. H. (1999), *A Third Culture Kid Bibliography*, East Lansing, MI. Available online: http://tckresearcher.net/RHU%20bib%20v2%20copy.pdf (accessed 1 April 2015).

Part 3

Comparative Settings – Federations, Shared Histories and Emerging Democracies

11

The Russian Federation and Australia: Comparing Like with Unlike

Tony Taylor

Introduction

When it comes to history education, John Howard and Vladimir Putin have more in common than each may think. From the beginning of both politicians' first terms of office as head of government, Howard in 1996 and Putin in 2000, each has displayed a special interest in how their nations' pasts have been represented in professional and in public forums, more particularly in how Australian and Russian national stories have been represented in school history classes. Within the period from 1996 to 2014, it is almost as if the leaders of these two nations were on parallel interventionist tracks, with, in terms of a chronology of events and actions, Australia slightly ahead (1996–2014) of Russia (2000–2015).

Howard's strategy was different from that of Putin. The Australian prime minister (and his successors) espoused changes in school history as a form of conservative cultural engineering. Their intention was to establish, as a fixed curriculum feature, a largely benign national narrative with assimilationist intentions. Putin, on the other hand, pressed for history education as an extension of an aggressive, nationalistic political strategy that has included territorial annexations. Both, however, favoured the idea that history curriculum policy should be directed towards shaping or even imposing a fact-based, essentialist and master narrative approach that would lead to a firmly outlined idea of what constitutes national identity in an Australian multicultural society and in a Russian multi-ethnic society.

There remain, of course, other substantive differences in political, social, cultural and educational circumstances between the two nations. Modern Australia is a federated liberal democracy with a democratic tradition (of varying sorts) that extends back to the establishment of a New South Wales legislative assembly in 1843. Russia, currently regarded by its critics as at best a federated illiberal democracy and at worst as a corrupt oligarchy, has a recorded history that goes back a thousand years but its genuinely democratic tradition only extends back to 1990: some would argue democracy in Russia ended a mere ten years later.

As for social character, Australia has a small population that is generally prosperous and is currently second highest (behind Norway) in the United Nations Human

Development Index (2014 estimates). Russia is fifty-seventh in the same healthy life/education/living standard index – just above Bulgaria. Culturally, modern Australia is a multicultural and multi-faith society founded on successive waves of immigration whereas modern Russia is a multi-ethnic society that has not yet espoused cultural pluralism and where 75 per cent of the population belongs to the Russian Orthodox Church, a denomination known for its intolerance of non-Russians, its dislike of other forms of worship and its hostility to Islam. Finally, when it comes to education, Australia has a strong late nineteenth- and twentieth-century tradition of mass public education whereas Russia's mass education policy only began under the post-revolutionary 'liquidation of illiteracy' campaign in the 1920s. When it comes to more modern times, the history curriculum in Australia was during the period from 1990 to 2010 subsumed within a generic, world-based social education framework in all states and territories except (temporarily) New South Wales. In Russia, history education almost invariably means the study of Russia's national history.

John Howard and History

Let us start with John Howard, who came into office as prime minister and leader of a conservative Coalition (Liberal Party in coalition with the rural/regional National Party) who took government in March 1996 after thirteen humiliating years in opposition at the federal level.

Howard has a strong personal attachment to Australia's past, especially to its military past. His father and grandfather served in the same Australian Imperial Force (AIF) division on the Western Front in the First World War. Howard's father Lyall was gassed and died prematurely as a result of chronic bronchitis at the age of 59.

This personal connection together with his conservative disposition has meant that Howard believes unswervingly in the honour of Australia's military past and has, in the persuasive view of historian Nick Dyrenfurth, 'hijacked' Australia's military history to help create an Anzac narrative of earlier, more reassuring times when 'mateship' was at the centre of Australian cultural, social and, most importantly, political values:

> Consciously or not, Howard was embarking on a revolutionary mission to change the meaning of mateship. The stress on practical mateship and volunteering seemed to decouple its meaning from state intervention in aid of a more egalitarian and equal society.
>
> Dyrenfurth 2015: 301

More generally, Howard's declared outlook prior to his 1996 elevation to office is recognizably that of a mid-twentieth-century working/middle-class, patriotic, patriarchal, conservative Australian male who doubts the value of multiculturalism and who has an interest in history as a narrative of positive progress (Taylor 2013). In his autobiography, Howard explains that 'History fascinates me. One of my real educational regrets was that I never did an arts or economics degree as a precursor to law. It would have allowed me to further indulge my passion for history' (Howard 2011: 18). Howard, whose heroes are Winston Churchill, (Australian Conservative Prime Minister) Robert Menzies and Margaret Thatcher, wanted 'balance'; that is, more room in school history for an appreciation of conservative and military contributions to Australia's foundation narrative.

Indeed, Howard's 1988 Liberal Party policy document *Future Directions* commented on what he perceived as the unjust behaviour of progressive left historians during the 1980s. This was his first major sortie into public commentary on historical representations of Australia's past. It came at the end of a decade when controversial and high-profile historian Geoffrey Blainey had publicly expressed anxiety about Indigenous activism, Asian migration, multiculturalism and the possibility of social and political disintegration in Australia. Howard admired Blainey, who had not, to Howard's annoyance, been reappointed Dean of Arts at the prestigious University of Melbourne in 1984.

Meanwhile, the influence of leftist historian Henry Reynolds' pioneering works (1981 and 1987) on ideas about Indigenous victimization and dispossession had led to a 1980s and 1990s conservative reaction against what Howard was later, in 2008, to call the 'fangs of the left'. Here is an excerpt from *Future Directions*:

> [P]eople's confidence in their nation's past came under attack as the professional purveyors of guilt attacked Australia's heritage and people were told they should apologise for pride in their culture, traditions, institutions and history. Taught to be ashamed of their past, apprehensive about their future, pessimistic about their ability to control their own lives let alone their ability to shape the character of the nation as a whole, many came to see change as being in control of them instead of them being in control of change.
>
> Howard 1988

After the publication of *Future Directions*, a series of historically framed controversies strengthened Howard's opinion that historical opinion was dominated by a leftist denigration of Australia's Anglo-European heritage. In his view, Australian history, neglected in a curriculum dominated since the early 1990s by generic and ahistorical social education (Taylor 2001) needed to be revived. Howard was just the politician to take on such a renewal, a personal sentiment firmed up by what he considered to be socialist provocations.

Howard and 'perverse myths'

In 1992, Labor Prime Minister Paul Keating's forceful pro-republican commentary on Australian–British relations led to an exacerbation of Howard's apprehensions about republicanism. Keating historicized his perspective, savaging the Liberal leadership's remembrance of the 1950s Menzies years as a 'golden age'. In a 1992 speech he gave what was then a heretical, if overstated, rendering of Second World War British–Australian relations:

> I learned one thing: I learned about self-respect and self-regard for Australia – not about some cultural cringe to a country which decided not to defend the Malayan peninsula, not to worry about Singapore and not to give us our troops back to keep ourselves free from Japanese domination.
>
> Hansard 1992

The raucous response of the Coalition benches opposite was so apoplectic that Speaker Leo McLeay intervened, commenting, 'I think the honourable member for Bennelong [Howard, shadow industrial relations spokesman] is going to have a heart attack if his face goes any redder' (Hansard 1992).

In the following year historian Geoffrey Blainey extended the scope of national history debates into Indigenous matters by adding an emotive phrase to Australian politics in his 1993 Sir John Latham Lecture when he referred to a progressive 'Black Armband' approach to the past:

> To some extent my generation was reared on the Three Cheers view of history. This patriotic view of our past had a long run. It saw Australian history as largely a success. While the convict era was a source of shame or unease, nearly everything that came after was believed to be pretty good. There is a rival view, which I call the Black Armband view of history.
>
> Blainey 1993

The speech was reprinted in the conservative journal *Quadrant* under the title 'Drawing Up a Balance Sheet of our History' (Blainey 1993), the year that the Coalition were defeated for the fifth successive time by the Australian Labor Party (ALP) in the March 1993 'unloseable election', a defeat which led to Howard's promotion to leader of the opposition. And a 'balance sheet' approach to Australia's history was now to become a Liberal Party motif, with the word 'balance' referring to a desired equality of representation of points of view that would offset any embarrassing emphasis on past misdemeanours.

During that pre-prime ministerial period, those politically sensitive historical issues, which had adversely impinged on Howard's professed worldview, were outlined succinctly in his ABC *Four Corners* interview on 19 February 1996:

> [B]y the Year 2000 I would like to see an Australian nation that feels comfortable and relaxed about three things: I would like to see them comfortable and relaxed about their history; I would like to see them comfortable and relaxed about the present and I'd also like to see them comfortable and relaxed about the future.
>
> Australian Broadcasting Corporation 1996

With Howard at last in power in 1996, his desideratum that Australians should feel 'comfortable and relaxed about their history' was in part a response to a period in Australian politics between 1984 and 1996 where contending notions of Australia's foundation as a colony and as a nation were the basis of increasingly angry differences of opinion between traditionalist opinion and what were seen by the Howard camp as battalions of progressive left historians who were overwhelming a heroic minority of victimized conservative commentators.

As it happens, this was not a paranoid vision. By the author's 2015 count (in consultation with other academic historians) there are just a handful of conservatively minded historians and writers of history at work in Australia, in a field of about 400 academic historians. However, these figures have to be counted against the pro-Liberal Party Newscorp (Murdoch) domination of the Australian mass media and the history-obsessed national Murdoch flagship newspaper *The Australian*'s remorseless public pursuit and excoriation of soft target academics with whom it disagrees (Taylor and Collins 2012).

Blainey's ideas had struck a chord with Howard, who picked up the black armband refrain after his 1996 general election victory. The Prime Minister wasted no time in affirming where he stood on historical issues. In his Sir Thomas Playford Memorial Lecture of 5 July 1996, his nearest equivalent to an inaugural speech, Howard (1996a) attacked Keating's views, pointing out that this 'partisan re-interpretation of Australia's past' was an 'insidious' attack on those who could not answer back. On 18 November 1996 he revisited the theme with an extended assault on leftist historical rewrites and 'perverse myths' about Australia's past in his Sir Robert Menzies Lecture on 'The Liberal Tradition: The Beliefs and Values which Guide the Federal Government' (Howard 1996b).

What had happened here was the elevation to power in 1996 of a prime minister who had spent thirteen harrowing years in opposition, seen five federal elections lost to the ALP, experienced a demeaning and self-destructive revolving door approach to Liberal Party leadership and witnessed the constant humiliation of his side of politics first by a canny Bob Hawke (ALP Prime Minister 1983–91) and then by the virtuosic Keating (1991–6). Paul Keating, an acerbic and virtually unassailable champion of debates in the House of Representatives and elsewhere, had been, from Howard's point of view, a purveyor of these perverse historical myths. With Howard in power, it was now time to balance the historical debate.

Howard's historical worldview

In summary, there were eight recurring motifs in Howard's rebalancing worldview. First, Anglo-Celtic (and later continental European) settlement in Australia had been a good thing even if Indigenous Australians had been, and were still, disadvantaged. Second, modern Australians may feel regret but need feel no responsibility for transgressions perpetrated by their ancestors. Third, attempts to disparage the historical achievements of Australia as a unique and successful nineteenth- and twentieth-century social laboratory were malicious challenges to the conventional Australian narrative by ideologically motivated historians wanting to undermine the reality of the nation's foundation story. Fourth, both the monarchy and the Christian religion had played, and continued to play, an important and valuable part in Australia's social and moral fabric. Fifth, multiculturalism was a relativistic and socially divisive leftist phenomenon. Sixth, it had been nineteenth-century classic liberal ideology that had led to change and progress in modern Australia, not socialist collectivism. Seventh, modern Australia had reached its position as a nation to be reckoned with, first within the secure boundaries of the mighty British Empire and later as a natural ally of the United States. Eighth, Australia had a proud military reputation that had started with the Gallipoli landing in 1915, had continued on throughout the Great War and had continued into the Second World War. This magnificent military record, based on Australia's unique foundation of mateship, was directly related to the nature of Australia's identity as a nation that was loyal to its friends and allies.

In that context Howard's anxiety was that the 'black armband' historians would use their 'perverse' myths to obscure and demonize what he considered to be the real foundation story of Australia, with its worthy but culturally and economically static Aboriginal societies, its sound British heritage, its ethical Christian character, its flourishing economic and social progress and its heroic military tradition. Howard, affronted by the historical tenor of the Keating era and its ideologized construction of an abhorrent narrative, was angry about what he considered to be a politically correct fabrication of the history of modern Australia, and was keen to see the contribution of the conservative side of politics brought into his country's creation story.

Howard's room for manoeuvre

As prime minister, Howard's options for remedial action were limited. He was unable to stifle a legitimate debate that had in any case been provoked by his favourite historian, Blainey. Not only that, but Blainey and his historically inclined supporters on the conservative side of politics still seemed to be massively outnumbered by professional commentators on the left. Moreover, Howard had no control at all over what the Liberals saw as the engine room of political correctness, the school classroom. It was the states and territories who designed and implemented curriculum even though the federal government was, at that time, subventing school education to the tune of six billion dollars per annum. Meanwhile, Howard had other distractions.

From 1996 to 2005, Howard's government had to deal with the aftermath of the Port Arthur massacre and an ensuing gun control debate, Indigenous native title arrangements, the rise of histrionic populist politician Pauline Hanson, the bitter 1998 dock strikes, the 1998 general election, the East Timor crisis, the 1999 referendum on the republic, the 2000 Sydney Olympics, the 2001 centenary of federation, the 2001 Tampa (refugee) crisis, 9/11, the 2001 general election, the 2002 Bali bombing, the 2003 Iraq war and a 2004 general election.

Even so, from 2003 to 2006 so-called 'history wars' occupied the attention of historians, public commentators and politicians, including John Howard (Macintyre and Clark 2003), whose government took time off from the larger crises to intervene where they could in, for example, correcting the perceived pro-Indigenous bias of the National Museum of Australia, supporting the work of ultra-conservative history warrior Keith Windschuttle and backing the journal *Quadrant*, described by Howard at an October 2006 fiftieth anniversary dinner as a publication whose causes against the 'black armband' view of history were 'close to my heart' (Errington and van Onselen 2007: 377).

Howard takes action

In December 2005, riots in Cronulla (Sydney) between mainly Lebanese-descent and Anglo-Celtic/Mediterranean males took place in Sydney, shocking Howard and motivating him into devising a systemic approach to Australian history that would act as a barrier against what he saw as spiteful and divisive leftist opposition to assimilation. The Prime Minister had been outraged by the Cronulla riots in what was effectively his home town. He saw this local conflict as a sign of social disintegration brought about, in part, by a lack of understanding of Australia's past (an unrivalled story of social, economic and political advancement) and by an absence of loyalty to its established cultural values. Howard wanted a national get-together to discuss Australian history and, in a single day, to construct for all schools an acceptable (to him) version of the nation's story.

On Australia Day eve, 25 January 2006, he gave a famous 'root and branch renewal' speech that foreshadowed changes in the school history curriculum (Howard 2006) and in July 2006 Education Minister Julie Bishop announced the convening of a one-day national history summit of the 'sensible centre' (twenty-four individuals, mainly historians, journalists, teacher representatives and curriculum officials) in Canberra on 17 August. As it happened, the summit was an attempt to impose a New South Wales-style (factually heavy) syllabus in Australian history across the nation. On the day, however, the plan backfired (for details see Taylor 2009).

The summit failed for two key reasons, political and organizational. First, Howard had deliberately shunned state and territory involvement in the summit, confident that media-inspired popular support for a specific curriculum in Australian history would force the jurisdictions into compliance. Not only that but Julie Bishop began to issue ill-considered warnings that federal funding would be cut to non-compliant jurisdictions unless they implemented the summit's proposals, ensuring that any Howardesque product of the summit would encounter a very rough passage at the jurisdictional level.

Second, organizationally, the day's discussion was to focus first on the commonly accepted iniquities of generic social education and then move on the details of a draft schema provided by relatively unknown academic historian Greg Melleuish from Wollongong University. Melleuish, it turned out, had close ties with a neoconservative think tank, the Institute for Public Affairs, had written for *Quadrant* and was publicly vocal as a strong Howard supporter. Unfortunately for both Melleuish and Howard, the draft plan, intended to provide the basis for a syllabus, was rejected by most of the summit's attendees because of its abstract nature. This left the summit with almost nowhere to go since the Howard initiative had been based, to continue the maritime metaphor, on expectations of smooth sailing and a safe arrival in harbour with a commonly agreed, fact-based syllabus. John Hirst, a highly regarded historian, then rescued the summit when he introduced a series of questions about Australian history as a framework for any next stage of curriculum development. A majority of attendees agreed and the day's work closed at 5 pm.

Post-summit criticism in the conservative media of Hirst's innovative questions-based proposals was followed by an astonishing claim in a Julie Bishop press release that curriculum officials took their ideas 'straight from Chairman Mao' (Topsfield and

Rood 2006) with 'ideologues experimenting with the education of young people from a comfortable position of unaccountability'. This bombshell came prior to a national conference of teachers in Fremantle on 6 October 2006 and the press release foreshadowed her conference speech. The ensuing furore provoked her own non-consulted department into insisting that the Mao reference be left out of her speech to the conference, but it was clear by late 2006 that the 'sensible centre' pitch had been replaced by what amounted to revived Cold War rhetoric.

Subsequently, during the early months of 2007, an inquiry-based curriculum in Australian history (K-10), commissioned by Bishop and designed by the author, was negotiated with the states and territories, with the final draft approved by Julie Bishop's department in April 2007. In June 2007, however, that draft was rejected by the Prime Minister's Office and shelved. A successor document was devised in a one-day meeting in September 2007 by a Blainey-led panel and published in October 2007 as a Howard-auspiced *Guide to the Teaching of Australian History in Years 9 and 10* (ages 15–16) (Department of Education, Science and Training 2007). The new curriculum document, the high point of Howardist history, was in reality a syllabus based on the study of seventy-seven essential or canonical Australian facts, including two references to cricket, Howard's favourite sport.

The Howard *Guide* was dropped by an incoming Rudd Labor government in 2008 at a time when the new Education Minister, Julia Gillard, was setting up a comprehensive national curriculum to be designed and overseen by the arm's length National Curriculum Board in 2008 and by its replacement, the Australian Curriculum, Assessment and Reporting Authority (ACARA), from 2009 onwards. In December 2010, with Gillard now as Prime Minister, the Labor government gained national agreement for the first stage of the new curriculum framework, of which history (Foundation to Year 10), with a world history (not just Australian) perspective and an inquiry-based approach, was a key part.

Howard's nadir

What had happened between 2005 and 2007 was a highly personalized, Howard-inspired attempt to introduce a history curriculum that was acceptable on a personal level to the Prime Minister. Such a curriculum would have strong support from the conservative media and would emphasize key Howard-approved elements in a traditionalist 'rebalancing' of the curriculum such as Australia's military past and its influence on national character. To make this happen, Howard had tried to circumvent the states and territories because both he and education minister Bishop saw state and territory curriculum designers as subversive leftist influences whose political masters had been captured by their officials.

In the Australian federal system, however, the Prime Minister has no direct authority over schooling, hence Howard's appeal to the public via the summit and use of its attendant publicity. Further, the Commonwealth Minister of Education had to gain the approval for major policy initiatives from a ministerial council dominated by eight state and territory education ministers, hence the funding threats, which were more bluster than promise. Ultimately, Howard's individualistic end run failed because of the workings of a liberal democracy. His idiosyncratic approach was replaced by a more systematic and professional national curriculum initiative which the 2007–13 Labor government left entirely to the newly formed ACARA, which conducted extensive consultation processes, hired experienced professional curriculum officials and worked closely with the states and territories.

Even so, in March 2010 the Coalition education spokesman (and former Howard cabinet minister) Christopher Pyne began a strident Howardist campaign against the new national history curriculum, accusing it, amongst other matters, of leftist political bias, ignoring Australia's 'Judeo-Christian tradition' [*sic*] and disregarding the historical importance in Australia of British and other Western influences. When the then Gillard ALP government was replaced by Tony Abbot's Coalition administration in late 2013, Pyne set up an inquiry into the national curriculum led by two personally appointed Liberal Party ideologues, Kevin Donnelly and Ken Wiltshire, who were to investigate the history curriculum for bias as well as lack of 'Judeo-Christian', British and Western tradition.

This inquiry, already under fire from a wide range of educators and other commentators for its unabashed ideological bias, took a farcical turn in July 2014 when Donnelly commented in a radio interview that he favoured corporal punishment in certain circumstances. Pyne was obliged to disown Donnelly's comments. To make matters worse for Pyne, in October 2014 it was revealed that the inquiry's senior English consultant, Professor Barry Spurr of Sydney University, had sent racist, sexist and homophobic emails to friends and colleagues. Pyne was also obliged to disown Spurr's remarks.

In the end, the review's report (Department of Education 2014) could find no political bias in the history curriculum but did complain about 'Judeo-Christian' and British and Western traditions being given a low priority, this despite the evidence-based research that the term 'Judeo-Christian' was a Cold War propaganda invention, and despite clear proof that the British and Western backgrounds to Australian history were incorporated in the 2010 national curriculum. The upshot was that Pyne was obliged to take his by now thoroughly discredited inquiry report to the ministerial council in December 2014. Consequently, the council all but ignored the report's complaints and produced non-controversial recommendations relating to an overcrowded curriculum, parent engagement, students with a disability and a vague reference to rebalancing the curriculum (adjusting the number of subjects on offer). There were no recommendations regarding the 'Judeo-Christian' tradition nor any about revamping the history curriculum (for details of this review episode see Taylor 2013).

Summary

During the Howard interventions of 2005 to 2007 and the Pyne initiatives of 2010 to 2014, the conventional democratically based curriculum implementation process in Australia was aided in three ways. First, Coalition governments of that period were mistaken in their belief that a personalized, ideologized and stubborn determination to circumvent process would triumph in the face of hostility from the education community at large. Second, the Coalition's manifestly uninformed and politicized view of what constituted history at the classroom level allowed critics of these putative Coalition interventions to gain traction in the public and professional arena (Taylor 2014). Third, the state/territory-dominated ministerial council barrier to individualistic action at the federal level remained firm in the face of political and media pressure by Canberra. At the end of this episode, at least, democracy had prevailed. Interestingly, in Howard's 728-page political autobiography, neither the 2005 Cronulla riots nor the 2006 history summit merit a mention in his narrative. Cricket, however, gets fifteen acknowledgements and two illustrations (Howard 2011).

Vladimir Putin

In 2000, Vladimir Putin started his presidency with a problem similar to Howard's. He was taking office after a long period of humiliation, but this time it was the humiliation of an entire nation and its people rather than just Howard's personal and party embarrassment. Putin's election as president came after a horror decade later known as the 'Roaring Nineties' when Russia had lost its superpower status and its people had suffered social degradation, economic collapse including hyperinflation (peaking at 5,000 per cent per annum in 1994), ideological and financial carpet-bagging by domestic and international opportunists and gloating by Russia's former geopolitical rivals. Putin had witnessed the first part of this collapse of the USSR from outside Russia, from the vantage point of an Andropovist KGB lieutenant colonel based for the most part in an East Germany which was busy celebrating its freedom from the Soviet yoke.

However, while Howard had been a party insider all his adult life, Putin was not. He had not even been a Communist Party of the Soviet Union (CPSU) fast-track apparatchik, the normal career route for an ambitious politician. Indeed, in his chosen career as a KGB officer, Putin was regarded as an enigmatic, not very competent outsider, the 'quiet Chekist' who was not a member of the CPSU *nomenklatura*. Moreover, he was not a metropolitan Muscovite but a St Petersburg interloper who was posted to the capital in 1996 at President Yeltsin's instigation to monitor Russia's wilful oligarchs (Hill and Gaddy 2012).

Putin's rise to power under the Yeltsin *krisha* (family's roof or patronage) was remarkable. In four years he rose from obscurity to become Yeltsin's head troubleshooter. Starting as an anonymous lieutenant colonel in the KGB who resigned his post in 1991, he became a senior official in the St Petersburg administration (1994–6), Yeltsin's Moscow-based deputy manager and later deputy chief of staff (1996–8), Director of the Federal Security Service (FSB) (1998–9), Prime Minister (1999), Acting President (1999–2000), President (2000–2007), Prime Minister (2008–12) and President again (2012–). During his rapid rise to power, Putin was, amongst other matters, anguished by Russia's loss of global status, the inability of the Kremlin to direct Russia's affairs with a firm hand, Gorbachev's relinquishment of Eastern Europe and by new, offensive interpretations of what he considered to be Russia's glorious imperial and military past.

As with Howard, Putin had a strong personal connection with his nation's military past. According to Putin, his father, Vladimir Spiridonovich Putin, who was wounded during the Second World War, had fought with an NKVD unit that operated behind German lines. His mother Mariya had apparently been left for dead during the Leningrad siege, only to be rescued by what seems to have been a variety of good Samaritans, if we believe Putin's own inconsistent tellings of the story (Putin 2000a: 6–7 and Macintyre 2014). In that family history context, over the decade that followed his inauguration as president, Putin's policy was to align Russia's past imperial greatness with its former military triumphs. As Putin's hold over the Russian state tightened in the second decade of his political elevation, he moved increasingly towards framing his idea of an old-but-new Russia in the national history curriculum.

In his 7 May 2000 inaugural speech, given two days before Victory Day, Putin dwelt on how he wanted Russia's past to be remembered, not as an abject victim of Western triumphalism but as a 'great, powerful and mighty state':

> For today's solemn event we are gathered here, in the Kremlin, a place which is sacred for our people. The Kremlin is the heart of our national memory. Our country's history has been shaped here, inside the Kremlin walls, over centuries. And we do not have the right to be heedless of our past. We must not forget anything. We must know our history, know it as it really is, draw lessons from it and always remember those who created the Russian state, championed its dignity and made it a great, powerful and mighty state. We shall preserve that memory, and we shall preserve that tradition through the ages. We shall hand down to our descendants all that is best in our history – all that is best.
>
> Putin 2000b

During the period from 2000 to 2007 Putin repeated this theme time and again, adding extra elements to the story as he went along. In 2003, in his annual address to members of the Russian Assembly he referred to their nation's former and never-to-be-forgotten glory:

> I would like to recall that throughout our history Russia and its people have accomplished and continue to accomplish a truly historical feat, a great work performed in the name of our country's integrity and in the name of bringing it peace and a stable life . . . It is our duty never to forget this, and we should remember it now, too, as we examine the threats we face today and the main challenges to which we must rise.
>
> Putin 2003

Putin and 'falsifications' of history

Amongst domestic and foreign historians and journalists, Yeltsin's presidency and the Putin regime had all come in for a great deal of criticism in the first decade of the twenty-first century, so much so that Putin became increasingly exasperated with the proliferation of these negative interpretations of Russia's past at the scholarly level. Not only that but a Yeltsin-era 1992 Education Act had, amongst other things, freed up schools from the constraints of compulsory classes in Marxism and Soviet-era historiography. This period of liberation led to interventions in Russian education and textbooks (1996–2005) by Council of Europe history education missionaries with their talk of multiple perspectives, inquiry learning, open-ended conclusions, teaching for multiculturalism and learning about controversial issues. Together with various other sorties by individual and EUROCLIO professional development teams these educational emancipators ranged from Archangelsk to Vladivostok. At the same time there had been a noticeable proliferation and liberalization of history textbooks, several of which, as history education researchers Liudmilla Aleksashkina and Joseph Zajda have each pointed out (Aleksashkina 2011; Zajda 2012), were critical of Russia's past.

In October 2003, Putin took time out from his many pressing crises to deal with the textbooks issue. He addressed Russian history teachers prior to the Duma elections of that year and, in referring to the wide range of history textbooks available to school students, his theme was clear. He was looking for factual emphasis combined with patriotism:

> It is good that we have a large diversity of literature of this kind. I think that we can be glad that we have left behind the single-party and single ideological interpretation of the history of our country. This is a major achievement, but I think you will agree that we should not go to the other extreme. Modern textbooks, especially textbooks for schools and institutions of higher education, should not become a platform for a new political and ideological struggle. These textbooks should really present historical facts; they should inspire, especially among young people, a feeling of pride for their own history and for their country.
>
> cited in Smith 2008: 1

In 2005, the same patriotic self-respect theme cropped up again in his annual address to the Federal Assembly, in which he commented on economic and political difficulties of the early years of his administration. He saw the history of the Roaring Nineties as a period of recovery from disintegration, not as a decade of deterioration:

> I will recall once more Russia's most recent history. Above all, we should acknowledge that the collapse of the Soviet Union was a major geopolitical disaster of the century. As for the Russian nation, it became a genuine drama. Tens of millions of our co-citizens and compatriots found themselves outside Russian territory. Moreover, the epidemic of disintegration infected Russia itself . . . Many thought or seemed to think at the time that our young democracy was not a continuation of Russian statehood, but its ultimate collapse, the prolonged agony of the Soviet system. But they were mistaken. That was precisely the period when the significant developments took place in Russia. Our society was generating not only the energy of self-preservation, but also the will for a new and free life.
>
> Putin 2005

This was not a view shared by all, however (see inter alia Satter 2003; Felshtinsky and Pribylovsky 2007; Gessen 2012).

Putin, whose major concerns were managing what was then a volatile state, re-establishing Russia's global presence, driving economic growth, dealing with Chechnya and promoting Russo-centric cultural and social cohesion, remained exasperated by this kind of freeing up of opinion and these critical histories which he saw as part of a subversive over-complication of Russia's grand narrative. The Putinist term that came to be used about this phenomenon was the 'falsification' of Russia's past, a term close to Howard's 1996 'perverse myths' about Australian history.

For Putin, these falsifications presented two problems. First, he was exasperated by those Russian and foreign historians who seemed to dwell on the 'black pages' of Russia's past (manifestly appalling incidents, for example the Katyn massacres), the 'bleak pages' (appalling but necessary incidents, for example the Gulags) and 'blank pages' (incidents not normally mentioned because they were too uncomfortable, for example the 1939 Molotov Pact with Nazi Germany). Putin wanted more emphasis on 'bright spots' (uplifting narratives) that would encourage patriotism and develop a sense of national identity; for example, Russia's 1812 victory at Borodino and its triumph over the Nazis in the Great Patriotic War of 1941–5.

Putin's worldview

In essence, there were seven historically based Putinist themes that developed during the period between 2000 and 2005. First, the sudden collapse of the USSR had led to traumatic economic, social and political instability which, although painful, led to renewal. Second, Russians had much to be proud of in their history, including key events of the Soviet era. Third, a common history, language and culture bound all Russians together whether they were in the Motherland or stranded (by implication) in the former USSR's border states such as Georgia, Ukraine and the Baltic states. Fourth, Russia was culturally and historically justified in its territorial ambitions regarding its border states. Fifth, Russian history needed to be rewritten to emphasize its former and present splendours, and he would do some of that historical rewriting in his speeches. Sixth, the new Russia was a vibrant and democratic *sovereign* nation. This new label, replacing the earlier term 'managed democracy', was the idea of Putin aide Vladislav Surkov. The Putin and Surkov view was that Russia had risen out of the chaos of the 1990s and should no longer be interfered with nor denigrated by external forces. Seventh, school students should focus on these positive bright spots in Russian history as well as quickly dealing with, and moving on from, the bleak spots, the black spots and the blank spots.

In Putin's world, the study of Russian history is seen therefore as an instrument of state power in the form of a politicized chronicle which must be based on a 'single flow' of a patriotic and exceptionalist narrative which will in the first instance proclaim Russia's status as a great power – past, present and future. Second, history will show that Russia can base its moral and geopolitical authority on the sacrifices made in the anti-fascist Great Patriotic War of 1941–5. Third, a study of the past will demonstrate that history is an important element in re-legitimizing a traditional

Tsarist framing of the political system, first espoused in the 1830s, of Orthodoxy, Autocracy and Nationality. Orthodoxy is represented by the Orthodox Church, whose Patriarch, Kirill, in February 2012 declared Putin to be a 'miracle of God'. The modern Orthodox Church is an ancillary arm of the state and acts as an extra-political but symbiotic spiritual agent in Putin's 'Russian world'. Autocracy manifests itself in the 'power vertical' while Nationality refers to the exceptional character of Slavic culture and its guaranteed preservation by the Kremlin. This final element in the political equation, Nationality, is a justification for the reclamation of the Russian strategic borderlands and social cohesion in a multi-ethnic (not a multicultural) society. Accordingly, Putin's historical ambitions can only be met if the nation's patriotic culture is supported by a school-level historical narrative that, amongst other matters, exalts these three Tsarist-era elements.

Putin's room for manoeuvre

Unlike Howard, who had been similarly concerned about Australia's own bright and black spots, Putin had it in his power to act when it came to influencing the curriculum. Under the terms of the 1993 constitution, Putin's presidential authority in domestic policy far exceeds that of the prime minister of a Western democratic federation. While not part of the executive branch of government in Russia, Putin can lay out guidelines which he and the government of Russia (dominated by the pro-Putin United Russia party) are able to implement. The conservative United Russia (UR) party's role in Russian government needs further explanation at this stage. With a large membership of teachers, public servants and other members of the middle classes, it sees its role as the supporter of governments that meet its needs, not as a Western-style partisan political party attached to a particular ideology. That being the case, Putin's position on domestic policy is outlined in his written pronouncements regarding draft federal laws, and these pronouncements influence UR's directions and policies. Equally importantly in the case of education, Putin can promulgate organizational and administrative regulations via decrees and executive orders.

Not only that, and bearing in mind that Putin's 'power vertical' arrangement was temporarily moderated by the intervening Medvedev presidency (2008–12), Putin, a president with cult-style popularity polls, more recently replaced his former exclusive but relatively wide governing cabal, narrowing down the actual decision-making caucus to a small clique of very close associates, giving him almost dictatorial powers.

Putin takes action

Pressured by forceful public utterances of Putin and his associates during the period from 2007 to 2013, the Russian Department of Education and Science and the Russian Academy of Education began to introduce significantly more politicized versions of Russia's post-1945 history, commencing with a 2007 history manual, *A Modern History of Russia: 1945–2006: A Manual for History Teachers* written in the main by Kremlin-friendly historian Alexander Filipov, a patriotic volume that was intended to guide textbook authors and teachers (Filipov 2007).

The 2007 manual argued, for example, that Stalin was a great but cruel leader who acted rationally in the best interests of the Russian people, and the Red Terror was an 'instrument of development'. Further, the USSR did not lose the Cold War; it ended it. Moreover, Gorbachev was seriously at fault for allowing the Soviet Union to lose its 'security belt', which a few years later would become 'a zone of foreign influence, with NATO bases an hour away from St Petersburg . . . We are talking about a new isolation of Russia' (cited in *The Economist*, 2007).

In the following year, during the August/September 2008 Russo-Georgian war, Putin claimed Russia was encircled, and in responding to the purported needs and demands of Russian citizens, fostering their development and ensuring their protection, South Ossetia was annexed by Russia.

The last chapter in the manual, on the topic of 'Sovereign Democracy', argued that the centralization of authority and the power of personal leadership are the driving factors in Russia's political culture, suggesting that a 'strong and wise leader is more important than [democratic] institutions' (cited in *The Economist*, 2007).

On 21 June 2007, Putin took up his single narrative theme again in an address to Russian humanities and social science teachers. In his speech, given just before the summer holidays, Putin referred to 'the muddle' caused in teachers' heads by differing interpretations of Russia's past. In this 2007 talk, he added an extra twist regarding Russia's history as measured against the histories of other nations, particularly against Russia's former enemies, the United States and Germany. His line was that Russia may have had a few bad moments but at least the Russians never went as far as some of its critics:

> Regarding the problematic pages in our history . . . In any event, we have never used nuclear weapons against civilians, and we have never dumped chemicals on thousands of kilometres of land or dropped more bombs on a tiny country than were dropped during the entire Second World War, as was the case in Vietnam. We have not had such bleak pages as was the case of Nazism, for example. All states and peoples have had their ups and downs through history. We must not allow others to impose a feeling of guilt on us.
>
> cited in Smith 2008: 2

The Russian government's next politico-historiographical move, in this case with Putin as prime minister, came early in 2009 with reports in the Russian media that the Kremlin was drawing up a law to ban statements denying that the USSR won the Second World War and liberated Eastern Europe. Those reports proved accurate, for in May 2009 the interim and more progressive Medvedev government set up a Historical Truth Commission to act against the 'falsification of Russian history'.

The anti-falsification campaign continued in July 2009 when Russian delegates stormed out of the Organization for Security and Cooperation in Europe (OSCE) meeting after Lithuania and Slovenia moved to equate Nazism with Stalinism. Russia lost that OSCE vote by 385–8, only confirming Putin's view that Russia was surrounded by hostile forces.

As soon as he resumed presidential duties in 2012, Putin restarted his history crusade, announcing that 2012 was to be the 'Year of Russian History' which would commemorate, in the main, Russia's 1812 victory at Borodino over the forces of Napoleonic France. In December 2012, Putin then gave a speech to the Russian Assembly, in which he announced that patriotism would be the ideological cornerstone of his next presidency, from 2012 to 2018, quoting Nobel prize-winning author Solzhenitsyn's nationalist argument that patriotism was a 'natural organic feeling' (Putin 2012).

Two months later, in February 2013, Putin convened a meeting of inter-ethnic relations at the Jewish Museum and Tolerance Centre in Moscow (the choice of venue was an implicit Putin criticism of Germany's Nazi past), where he denounced 'all kinds of pseudoscientific, biased speculations on the subject [of Russia's history]', at the same time commissioning an approved panel of historians to develop a single model school textbook (for each year of secondary school) free from 'internal contradictions and ambiguities' (Putin 2013).

This chronicle of Putin's politico-historical moves continues in March 2013. In presenting awards at the newly set-up Russian Military History Society, Putin told its members they should strive to 'preserve Russia's distinctive national character by extolling its traditions and roots, its spiritual and cultural heritage', pointing out that he has also 'overseen the creation of the Directorate for Social Projects, a body tasked with strengthening "government policies in the field of patriotic upbringing"' (cited in Winning 2013), and a Putin-backed bill submitted to the State Duma on 9 March that would increase funding for NGOs engaged in 'patriotic education'.

Later that year, in a September *coup de main* that tightened Kremlin control of a money-spinning and corrupt school textbook business, Putin crony and oligarch Arkady Rotenberg took over as chair of *Prosveshcheniye* ('Enlightenment'), Russia's largest textbook publisher with a reputation for producing uncritical rote texts. In October 2013 the Russian Historical Society then approved the new draft plan for what were now 'single concept' history textbooks for secondary schools, to be implemented by September 2016. In November that year, State Duma speaker and chair of the Russian Historical Society Sergei Naryshkin launched an outline manual for new approved textbooks which was slightly less provocative than the 2007 version but still had some issues. For example, the 1939 Molotov–Ribbentrop pact was omitted and Putin's role in modern Russia was framed in heroic terms, notwithstanding unmentioned protests in 2011 and 2012 over vote rigging and allegations about Putin's leadership style.

A Putinist apotheosis

It was at this point that Putin's nationalist educational policy was used to shore up his security emphasis and his territorial ambitions. In late February 2014, the annexation by ethnic Russian proxies of the Donbas region of Ukraine began and in March 2014 Russia annexed Crimea. During that April, the Russian Ministry of Education and Science allowed the introduction of a high school course called 'We are together' in which selected United Russia party members and teachers would 'talk to' students about events in Georgia, Crimea and Ukraine. During April, too, the Ministry of

Education and Science banned more than 50 per cent of Russian textbooks for conveying 'foreign influences' and a lack of patriotism. These bans cleared the way for a profitable and a Putin-friendly *Prosveshcheniye* monopoly from the next school year onwards. School books published by *Fyodorov*, a publishing company that used modern, Leonid Zankov (Deweyan) pedagogy, were amongst those banned. Teacher protests followed (Becker and Myers 2014).

It was not just the teachers who were protesting. During the spring period that saw Putin's March 2014 annexation of Crimea, academic historian Andrei Zubov of the Moscow State Institute of International Relations published an article in the respected Russian daily *Vedomosti* in which he compared Putin's 2014 Crimean annexation to Hitler's 1938 takeover of Austria. Putin entered the debate elliptically but unmistakably on 18 March 2014 in a speech to the Duma in which he referred to a 'fifth column' and a subversive 'disparate bunch of national traitors'. On the Monday following that speech, Zubov was dismissed by his university for 'an immoral act incompatible with the continuation of work' (Yaffa 2014).

Although Zubov was later reinstated, the national and international uproar that followed his dismissal was inflamed by New York-based but very Kremlin-friendly academic Andranik Migranyan, who published an article on 3 April 2014 in pro-government daily *Izvestia* pointing out that Zubov was guilty of 'monstrous distortions, fabrications and falsifications' (Migranyan 2014). In a strange turn of events, Migranyan then went on to argue that Hitler had been a 'politician of the highest order' – until 1939 at least. This episode, combining an attack on Zubov with this bizarre, new party line defence of the 1939 Molotov Pact, became known as the 'Good Hitler: Bad Hitler' debate.

These 2014 incidents were a clear example of how Putin, directly or indirectly, held most of Russia's media cards, controlled the legal authorities and held sway over academic organizations, encouraging aggressive countermeasures against historically based dissent, a tactic which it was expected would have a trickle-down effect amongst teachers whose continuing employment or promotion was often at the behest of officials who were members of the United Russia party and who, at the least, were expected to second-guess the President's intentions.

Having virtually shut down academic discussion of the Crimea issue, Putin's history-as-politics campaign opened up a new front. The first day of August 2014 was the hundredth anniversary of the beginning of the First World War and Putin, while unveiling a memorial to Russia's Great War heroes at Moscow memorial site Poklonnaya Gora, revised history yet again, this time with a Kremlin revisitation of the 1917 White Russian worldview, a variation on Germany's 1918 *Dolchstoss* (stab in the back) conspiracy theory. He commented:

> Today we are restoring the historical truth about World War I . . . this victory was stolen from our country. It was stolen by those [Bolsheviks] who called for the defeat of their homeland and army, who sowed division inside Russia and sought only power for themselves, betraying the national interests . . . Today, we are restoring the kinks in time, making history a single flow once more.
>
> Putin 2014; see also Lipman 2014

This was nothing less than a politically motivated attempt to portray Russia's disastrous involvement in the First World War as a stolen victory, with Putin egregiously putting the blame for Russia's defeat on the 1917 anti-nationalist Communists. It was no coincidence that these accusations came at a time when the Communist Party of the Russian Federation was very slowly chipping away at the UR majority.

Summary

Putin's highly personalized and highly politicized view of history, as developed in the period from 2000 to 2014, combined an aggressive blend of Tsarist-era historical consciousness with a White Russian anti-Bolshevik historical ideology together with elements of a Soviet-style rigid pedagogy. Because of his ability to intervene directly in educational policy and in publishing, within a system where over 90 per cent of Russian history teachers are heavily dependent on textbooks as a classroom resource, where teachers are aware that their employment security can depend on government approval for their actions and where the seemingly ever-popular Putin holds sway over a mass media and a Russian political system which approves of his nationalistic policies, the Russian president can do much as he likes. That being the case, Putin has made it quite clear that he intends to keep on doing precisely that until 2024, the final year he can remain in power, if he succeeds in the 2018 presidential election. As for the 'single concept' textbook series, at the time of writing it is still on track for publication in mid-2016 by *Prosveshcheniye*, educational specialists in rote learning.

References

Aleksashkina, L. (2011), 'National Standards and Development of Historical Education: Experiences of Secondary Schools in the Russian Federation', *Curriculum and Teaching* 26 (2): 7–92.

Australian Broadcasting Corporation (1996), 'Howard An Average Australian Bloke', *Four Corners*, 19 February. Available online: http://www.abc.net.au/4corners/content/2004/s1212701.htm (accessed 11 February 2015).

Becker, J. and Myers, S. L. (2014), 'Putin's Friend Profits in Purge of Schoolbooks', *New York Times*, 1 November. Available online: http://www.nytimes.com/2014/11/02/world/europe/putins-friend-profits-in-purge-of-schoolbooks.html (accessed 11 February 2015).

Blainey, G. (1993), Sir John Latham Memorial Lecture, 30 July, later published as 'Drawing Up a Balance Sheet of our History', *Quadrant*, July: 10–15. Available online: http://search.informit.com.au/documentSummary;dn=096284804696129;res=IELLCC (accessed 11 February 2015).

Department of Education, Science and Training (2007), *Guide to the Teaching of Australian History in Years 9 and 10*, Canberra: AGPS.

Department of Education (2014), *Review of the Australian Curriculum*, October 2014. Available online: http://www.studentsfirst.gov.au/review-australian-curriculum (accessed 11 February 2015).

Dyrenfurth, N. (2015), *Mateship: A Very Australian History*, Brunswick, Victoria: Scribe.

Economist (2007), 'Russia's Past: The Rewriting of History', 8 November. Available online: http://www.economist.com/node/10102921 (accessed 11 February 2015).

Errington, W. and van Onselen, P. (2007), *John Winston Howard: The Biography*, Carlton, Victoria: Melbourne University Press.

Felshtinsky, Y. and Pribylovsky, V. (2007), *The Age of Assassins: The Rise of Vladimir Putin*, London: Gibson Square.

Filipov, A. (2007), *A Modern History of Russia: 1945–2006: A Manual for History Teachers*, Moscow: Prosveshcheniye.

Gessen, M. (2012), *The Man Without a Face: The Unlikely Rise of Vladimir Putin*, London: Granta.

Hansard [Parliament of Australia] (1992), 27 February. Available online: http://parlinfo.aph.gov.au/parlInfo/search/display/display.w3p;query=Id%3A%22chamber%2Fhansardr%2F1992-02-27%2F0094%22 (accessed 11 February 2015).

Hill, F. and Gaddy, C. G. (2012), *Mr Putin: Operative in the Kremlin*, Washington, DC: Brookings Institution Press.

Howard, J. (1988), *Future Directions*, Barton, ACT: Liberal Party of Australia, December.

Howard, J. (1996a), Sir Thomas Playford Memorial Lecture (no title), 5 July. Available online: http://pmtranscripts.dpmc.gov.au/browse.php?did=10041 (accessed 11 February 2015).

Howard, J. (1996b), Sir Robert Menzies Lecture, 'The Liberal Tradition: The Beliefs and Values which Guide the Federal Government', 18 November. Available online: http://menzieslecture.org/1996.html (accessed 11 February 2015).

Howard, J. (2006), Address to the National Press Club, Great Hall, Parliament House (no title), 25 January. Available online: http://australianpolitics.com/2006/01/25/john-howard-australia-day-address.html (accessed 11 February 2015).

Howard, J. (2011), *Lazarus Rising: A Personal and Political Autobiography*, Sydney: HarperCollins.

Lipman, M. (2014), 'Putin Disses Lenin', *New Yorker*, 3 September. Available online: http://www.newyorker.com/news/news-desk/putin-disses-lenin (accessed 11 February 2015).

Macintyre, B. (2014), 'The Moving Tale of Putin's Mother is a Myth', *The Times*, 13 June. Available online: http://www.thetimes.co.uk/tto/opinion/columnists/article4117430.ece (accessed 11 February 2015).

Macintyre, S. and Clark, A. (2003), *The History Wars*, Carlton, Victoria: Melbourne University Publishing

Migranyan, A. (2014), 'About a Certain False Analogy and its Russian Advocates', *Izvestia*, 3 April.

Putin, V. (2000a), *First Person*, New York: Public Affairs.

Putin, V. (2000b), Inauguration Speech of President of the Russian Federation, 7 May. Available online: http://eng.kremlin.ru/transcripts/8644 (accessed 11 February 2015).

Putin, V. (2003), Annual Presidential Address to the Federal Assembly of the Russian Federation, 16 May. Available online: http://eng.kremlin.ru/transcripts/7312 (accessed 11 February 2015).

Putin, V. (2005), Annual Address to the Federal Assembly of the Russian Federation, 25 April. Available online: http://archive.kremlin.ru/eng/speeches/2005/04/25/2031_type70029type82912_87086.shtml (accessed 11 February 2015).

Putin, V. (2012), Annual Presidential Address to the Federal Assembly of the Russian Federation, 12 December. Available online: http://eng.kremlin.ru/news/4739 (accessed 11 February 2015).

Putin, V. (2013), Address, Meeting of Council for Interethnic Relations, 19 February. Available online: http://eng.kremlin.ru/news/5017 (accessed 11 February 2015).
Putin, V. (2014), Speech at Ceremony Unveiling a Monument to World War I Heroes, 1 August. Available online: http://eng.kremlin.ru/transcripts/22756 (accessed 11 February 2015).
Reynolds, H. (1981), *The Other Side of the Frontier: Aboriginal Resistance to the European Invasion of Australia*, Sydney: University of New South Wales Press.
Reynolds, H. (1987), *Frontier: Aborigines, Settlers and Land*, Sydney: Allen & Unwin.
Satter, D. (2003), *Darkness at Noon: The Rise of the Russian Criminal State*, New Haven: Yale University Press.
Smith, M. (2008), 'The Politicisation of History in the Russian Federation', *Advanced Research and Assessment Group: Russian Series*, Shrivenham: Defence Academy of the United Kingdom, May.
Taylor, T. (2001), *The Future of the Past: The Final Report on the Teaching and Learning of History in Australian Schools*, Canberra: Department of Education, Training and Youth Affairs.
Taylor, T. (2009), 'Howard's End: A Narrative Memoir of Political Contrivance, Neoconservative Ideology and the Australian History Curriculum', *Curriculum Journal* 20 (4): 317–29.
Taylor, T. (2013), 'Neoconservative Progressivism, Knowledgeable Ignorance and the Origins of the Next History War', *History Australia* 10 (2): 227–40.
Taylor, T. (2014), 'Pyne's Curriculum Review Should Have Learnt from History', *Crikey.com*, 23 October. Available online: http://www.crikey.com.au/2014/10/23/pynes-curriculum-review-should-have-learnt-from-history (accessed 11 February 2015).
Taylor, T. and Collins, S. (2012), 'The Politics are Personal: *The Australian* vs the Australian History Curriculum', *Curriculum Journal* 23 (4): 531–52.
Topsfield, J. and Rood, D. (2006), 'Lib Calls for National Curriculum', *The Age*, 6 October. Available online: http://www.theage.com.au/news/national/lib-calls-for-national-curriculum/2006/10/05/1159641461872.html (accessed 11 February 2015).
Winning, A. (2013), 'Putin's Patriotism Campaign Gathers Momentum', *Moscow Times*, 21 March. Available online: http://www.themoscowtimes.com/news/article/putins-patriotism-campaign-gathers-momentum/477231.html (accessed 11 February 2015).
Yaffa, J. (2014), 'Putin's New War on Traitors', *New Yorker*, 28 March. Available online: http://www.newyorker.com/news/news-desk/putins-new-war-on-traitors (accessed 11 February 2015).
Zajda, J. (2012), 'Transforming Images of Nation-Building: Ideology and Nationalism in History School Textbooks in Putin's Russia, 2001–2010', in T. Taylor and R. Guyver (eds), *History Wars and the Classroom: Global Perspectives*, 125–42, Charlotte, NC: Information Age Publishing.

12

Spain: History Education and Nationalism Conflicts

Ramón López Facal and Jorge Sáiz Serrano

The nation, politics and transnational dimensions in history education in Spain

No political power can be maintained for long by using the exclusive resource of coercion.* It needs to achieve a certain level of social cohesion if it is to establish its claim. During the *ancien régime*, religion assumed the role of spreading values of subjugation to the social order, which was accepted as being both natural and everlasting. After the liberal revolutions (1776–1830), nationalism imposed its ideas as a lay substitute that redirected loyalty towards a new image: the nation. Since ancient times, the use of history had been justified as a moral example for individuals. From the nineteenth century it was applied to nations, which were transformed into the protagonists of history. Romantic history became more than just a chronological tale of kingdoms and dynasties, and turned the people into the real protagonists. The idea of a common nation was developed, shared and conceived as an organism with an everlasting soul or formed in a distant past, evident in the continuity of legal institutions and the actions of unique individuals who, at certain times, expressed the collective will and national character. The nation became the historical subject towards which the sense of loyalty was directed, and the monarchy was exalted in accordance with the subject. Many historians continued to be providentialists, but now refined the divine predilection for the nation rather than for a specific dynasty, such as the *ancien régime*.

History education was not institutionalized until the consolidation of the liberal states.[1] The triumph of a constitutional state, based on legal equality and individual freedom, was possible only if it were based on citizens. Education was to be used to form citizens who were equal in the eyes of the law and, at the same time, to make 'natural' inequalities legitimate. The educational system was institutionalized after the final defeat of those who supported the *ancien régime* in the mid-nineteenth century and it also changed the perception of history.

Following the second half of the nineteenth century, a canonical interpretation of the past of Spain was designed that stood on four pillars (traits):

1. Territorial sovereignty: the nation, Spain, is made up of a territory marked out by 'natural' borders. The abstract idea of nation was visible on the maps used in school and those that could be seen displayed presiding over the public institutions and bodies of the day.
2. Legislative and political unity: the nation could be associated at any time in the past with a certain degree of political unity, central government and a common legal system.
3. The national identity is based on a common character. Spaniards have always shown similar behaviours and attitudes, mainly because they share one single territorial framework that is essentially consistent despite its diversity. For example, landforms have led to individualism.
4. Catholic religious unity: Catholicism, with the Catholic Church as an institution, has helped forge the Spanish identity. This idea, shared by moderate liberalism and traditionalism, was also imposed on progressivists and democrats.

These four elements provided the key factors behind the image of the past of Spain, which remained evident in textbooks for more than a century: the 'Spanish character' (3) was revealed for the first time in the 'original Iberian settlers' (courage, austerity, individualism, generosity, a love for independence, resistance to outsiders), as 'confirmed' by the struggles for 'independence' from Phoenicians, Carthaginians and, above all, Romans. Although initially hated as foreign conquerors, the Romans were appreciated highly following the Imperial period (after the conquest) insofar as they brought political and linguistic unity (2) and stability to the peninsula (1) and thanks to the providential role they played in the spreading of Christianity (4).

The Visigoth monarchy was exalted as the founder of the first 'national' state after it unified the peninsula on a legal and political scale, giving it one single religious identity (1, 2 and 4).

In the Middle Ages, the 'reconquest' of Moslem Al Andalus by Christian kingdoms in the Peninsula stands as a great 'trial' in which 'Spaniards' (including only Christians within this term) suffered for the sins of their previous disunity and vices and managed to rebuild the permanently longed-for 'lost unity' (1 and 2) only through unity and eight centuries of courage. The Moslems of Al Andalus are 'the others', the invaders, even after being there for eight centuries (711–1492), against whom the national identity is defined (3).

History reached its height when the Catholic Monarchs (Isabella of Castile and Ferdinand of Aragon) conquered Granada in 1492, finished the 'Reconquista' and restored the 'national unity' of Spain (1, 2, 3 and 4). Furthermore, from the point of view of nineteenth-century liberals, the symbolic value of those monarchs was emphasized by the fact that they subjugated the 'unsupportive' nobility.

The monarchy of the Hapsburgs (sixteenth and seventeenth centuries) brought Spanish 'decadence' by focusing mainly on foreign enterprises and forgetting the nation's real problems.

However, this basic agreement about the interpretation of national past periods was not easily achieved. The appreciation of the liberal transformations taking place during the nineteenth century led to a great deal of ideological confrontation, which, however, basically coincided on the approval of the so-called War of 'Independence' against Napoleon's troops (known by the British as the 'Peninsular War'); from the middle of the century, it was magnified and turned into a myth by every ideological stance, albeit from significantly different standpoints.

The Catholic traditionalist sectors proposed no alternative whatsoever during the nineteenth century. From the reactionary yearning for an idealized past, they aspired to subordinating society as a whole to maintain and/or recover the privileges the Church had lost. Until the end of the nineteenth century, they rejected the very idea of nation and forms of schooling other than that which corresponded with Catholic doctrine, clearly seen by its opponents as indoctrination. It was the arrival of the Bourbon restoration in 1875, finally consolidating the conservative liberal state, which made it possible for traditionalist thought to assume the concept of nation. Thus it associated the idea of country with the anti-modern, anti-liberal essence of Catholicism, linked to the French and Italian counter-revolutionary thought of the period. Traditionalist thought was characterized by their mythological archaism and the maintenance of old myths questioned since the eighteenth century, such as the idea that the first Spaniards were of biblical origin. However, above all, the idea was to value the various stages of history according to the supremacy achieved by the Catholic Church over political powers. In this period of the Bourbon restoration the academic concept of 'reconquest' crystallized as a struggle to build Spanish religious and national unity. The fact that traditionalist thought differs from liberal romantic historiography, insofar as it rejects modernity and progress, has concealed the reality that they have many stereotypes in common. One common belief is that there is an alleged Spanish character with particular attributes (ascetic, spiritual, individualistic, intuitive, warring) and that territorial sovereignty is a timeless truth.

Liberal-progressivist thought was also renewed after the restoration. Its main educational reference was the *Institución Libre de Enseñanza* (Spanish acronym: ILE, Institute of Free Education). The frustration of the intellectual elites at the end of the nineteenth century, when they confirmed Spain's 'decadence', increased notably after the defeat of 1898, a date whose symbolism and consequences in Spanish intellectual circles is comparable to the defeat of 1870 in Sedan for the French intellectuals of the Third Republic. For the progressivists, the search for the desired progress that would put Spain in a position similar to the great powers involved an awakening of national awareness, forming a ruling minority that would assume its role in the country's modernization as a patriotic duty and help the popular masses identify with a common political project. This project was associated with the extension and improvement of education and, particularly, the teaching of history. The work that was ongoing in France and Germany became a model that was to be copied.

Rafael Altamira (1866–1951) was the intellectual associated with the ILE who led the renovation of historiography and pedagogy for the building of the nation. He is largely responsible for disseminating the historical method or historiographical positivism and, above all, modernizing what was taught in schools. His idea was for history at school to refer to the 'Spanish civilization', to take in what at the time was called 'internal history' (economics, culture) rather than the traditional 'external history', which was limited to a list of political events. He incorporated recent studies on prehistory, including the theories of evolution, and ancient history, bringing in subjects from archaeology; he offered a positive view of the colonial expansion in the Americas and the modernization process of the nineteenth century, together with the contributions made to Spanish national culture from within Al Andalus.

However, he also coincided with other stereotypes of the romantic discourse, modified only slightly by his greater historical precision: the evolutionist perspective of history, conceived as a process of continued progress from the divisions of the *ancien régime* to a centralized national state, is quite similar to earlier romantic ideas. The appreciation of the Visigoths (religious unity, overcoming cultural division) is also similar, but he criticizes the political practice of an unsupportive, warring aristocracy. His criterion for defending the past, especially the Middle Ages, is the greater or lesser degree of political unity achieved at any given time: the kingdom of the Catholic Monarchs therefore represents the 'crystallization of the national ideal' that put an end to medieval division. Indeed, despite his democratic convictions, he justifies the expulsion of the Jews, even though he considers it morally incorrect, because it helped achieve national unity.

Traditionalism and progressive liberalism before the Spanish Civil War thus shared similar nationalist stereotypes, such as believing in the existence of a hardened collective identity expressed through time, visible in one common language: Castilian Spanish (in the mid-nineteenth century, less than 50 per cent of the Spanish population spoke Castilian Spanish; in some regions, such as Galicia, the language was spoken by less than 3 per cent of the population), as an expression of the character of Spanish people; the idea of the Spanish 'race' as a cultural or spiritual community rather than a biological one, explicitly assumed by traditionalists (Menéndez Pelayo) and liberals (Ortega y Gasset); the idea of 'sacred territorial unity' that looks to the past; the conviction that there is a collective 'soul' of the Spanish people that transcends its individuals; the mythologization of traditions and customs that supposedly reflect that common soul (the austerity of the Castilian peasant); and also the religious, Catholic dimension of the Spanish character. In the first third of the twentieth century, the clichés taught in history at school were cemented in place and lasted until the 1970s. During the Second Republic (1931–36), school manuals issued by Catholic traditionalist publishers continued to be widely used in schools but there were also textbooks that followed the progressivist thought left behind by Altamira.

Franco's regime brutally eradicated the liberal tradition and imposed the traditionalist version, taking *National Catholicism* as the core of its ideology. This was a form of nationalism that referred to those who did not share its point of view not merely as non-Spanish, but rather as anti-Spanish: the positive Spanish value was identified with the Catholic value that accepts the supremacy of the Church over civil powers; any other attitude was considered negative, anti-Catholic and, therefore, anti-Spanish. The few differences from pre-1930s Catholic traditionalism were limited to certain external formulas adopted from Italian fascism (exaltation of the Empire, and the *caudillo* [leader]) or to avoiding opinions about the option of monarchy as a desirable form of government. Franco was only in formal and superficial ways inspired by the fascism of the time, whereas Hitler and Mussolini were wholly influenced by it. In essence Franco is a reactionary – ultra-conservative and anti-modern. His policies had more in common with the counter-revolutionary French Catholicism of the nineteenth century than with the 'modernization' and 'futuristic' stance of Mussolini.

After the Second World War, most Western European countries began a process for extending secondary education in response to new economic demands and a well-intentioned aim of achieving 'equal opportunities' and social and personal emancipation through education. For its part, while that was happening, the early years of Franco's regime did away with the progress made during the Second Republic. Educational contents were supervised by ecclesiastic censorship, and the function of educating the 'ruling minority' was given back to the Church. In 1937, an order was handed down for the closure of thirty-seven secondary education state schools that were 'obviously unnecessary', and the number of such schools was reduced to 113 in all of Spain; twenty years after the War had ended, in 1959, there were only 119. However, the number of schools offering private education grew sixfold in that period, with the same growth rate in the number of students registered: from 28.9 per cent of students in 1931 to 70.7 per cent in 1943.

From the abandonment of Franco-regime clichés to the questioning of the education system

The National Catholicism of Franco's regime sought to do away with any remains of other alternative nationalisms that had achieved political recognition during the Second Republic. However, the refusal to accept the smallest token of reconciliation or tolerate the slightest show of pluralism during almost forty years of the regime finally gave way to a crisis of the national identity it had tried to foster. By linking the idea of nation to pre-modern values, in open confrontation with the idea of progress, it contributed to the very crisis by which it was affected as soon as a process for modernizing Spanish society began in the 1960s. This, paradoxically, favoured the other nationalisms that acquired greater social legitimacy owing to the fact that they were associated with democratic, modernizing ideologies that were also anti-Franco.

In education, the change started to show itself with the adoption of the General Education Act (Spanish acronym: LGE) in 1970, five years before the dictator's death. As one of us has argued elsewhere (López Facal 2000), the technocratic sectors tried to use the LGE to adapt Franco's regime to the dominant models in place in the developed capitalist world, opening doors to values that were associated with liberalism and the democracies that had been rejected and persecuted for more than thirty years. As far as the teaching of history is concerned, the result was a breakaway from the nationalist narrative that had been maintained for fifteen hundred years beyond any ideological differences.

With the onset of the LGE, the main historiographical reference of history education was the Annales School of Thought and, to a lesser extent, a number of contributions from Marxist tradition. Political history drastically reduced its presence in the school curriculum and the economic and social dimension was increased notably. The more clichéd references to the founding of the Spanish nation in past times (the Iberians, Visigoths, Catholic Monarchs) disappeared, albeit with the odd exception, and the construction of the national state was not related to any period of time, not even to the liberal transformations of the nineteenth century; the problem was simply avoided. However, with the absence of the smallest amount of information and reflection on the process for national construction in Spain and the corresponding Spanish nationalism – which had been the driving force behind the process – it has been possible implicitly to maintain the traditional ideas about the Spanish nation, for example through historical maps, many of which, including those that referred to Roman times, showed the Pyrenean border. The current border was set by the Peace of Westphalia in 1648. Attempts to link this with a border that might have existed there at the time of the Roman Empire are anachronistic because this border did not exist until the seventeenth century. It is a projection into the past of the current image of the nation. The current linguistic boundaries are for some nationalists also national borders. However, the territories where different languages are spoken have a medieval origin and language barriers are a fallacy. The territories whose residents identify themselves as nations or regions are never homogeneous from the linguistic point of view.

The end of Franco's dictatorship was followed by an immediate and widespread popular rejection of the symbols it had tried to impose by force. The desire to overcome the recently disappeared regime as soon as possible enabled the abandonment of the ideas that had upheld Spanish nationalism since its origin, including the myths of how the nation was founded and the very idea of national unity. At the same time, alternative ideas and practices to the old Spanish centralist nationalism acquired democratic legitimacy. This can be partially explained by the almost non-existent popular opposition to the profound political and administrative decentralization of the state. The new regional powers that appeared with the transition to democracy hurried to create the symbolic elements that would legitimate their existence, again resorting to the 'discovery' of regional or national substance through elements of historicism and organicism. In a few years, all the autonomous communities had their own history and geography to 'demonstrate' their organic unity in time and space. Andalusia paid special attention to the legacy of Al Andalus; Catalonia, Aragon and Valencia turned to their medieval splendour prior to the unification of their dynasties with Castile; Galicia looked to the pre-Roman culture of its hill-forts, and so on.

Survival was difficult for the commemorations and anniversaries of old Spanish nationalism: 12 October ('Hispanic Race' day or 'Hispanic World' day) has been kept as a national public holiday, limited to a military parade in Madrid and low-level enthusiasm from the population; and 2 May, a symbolic date that commemorated the 'War of Independence' against the French in 1808, has been reduced to a regional holiday in Madrid, more to do with festivities than with patriotism. However, certain alternative commemorations to Spanish nationalism, such as the National Day of Catalonia (11 September) to commemorate the conquest of Barcelona in 1714 by the Bourbon troops, or the Day of the Basque Country (Easter Sunday) are of considerable political interest for large crowds in the corresponding territories each year.

Nation is an idea, a feeling, not a tangible reality; it is a political-ideological construction that was developed in the nineteenth century, seeking to guarantee the social cohesion of a collective based on belief in a shared identity. All forms of European nationalism owe themselves more or less to the romantic essentialist tradition, and history education has been at the service of this idea. This was so until the international context (as seen in the process for the integration of Western Europe in the framework of the Cold War) made it possible to overcome this situation, at least its more xenophobic and bellicose aspects. However, this transformation has also included a critical reflection on the nature of the concept of nation, its genesis and evolution. It has simply been hidden, in view of an avalanche of new contents and focuses that tended to 'demonstrate' the common identity of the democratic countries of Western Europe (the Greco-Roman past, the desired uniformity of feudal societies, the Enlightenment or the Industrial Revolution).

The survival of essentialist concepts, shamefully hidden by old European nationalisms, appeared openly in other alternatives which, in Spain, also carried democratic legitimacy as a result of their anti-Franco past. The result was a declaration of Spain that is much more plurinational than in the past. The construction of the so-called 'state of autonomous communities' during the transition to democracy helped discredit the centralist variant of Spanish nationalism, but, when the national dispute was a low-level conflict, it made relations between the sub-state entities and the state constantly contentious.

These circumstances led to the sensation of crisis and discontent among Spanish nationalists, who considered they had made notable and even excessive efforts in their competitors' favour. They also felt orphaned from the only national references they had known and in which they had been educated (the common history, common territory, common character, etc. of the Spanish), questioned by those who had an alternative national reference based on a permanent something that was specific and different. Spanish nationalists were uneasy with the crisis of the idea of a Spain that was not unanimously accepted and never had been, but that was now also questioned not only by historical nationalisms but also by regionalisms that had arisen from the new structure of the state. This was joined by the restlessness caused by the growing influx of immigrants seen as a threat for the survival of a cultural identity considered consubstantial to their idea of nation. The reaction of Spanish nationalists was to try to impose a return to old national essences associated with the nationalizing function of history. They failed to grasp that the crisis had nothing to do with the history of Spain, but rather with a certain feeling of the Spanish nation born from very different circumstances.[2]

The attempts to set new Spanish nationalism on a more pluralist and integrating discourse based on 'constitutional patriotism', which, except for the name, was far removed from the discourse on this concept offered by Sternberger (1990) and Habermas (1997), have not managed to overcome old stereotypes. They have been limited to removing events such as the medieval battles between Christians and Muslims from school textbooks and, in their place, disseminating a well-intentioned but not so rigorous tale of the harmonious co-existence of the three cultures (Christians, Muslims and Jews). The emphasis is placed on the cultural additions of the past rather than on military achievements. And, to top it off, the transition to democracy is magnified as a happy ending to the process for outdoing Franco's dictatorship and the division of the 'two Spains', consecrating the 1978 Constitution to the point where it is considered almost untouchable.

Today, there is a feeling of crisis in education that is not limited to the contents of history. Without going into great detail here to explain the new education policies that are being applied in the world, it is at least necessary to link the current media offensive in much of the Western world against state schools and current teaching plans in view of the new socio-economic context.

Neoconservative education policies call for an education that is allegedly efficient and competitive and focused on the market. However, at the same time, there is concern for guaranteeing social cohesion around one political system. In a plural society with various national references in competition with each other, we look to the teaching of history or language in the belief that it would be possible, as in the past, to guarantee cohesion in a society that is becoming increasingly unequal and, at the same time, neutralize the 'other' opposing nationalisms. Yet, despite the increase in 'nationalizing' contents in these subjects, the national options of the population do not seem to be modified.

National history in crisis: education, democracy and dialogue

Spain, which became a state at the end of the fifteenth century and a nation state with the liberal revolutions of the nineteenth century, shares numerous cultural references with other neighbouring states, but there are also notable differences. After the nineteenth century, the cultural elites drew up a nationalist discourse similar to that which was built in France, Italy and Germany; however, unlike in those countries, the different role played in the past by the national military in the case of Spain was not understood by many layers of the population owing to limitations on schooling and, as well as other reasons. The Spanish army during the nineteenth and twentieth centuries had hardly participated in wars against other European nations. Civilians were unable to identify with 'their' army or 'their' nation against other armies and other nations. The Spanish army had been regularly used as an internal instrument of repression and had been active in politics, holding power on numerous occasions. It had not been a national army, nationwide. Furthermore the education of the masses had been very poor and reached only a minority. The most powerful tools in the nationalization pre-audio-visual media age had been school, the army and the press, but most of the population lived outside them. This is the reason for asserting that Spanish nationalism was not assumed by most of the population. It is a complex issue. Most of the research into the processes behind the construction of the 'nation' (Smith 1991; Gellner 2006; and especially Weber 1976) highlights the military's role in nation-building. In this sense the Spanish case is very different and, for many Spanish historians (e.g. Álvarez-Junco 2011), one of the causes of weak Spanish 'nationalization'.

Furthermore, the relative 'failure' of Spanish nationalism has enabled greater development of nationalisms with an alternative reference (Catalonia, Galicia, the Basque Country and Valencia), although they have not managed to defeat, eliminate or overcome the Spanish national feeling in their respective territories. We now stand at the crossroads of a 'historical draw' between Spanish nationalism and peripheral nationalisms, 'if not with the confirmation of a dual and paradoxical failure' (Núñez Seixas 1999) in which they block each other out in view of the impossibility of one of them being implanted in an exclusive or hegemonic way.

Most of the population of the autonomous communities in which the presence of alternative nationalisms to Spanish nationalism is particularly significant assume the compatibility of their dual Spanish and regional identities. This situation is not necessarily stable or permanent and is changing for various reasons: an institutional or economic crisis like the present one can have unforeseeable effects. The instability of this situation can be seen, or at least felt, in circles that are more aware of one national identity or the other, and affects the overvaluation of the importance they give to the population's education in history.

The importance given to history in nationalist worlds (Spanish or alternative) means that the content and focus of the subject constitute a permanent field for ideological confrontation. The frequent controversies involving the teaching of history are limited to some claiming the presence of a 'common historical legacy' and others claiming the knowledge of their 'specific roots'. It is wrong to consider that education in general and that of history in particular is today the main instrument for shaping a national identity. Other areas are much more decisive and make up the social representation (common thought) of the population, such as the media and, above all, sports events, which play an increasingly important role in the development of a sense of identity.

In 1998, a Spanish historian, Carlos Forcadell, said that, in what he referred to as the professional community of historians, 'no one seems to contradict that there is no need for teaching (nationally) educated students, but rather citizens educated to criticize, the exercise of personal and intellectual freedom and the changing demands of the global village' (Forcadell 1998: 147). Perhaps his words are generically correct if they refer to academic research, but there are also historians who defend the need for 'renationalizing' and increasing the content of Spanish history in secondary education. It might be thought that they only consider historical precision necessary for university education while, for most of the population, the main purpose of history should be to pass on the myths of nationalism. These viewpoints have been imposed with the latest educational reforms and counter-reforms. Spanish neo-nationalism seeks to return to the 'good old days' when students learned the nation's glorious achievements by heart and with discipline.

The historiographical archaism of the reformed curricula in secondary schools is joined by the archaism of the methodology and pedagogy. Debates on the history of schooling in Spain since the 1990s have focused more on the contents of the discourse: on what to teach, rather than on how to teach and learn to think in a historical way. The teaching–learning processes are understood as a mere act of transmission of contents (emission–reception). The new programmes include notable increases in the number of events that have to be memorized. Thus, in the (to date) latest conservative reform of education, which is to be applied as from 2015, the subject of History of Spain is compulsory for all students in their last baccalaureate year (17–18 years). Contents range from the Palaeolithic period to the present day and include the following, among others:

> Explain the differences between the economy and the social organization of the Palaeolithic and Neolithic periods and the causes of the change . . . Summarize the main characteristics of the Kingdom of Tartessos and quote the historical sources used. Explain the different level of development of the Celtic and Iberian areas before the Roman conquest in relation to the influence received from Indo-Europeans, the Kingdom of Tartessos and the Phoenician and Greek colonizers . . . Compare the rate and degree of Romanization of the different territories on the peninsula. Summarize the characteristics of the Visigoth monarchy and explain why the Church and nobility obtained so much power. Find useful information (in books or on the internet) on the culture and art that has survived from Roman times in Spain today and give a brief explanation. Draw a schematic map of the Iberian peninsula and mark the Iberian and Celtic areas on it. Draw a timeline from 250 BC to AD 711, placing the main events of history on it.
>
> López Facal 2014

The programme requires tasks that are impossible in the time available, but which are to be evaluated in a final external examination. It includes 161 learning standards, which involve drawing twelve timelines; twelve explanations in the classroom; drawing or commenting on a dozen maps, charts, images and texts; half a dozen summaries, comparison tables, diagrams and much more. This excessive number of activities and the complexity of the knowledge that is demanded do not guarantee an understanding of history or the acquisition of useful knowledge. They reveal continuity with earlier programmes that do not teach students to reflect on the content in a historical way. If we add to this the concealment in education of nationalisms and the processes of nationalization in Spain, it comes as no surprise to find that the vision of the Spanish national identity shown by students at the end of their baccalaureate studies maintains essentialist and organicist elements of the Spanish nation, the same ones that are present in the social representations of the collective world (Sáiz Serrano and López Facal 2012).

A different educational culture for a different society

The profound changes that have taken place in modern societies, including those that have affected the communication and dissemination of information, mean that any education based on the transmission of information is sterile and doomed to failure. Nowadays, any teenager has a huge amount of information available on any subject but, at the same time, they have no criteria for selecting, organizing, structuring and appreciating that information. No school can compete with these sources of extracurricular information. The function of education cannot go on being that of transmitting more information, but rather that of helping students learn to critically analyse the information that is offered to them and make value judgements based on sound reasoning on the aspects of human co-existence that society considers most important or problematic at any given time. That capacity for critical analysis affects a historical dimension for understanding its genesis and evolution. Too much curricular content leads to superficiality and simplification, i.e. the opposite to developing the capacity for criticism.

Since the eighteenth century, Western culture has been underpinned by the idea that humanity was in constant progress thanks to the development of science and technology; their mission was to subjugate the irrational forces of nature and eradicate ignorance and barbarity. History was there to document progress towards civilization, represented by the national states that guaranteed stability, order, economic growth and cultural development, culminating in their achievements with colonialist expansionism. These cultural stereotypes, which respond to a bourgeois mentality,[3] have been questioned for some time now but they continue to integrate the social representations assumed by a high number of individuals. It is very difficult to overcome them if there is no critical thought based on knowledge.

A new form of history education: post-national history

> The centre of historiography is no longer taken up by the actions of important personalities or the impersonal structures or processes of the economy or society, but rather by the existential experiences of specific individuals, some of whom, as they had no power, had been excluded from traditional history.
>
> Iggers 1998: 15

History education can help develop a capacity for criticism, but not based on just any content. The history that is taught still focuses fundamentally on Europe, with an inflexible chronological structure that is nationalist and androcentric and justified teleologically. There is a sense of crisis in these out-of-date patterns that cause unease among those who still see history as a justification of the present order. The spheres of power, academia and politics do not usually question new emerging social values openly, but they are rejected in practice by excluding them from historical reflection or the school curriculum.

In our opinion, the old historiographical stereotypes must be withdrawn from secondary education, which must play its part in the individual, social education of people. We need to question whether or not the present contents of today's curricula are adequate for educating citizens who are capable of building a more democratic, supportive society. We also need to decide whether or not history education should focus on analysing the genesis and evolution of the major problems that affect us today: those that affect the lives of people, the resources and survival of human beings; their forms of social organization in terms of the family and relations between genders and classes and, of course, those that refer to political co-existence; the relations of power and domination; beliefs, knowledge, culture and art; the reasons why large collectives have been excluded from official history when they reflect and condition the perception of the world. When considering which new contents correspond to the purposes and values we want to develop in our society to overcome the nationalist myths of the past, we also need to examine whether or not traditional strategies are adequate for most of the population to think about their surroundings in a historical way.

Our thesis is that the teaching of history (along with other instruments such as the press and military service) has played a role in the (nationalist) socialization of the population that is inappropriate at the present moment. We therefore propose a teaching of history that fosters critical skills for a new citizenship based on shared democratic values and not on national or religious 'essences'. The process for selecting contents must necessarily take into account chronological and spatial criteria. The importance of contemporary history is fundamental, but events from far-off times can also be highly relevant. As far as spatial criteria are concerned, the relationship between local and global, focused on 'thinking globally and acting locally', is essential. There are few things more universal than the local perspective: we identify and recognize ourselves as part of it. A rigorous, contextualized explanation in our local references is a tool of universality.

According to José A. Marina and María de la Válgoma (2000), 'praising the past is a trick played by those who aspire to become privileged members of society', and we can reformulate it by saying that the rigorous criticism of the past protects us from the deceit of those who seek to perpetuate their privileges. Education cannot relinquish its goal of educating free individuals who are capable of taking their own decisions based on appropriate reasoning feeling that they take part in and are jointly responsible for a project for a free, supportive society in which justice means equality and pluralism means tolerance. Fortunately, we have more and more research on social groups that had been excluded from the traditional discourse of history.

Social exclusion is an important educational problem, concerning which history offers an unfortunate array of tragedies. The best known is that of the Nazi genocides, but in Spain we must not forget the brutal dictatorship maintained by Franco, of which many textbooks continue to exclude the most criminal aspects. Habermas argues (1997: 45–6) that the past, history, can only become *magistra vitae*[4] when it is criticism. At best, it tells us what we shouldn't do. What we learn from are negative experiences.

Being aware of the struggles and difficulties that have existed to achieve certain personal liberties and social rights can help them to be more highly valued by a generation that sees them as something that 'was always there'. To take up their defence, it is important to understand that they are somewhat fragile, recent and not necessarily permanent or the natural result of progress. The desire for a better society in which rights and liberties are augmented and certain limitations and discriminations are overcome is easier if history is analysed to discover what made it possible for other individuals in the past to dream of rights that were unimaginable in their day but which exist at the present time, at least to a certain extent, in our society. Reflecting on forms of violence against women, ethnic, religious or other minorities makes more sense when they are related to the different forms of organization of political power humanity has assumed or that have been imposed on it.

Relations of co-existence established in the core of every human community have always been a source of conflict. The forms of political organization are the expression of how that social conflict has been resolved. An educational proposal that seeks to eradicate the illegitimate use of violence in social and interpersonal relations must present the areas in which conflicts have more frequently been solved by resorting to abuse, terror and force as food for thought at school.

In recent centuries, many people have killed others or have let themselves be killed to promote certain projects of state or to identify themselves with opposing nationalist ideologies. The twenty-first century has begun in a similar way. Although nationalist ideas have not been the only cause, they have been part of almost every armed conflict of the last 150 years. That is why it is urgently necessary for school curricula to include the rational analysis of the different forms of political organization and their consequences for people and, more immediately, the process for building the state and the development of different territorial nationalisms that compete with each other.

The modern states that were the first to consolidate their position did so thanks to coercion and the mobilization of resources for war (Tilly 1990) and not in response to any preliminary project. However, this could be drawn from the teleological explanations that usually fill school textbooks on history and the everyday thought reflected in the media. Providing rigorous information that helps counter these deep-rooted myths is an important task for education. The same thing happens with the essentialism that forms part of most ideas of what the nation is.

The teaching of history must help play down the construction of national identities from a historical point of view and foster the understanding of nationalist phenomena today and the new supranational frameworks. It must also develop the capacity for identifying and (historically) criticizing the mechanisms of integration, subjugation and political participation, involving aspects that cover the analysis of control and participation mechanisms and relations between violence and power. The history of power and nationalisms could stand as a good antidote to state and nationalist essentialisms and as a salutary lesson for the self-satisfied alienation that results from living in the best possible world.

Final considerations

History education is a field of ideological confrontation because it is not neutral and involves choosing between opposing social models. It has often been and still is at the service of power. Those in power will never voluntarily relinquish a form of history education that focuses on generating loyalty or acritical subjugation. The current neoconservative policies represent absolute regression in this sense. The historians and history teachers who assume a commitment to freedom and the rights of most of the population have the difficult task of building a different type of discourse and practice and finding the spaces in which they can be developed. It is a question of providing the key factors behind the problems that most directly affect or concern the majority, building not a history of power, but rather the history of people.

- Can we promote a post-national history education that opposes the survival of teaching routines and age-old cultural traditions based on nationalist myths?
- Should history education question the dominant thought that seeks to become the only form of thought through exclusion or the rejection of any possible alternatives or different points of view?

- Can this task be carried out from the territorial framework of national states?
- Is world history the alternative to national histories? How can we integrate the local dimension into it?

Notes

* This chapter forms part of the COMPSOCIALES (EDU2012-37909-C03-01) project financed by the Ministry of the Economy and Competitiveness of the Spanish Government. The English translation has been subsidized by the *Novos enfoques da análise territorial: implicacións sociais, económicas e formativas* network financed by Xunta de Galicia (Government of the Autonomous Community of Galicia).

1 In most countries; in Spain from 1857.

2 The crisis of national feeling did not exist only in Spain. During a session of the House of Commons on 29 March 1990, the MP John Stokes said, 'At the present time, there is great concern for history education in our schools. Instead of teaching general subjects and important affairs, why don't we return to the good old times when we learned the names of the Kings and Queens of England, battles, facts and all the glorious events of our past by heart?' Prime Minister Margaret Thatcher backed her colleague by insisting on the importance of establishing 'what children should be taught in history' and the convenience of 'children learning about the great events of history' (Stokes 1990, cited in Maestro 1997: 54; See also Thatcher 1993: 595–6, and Phillips 1998: 83–109).

3 Here, we do not use the term 'bourgeois' in the sense used by Marx – a class defined above all by its relationship with means of production – but rather a vital world, a way of thinking and acting which, although related to the circumstances of political and economic power, goes beyond them and influences them (Iggers 1998: 18).

4 *Historia magistra vitae est* is a Latin expression, taken from *De Oratore* (Cicero, 55 BCE), which suggests that 'history is life's teacher'.

References

Álvarez-Junco, J. (2011), *Spanish Identity in the Age of Nations*, Manchester: Manchester University Press.

Forcadell Álvarez, C. (1998), 'Historiografía española e historia nacional: la caída de los mitos nacionalistas [Spanish Historiography and National History: The Fall of Nationalist Myths]', in J. M. Ortiz de Orruño (ed.), *Historia y Sistema Educativo* [History and the Education System], *Ayer* 30 (1998): 141–58. Available online: http://www.ahistcon.org/PDF/numeros/ayer30_HistoriaySistemaEducativo_OrtizdeOrruno.pdf (accessed 24 March 2015).

Gellner, E. (2006), *Nations and Nationalism (New Perspectives on the Past)*, 2nd edn, London: Wiley-Blackwell.

Habermas, J. (1997), *Más allá del Estado Nacional* [Beyond the National State], Madrid: Trotta. (Original title: *Die Normalität einer Berliner Republik: Kleine Politische Schriften VII*. [The Normality of a Berlin Republic: Lesser Political Writings VII], Frankfurt am Main: Suhrkamp Verlag, 1995).

Iggers, G. (1998), *La Ciencia Histórica en el Siglo XX: Las Tendencias Actuales* [The Historical Science in the Twentieth Century: Current Trends], Barcelona: Idea Books.

(Original title: *Geschichtswissenschaft im 20. Jahrhundert: Ein Kritischer Uberblick im Internationalen Zusammenhang* [History in the 20th Century: A Critical Survey of the International Context]), Göttingen: Vandenhoeck und Ruprecht, 1993 (new edition 2007).

López Facal, R. (2000), 'La nación ocultada [The Hidden Nation]', in S. Pérez Garzón (ed.), *La Gestión de la Memoria* [The Management of Memory], Barcelona: Crítica.

López Facal, R. (2014), 'La LOMCE y la competencia histórica [The Ley Orgánica para la Mejora de la Calidad Educativa/the Organic Law for the Improvement of Educational Quality and Historical Competence]', *Ayer* 94 (2): 273–85.

Maestro, P. (1997), 'Historiografía y Enseñanza de la Historia [Historiography and History Teaching]', unpublished doctoral thesis, Alicante: Universidad de Alicante.

Marina, J. A. and Válgoma, M. de la (2000), *La Lucha por la Dignidad* [The Struggle for Dignity], Barcelona: Anagrama.

Núñez Seixas, X. M. (1999), *Los Nacionalismos en la España Contemporánea (siglos XIX y XX)* [Nationalism in Contemporary Spain (XIX and XX Centuries)], Barcelona: Hipòtesi.

Phillips, R. (1998), *History Teaching, Nationhood and the State – A Study in Educational Politics*, London: Cassell.

Sáiz Serrano, J. and López Facal, R. (2012), 'Aprender y argumentar España. La visión de la identidad nacional entre el alumnado al finalizar el bachillerato [Learn and Argue Spain. The Vision of National Identity among Students Finishing High School]', *Didáctica de las Ciencias Experimentales y Sociales* [Teaching Experimental and Social Sciences] 26: 95–120.

Smith, A. D. (1991), *National Identity*, Harmondsworth: Penguin.

Sternberger, D. (1990), *Verfassungspatriotismus* [Constitutional Patriotism], Berlin: Insel Verlag.

Stokes, J. (1990), Prime Minister [Q4 in Question Time], Hansard, Column 668, 29 March. Available online: http://www.publications.parliament.uk/pa/cm198990/cmhansrd/1990-03-29/Orals-2.html (accessed 7 August 2015).

Thatcher, M. (1993), *The Downing Street Years*, London: HarperCollins*Publishers*.

Tilly, C. (1990), *Coercion, Capital and European States. A.D. 990–1990*, Oxford and Cambridge: Basil Blackwell (Spanish translation: *Coerción, capital y los Estados europeos*, 900–1990, Madrid: Alianza).

Weber, E. (1976), *Peasants into Frenchmen: Modernization of Rural France, 1870–1914*, Stanford, CA: Stanford University Press.

13

Discussant on Part 3 – Comparative Settings – Federations, Shared Histories and Emerging Democracies

Robert Guyver

The third part of the book is relatively short but includes broad transnational comparisons, Australia with Russia and an intranational case study, Spain. Tony Taylor uses the descriptions 'liberal' democracy and 'illiberal' democracy, and in his chapter draws parallels between the political lives of John Howard and Vladimir Putin. The workings of Australia's kind of democracy prevented John Howard from imposing a certain kind of history curriculum on Australia's states. What followed his departure from power in December 2007 was the setting up of a curriculum body (ultimately, ACARA: Australian Curriculum Assessment and Reporting Authority) which became operational from May 2009, and prided itself on its professionalism, neutrality and distance from central political power.

Spain, Russia and Australia have all experienced political change since the beginning of the last quarter of the twentieth century. In Spain there was a transition from dictatorship under Franco to a constitutional monarchy with more features of democracy. Australia's rather harsh attitudes towards its Indigenous peoples and towards immigrants softened with such developments as the initiation of 'Sorry Day' (26 May, from 1998). In some academic circles this went even further, and questions were being asked about whether Australia's espoused values were in fact false, based as they were on mistreatment or even 'genocide' of Aboriginal and Torres Strait Islander peoples. Right-wing political opposition to liberal trends in Australia was, according to Taylor, similar to such trends seen in Russia, especially after Russia's loss of political prestige following the break-up of the Soviet Union in the early 1990s.

Spain, rather along the same lines as Greece and Turkey, at various stages sought to reinvent itself by reclaiming heroic eras of its past and appropriating them to the present. However, going against these trends, Ramón López Facal and Jorge Sáiz Serrano make a strong case for a different kind of history education to support principles of co-existence in what has become a plurinational, even post-national Spain. They examine how peripheral nationalisms as autonomous communities have become a political reality alongside a central nationalism, providing flexible and to a large extent tolerated alternatives which also work – perhaps, as forms of resistance to it. Again, like the authors of the chapter on Turkey and Greece, what they recommend is a history education the main focus of which is not on political or military power, but on the lives of ordinary people across these intranational communities, and setting their experiences not just in the local or the national but also in global contexts.

Ramón López Facal and Jorge Sáiz Serrano see the importance of another strand which has emerged as important not only in Australia but also elsewhere, for example in England, Northern Ireland, New Zealand, the Republic of Ireland and South Africa, in debates about the relationship between national history and the principles of democratic citizenship. This is the idea of using a critical pedagogy, historical thinking and historical literacy to educate future citizens who can use critical powers to exercise discriminating judgement in deciding whether or not history is being presented by politicians in a distortingly hegemonic way. This runs counter to the notion of creating a canon or list of events which shows a 'glorious' past, but here the authors are emphasizing a different kind of exceptionalism, in that the development of a society in which such debates can happen, rather in the way that Simon Schama noted that difference and division were to be celebrated as Britain's strengths, is a kind of counter-canon. Thus debate itself is something that needs to be seen both as an outcome of democratic development and as the very process whereby a liberal democracy is established.

In Tony Taylor's comparison of John Howard and Vladimir Putin it becomes clear that both men had a strong belief in the role of history education to seal a link between an exceptionalist national narrative and the creation of loyal, patriotic citizens who had a certainty and clarity about the trajectory of the nation, based to a large extent on an honourable past, if not an always glorious one. The element of military history is combined in this with what Anna Clark refers to as a form of 'national spiritualism' (see Chapter 15), which may well be reinforced through connections with family members' experiences of wars fought on behalf of the nation. Both men had fathers who had fought in World Wars. Both men had a pride in their homelands which they regarded as being under threat: in Australia from within; in Russia from both within and without.

There is a political story and a curriculum story behind what happened in Australia. The first is marked by how the development of Australia's national history curriculum from the time of the Cronulla riots (December 2005) through to the history curriculum summit of August 2006, and beyond to John Howard's loss of power and the setting up of ACARA, became an example of a liberal democracy in action, with certain groups ensuring that there are checks and balances preventing politicians from imposing their will on federal governments. The curriculum story in Australia is one very similar to what happened to Michael Gove's draft curriculum in the UK in February 2013: a very detailed canon of national events was rewritten by historians and curriculum experts to transform it into a framework for enquiry that provided a chronological core with exits and entrances. John Hirst, a respected Australian historian based at La Trobe University in Melbourne, said at the famous summit that what was needed was a structure for 'landmarks with questions'. This in essence offers a bridge between that part of a history curriculum that is nationally focused and a democratic approach.

John Howard did not get his way because of the political system in Australia, and ultimately also its electoral system, through the workings of which his party lost office and he personally lost his parliamentary seat. Vladimir Putin, however, was in succession president, prime minister and president again in a nation state with very limited checks on his power. His wish for school textbooks to be in general use which would reflect his own interpretation of Russian history could be translated quite easily into action. His motives seemed to be laudable – he did not want the Russian people or even their history teachers to be confused about the Russian past. This ties in with what Tamara Eidelman, Polina Verbytska and Jonathan Even-Zohar wrote in Chapter 2 about the Russian film director, Karen Shakhnazarov, who was reported to say that he did not want Russian children to be told the national equivalent of very bad things about their parents' lives. But of course this is a form of denial and ties in with Vladimir Putin's wish to stress the 'bright spots' of Russia's past. The impossibility of discussing events which have contributed to a traumatic past has been seen in other chapters (especially the chapter on South Africa and Rwanda) as ultimately having a negative effect when these events should be remembered and not forgotten.

Observations about developments in post-Franco Spain are useful when trying to analyse what is *not* happening in Russia, and in a way by providing a counter-narrative also suggest some ways ahead. For historical reasons Spain has avoided the word 'federalism', which is associated with the (anti-monarchist) Republican historical tradition. Currently, political parties of the left, from the PSOE (Partido Socialista Obrero Español, the Spanish Socialist Workers' Party) to the leftmost, are calling for a federal constitutional amendment. Clearly Russia is seeking to assert a strong centralizing power and the idea of relinquishing influence over the constituent parts of the Federation would seem to have economic as well as intellectual and educational consequences.

Ramón López Facal and Jorge Sáiz Serrano touch on a theme which is running through this whole book when they stress that it is important to look at the lives of ordinary people across internal borders, and to assess the impact on their lives of the decisions of politicians or military figures.

The fact that there is a strong national public discourse about the history curriculum in Australia and in Spain contrasts with the situation in Russia, although in Chapter 2 it has been seen that a famous Russian psychologist, Lyudmila Petranovskaya (2014), has warned the country about the negative effects of the 'Weimar syndrome'. The comments noted by Forcadell (1998) in the Spain chapter that the whole purpose of history education was to produce critical citizens capable of sustaining a democracy are deeply significant.

References

Forcadell Álvarez, C. (1998), 'Spanish Historiography and National History: The Fall of Nationalist Myths', in J. M. Ortiz de Orruño (ed.), *Historia y Sistema Educativo* [History and the Education System], *Ayer* 30: 141–58 (Spanish text).

Petranovskaya, L. (2014), Blog entry, 28 June. Available online: http://ludmilapsyholog.livejournal.com/235045.html (accessed 9 March 2015).

Part 4

Shared History as a Transnational and Intranational Landmark with Questions

14

Turkey, Australia and Gallipoli: The Challenges of a Shared History

Jennifer Lawless and Sedat Bulgu

Gallipoli and the Anzac legend

Australia and Turkey share a momentous historical event that occurred at the beginning of the First World War – the Gallipoli campaign of 1915. For both countries, this campaign has taken on considerable importance in the development of each nation state. In Australia, the day of the invasion of the Gallipoli peninsula, 25 April, is a national holiday, Anzac Day.[1] The aim of the day is to remember and honour Australians who died in all wars. The major focus of the day is the dawn service held near the site of the original landing on the Gallipoli peninsula in Turkey and has become an ideal venue for Australian politicians to reinforce a sense of Australian nationalism. The celebration of Anzac Day declined in popularity during Australia's involvement in the Vietnam War during the 1960s and early 1970s. However, since the 1980s, politicians have been keen to promote this idealist image of the Gallipoli campaign as an integral part of Australia's national identity. All capital cities in Australia host Anzac ceremonies and marches on the day. Suburbs and country towns throughout Australia also commemorate Anzac Day with a dawn service often centring around a local war memorial recording the names of local men who died in wars.

In Turkey, the victory against the invading Allied navy is celebrated on 18 March and is known as the Çanakkale Victory. The Gallipoli campaign is also linked closely to the creation of the Turkish Republic, as its founder, Mustafa Kemal, was a prominent commander in defence of the Gallipoli peninsula. He became the first Turkish Republic President, known as Atatürk – the father of the Turks. With the centenary of the campaign in 2015, there will be more focus on this event than ever before in both countries.

A large part of the Australian Anzac Day celebrations is the underpinning 'Anzac legend'. In Australia, this tradition has developed since the fateful landing in 1915. It celebrates the alleged 'typical' qualities of the Australian soldier as displayed during the Gallipoli campaign, based on the characteristics of the Australian bushman – resourceful and courageous, with a dislike of authority, a sense of humour and a strong sense of 'mateship'. Part of the legend argues that the Gallipoli campaign was a 'baptism of fire' for the young nation, only thirteen years old, and that Australia proved itself internationally on the shores of the peninsula. The legend was developed and supported by the official First World War historian, Charles Bean. It was also exploited by the Australian government of the time as official propaganda to encourage recruitment to the army. Bean went on to help establish the Australian War Memorial, Canberra, further enshrining the legend and ensuring its continuation.

Generally the Turkish experience of the campaign is not part of the Anzac legend, and little is said of the bravery of the Turkish soldiers defending their homeland from invasion. In Australia, the enormous casualty rates among the Turkish soldiers is often overlooked. Approximately 86,000 Turks were killed and 251,000 were either wounded or were missing. Little has been said of the number of farms, villages, towns and hospitals damaged or destroyed by Allied bombardments, resulting in the deaths of many citizens. In comparison, 8,700 Australians were killed and 27,700 wounded. Australian casualty rates were much higher when the troops went on to fight on the Western Front in Europe.

How did two countries so far removed by distance, history, culture and religion come to share a history so important to both country's concept of national identity?

What was known of 'the other'?

For centuries the Ottoman Empire occupied a vast territory that stretched from Iran to Vienna. In the Crimean War (1854–6) Turkey sided with Britain and France against Russia. However, in the years leading up to the First World War, relations with Britain soured and the Empire was weakened by a series of nationalist revolts and uprisings. Prior to the outbreak of war, Germany actively wooed Turkey and it became a German ally. Britain declared war on Turkey on 31 October 1914 and Australians joined the Allied invasion of the Gallipoli peninsula on 25 April 1915. This followed an unsuccessful Allied naval attack in March that was planned to pave the way for the capture of the Turkish capital, İstanbul.

Prior to the Gallipoli campaign in 1915, Turks and Australians knew little about each other and certainly had no reason to go to war. There were few Turks living in Australia, and, as a member of the British Empire, Australian attitudes to the Turks reflected British views. Whilst researching Gallipoli veterans in 1991, Turkish Professor Mete Tunçoku found that the majority of Australian Gallipoli veterans admitted knowing nothing of Turks before being sent to fight at Gallipoli. 'I must confess that the only thing I knew about the Turks was Turkish cigarettes,' stated one veteran (Tunçoku 2005).[2] The Muslim world was also regarded with suspicion by the Western Christian nations. Contemporary Australian attitudes are suggested by a description of Turks in an Australian primary school textbook written in 1899: 'A cruel and ignorant race . . . one of the most fanatical of the Mohammedan race, the ferocity of the "unspeakable Turk" in gaining converts being unsurpassed by any other race' (Firth 1970: 130).

Generally, the Turkish population knew very little about Australians. Initially, they believed that the invading army was British. When several of the Australians captured as prisoners of war at Gallipoli were initially interrogated, their Turkish captors often asked why they had travelled halfway around the world to invade their land (Conk 1947).

Teaching of Gallipoli in New South Wales, Australia

The focus on Gallipoli in school history in Australia has increased over the years. The state of New South Wales (NSW) will be the focus of the following discussion as it is the most populous state and the only state to mandate history studies in secondary schools for the past three decades. Other states during this period adopted an integrated approach to teaching Social Science, including history and geography, generally labelled SOSE – Studies of Society and the Environment.

In NSW, the study of the First World War, including Gallipoli, has been a focus for over seventy years. In 1954 the senior Modern History syllabus offered the topic 'The World War: causes, events and results'. Content suggested for the study of the First World War changed little over the next few decades. However, in 1992, the Years 7–10 NSW History syllabus introduced broad thematic topics, two of which included a study of 'Gallipoli and the Anzac tradition':

- What have been the major influences on how Australians regard themselves today?
- What have been the significant relationships between Australian and other countries over the last two centuries?

In 1999, a revised NSW Years 7–10 History syllabus eliminated the study of broad themes and comprised specific topics organized chronologically, including *Australia and World War I*. Within that topic was a mandatory study of the Gallipoli campaign and an analysis of the Anzac legend. This topic also included the following Inquiry Questions:

- Why did Australia become involved in World War I?
- What were the main aspects of Australia's involvement in the Gallipoli campaign?
- How did events at Gallipoli create the Anzac legend?

After teacher complaints of the crowded nature of the content in this syllabus, a revised syllabus was written in 2002. However, little was changed on the topic of the First World War and Gallipoli. The topic continued to be called *Australia and World War I*, retaining the first Inquiry Question and rewording the other two:

- What were the experiences of Australians in the Gallipoli campaign?
- How and why was the Anzac legend created?

The specific content concerning the Gallipoli campaign focused on the use of a variety of historical sources including a database or website, encouraging a more analytical approach to the 'legend'.

As well as content, over the past few decades NSW students also learned to apply historical skills and develop an understanding of historical concepts, in line with best practice in historical teaching, particularly influenced by reforms in historical teaching in Britain, the United States and Canada.[3] An enquiry approach was encouraged, together with a greater focus on source analysis and historical thinking. The skills of the 2002 syllabus were specified as:

- comprehension
- analysis and use of sources
- perspectives and interpretations
- empathetic understanding
- research skills
- communication skills.

Historical skills were clarified further for each topic, including for the topic *World War I*:

- sequence events within the time period;
- identify perspectives of different individuals and groups;
- interpret history within the context of the actions, values, attitudes and motives of people from the past;
- identify, comprehend and use historical sources as part of an historical inquiry;
- select and use appropriate text forms to communicate effectively about the past.

In December 2010, an Australia-wide history curriculum was published after considerable political debate over the years.

Debate over the Australian curriculum

The national political debate over what should be taught in Australian history in every state has raised its head on several occasions over the years. Debate heated up in 2003 with the so-called 'history wars', with conservative claims that school history was inadequate and taught by left-wing demagogues. In 2006 the conservative Prime Minister, John Howard declared that it was time for a renewal of the teaching of Australian history in schools, as it was too concerned with 'a fragmented stew' of themes and issues. Soon after (August 2006), a National History Summit was convened in Canberra to develop a national, narrative-based and chronological school history. The suggestions that arose from the summit were widely debated but finally did not produce a national curriculum, though a *Guide to the Teaching of Australian History in Years 9 and 10* (11 October 2007) was published with 77 mandatory 'Milestone' events, including the Gallipoli campaign.[4]

In November 2007, a Labor government came to power and the development of a National Curriculum for English, Mathematics, Science and History commenced. The new Australian History Curriculum, Kindergarten to Year 10, was published in 2010. It includes a Depth Study on the First World War, with the specific content 'The commemoration of World War I, including debates about the nature and significance of the Anzac legend'. New South Wales adopted the Australian curriculum but made some minor adjustments. The following content concerning the Gallipoli campaign in NSW is mandatory:

- describe the nature of warfare during the Gallipoli campaign;
- explain the outcome of the Gallipoli campaign;
- commemorations and the nature of the Anzac legend;
- explain how and why Australians have commemorated the wars;
- explain different perspectives on the Anzac legend.

There is still a strong focus on the development of historical skills and further focus on developing an understanding of historical concepts. There is considerable scope for teaching a Turkish perspective of the campaign. The understanding of specific concepts is a mandatory part of the syllabus and for each stage of learning, and examples of the concepts to be taught are suggested, including specific references to Gallipoli for Years 9 and 10:

- **perspectives**: the reasons for different perspectives in a particular historical context e.g. Turkish and Australian views of the Gallipoli campaign;
- **significance**: the reasons why the importance of an event, development or individual may change over time, e.g. commemoration of Anzac Day;
- **contestability**: historical sources, events or issues may be interpreted differently by historians depending on their perspectives and methods of inquiry.

Board of Studies, NSW 2012: 21

However, the current conservative Liberal government once again commenced a review of this National Curriculum in January 2014 with an aim to 'strengthen the curriculum'. The final report was published in October 2014 with the recommendation for History:

- History should be revised in order to properly recognise the impact and significance of Western civilisation and Australia's Judeo-Christian heritage, values and beliefs.
- A revision of the choice available throughout the curriculum should be conducted to ensure that students are covering all the key periods of Australian history, especially that of the nineteenth century.

Department of Education 2014: 181

It is not probable that NSW will heed any likely changes to arise from this promised review. So, currently, a study of the Gallipoli campaign is mandatory for all NSW students, with a focus not just on the content but also on enquiry learning based on the development of historical skills and concepts, and, particularly relevant for a Gallipoli study, perspectives and empathetic understanding.

In reality, how does this play out in the classroom for students of Turkish heritage?

Turks in Australia

For a multicultural nation, the notion of a 'shared' history becomes a complex one in the classroom. The 2011 Australian census noted 66,919 Australian residents claiming

Turkish ancestry, with 32,847 having been born in Turkey. Over the years, Turks and Australians have come to know each other better. A Turkish Embassy in Canberra was opened in 1967 and an Australian Embassy in Ankara in 1968. The first official Australian government-sponsored Turkish migrants arrived in Australia in 1968. Many were unskilled and worked in factories, providing labour for the much-needed manufacturing workforce. A number of governmental visits have been made to both Australia and Turkey over the years, with increased trade developing between the two countries.

Being regarded as a former enemy, initially citizens of Turkish descent were not allowed to march on Anzac Day. In Sydney in 1972, nine Turks marched in the Anzac parade under the banner 'Turkish Australians. Friendship will never die' (Fewster et al. 2003: 17). It took some time for Turkish marchers to be accepted in all cities. Some Turkish organizations commemorated their own ceremonies for Anzac Day. The mosque in the Sydney suburb of Auburn was named the 'Gallipoli Mosque' in a generous gesture by the local Muslim community.

The challenge for teachers of history lies in the dilemma of how this topic may be taught in a democratic setting that includes citizens from 'the other side'. How can the notion of 'nation' deeply embedded in the curriculum be made accessible for all? Should the topic be approached in the classroom from a national point of view or through a transnational lens? Gallipoli is certainly a national 'landmark' for both Australia and Turkey. It requires a range of teaching approaches based on an understanding of the issues and content knowledge of the Gallipoli campaign.

How is a Turkish perspective included?

Considering the political and nationalistic focus on Gallipoli in the history syllabus over the years in NSW, how encompassing is the inclusion of Turkish material, sources and perspectives in the classroom, considering that the relevant historical skills and concepts have been mandatory for some time? An analysis of a range of textbooks reveals that little is included on the Turkish experience. In Australia, there are no government-sponsored textbooks. Large publishing firms vie with each other for the secondary history textbook market. Over time, textbooks have gradually included more content on Gallipoli, in line with changes to the NSW History syllabuses and now the Australian curriculum since 2010.

In 1994, typically textbooks devoted approximately two pages to the topic, with only passing reference to the Turks: 'The landing at Gallipoli took place on 25 April and cost 2,300 Australian lives'; the cliffs above the beach landing were 'defended by Turks with machine guns' (Nichols et al. 1994: 184). There is never a hint that the 'landing' was in fact an invasion of another land. Similar treatment of the topic was included in a text published in 1998. Two pages were devoted to Gallipoli, including: 'On 25 April 1915, the Allied forces rowed ashore at a place later called Anzac Cove, where they met with fierce initial resistance from waiting Turkish gunmen.' Accompanying student exercises, including an empathetic task, were based solely on the Australian experience (Engwerda and Cotter 1998: 152).

In response to the revised 1999 NSW History syllabus, which included an examination of the Anzac legend, textbooks began to include more detail on Gallipoli.

In 2000, a popular text focused on the Anzac legend and devoted eight pages to the campaign, which was actually referred to as an 'invasion'. In an attempt to include a Turkish perspective, an empathetic writing task asked students to 'rewrite the source from the point of view of a Turkish soldier or reporter'. However, with no earlier reference to Turkish experiences or inclusion of any Turkish sources, the exercise encouraged creative or imaginative writing rather than an exercise in historical empathy. No Turkish perspective is offered in the discussion of the 'legend' (Anderson and Ashton 2000: 87–9).

One text attempted to include more Turkish material for the 1999 syllabus. The Gallipoli campaign took up twelve pages, and included a reference to the British command underestimating the Turkish forces at Gallipoli and a note that the Turkish celebrations of the campaign took place on 18 March. It refers to the site of Gallipoli, including mention of the various Turkish war monuments and cemeteries, and describes the campaign as an invasion: 'Thus the Australian forces were to take part in the invasion of another land – an aspect of the Anzac tradition that is often forgotten.' Using several Turkish sources, an exercise on differing perspectives is included. Accompanying photos include those of Turkish soldiers and Turkish monuments to the dead at Gallipoli. The words of Atatürk that are inscribed on a monument above Anzac Cove are also included. A final task requires students to 'Design an inscription for a monument at Anzac Cove for both the Australian and Turkish soldiers killed' (Cameron, Lawless and Young 2000: 44–52).

In response to the revised 2002 NSW History syllabus, one text attempted to involve students in an analysis of the Turkish experience; yet, without any background content or sources, it would have been difficult for students to go beyond a creative writing task. Under the heading *Perspectives*, students are asked 'In what ways would a Turkish soldier's experience at Gallipoli be similar to and different from that of an Australian soldier?' Again, in dealing with *Empathetic Understanding*, students are asked: 'What do you think would have been the attitude of the ANZACs towards the Turks at this time?' Despite the attempt to include a Turkish perspective, with the lack again of specific relevant content or sources, the exercises are not reflecting historical empathy or perspectives (Anderson and Ashton 2004: 65).

Over the past few decades, the Australian government, through the Department of Veterans' Affairs, has published a number of resources on the Australian experiences of war, and of Gallipoli in particular. These resources have been sent to all schools throughout Australia and celebrate Australia's military history. In 2005 it published a comprehensive resource focusing on both the First and Second World Wars, called *Operation CLICK: Anzac to Kokoda*, which was closely connected to a website, *Visit Gallipoli* (www.anzacsite.gov.au). By linking this resource to a website, material could be updated and altered over time. Student exercises encouraged a broad and analytical use of sources and the application of research skills. A major innovation was introduced from 2005 with the material on the website translated into Turkish by the author (Sedat Bulgu). This resulted in thousands of 'hits' from Turkish speakers and hopefully from Australian students of Turkish heritage. Further material in Turkish is to be added in the future and it is hoped that more Turkish sources may also be included.

In 2012, to meet the needs of the Australian curriculum, another popular text attempted to broaden the Turkish content, devoting nine pages to the campaign. It included a photo of Mustafa Kemal and an attempt to include a Turkish perspective:

> For the ordinary Turkish soldier it was very clear why they were fighting – enemies were attempting to defeat them and to take their land. Like all attacking armies in World War I, the Turks suffered terribly from the power of Allied machine guns, artillery and rifle fire. In addition, the Turkish soldiers faced the same environmental hardships as the ANZACs, including the lack of water, the swarms of flies, the cold and the heat.
>
> The ANZACs developed a grudging respect for the Turkish soldiers. During the major Turkish offensive of May 1915, in which approximately 3,000 Turkish soldiers died and 7,000 were wounded, the Turks had shown great courage and determination in persisting with their attacks. It is estimated that 100,000 Turks were killed and another 250,000 wounded in the Dardanelles campaign. These figures dwarf the losses incurred by the Allied countries. (Greer et al. 2012: 335–43)

In the lead-up to the centenary celebration of the campaign in 2015, the Australian government, again through the Department of Veterans' Affairs, published two teaching kits distributed to every school in Australia – both primary and secondary schools. Beautifully presented, they focused on how schools might conduct the commemorative events of Anzac Day 2015, various 'investigations' that students could undertake and some sources to be used. There is also an excellent guide on preserving and presenting war memorabilia. Various exercises are aligned with the Australian History Curriculum, focusing on the First World War Depth Study. It acknowledges that 'the Turks were defending their homeland'. A classroom exercise in writing about 'different perspectives' includes a photo of a Turkish soldier, an Australian soldier and a senior British officer. Students may choose one to write about, However, sources are provided for the Australian experience and some British, but there are no sources for the Turkish experience. Thus if students chose the Turkish experience they would have no relevant sources upon which to base their writing (Department of Veterans' Affairs 2014)

So, from a Turkish perspective, though textbooks have improved somewhat over the years, there is still limited material for teachers to draw upon. Even if Turkish students choose to read the official Gallipoli website in their own language, there is a need for ready access to Turkish sources to enable a more detailed understanding of the Turkish experiences at Gallipoli.

A random sample of fifteen NSW history teachers were asked in December 2014 about their attempts at introducing a Turkish perspective in their classrooms and their responses varied. An experienced Head of History teacher from a semi-rural secondary school had travelled widely in the Middle East, including Turkey. His school has no students with Turkish ancestry, yet he strongly felt the specific need to introduce a Turkish perspective to challenge their Anglo-Australian views. He noted: 'Some feel uncomfortable with this, yet they need to be challenged.' He drew resources from articles published by the Australian War Memorial magazine *Wartime*, the Atatürk memorial at Anzac Cove and resources from a Turkish colleague. He also used a Turkish film, *Çanakkale 1915* (2012), with English subtitles and the Peter Weir film *Gallipoli* (1981), starring Mel Gibson, as a comparative film study analysing historical accuracy, with the comment 'I like myth-busting!' For the 2015 Anzac Day school ceremony, he planned to fly the Australian, New Zealand and Turkish flags.

Another experienced history teacher noted that her approach to teaching Gallipoli changed dramatically after she had visited the site. 'I became much more aware of the Turkish experience and was overwhelmed by the generosity of the Turkish people, welcoming the ancestors of their former enemy. I try to explain to my students that it is a very unusual situation to have a country welcoming a former enemy each year to commemorate the invasion of their land.' Students reacted very positively to her personal stories and photographs from Gallipoli. She noted that teachers generally needed more resources to teach the Turkish side of the campaign adequately.

Most of the teachers interviewed stated that they generally used textbooks for this topic and that the Turkish perspective was often lacking. They were not aware of any other resource that might provide an alternative view. One stated that they used Atatürk's inscription, and some used Weir's film *Gallipoli*. Some used the official Gallipoli website to conduct a site study online. However, several stated that they hadn't even considered a Turkish perspective and had not studied the First World War at university and felt inadequate in the content knowledge required. Several stated that further professional development for teachers was required and access to Turkish sources needed to be made available.

Two history teachers of Turkish ancestry were determined to provide more depth in addressing varying perspectives and interpretations. One who had received an NSW Premier's History Scholarship utilized the funding to further research a Turkish view of Gallipoli at Çanakkale. She explained: 'I endeavour to echo the sentiments and great vision of Mustafa Kemal Atatürk. My programmes aim to provide a balanced perspective of the Gallipoli campaign during the First World War. My lessons attempt to address conditions for both sides of the war. The difficulty I face is the lack of published Turkish material in the English language.' She introduced several documentaries, including *Gallipoli: The First Day* (2009) and Turkish director Tolga Örnek's *Gelibolu* [*Gallipoli*] (2005). She added: 'I am very proud to be Australian; but I am also aware of trying to demonstrate the very important skills of balance and perspectives to my students. I would like to think that I allow my students to soak up both sides of the campaign.' Generally there are no Turkish heritage students in her middle-class urban school.

The second teacher of Turkish ancestry teaches in a lower socio-economic suburb of Sydney with students from a variety of ethnic backgrounds. He stated that he 'always provided a Turkish perspective', referring to place names on the peninsula with both their Turkish and English names.

> Although our syllabus doesn't necessarily have an option for the Turkish perspective, I feel it is very important for students to gain an understanding of who the ANZACs were fighting against and how the Turks came out of the war. Also,

> as the person responsible for our Anzac Day ceremony at school, I usually provide a short speech from the Turkish perspective and mention a few of Atatürk's words.

He also noted that few teachers he had taught with presented a Turkish view of Gallipoli and that the lack of specific education and the lack of resources was an issue.

So what have been the experiences of Turkish students studying Gallipoli in NSW classrooms?

A brief review of fifteen Turkish students has indicated some disquiet. Many felt uncomfortable in class at being described as 'the enemy' and lamented the 'lack of a Turkish perspective and biased treatment of the campaign'. One noted that 'he complained strongly about the negative view presented in the textbooks when it was Australians who travelled all the way to Turkey, to attack them and then called us enemies'.

One recalled an incident in class:

> I remember clearly that my Year 9 teacher said that Australians won the war! She was so passionate when she said this. I couldn't take it anymore and I stood up and questioned her: 'In what aspect do you believe that Australians won the war?' She literally froze and could not answer my question. I told her if there is a winner that is Turkey, a country that was isolated and fighting against many countries and Turks trying to protect their land with minimal food and with hardly any weapons are the ones who can be called the winners. In all due respect your coming to invade a country and as a result Turkey was not invaded hence you cannot say that Australians won the war!' She apologized.
>
> When I stood up and defended how Turkey won the war an Australian boy in my class told me to go back to where I came from, and I replied saying 'at least I have a country to go back to which I'm proud of'. Even though my teacher was Australian, she sent him to be disciplined for being a racist. Racism was definitely not tolerated. However, I strongly believe that young Turkish Australians with little knowledge about what happened in Gallipoli will find it difficult to stand up front and stop misleading information from being taught in schools.

Another group of students recalled that the overall impression they had gained was that 'the Turks slaughtered everyone and mistreated them'. One student noted that 'even though they are the ones who invaded Turkey, they still made it out as if we were the bad guys'.

The sample of fifteen Turkish students was obviously a small one and their experiences may not be typical of all. However, they were drawn from schools of differing locations and cohorts and their comments suggest that their collective experience of Gallipoli in the classroom was not a comfortable one. It demonstrates that again further resources and teacher professional development are needed.

An interesting resource that may be introduced into future history lessons on Gallipoli is the film *The Water Diviner*, directed by Russell Crowe, screened first in

Australian theatres on 26 December 2014. It presents the Turks at Gallipoli in a more favourable light and could be an interesting addition to the study of perspectives. In an interview in a popular Australian magazine, Crowe acknowledged that he knew little about the Turkish experiences before he commenced the film:

> We all know how many ANZACs were lost at Gallipoli, but I didn't know about the Turks. And it wasn't the number that I was surprised by, it was the fact that I didn't know. It was intriguing to me, embarrassing, I suppose, that I didn't know the number. And 100 years later, it's time to be a little bit more open in terms of the Turkish perspective. They have shown us great kindness over time, allowing us to have the bodies of our children buried in their soil . . . It's OK, 100 years later, to understand that we invaded a sovereign country that had never done anything wrong to us.
>
> quoted in Overington 2015: 60–65

This quite extraordinary statement coming from a respected actor may contribute to changed perceptions of the Turkish experience in the broader Australian community and classrooms.

The unique yearly pilgrimage of thousands of Australians to the dawn service for Anzac Day at Gallipoli is also experienced by school groups each year, contributing to a broader understanding of the Turkish experience. In 2015, one hundred school students were sponsored by the Australian government to attend. Most local Turks are intrigued by the numbers of Australians who attend the Anzac ceremony each year. Despite the misgivings some teachers and students of Turkish heritage have about the teaching of Gallipoli in Australia, it is interesting to read one Turkish observer's comment. The following is a newspaper account of Australians attending the ceremony in 2012, written by Turkish journalist Mehmet Tez:

> It is almost entirely a young group. They uphold their history and remember their losses with emotion in an entirely positive way. I don't know what the *Plus 4* [the Turkish education system is divided into four-year periods] in their education system is, but it doesn't look half bad to me. During the dawn ceremony one feels that they do not just remember the ANZACs but everybody who died in all wars. Humanity is the real theme of the ceremony . . . Another success of this ceremony worth appreciating was during the commemoration, there is always a reminder that Turks lost their lives here . . . To cut it short: 100 years ago these people were killing one another at this very place. Today one wearing a 'Çanakkale is impassable' hat is selling chicken rolls to the one wearing an 'Anzac Day' T-shirt at 4 am. The moral of all these things for me is: Whoever said 'Make love not war' was right.

Conclusion

With the introduction of the new Australian History Curriculum and its mandatory inclusion of the Gallipoli campaign, it is timely to consider emphasizing the importance of a Turkish perspective in the classroom for the edification of both Australian and Turkish-heritage students. A brief review of a number of textbooks in New South Wales shows a gradual increase in awareness of the need to introduce varying perspectives in the study of the Gallipoli campaign. Many experienced teachers attempt to broaden their lessons on Gallipoli to include a Turkish perspective. However, it is obvious that some teachers do not present a Turkish perspective of Gallipoli in their classrooms, and some Turkish students feel uncomfortable with the views presented. It is hoped that with the increased focus on the Gallipoli campaign's centenary in 2015 there will be an increased awareness of the need for more Turkish resources to be made available for the classroom. As the NSW syllabus and Australian curriculum have increased the emphasis on the understanding of historical concepts such as perspectives and historical empathy, there is considerable scope for increasing the focus on the Turkish experience. The authors plan to publish a collection of translated Turkish sources and student activities for use in the classroom that will hopefully make the teaching of this shared history more accessible – for all students.

Notes

1 The term 'ANZAC' refers to the combined military forces of Australia and New Zealand – the Australian and New Zealand Army Corps.
2 *Mehmetçik* is a Turkish word for soldier based on the diminutive form of a very common name in Turkey, Mehmet; this usage has a similar connotation to 'Tommy' in the UK, i.e. an ordinary soldier. In the context of the Tunçoku book title it also has the meaning of 'anonymous', as in the concept of the 'unknown warrior'; one of several Mehmetçik monuments in Turkey is on the Gallipoli Peninsula.
3 NSW History teaching was greatly influenced by the innovations of the British Schools History Project and history educators such as D. Shemilt, P. Seixas, S. Wineburg, P. Lee and R. Ashby.
4 For further reading on this development, see Taylor (2012) and Chapter 11 in this volume.

References

Anderson, M. and Ashton, P. (2000), *Australian History and Citizenship*, Melbourne: Macmillan.
Anderson, M. and Ashton, P. (2004), *Australia in the Twentieth Century: Working Historically*, Melbourne: Macmillan.
Board of Studies, New South Wales (2012), *NSW Syllabus for the Australian Curriculum: History K-10*, NSW Board of Studies.
Cameron, K., Lawless, J. and Young, C. (2000), *Investigating Australia's 20th Century History*, Melbourne: Nelson.
Çanakkale 1915 (2012), [Film] Dir. Yesim Sezgin, Turkey: Tiglon Film (Theatrical).
Conk, C. (1947), *Memoirs*, İstanbul: Canli Tarihler.
Department of Education (2014), *Review of the Australian Curriculum: Final Report*, Canberra: Department of Education, Australian Government.

Department of Veterans' Affairs (2005a), *Gallipoli and the Anzacs*, Department of Veterans' Affairs, Australian Government. Available online: http://www.anzacsite.gov.au (accessed 12 March 2015).

Department of Veterans' Affairs (2005b), 'Operation CLICK: Anzac to Kokoda', *Gallipoli and the Anzacs*, Department of Veterans' Affairs, Australian Government. Available online: http://www.anzacsite.gov.au/operationclick (accessed 12 March 2015).

Department of Veterans' Affairs (2014) *We Remember Anzac*, Secondary Resource, Canberra: Department of Veterans' Affairs, Australian Government. Available online: http://www.anzacportal.dva.gov.au/sites/default/files/publication-attachments/WE%20REMEMBER%20ANZAC%20(SEC)_0.pdf (accessed 3 January 2015).

Engwerda, R. and Cotter, R. (1998), *Australian History to 1957*, Queensland: Jacaranda.

Fewster, K., Başarin, H. and Başarin, V. (2003), *Gallipoli: The Turkish Story*, Sydney: Allen & Unwin.

Firth, S. G. (1970), 'Social Values in the NSW Primary School, 1880–1914: An Analysis of School Texts', in R.J.W. Selleck (ed.), *Melbourne Studies in Education*, 123–59, Carlton: Melbourne University Press.

Gallipoli (1981), [Film] Dir. Peter Weir, Australia and New Zealand: Village Roadshow.

Gallipoli: The First Day (2009), [Documentary film] Dir. Sam Doust, Australia: Australian Broadcasting Corporation (ABC). Available online: www.abc.net.au/gallipoli (accessed 5 January 2015).

Gelibolu [Gallipoli] (2005) [Documentary film] Dir. Tolga Örnek, Turkey: Dogus Group (released in Australia as *Gallipoli: The Frontline Experience*).

Greer, V., with Bowman, R., Cameron, K., Fielden, P., Gates, C., Phillips, L. and Southee, M. (2012), *Connect With History 9*, South Melbourne, Victoria: Cengage Learning Australia.

Nichols, G., Emmelkamp, M., Prince, F. and Pollock, A. (1994), *Images of Australian History*, South Melbourne: Thomas Nelson.

Overington, C. (2015), 'Hollywood Actresses Need to Act Their Age', *Australian Women's Weekly*, January.

Taylor, T. (2012), 'Under Siege from Left and Right: A Tale of the Australian School History Wars', in T. Taylor and R. Guyver (eds), *History Wars and the Classroom: Global Perspectives*, 25–50, Charlotte, NC: Information Age Publishing.

Tez, M. (2012), 'Anma günü değil anma festivali!' ['A Memorial Festival not a Memorial Day!'], *Milliyet*, 26 April. Available online: http://www.milliyet.com.tr/anma-gunu-degil-anma-festivali-/gundem/gundemdetay/26.04.2012/1532763/default.htm?ref%3DOtherNews (accessed 3 January 2015) (Turkish text).

The Water Diviner (2014), [Film] Dir. Russell Crowe, Australia: Fear of God Films.

Tunçoku, A. M. (2005), *Anzaklarin Kaleminden Mehmetcik. Çanakkale 1915* [The Anonymous Turkish Soldier as Narrated by ANZACs. Çannakale (Gallipoli) 1915], Ankara: TBMM [Türkiye Büyük Millet Meclis – Grand National Assembly of Turkey] Kültür Sanat ve Yayin Kurulu Yayinlari [Culture, Art and Publishing Editorial Board] (Turkish text).

15

Australia and New Zealand: ANZAC and Gallipoli in the Twenty-First Century

Mark Sheehan and Tony Taylor

Introduction

Gallipoli is a central feature of war commemoration and remembrance in New Zealand and Australia, but although the ANZACs' experience of the campaign (and the First World War generally) was not dissimilar, both nations have adopted different ways of historicizing and making meaning out of this event. New Zealand and Australia were both white settler colonies who had recently acquired dominion status and were enthusiastic participants in the First World War despite neither nation being directly threatened by the Turkish Empire or the Central Powers. However, while they shared the collective trauma at the enormously high casualties suffered in the campaign (and a sense of pride in the exploits and bravery of the ANZACs), New Zealand and Australia have been selective in how they have aligned this event with national identity. These differences are reflected in wider questions over how each country has seen its place in the world over the last century and has linked this with the Anzac mythology. They are evident in approaches to teaching and learning history in both countries and are the focus of this chapter.

The Australian experience

Commemorating and investigating the Anzac legend

Anzac Day, 25 April 1915, is honoured throughout Australia as the day that the all-volunteer troops of the Australia and New Zealand Army Corps landed at dawn on the Gallipoli peninsula at what, as of that day, was to become Anzac Cove. It was reported at the time by experienced British journalist and war correspondent Ellis Ashmead-Bartlett in the following terms:

> There has been no finer feat in this war than this sudden landing in the dark and the storming of the heights, and above all, the holding on whilst reinforcements were landing. These raw colonial troops in these desperate hours proved worthy to fight side by side with the heroes of Mons, the Aisne, Ypres and Neuve Chapelle.
>
> Ashmead-Bartlett 1915

The Gallipoli landing has become for many Australians a defining moment in their nation's history which has featured in various forms in the different state and territory school history curricula that preceded the 2010 National Curriculum, Australia's first successful attempt at standardizing curricula across the federation of six states and two territories.

The 2010 Australian school history curriculum (Version 7.2) was based on a national framework that has a world history perspective and uses inquiry-based pedagogy. Each year level was therefore based on a series of inquiry questions and in Year 9 (age 15–16) students study the First World War as a mandatory depth study. The 2010 framework as a whole had a mere two Anzac mentions, but the detail of this has changed slightly in the current version of the Australian Curriculum (8.1). The first (Version 7.2) was in Year 3 (age 8–9) as a comparative examination of celebrated or commemorated days in Australia, days that include Australia Day, Anzac Day, Harmony Week, National Reconciliation Week, NAIDOC' (Indigenous) Week and National (Indigenous) Sorry Day[1]. The second Anzac mention occurs in Year 9 (unchanged from Version 7.2 to 8.1), where students conduct an investigation of the commemoration of the First World War, including debates about the nature and significance of the 'Anzac legend'.

This Year 9 investigation takes into account one of the seven historical understandings that underlie the history curriculum for Years 7 to 10, contestability – defined as occurring 'when particular interpretations about the past are open to debate, for example, as a result of a lack of evidence or different perspectives' (the other understandings are evidence, continuity and change, cause and effect, perspectives, empathy and significance). These understandings, a compilation of research into history education from the 1970s onwards, are based on the historical literacies published in Australia as part of the Commonwealth History Project of 2001–6 (see Taylor and Young 2003). Contestability as an explicit understanding, however, appears to be unique to the Australian history curriculum.

On the face of it, this is a simple enough approach to teaching students about the important topic of Australia's involvement in the First World War, but the notion of an Anzac legend complicates matters, shifting a straightforward secondary school historical investigation firmly into contested areas of historical remembrance and pedagogy since the Anzac legend narrative is commonly understood to include the uniquely Australian 'Anzac spirit' and is said to comprise part of a contentious 'Anzac myth' in a phenomenon satirically referred to by its critics as 'Anzackery'.

The Anzac legend

In short, the 'Anzac spirit' can be summed up in the words of the Australian official war historian Charles Bean (1879–1968), who was responsible, together with Ashmead-Bartlett, for the birth of the concept. It was Bean who summarized the Anzac spirit in his 1946 official history *Anzac to Amiens*: 'Anzac stood, and still stands, for reckless valour in a good cause, for enterprise, resourcefulness, fidelity, comradeship, and endurance that will never own defeat' (Bean 1946: 181).

This was a strong and a persuasive assertion and over time the Anzac spirit became a component part of the Anzac legend in popular consciousness, with 25 April having been established as a day of national foundation in the 1920s, and now arousing more public, cultural and political fervour than any other key Australian commemorative day. Indeed, the Anzac Day tribute is now considered to be more important than Remembrance Day (11 November), than Australia Day (26 January), which generally marks the end of the summer holiday, and far more important than the Queen of Australia's official birthday (early June except Western Australia), celebrated in the temperate south-east of Australia less as a monarchical landmark and more as the beginning of the ski season.

Having said that, Anzac Day is an oddity amongst military commemorative days since it celebrates a great defeat rather than a great victory. Australia and New Zealand share this reversed approach to commemoration with the Irish republicans' failed 1916 Easter Rising, honoured in the Republic of Ireland on Easter Sunday, and Serbia's 1389 defeat at the hands of the Ottomans at Kosovo, remembered on 13 June. There is another oddity which Australia and New Zealand share with Serbia. Their commemorative events occurred beyond the modern borders of the three nations concerned.

Defeat or no defeat, Anzac Day is a high-profile public holiday in Australia, with a school holiday; opinion, feature and editorial articles in the major and minor newspapers; extensive television coverage of attendees at dawn services (80,000 at Melbourne's Shrine of Remembrance in 2014); street marches; speeches at war memorials by politicians and by other notable figures; and annual outbursts of anguish by historians about the patriotic misuse of history. Meanwhile, at Gallipoli itself anything up to 40,000 mainly young Australians have attended what is a carefully stage-managed dawn service in and around Anzac Cove, a ritual that has become an integral part of a youthful twenty-first-century version of a Grand Tour.

This is the modern atmosphere in which Australia's twentieth-century creation myth based on the Bean version of Anzac spirit, was, until recently, situated generally as a populist and exceptionalist narrative of self-sacrifice, stoic camaraderie (mateship), colonial exploitation (by the British) and combat with a fierce but honourable enemy (Johnny Turk).

Largely omitted from this narrative is the participation of New Zealanders in the Anzac legend and, until recently, the contribution to the Anzac story of women in war service. There is little mention too of Indigenous Australian army recruits in the AIF (Australian Imperial Force) and the involvement and character of the 30 per cent British-born Australian troops at Anzac Cove. Absent also from popular historical consciousness has been the contribution of British regiments to the Gallipoli landings, including that of the 'six VCs before breakfast' Lancashire Fusiliers. Even today, the French, French African, Imperial Indian and Newfoundlanders' participation likewise rarely rates a mention in modern tabloid despatches, nor in school textbooks. To be fair, on the latter point, textbook space tends to be very limited.

Not only that but, in an act of commission, the Anzac legend incorporated into its narrative an 'Australian' hero, English-born Private John Simpson Kirkpatrick, better known as John Simpson, who was part of a Gallipoli stretcher-bearing double act that featured Private Simpson and a string of Turkish donkeys. Simpson's transformation from a knockabout English ship-jumper and illegal immigrant into an Australian recruitment icon began a mere six weeks after his death on 19 May 1915 with Australian newspaper accounts then describing this five-foot eight-inch Geordie with a thick South Shields accent as a six-foot Australian who allegedly spoke broad Australian English (Ward 2010: 39).

Having said that, there is little doubt that the generality of Australian troops involved in the ANZAC campaign at Gallipoli were fierce fighters who had a sardonic worldview, a contempt for unearned respect and a preference for operating independently and pragmatically, a long-standing stereotype summed up neatly in a scene in Richard Attenborough's British-made 1969 film adaptation of pacifist Joan Littlewood's 1963 satirical workshop version of *Oh! What a Lovely War*. In this instance, a squad of grimy and battle-weary Western Front AIF soldiers are depicted lounging on the grass in front of a stately home being used as a British army HQ. Two platoons of British infantrymen are lined up for inspection by Field Marshal Haig and by several general staff officers who begin a surrealistic hopping choreography as the Australians take up the derisive refrain, 'They were only playing leapfrog'. Symbolizing a more general transnational (ANZAC and British infantrymen's) contempt for what they saw as the British army's pompous and ineffectual hierarchies, the song is a mocking reference to Field Marshal Douglas Haig's late 1915 takeover from his predecessor Sir John French, Haig's distance from actual combat and his lack of care for his men; and, in the film, it is the irreverent AIF troops who are given the task of providing a derisive commentary.[2]

The *Gallipoli* turning point

In the decades prior to the 1980s, Anzac Day was far from a mass cultural phenomenon. Indeed, it was generally celebrated quietly by small numbers of marchers and spectators partly because many First World War veterans, who would have been in their late seventies or early eighties, were in declining health, partly because Second World War veterans seemed to join the parades mainly as an occasion for low-key unit reunions, often followed by drinks at the pub, and partly because the younger veterans of the Korean and Vietnam wars had shamefully (and shame-makingly) been largely ignored in the cyclical media tales of the Anzacs. Not only that but in the 1960s and 1970s the unpopularity of the Vietnam War amongst the general population, especially amongst those in their twenties and thirties, meant that crowds were frequently sparse, anti-war demonstrations were not uncommon and media coverage was meagre.

A turning point came in 1981 with the release of Australian director Peter Weir's film version of events at Gallipoli which starred a young Mel Gibson. As it happened, *Gallipoli* turned out to be the first of a three-part sequence of Gibson anti-colonialist vehicles that included *Braveheart* (1995) and *The Patriot* (2000). *Gallipoli* followed the adventures of two young volunteers from Western Australia, Frank Dunne (Gibson) and Archy Hamilton (Mark Lee), and culminated in a visually gripping, musically charged and very moving depiction of their ill-fated participation in the failed dawn attack at the Nek by the dismounted 3rd Light Horse Brigade (which included Western Australia's 10th Light Horse Regiment) on 7 August 1915. This attack turned into a slaughter, with the Australians suffering 234 fatalities.

Written by playwright David Williamson and based on the work of consultant historian Bill Gammage as well as on the first two volumes of Charles Bean's six volumes (of a twelve-volume) official history, the general tenor of *Gallipoli* is to do with loss of innocence (as in unstinted devotion to empire), growth into manhood (independence from Britain) and the futility of war (heroic deaths caused by poor communications, reminiscent of the 1854 Charge of the Light Brigade). Further, according to film historian John Reynaud, *Gallipoli* pulls together various strands of stereotypical Australian male culture: 'It contained all the essential elements of the Anzac, and Australian, myth: the importance of sport, the anti-British sentiment, the metaphorical use of the Australian landscape, but most of all the bushmen archetypes, including the wowser and the larrikin, the emphasis on mateship, and the almost complete absence of women' (Reynaud 2007).[3]

There are indeed several incidents in the film which seem to have an anti-British sensibility, including the mistaken understanding that the fictional brigade commander Colonel Robinson's accent is English (it was meant to be early twentieth-century genteel Australian English) and that the ANZACs went over the top just as tea-drinking British troops were consolidating a tranquil landing at Suvla Bay. As it happened, the charge at the Nek was undertaken to support a New Zealand attack on the Chunuk Bair range, an intense battle in which the New Zealanders suffered severe casualties, and the fiercely contested British landing at Helles peninsula on 25 April was the offensive that saw the Lancashire Fusiliers gain their six VCs.

In Australia, the film's early 1980s timing was perfect since it followed on from director Bruce Beresford's highly regarded 1980 film *Breaker Morant*, a rant about toxic Australian–British imperial relationships during the Boer War. *Gallipoli* then fed into lingering baby-boomer anti-war sentiment as well as hostility towards what was then perceived as Australia's kowtowing to US (British in the film) foreign policy interests in South-East Asia. More importantly, the film safely allowed audiences to empathize with the plight of Australia's 1915 volunteer soldiers at a time when many young filmgoers were less than charitable about the plight of hapless 1964–72 Vietnam conscripts.

Gallipoli became a huge national success ($A11.7m box office takings) and was critically acclaimed in Australia and in the USA, where it was nominated for the 1982 Golden Globe Award for Best Foreign Film. It was followed in 1985 by a successful TV mini-series, *Anzacs*, and by *The Lighthorsemen* (1987), yet another ANZAC movie, which, in its case, received mixed reviews. With the Vietnam War long settled, the 1980s were therefore the decade of ANZACs on film. During that decade there was a federal Labor government in power (1983–96) led by prime minister Bob Hawke (1983–91), who was determined to pay tribute to Vietnam War veterans by upgrading federal government support for ANZAC commemorations. This meant that the generational anti-war sentiment could now be replaced by a growing pro-ANZAC sensibility fuelled by, amongst other things, *Gallipoli*, the Hawke campaign and by the continuing success (seventeen editions) of Patsy Adam-Smith's popular 1978 book, *The Anzacs*, which had provided the historical material for the 1985 mini-series.

In schools during the 1980s there was a noticeable post-*Gallipoli* turnaround in attitudes, with a growing shift towards a closer examination of Australia's role in the

First World War I. Rosalie Triolo, former history teacher and now history educator with a research background in Great War military history, comments on her own experiences in Victorian government schools where, unlike in the New South Wales education system (see Chapter 14), post-1945 Victorian curriculum interest in Anzac had waned, until 1981at least:

> [T]he film [*Gallipoli*] had a huge impact in the growth of WWI history in schools. The film was as if compulsory viewing at Year 10 in the four government schools in which I taught at that time. I won't say it caused the 'resurgence'; rather, with the passing of the WWI generation, I'd go out on a limb and say that WWI history was taught more in the 80s and 90s than it had ever been taught before – it was a 'birth' – because, I believe that the history [of the First World War] had rarely been comprehensively taught. I had none of it in my [1960s–70s] primary and secondary schooling . . . except for some . . . Gallipoli-related [teaching], always around and for Anzac Day commemorations.
>
> Triolo 2015

Bearing in mind the organizational difficulties of showing a movie in early 1980s school classrooms using cumbersome 16mm projectors, the impact of *Gallipoli* the film seems even greater from a twenty-first-century distance, at a time when smart information technology now means a teacher can show a feature film at the press of a button. And, bringing the *Gallipoli* success story into the twenty-first century, more than thirty years after the film was released, surveys of 203 Australian government and non-government schools by New South Wales history educator Debra Donnelly show that it still remains the most popular history film used in schools (Donnelly 2012).

Media interest

It was not just the film that sparked a surge of interest in Anzac matters. Feeding off the film's success, the mainstream press media and television news reporting began to feature more stories about Anzacs during what might be called the Anzac season, throughout April in the lead up to 25 April. One way of tracking this phenomenon is an examination of press mentions of Anzac from 1986 to 2014.

Newspapers surveyed were Fairfax's *The Sydney Morning Herald*; *The Age*; *The Australian Financial Review*; *The Sunday Age* and Newscorp's (Murdoch outlets) *The Herald Sun*; *The Australian*; *The Sunday Herald Sun* and *The Business Review Weekly*, as well as other minor media sources but excluding Sydney's major Newscorp tabloid *The Daily Telegraph*. From a 1986 base of 162 mentions of Anzac in major Australian newspapers there was a rising level interest in articles to a 2005 peak of 1,315 mentions (*Factiva* 2015). Overall, between 1986 and 2014 there were 18,913 mentions of Anzac, with the 2014 figure steadying off at 1,015 mentions.

Interestingly, when there might be an expectation that the conservative and more patriotic Newscorp (Murdoch) press might outweigh the slightly left-of-centre Fairfax press in mentions, the combined Fairfax totals for 1986–2014 were 11,517 mentions compared with 7,888 mentions in the Murdoch press surveyed, but the exclusion of

Newscorp's *Daily Telegraph*, Adelaide's *The Advertiser* and its Brisbane equivalent *The Courier Mail* from the survey skews the figures and we can assume that the Newscorp totals would have had a higher proportion of mentions, arguably putting Newscorp mentions at about 12,000, slightly more than Fairfax.

This 2005 peak can be explained as a response to conservative prime minister John Howard's rebooted and assimilationist 'National Framework for Values Education in Australian Schools', launched in mid-2005. The framework, a highly controversial policy initiative, used a poster featuring Simpson and his donkey that included a list of values as a publicity item, with one copy allocated to each classroom in the nation. The nine values listed on the poster were 'care and compassion; doing your best; fair go; freedom, honesty and trustworthiness; integrity; respect; responsibility; understanding and tolerance; and inclusion'. Federal education minister Brendan Nelson, instigator of the 2005 Simpson-as-icon campaign, spoke to ABC radio about his intention, which, it seemed, was (intolerantly and non-inclusively) aimed at Islamic faith schools which were supported by federal funding but even then were regarded with unease by national and local politicians as well as by education bureaucrats: 'If [migrants] accept the privilege and the responsibilities of citizenship in our country, then they're the values essentially, which I might add under-ride the major religions of the world, which we embrace. And if people don't want to accept and embrace those values, then they ought to clear off. I don't care where they're from.'

Nelson's provocative comments led to a media uproar and this, as well as the previous and subsequent rise in Anzac sentimentalism, provoked academic historians Marilyn Lake and Henry Reynolds, no strangers to controversy themselves, into writing and editing *What's Wrong with Anzac*? (Lake and Reynolds 2010).

What's Wrong with Anzac?

The Lake and Reynolds book criticized, with some authority and justification, what was referred to as the militarization of history, and paid particular attention to 'Federal government departments and instrumentalities [which] have been involved in unprecedented ways in the creation and dissemination of curriculum materials relating to war in a direct attempt to influence the content of classroom teaching' (Lake and Reynolds 2010: 158), a reference amongst other things to education minister Brendan Nelson's Simpson poster, to the long-standing Commonwealth Simpson Essay Prize and to the Department of Veterans' Affairs (DVA) educational unit which (frugally) sends out a mere two copies of each of their booklets and kits to every school in Australia, a move described in *What's Wrong with Anzac?* as a 'veritable tidal wave of military history [which] has engulfed our nation', with the DVA generating a 'torrent of curriculum materials' (Lake and Reynolds 2010: 135.)

In this case however, the *What's Wrong with Anzac?* point of view was based on three unsustainable propositions. First, that this rise in interest in military history (not just ANZAC) is uniquely Australian, forecasting that 360 titles on military subjects alone would have been published in Australia during the decade up to 2009. However, if we compare this figure with three similarly significant military events in Britain, the USA and France, as a simple measure (2015 figures) amazon.co.uk carries 15,381 titles on the Battle of Britain, amazon.com carries 9,002 titles on the Battle of Gettysburg, while amazon.fr carries a comparatively paltry 3,690 titles on the nation-defining Battle of Verdun. There is no amazon.co.aus but amazon.co.uk carries 1,281 Australian, British and other foreign titles about the Gallipoli campaign.

The second proposition is that teachers are willing accomplices in the militarization of Australian history in schools. This is a manifestly absurd notion, making assumptions about a right-wing conspiracy which are unsustainable if we look at the idea of a teacher-moderated curriculum and, for example, at the mainly left-of-centre political disposition of secondary history teachers in Victoria who are hardly going to be passive recipients or active purveyors of militaristic propaganda (Taylor 2009).

The third proposition is the view that students are passive recipients of militaristic propaganda. As it happens, Anna Clark in her 2008 book, *History's Children: History Wars in the Classroom*, considered student responses to the study of military topics in history and concluded that while there has been a growth in student interest and involvement in Australia's military past, this is more about what she calls 'national spiritualism' than any genuine interest in military history or in a militaristic Anzac spirit as an authentic foundational set of national values. Indeed, a highly experienced history teacher involved in the Simpson Prize related to this author a vignette about student attitudes:

> I was at a recent dinner at Duntroon [military academy] officers' mess where one of the [Simpson] winners gave a wonderful address on the lack of recognition for Aboriginal service folk. I later overheard the Brigadier say to the Colonel that there didn't appear to be any potential recruits amongst the winners . . . Anyhow, the kids then go off to Gallipoli where they engage with the personal tragedies and come back full of feeling about the futility of war.
>
> Anon. 2010

Leaving aside these points of view about the purported influence of military narratives on students and the failure to understand just how little influence two booklets per school might have on curriculum, the Lake and Reynolds propositions did focus further debate on the Anzackery issue and did contain strong argument once they left school curriculum territory. It is no coincidence that most of the counter-narrative histories cited below follow on from that 2009 furore, and their influence can be seen in the mainstream media's new and more subtle approach to memorializing Anzac Day.

Revision and contestation

From 2005 onwards, successive revisions of the Anzac myth have led to media, public and school-level questioning of the essentials of this national folk tale, that the character of the Australian homeland was created in war rather than in its peaceful (but far less gripping) birth on 1 January 1901 as a federated colonial nation. Not only that but the narrative of the contribution of the Australian Imperial Force and its 'larrikin diggers' (irreverent soldiers) to the war effort has of late been extended by professional historians and by others to include a more intensive assessment of the AIF's Western Front campaigns of 1916 to 1918.

Counter-narratives provide a more nuanced approach to the populist historical narratives and they are at the same time a refutation of simplistic media and classroom narratives. These revisions take several forms beginning really with Graham Seal's 2004 book, *Inventing Anzac: The Digger and National Mythology*, and moving on to new research into the character and background of the Anzacs that deals with a more comprehensively gendered and more racially inclusive version of events (Rees 2008; Scarlett 2011). Second, we have revisions to simplistic views of Diggers as consistently and exceptionally heroic. This research deals, for example, with the historical realities of the Simpson legend, the activities of small minorities of AIF soldiers who were deserters, mutineers, rapists, criminals, murderers or any combination of these, as well as the large minority (60,000) who were sufferers from venereal disease (Cochrane 2014; Pedersen 2007; Stanley 2010; Dunbar 2014). Third, there is the research into post-war events and how Australian authorities failed to handle the problems of many of the nation's returning soldiers (Crotty and Larsson 2010). Finally there is former army officer James Brown's persuasive commentary on the commodification and politicization of ANZAC history (Brown 2014).

Conclusion

All of these publications (and more) are responses to late twentieth and early twenty-first-century media and political interest in 'Anzackery' at a time when the centenary of the Gallipoli landing is, arguably, to be celebrated as a politicized, expensive and sententious public relations exercise (Brown 2014). Indeed, there is a very strong argument that the mythology of Anzac is a combined media and political creation that began with the 1980 film and television representations of the campaign, was carried on through the annual cycles of newspaper and electronic media repetitions of the Anzac legend and, with the support of conservative coalition prime minister John Howard (1996–2007) (see Taylor 2012) grew into the mass cultural phenomenon that it is today.

Fortunately, the Australian curriculum's emphasis on contestability as well as the gradual shift in professional historical and media commentary towards a more closely examined view of the Anzac legend provides history teachers and students with the opportunity to broaden the scope of their historical understanding of the topic and arrive at their own, rather than any government-auspiced, set of conclusions about Anzac's place in Australian and world history.

As for an alternative day commemorating the nation's foundation, Australia has a limited number of choices since Australia Day is a controversial and awkward reminder of an eighteenth-century appropriation of Indigenous territory and the creation of a penal settlement in New South Wales. That leaves 1 January, an uncelebrated, untraumatic and probably unfilmable federation day with its unglamorous 1901 commemorative photographic and engraved images of heavily bearded burghers, other notables, a stern English governor general, Lord Hopetoun and an elderly Queen Victoria. That being the case, Anzac Day, politicized, commercialized and bowdlerized as it is, seems unlikely to lose its place as Australia's day of creation, but at least teachers' and students' classrooms will have a great deal of primary and secondary source material ammunition when it comes to dealing with, challenging and even disproving ahistorical myths.

The New Zealand experience

Introduction

The selective remembrance of war is a key feature of how nation states commemorate historical events that are aligned with notions of heritage and identity. School history is a core aspect of this feature of 'organized memory' and typically this is characterized by 'a heroic past . . . expunged of embarrassing episodes' (Füredi 1992: 27). Australia and New Zealand have historicized this event that is bounded by the notion of the nation state with a strong strand of exceptionalism. The version of the Anzac narrative that is taught in New Zealand schools is a selective, partial view of that campaign that minimalizes the controversial aspects of this event, and seldom requires students to engage with divergent perspectives or place Gallipoli into the wider global context of the First World War. This has seen the role of 'the other' ANZAC partner minimalized and has largely excluded other Allied participants as well as the experiences of Turkish soldiers and civilians.

Australia and New Zealand have differed in the way they have made meaning out of Gallipoli, but their experiences of the campaign were not dissimilar. Both Dominions suffered an almost 80 per cent casualty rate in what was their 'baptism of fire' and although not directly threatened by the Turks (or the Germans) they enthusiastically supported the British war effort and initially volunteered in great numbers. They also identified the initial landings on 25 April as the focus of war remembrance (Anzac Day) rather than Armistice Day on 11 November. The first Anzac Day commemorations were held in 1916 and by the mid-1920s the day was a public holiday in both nations with similar restrictions to Christmas and Easter (Thompson 1994). In doing so New Zealand and Australia are unique in that they choose to make the focus of war remembrance a poorly planned, unsuccessful attempt by Allied forces to invade a country with which neither Australia nor New Zealand had a quarrel. Despite the experiences of the ANZACs being similar, however, Australia and New Zealand differ in how they have made meaning of this event. These differences do not reflect the experiences of the ANZACs at Gallipoli but rather how each country has seen its place in the world and how the notion of Anzac has been linked with national identity.

Anzac and Gallipoli had a lower profile in New Zealand than in Australia. In Australia the idealized notion of the 'Digger' as a natural soldier who had the unique qualities of the Australian bushman emerged in the 1920s with C. W. Bean's multi-volume official history. It was untypical of First World War official histories in that it drew on diaries and oral interviews of the soldiers who fought at Gallipoli rather than simply concentrating on battle plans. Bean was especially critical of the hierarchical nature of the British command structure and compared British troops unfavourably with the ANZACs. Bean's account was a social history and was widely read. It was reprinted several times (the last time being in 1981). His version of the Anzac legend with its idealized notion of Australian manhood became a core feature of Australian identity that, while questioned in recent years (Thompson 1994), still resonates as a central feature of Australian identity.

The culture of the New Zealand soldiers on Gallipoli was similar to the Australians. They were typically contemptuous of the British commanders and soldiers but there was no equivalent of Bean to generate and maintain a nationalistic Anzac myth in New Zealand (Reynolds 2013). Nor were New Zealanders especially critical of the British Empire after the war. Despite the economic depression of the 1930s and the election of the socialist Labour government (1935–49) New Zealanders were steadfast in their commitment to Britain (including during the Second World War). This remained the case until the 1970s (Belich 2001). The attitude of New Zealand to the British Empire in these years is reflected in the response by Prime Minister Michael Joseph Savage to the outbreak of the Second World War in 1939: 'Both with gratitude for the past and confidence in the future, we range ourselves without fear beside Britain. Where she goes, we go. Where she stands, we stand' (McKinnon 2013: 31). New Zealand began to align itself with the USA in the 1950s (joining the military ANZUS alliance with Australia and USA in 1951) but it was reluctant to fully participate in the USA's foreign initiatives. Wherever possible New Zealand preferred to align itself with British interests. In the case of Vietnam, for example, only a small force of regular forces served (unlike Australia who also sent conscripts). Until the early 1970s New Zealand's prosperity was primarily based on a exporting a narrow range of primary products for the British market. Royal visits were enormously popular, there was an admiration for things British and in a country with almost no manufacturing the bulk of manufactured commodities (such as cars) were imported from Britain.

The first comprehensive, detailed history of the New Zealand experience at Gallipoli appeared in 1984 with the publication of *Gallipoli: The New Zealand Story* by Chris Pugsley. This coincided with a radical reorientation in New Zealand's social, economic and foreign policy in the 1980s and an increasing interest in national identity (Belich 2001). Although Pugsley was a serving colonel in the army and *Gallipoli: The New Zealand Story* was essentially a military history, it appeared in the context of increasing anti-militarism (James 1992) and a major shift in how New Zealanders saw their place in the world. By 1990 New Zealand had left the ANZUS alliance and adopted an anti-nuclear stance that banned nuclear ship visits. The focus of overseas involvements since this time has been predominantly on United Nations peacekeeping initiatives. For example, (unlike Australia) New Zealand refused to join the 'coalition of the willing' (with the United States and the United Kingdom) for the war in Iraq in 2003.

Gallipoli: The New Zealand Story was more than simply a military history. It was part of a wider body of plays, novels and films that emerged in the late twentieth century in New Zealand which were linked to notions of national identity. It also provided a distinctive perspective on the New Zealand experience by focusing on the successful assault by the New Zealanders on Chunuk Bair on 7 and 8 August 1915. This was the closest that the Allied forces came to breaking out of Anzac Cove, and if the position could have been held it potentially could have seen an Allied victory and changed the course of the war (Pugsley 1984). It was the subject of the film *Chunuk Bair* (1991) that, while not as commercially successful as Peter Weir's *Gallipoli*, provided a New Zealand perspective on the campaign. Drawing on *Gallipoli: The New Zealand*

Story (Pugsley acted as historical advisor) *Chunuk Bair* was the story of brave, idealistic New Zealand soldiers who successfully won the heights of Chunuk Bair at great cost but were ultimately let down by the poor leadership of the British commanders and the lack of adequate reinforcements. Most controversial was the claim made in the film (which was not in *Gallipoli: The New Zealand Story*) that the British navy mistakenly shelled the New Zealanders on the ridge.

The last twenty years has seen a growing interest in Gallipoli, with increasing numbers attending Anzac Day commemorations and government-sponsored events such as the return of the 'unknown soldier' in 2008 that was greeted with public euphoria. The current fascination with New Zealand's wartime past has seen the First World War being the focus of museum exhibitions, television period-dramas, theatrical productions and feature films as well as an increasing personal interest in the wartime experiences of family members. Popular narratives of the First World War are enormously important in engaging young people to think about the past at an emotional and imaginative level. However, although they can bring history alive and encourage them to empathize with people in the past they seldom encourage them to ask difficult questions (Timmons, Vernon and Kinealy 2005: 25–8). This is especially apparent when historical events are fictionalized. Films and television dramas such as *Gallipoli* and *Chunuk Bair* seek moral clarity and eschew complexity (Black 2005: 33). This is history as memory, and the tone of the official commemorations of the First World War in New Zealand reflects a focus on an Anzac narrative that is explicitly aligned with national identity and discourages any form of critique. The 'ANZAC as New Zealand identity' narrative is central to the commemorative activities of New Zealand's experiences of the First World War, such as the 'recreation' of the Quinn's Post trench at Te Papa (overseen by Sir Peter Jackson; Te Papa n.d.) and the inclusion of ANZAC aspects in the Pukeahu National Memorial Park in Wellington, such as the building of the 'Arras Tunnel' under the Memorial Park.[4]

Historical thinking and Anzac

The focus on Anzac and national identity has implications for how young people are educated to make independent judgements about the way that historical events such as Gallipoli are linked with present concerns. The New Zealand curriculum allows teachers considerable autonomy in what they choose to teach. It blends particular outcome-based 'learning areas' (that do not prioritize subject-specific knowledge) with generic competencies such as 'thinking' (Ministry of Education 2007). History is not a core subject as it is in Australia. In the compulsory curriculum (ages 1 to 10) it is subsumed in the integrated subject of social studies, where students are unlikely to engage with historical ideas. For young people to be able to think critically about questions such as the alignment between national identity and Anzac they need to be taught how to think historically and engage with history as a discipline-informed subject. Only a minority of students, however, learn to think critically about the past. Although historical thinking is a prominent feature of senior secondary school history programmes in New Zealand (Harcourt and Sheehan 2012; Davison, Enright and Sheehan 2014), the subject is only offered as an option in Years 11–13 (Ministry of Education 2011).

The minimalist place of history in the New Zealand curriculum reflects the declining emphasis over the last twenty years on discipline-informed subjects that develop critical thinking. The current orthodoxy in educational circles in New Zealand is that young people require generic, transferable thinking skills rather than disciplinary-based subject knowledge (Claxton 2007: 115–34). Generic thinking skills approaches, however, make little reference to knowledge and as such they have little to contribute to young people learning to think critically or independently about the abstract questions that history students address (Counsell 2011: 201–25). Thinking critically is contextual (McPeck 1981, 1990: 10–12; Brown, Collins and Duguid 1989: 32–41). It is always about something and it is most effectively developed within disciplinary frameworks of academic disciplines (or in the case of history through historical thinking).

If young people are to learn how to interrogate the underlying assumptions that underpin popular narratives of Gallipoli and national identity they need to learn to think critically about the past. This requires the ability to problematize questions related to identity and war by adopting an historical thinking enquiry approach that places Gallipoli and Anzac into both local and global contexts. Learning to think historically not only provides young people with knowledge that contributes to their understanding of questions to do with identity, place and heritage, but it also prepares them to be informed, critical thinkers who can participate constructively in conversations about the past, the present and the future. Thinking historically, however, is counter-intuitive. It has been described as an 'unnatural act' (Wineburg 1996, 2001). Typically young people make sense of national events such as Gallipoli based on the official narratives presented in the popular media as well as 'common sense' notions influenced by community and family memories.

Historical thinking is at odds with the uncritical nature of popular approaches to history. It challenges 'common sense' beliefs and uninformed opinions about the past. Historians put forward evidence-based arguments that address particular questions and, while their interpretations contribute to our understanding of the past, they may be contested by other experts in the field. Historical explanations draw on evidence and follow accepted methodological approaches of the discipline, but like all disciplinary knowledge they are fallible and open to question. History is, as Pieter Geyl so succinctly put it, 'an argument without end' (in Hughes-Warrington 2000: 119). It is the fallibility of disciplinary knowledge and its openness to alternative viewpoints (Young and Lambert 2014) that is the core contribution that historical thinking makes to young people, enabling them to unpack how events such as Gallipoli are used in the contemporary world. For example, it equips them to critique a recent speech by Prime Minister John Key that explicitly aligned the 'ANZAC spirit' with New Zealand's decision to contribute to an international force fighting against Islamic militants in Syria.

Teaching and learning about Anzac, Gallipoli and national identity

Disciplinary thinking has been developed (usually over a long period of time) by specialists with a clearly defined focus and relatively fixed boundaries that separate their form of expertise from other forms (Young and Lambert 2014). What makes historians experts in how they think about an event such as Gallipoli is not only that they have a vast knowledge of the details of this event but how they use core historical concepts such as evidence and significance to examine why this event has meaning at this point in time. In particular what young people can take from this is to develop understandings as to why there are different interpretations of Gallipoli as well as to understand how to adjudicate between these. They learn these ways of thinking by mastering the intellectual tools that historians use when they produce and critique knowledge (Seixas and Morton 2013). In the case of Gallipoli students need to be exposed to a variety of different accounts of this campaign, and how it has been remembered, to develop the 'means to assess the relative strengths and weaknesses of these interpretations' (Seixas 2000: 25).

Rather than simply learning an orthodox, officially sanctioned historical narrative of what Gallipoli says to New Zealanders, young people need to be able to make informed, analytical judgements about Gallipoli and adjudicate between competing claims to historical 'truth' if they are to participate confidently in society as critical citizens (Johnson and Morris 2010). If they are considering the question of why Gallipoli has meaning in the second decade of the twenty-first century a body of factual information on its own is insufficient. Knowing that a considerable number of New Zealanders fought and died in this campaign and that the anniversary of the initial landings on 25 April is commemorated on Anzac Day is to know factually correct details, but they tell us little as to why this event is still seen as important one hundred years after it occurred. For young people to make sense of the current commemorations of Gallipoli requires more than simply recalling a myriad of details about battles, strategies, and recruitment and casualty rates.

Learning how to think historically distinguishes it from ideas about the past that are based on dogmatic and fixed beliefs, and this is especially important with national narratives such as Anzac. If they are to understand why Gallipoli has meaning to people in the twenty-first century young people need to learn to think about this event from a historical thinking perspective. One way to do this is by using the core concepts that historians draw on to examine past events such as historical significance. Because they cannot study everything that happened in the past, historians select particular events, people, dates or phenomena that are more important to their studies than others. Addressing the question of Gallipoli through the lens of historical thinking demands that young people interrogate how this event has been memorialized and what particular version of Gallipoli is presented. They might ask why New Zealanders enthusiastically commemorate the unsuccessful attempt to invade a country which did not pose a direct threat to them and with which they had no quarrel; or why this event is significant given that the number of New Zealanders who were killed at Gallipoli was only a small proportion of those on both sides who died in the mass slaughter of the First World War. Even if Gallipoli is considered from the perspective of New Zealanders in the First World War, there were far more New Zealanders who died on the Western Front than at Gallipoli. Approaching this event through the lens of historical thinking, young people may ask what sorts of ideas informed the soldiers who went to fight in this campaign. Were they fighting for 'King and Country' or was it a 'Great Adventure'? And given the thousands of Turkish people who died at Gallipoli in defence of their country, how has this event been memorialized in Turkey?

Not all New Zealanders supported the Imperial war effort, and if they are to think critically about this event students may consider why the experience of conscientious objectors is not a prominent feature of the official narrative about Gallipoli or why some Maori enthusiastically supported the war effort while others did not. The latter point is especially of interest because there is a reluctance to commemorate the colonial wars in the same way as Gallipoli. The legacy of the conflicts during the nineteenth century between the British and Maori in New Zealand has direct implications for how non-Indigenous New Zealanders and Maori renegotiate their future relationship, yet these wars have a much lower profile in the national narrative. While New Zealand does commemorate the colonial conflicts in a localized manner they are not seen as contributing to questions to do with identity.

These are the sorts of questions to which there are no right and wrong answers, and engaging with this sort of thinking prepares young people to think independently about a complex past and make well-informed decisions about what events such as Gallipoli mean to us today. For example, a local historical thinking approach could see students examine the Waikato resistance to conscription in 1916 in the context of the New Zealand wars in the 1860s that had seen their defeat by the British and the confiscation of their lands. For the global approach students could be encouraged to examine the wide range of participants in the Gallipoli campaign besides New Zealanders and Australians (English, Scottish, Irish, Welsh, Indian, Jewish, French, Turks and Arabs).

Conclusion

The way that Gallipoli and Anzac is increasingly aligned with national identity in New Zealand offers the potential for students and teachers to problematize how official narratives select a particular version of the past that maintains social cohesion. New Zealand (and Australia) are well placed to do this with Gallipoli being the focus of war remembrance. The campaign cannot be historicized as being about the defence of homeland or of a worthy ideal. It was a military disaster that achieved little for the Allies and saw the deaths of thousands of participants. It was not fought in defence of New Zealand and Australia. Indeed the ANZACs were the aggressors in the conflict, attempting to invade a nation with whom they had no quarrel and who posed no direct threat to their part of the world. The non-prescriptive New Zealand secondary school history curriculum allows teachers who are intellectually confident in the disciplinary knowledge of their subject the opportunity to interrogate these sorts of questions and think critically about what this means for New Zealand in the twenty-first century. The ability to critique interpretations of past events such as Gallipoli prepares young people to think critically about contemporary concerns and understand how the past is used to support some initiatives and denigrate others. It is an emancipatory process. It fosters a healthy intellectual scepticism and contributes to young people becoming critical, informed learners who can make a meaningful contribution to the sorts of conversations and debates that shape New Zealand's future.

Notes

1 NAIDOC stands for National Aborigines and Islanders Day Observance Committee. The dates of observance are as follows: Australia Day (Tuesday 26 January 2016); Anzac

Day (April 25); Harmony Week (15–21 March annually); National Reconciliation Week (27 May–3 June 2015); NAIDOC (Indigenous) Week 2015 (5–12 July 2015, 3–10 July 2016; observed since 1975); National (Indigenous) Sorry Day (26 May, observed since 1998). In Version 8.2 there is no specific mention of Harmony Week, National Reconciliation Week or NAIDOC week.

2 A re-evaluation of Haig has recently appeared written by Gary Sheffield (2011), *The Chief–Douglas Haig and the British Army*, London: Aurum Press, which presents a different view.

3 A wowser is a puritanical killjoy or spoilsport and a larrikin is a mischief-making youth with a disregard for social and political conventions.

4 See http://ww100.govt.nz and http://www.nzhistory.net.nz as well as http://www.mch.govt.nz/pukeahu/park/australian-memorial/anzacs for details of activities associated with ANZAC commemorations; for the 'Arras Tunnel' see http://www.mch.govt.nz/pukeahu/park/significant-sites/arras-tunnel (all accessed 4 August 2015).

References

Adam-Smith, P. (1978), *The Anzacs*, West Melbourne: Nelson.

Anon. (2010), correspondence with the author [Tony Taylor], 9 May.

Anzacs (1985), [TV series] Nine Network, Australia, 27 October [followed by four more episodes all of two hours].

Ashmead-Bartlett, E. (1915), 'Mr Ashmead-Bartlett's Story', *Sydney Morning Herald*, 7 May.

Australian Government Department of Education, Science and Training (2005), *National Framework for Values Education in Australian Schools*. Canberra: Commonwealth of Australia. Available online: http://www.curriculum.edu.au/verve/_resources/Framework_PDF_version_for_the_web.pdf (accessed 22 October 2015).

Bean, C. E. W. (1946), *Anzac to Amiens*, Canberra: Australian War Memorial.

Belich, J. (2001), *Paradise Reforged*, Auckland: Auckland University Press.

Black, J. (2005), *Using History*, London: Bloomsbury.

Braveheart (1995), [Film] Dir. Mel Gibson, USA and Canada: Paramount Pictures.

Breaker Morant (1980), [Film] Dir. Bruce Beresford, Australia: Village Roadshow.

Brown, J. (2014), *Anzac's Long Shadow: The Ghost of Our National Obsession*, Collingwood: Redback.

Brown, J. S., Collins, A. and Duguid, P. (1989), 'Situated Cognition and the Culture of Learning', *Educational Researcher* 18 (1): 32–41.

Chunuk Bair (1991), [Film] Dir. Dale G. Bradley, New Zealand: Avalon/NFU Studios and Daybreak Pictures.

Clark, A. (2008), *History's Children: History Wars in the Classroom*, Sydney: University of New South Wales.

Claxton, G. (2007), 'Expanding Young People's Capacity to Learn', *British Journal of Educational Studies* 55 (2): 115–34.

Cochrane, P. (2014), *Simpson and the Donkey: The Making of a Legend*, Carlton: Melbourne University Press.

Counsell, C. (2011), 'Disciplinary Knowledge For All, The Secondary History Curriculum and History Teachers' Achievement', *Curriculum Journal* 22 (2): 201–25.

Crotty, M. and Larsson, M. (eds) (2010), *Anzac Legacies: Australians and the Aftermath of War*, North Melbourne: Australian Scholarly Press.

Davison, M., Enright, P. and Sheehan, M. (2014), *History Matters 2: A Handbook for Teaching and Learning How to Think Historically*, Wellington: NZCER Press.
Donnelly, D. (2012), 'Adventures in Flawed Time Machines: Feature Films, Teacher Pedagogy and Deep Historical Understanding', unpublished PhD dissertation, Monash University, Gippsland Campus, Victoria.
Dunbar, R. (2014), *The Secrets of the ANZACs: The Untold Story of Venereal Disease in the Australian Army, 1914–1919*, Brunswick, Victoria: Scribe.
Factiva (2015) Dow Jones database. Available online: https://global.factiva.com/factivalogin/login.asp?productname=global (accessed 4 August 2015).
Füredi, F. (1992), *Mythical Past, Elusive Future: History and Society in an Anxious Age*, London: Pluto Press.
Gallipoli (1981), [Film] Dir. Peter Weir, Australia and New Zealand: Village Roadshow.
Harcourt, M. and Sheehan, M. (eds) (2012), *History Matters: Teaching and Learning History in 21st Century New Zealand*, Wellington: NZCER Press.
Hughes-Warrington, M. (2000), *Fifty Thinkers on History*, London: Routledge.
James, C. (1992), *New Territory: The Transformation of New Zealand 1984–1992*, Wellington: Bridget Williams Books.
Johnson, L. and Morris, P. (2010), 'Towards a Framework for Critical Citizenship Education', *Curriculum Journal* 21 (1): 77–96.
Lake, M. and Reynolds, H. (eds) (2010), *What's Wrong with Anzac?*, Sydney: University of New South Wales Press.
McKinnon, M. (2013), *Independence and Foreign Policy*, Auckland: Auckland University Press.
McPeck, J. E. (1981), *Critical Thinking Education*, New York: St Martin's Press.
McPeck, J. E. (1990), 'Critical Thinking and Subject Specificity: A Reply to Ennis', *Educational Researcher* 19 (4): 10–12.
Ministry of Education (2007), *The New Zealand Curriculum*, Wellington: Learning Media. Available online: http://nzcurriculum.tki.org.nz/The-New-Zealand-Curriculum (accessed 5 February 2015).
Ministry of Education (2011), *New Zealand Curriculum Guides: Senior Secondary, History*. Available online: http://seniorsecondary.tki.org.nz/Social-sciences/History (accessed 5 February 2015).
Oh! What a Lovely War (1969), [Film] Dir. Richard Attenborough, UK: Accord Productions.
Pedersen, P. (2007), *The Anzacs: Gallipoli to the Western Front*, Camberwell, Victoria: Penguin.
Pugsley, C. (1984), *Gallipoli: The New Zealand Story*, Auckland: Hodder and Stoughton.
Rees, P. (2008), *The Other Anzacs: Nurses at War, 1914–18*, Crows Nest, NSW: Allen & Unwin.
Reynaud, D. (2007), 'The Changing Anzac Legend in Three Key Australian Films', *Screening the Past* 22, December. Available online: http://tlweb.latrobe.edu.au/humanities/screeningthepast/22/anzac-legend-australian-films.html (accessed 5 February 2015).
Reynolds, D. (2013), *The Long Shadow: The Great War and the 20th Century*, London: Simon and Schuster.
Scarlett, P. (2011), *Aboriginal and Torres Strait Islander Volunteers for the AIF: The Indigenous Response to World War One*, Sydney: Macquarie University.
Seal, G. (2004), *Inventing Anzac: The Digger and National Mythology*, Brisbane: University of Queensland Press.
Seixas, P. (2000), 'Schweigen! die Kinder! or, Does Postmodern History have a Place in

Schools?', in P. Stearns, P. Seixas and S. Wineburg (eds), *Knowing, Teaching and Learning History: National and International Perspectives*, 19–37, New York: New York University Press.

Seixas, P. and Morton, T. (2013), *The Big Six Historical Thinking Concepts*, Toronto: Nelson Education.

Stanley, P. (2010), *Bad Characters: Sex, Crime, Mutiny, Murder and the Australian Imperial Force*, Sydney: Pier 9.

Taylor, T. (2009), 'Teacher Politics', *Agora* 44 (2): 17–19.

Taylor, T. (2012), 'Under Siege from Right and Left: A Tale of the Australian School History Wars', in T. Taylor and R. Guyver, *History Wars and the Classroom: Global Perspectives*, 25–50, Charlotte, NC: Information Age Publishing.

Taylor, T. and Young, C. (2003), *Making History: A Guide for the Teaching and Learning of History in Australian Schools*, Melbourne: Curriculum Corporation.

Te Papa (n.d.), 'Gallipoli: The Scale of Our War', Museum of New Zealand Te Papa Tongarewa. Available online: http://www.gallipoli.tepapa.govt.nz/order-from-chaos-five-yards (accessed 10 August 2015).

The Lighthorsemen (1987), [Film] Dir. S. Wincer, Australia: Hoyts.

The Patriot (2000), [Film] Dir. R. Emmerich, USA: Columbia Pictures.

Thompson, A. (1994), *Anzac Memories: Living with the Legend*, Melbourne: Oxford University Press.

Timmons, G., Vernon, K. and Kinealy, C. (2005), *Teaching and Learning History*, London: Sage.

Triolo, R. (2015), correspondence with the author [Tony Taylor], 14 January.

Ward, T. (2010), *Sport in Australian Identity: Kicking Goals*, London: Routledge.

Wineburg, S. (1996), 'The Psychology of Learning and Teaching History', in D. Berliner and R. Calfee (eds), *Handbook of Educational Psychology*, 423–37, London: Macmillan.

Wineburg, S. (2001), *Historical Thinking and Other Unnatural Acts: Charting the Future of Teaching the Past*, Philadelphia: Temple University Press.

Young, M. and Lambert, D. (2014), *Knowledge and the Future School: Curriculum and Social Justice*, London: Bloomsbury.

16

Discussant on Part 4 – Shared History as a Transnational and Intranational Landmark with Questions

Robert Guyver

There are three separate and main contributory jurisdictions in Part 4 of this book: Australia, New Zealand and Turkey. We have of course already come across Turkey and will realize that at the time of the Gallipoli campaign of 1915 Turkey did not exist as a separate nation state but was still part of the Ottoman Empire, although there would be further traumatic events in store within Anatolia before Turkey became a nation 'in its own right' in 1923. The arguments in chapters 14 and 15 include discussion of the role that Gallipoli played and still plays in the construction of national identity for all three countries. Of course for the Australians and New Zealanders it was a military defeat, and for the Turks, although it was not a defeat, it involved very heavy losses. For them of course, and for the others, it was an invasion of sovereign territory by a coalition of enemy forces. The Anzac–Gallipoli myth, however, seems to transcend any talk of victory or defeat and symbolizes the coming of age and perhaps loss of innocence of two states with strong links to Britain. On 1 January 1901, Australia's six colonies (New South Wales, Queensland, South Australia, Tasmania, Victoria and Western Australia) federated, forming the Commonwealth of Australia as an independent state. New Zealand became a Dominion in 1907. Both countries had their Dominion status re-affirmed in the Statute of Westminster in 1931.

A transformation seems to be happening in the way that this mythic event is used as a teaching object, reflecting developments and indeed concerns which have been touched upon elsewhere in this book. Fundamental to this change is a review of the very nature of patriotism and identity, especially as commemorating the losses at Gallipoli has been seen as contributing to a sense of identity but with some rather unusual features that do not entirely fit traditional notions of patriotism. Mark Sheehan and Tony Taylor note that in school the study of the event has become a rich source for examining contestability and other aspects of historical thinking and historical literacy.

The 1981 film *Gallipoli* which starred Mel Gibson and Mark Lee was clearly a landmark as its interpretation of this part of the First World War touched a note of irreverence for the stuffy hierarchies of class and empire which resonated with the youth culture of the 1980s. It managed somehow to be at the same time anti-war and sympathetic to the bravery and spirit of the volunteers. The stars of the film were anti-heroes, pitting their 'larrikin' culture against 'wowser' targets, mainly snooty officers who seemed to be very British. If this was patriotism then it was a very different animal to the traditional unquestioning loyalties of the late nineteenth century.

Nevertheless linking these elements is a fresh look at the role that history plays in citizenship education. Tony Taylor tracks reactions both to the film *Gallipoli* and to the way the Anzac myth and legend has been used in history education. These reflections in turn are used to feed back into the debate about students being prepared in schools to recognize elements of controversy and thus how they can be empowered to handle contestability. The 'militarization' of the curriculum is an accusation that is examined and largely dismissed as a criticism. In fact Anna Clark described the interest in Anzac-related military matters as an example of 'national spiritualism' (2008). Taylor also looks at how the Gallipoli narrative has been widened, for example, by Graham Seal (2004) to include 'deserters, mutineers, rapists, criminals or murderers' among the AIF soldiers as well as 'the large minority (60,000) who were sufferers from venereal disease'. Taylor also examines through a review of critical literature how the Anzac experience and legend has been commodified and politicized.

Mark Sheehan raises the question of the status of critical citizenship in New Zealand and deconstructs this on several fronts. The study of Gallipoli is seen as inadequate when it is not put into a wider context with an awareness of other combatants apart from the ANZAC forces. The campaign's uncertain relationship with the rest of the First World War, especially the action on the Western Front where heavier ANZAC losses were incurred, are aspects that are seen as needing to be addressed. Moreover, other conflicts closer to home, equally important for the construction of a shared national identity with Maori, New Zealand's Indigenous population, have been neglected, and Sheehan raises the issue of significance for New Zealanders. Foremost among these are the New Zealand Wars of 1845–1872 (with an escalation of hostilities in the 1860s) which resulted in land loss and traumatic memory for Maori, who nevertheless distinguished themselves by their prowess in battle, noted in James Belich's groundbreaking revisionist text of 1986, followed by a television series on the wars (*The New Zealand Wars* 1998). This is an example of a shared history involving conflict between New Zealand as a colonial power of Britain, and different citizen groups within the colony. To underpin greater understanding in support of the full working of history as a discipline there is a need for stronger local and global contextualization, of both Anzac *and* these internal colonial wars, and this requires recognition of the benefits that this approach has for critical citizenship. Such a realization of the interrelationship of these factors might improve history's low visibility in New Zealand's national curriculum.

Tony Taylor similarly notes that the phenomenon of memorializing the Anzac myth, relating this to events that happened outside Australia, and in such a mammoth way as a founding moment is somewhat at odds with sets of alternative internal facts on the ground. Australia Day is seen by Taylor as 'a controversial and awkward reminder of an eighteenth-century appropriation of Indigenous territory and the creation of a penal settlement in New South Wales', and Federation Day as 'uncelebrated, untraumatic and probably unfilmable . . . with its unglamorous 1901 commemorative photographic and engraved images of heavily bearded burghers, other notables, a stern English governor general, Lord Hopetoun and an elderly Queen Victoria', bearing in mind of course that she never visited Australia. It seems unlikely in these circumstances that Anzac Day will be replaced.

Jennifer Lawless and Sedat Bulgu comment that the '2011 Australian census noted 66,919 Australian residents claiming Turkish ancestry, with 32,847 being born in Turkey'. This raises important questions about how the narrative should be approached. Lawless and Bulgu report on some significant findings about how students of Turkish ethnicity engage with their fellow students in debates about the military campaign. Any tendency towards Australian national exceptionalism is clearly problematic when there are students of Turkish ancestry in the classes. Lawless and Bulgu also raise the matter of Turkish representation in commemorative marches and events. Although not a group indigenous to Australia (as for example Maori are to New Zealand) the Turkish population have their own collective memory, and the fact that in a democracy groups who once fought on opposing sides in a war can come together to co-construct a narrative which includes both viewpoints is healthy indeed. To this end it is significant that more Turkish-language sources about Gallipoli are being made available in translation. This is an example of an approach examined and recommended by Gülçin Dilek and Eleni Filippidou that, in order to avoid an over-nationalistic interpretation, some aspects of conflict are set in a macro-historical context and some are supported by micro-historical sources like oral history and autobiography. Bearing in mind other aspects of their chapter (Chapter 4) it can be seen that for Turkey the period between 1915 and 1923 was one of intense change, characterized by the Greco-Turkish Wars (1919–22), the end of the Ottoman Empire, the birth of the Turkish Republic in 1923, but also internal turmoil and displacement, with another significant battle (Dumlupınar, 1922) fought not against Western European powers, but against its neighbour, Greece.

The chapter by Sedat and Lawless also draws on the existence of other films apart from the Mel Gibson *Gallipoli*. There are the Turkish films like *Çannakale 1915* and *Gelibolu*, and available in Australia are web-based interactive sites which tell the story of the campaign visually. Jennifer Lawless's own PhD, 'Kizmet: The Fate of Australian Gallipoli POWs' (2011), has demonstrated how a historian can draw on transnational situations to illustrate the histories of both 'sides'. This has now been published as a book (Lawless 2015). Lawless examines the historical context of Western 'orientalist' attitudes towards the Ottomans that underpinned many contemporary sources. A central theme was to challenge 'the myths that have developed since the end of World War I, including the belief that few of the captured Australians returned home and that their experiences mirrored that of the brutal World War II POW experience under the Japanese'.

The habit of visiting the original site at Anzac Cove in Turkey has become a compulsory part of the OE (Overseas Experience), the twenty-first-century Australian and Kiwi equivalent of the Grand Tour of the eighteenth century. This has been noted in the Turkish press as an interesting phenomenon in its own right, and the comments are a reflection on the narrative itself. Turkish journalist Mehmet Tez writes, 'During the dawn ceremony [on 25 April] one feels that they do not just remember the ANZACs but everybody who died in all wars. Humanity is the real theme of the ceremony' (Tez 2012).

The way in which so many different perspectives have been brought to bear on Gallipoli as a campaign, a set of films, a myth, a memorialization, and as the subject (and object) of revisionist and critical texts, shows how a single landmark event can be appropriated by diverse interest groups and nations. What is remarkable and indeed democratic is the way in which it is possible in a single classroom to incorporate both Australian and Turkish perspectives about a 'national' conflict without losing sight of the principles of a democracy that has, after years of problems in this area, a more promising and potentially much more inclusive policy on citizenship. There are quite serious lessons here for whole countries and for different ethnic groups within nations, and indeed for writers of history curricula where there continue to be tensions between a strictly national interpretation of national history and an inclusively democratic interpretation that looks for opportunities to layer the transnational and intranational alongside the national.

References

Belich, J. (1986), *The New Zealand Wars and the Victorian Interpretation of Racial Conflict*, Auckland: Penguin.

Çanakkale 1915 (2012), [Film] Dir. Yesim Sezgin, Turkey: Tiglon Film (Theatrical).

Clark, A. (2008), *History's Children: History Wars in the Classroom*, Sydney: University of New South Wales.

Gallipoli (1981), [Film] Dir. Peter Weir, Australia and New Zealand: Village Roadshow.

Gelibolu (2005), [Documentary film] Dir. Tolga Örnek, Turkey: Dogus Group (released in Australia as *Gallipoli: The Frontline Experience*).

Lawless, J. (2011), 'Kizmet: The Fate of Australian Gallipoli POWs', unpublished PhD thesis, University of New England, Armidale, Australia.

Lawless, J. (2015), *Kizmet: The Story of the Gallipoli POWs*, Melbourne: Australian Scholarly Publishing.

Seal, G. (2004), *Inventing Anzac: The Digger and National Mythology*, Brisbane: University of Queensland Press.

Tez, M. (2012), 'Anma günü değil anma festivali! [A Memorial Festival not a Memorial Day!]', *Milliyet*, 26 April. Available online: http://www.milliyet.com.tr/anma-gunu-degil-anma-festivali-/gundem/gundemdetay/26.04.2012/1532763/default.htm?ref%3DOtherNews (accessed 3 January 2015) (Turkish text).

The New Zealand Wars (1998), [TV series] Television New Zealand [five episodes].

Conclusions

Robert Guyver

Shared histories

As has been seen in several cases, but is perhaps best illustrated in the overlapping and shared histories of Turkey and Greece, a retrospective look at history strictly or only from within the current borders of nation states provides an inadequate paradigm for the study of those national pasts. Portugal and Brazil, the Republic of Ireland and Northern Ireland, Russia and Ukraine, Australia and New Zealand, Israel and Palestine, England and Scotland (and of course Wales) – all have shared histories, their interpretations influenced by seeing them though the different lenses of identity and belonging. At different chronological stages the relationships have been characterized by both change and continuity, but a long view, bearing in mind the fickle nature of national borders, must be a more enlightened one.

Landmarks with questions – the military dimension of national pasts

Gallipoli is the focus of the last two chapters in the context of the development of critical perspectives on a landmark 'mythic' event. It was a military defeat for the Allies, but when it was re-appropriated under the influence of the Peter Weir film starring Mel Gibson, *Gallipoli* (1981), it engendered a new and strangely ironical kind of national identity in Australia, in that it coincided with a time of anti-war sentiment and its popular reclamation managed to encapsulate many aspects of the Australian character in the name of memorializing a past event as a 'coming of age' landmark in Australia's history. Against claims of an over-militarization of Australian history in schools, Tony Taylor uses a significant quote from Anna Clark (2008), who points to a kind of 'national spiritualism' in the appreciation of the human sacrifices made at times of war, a state of mind that is not celebratory but commemorative, but also, in the case of the Australians and indeed New Zealanders who attend the dawn service on 25 April at the original landing site, characterized by an empathetic universalism about human sacrifice that embraces the experiences and indeed losses of the former 'enemy' nation, Turkey.

The case of New Zealand's internal military past is raised in Chapter 15, especially when considering the comparative significance for New Zealanders of the distant events of Gallipoli set against New Zealand's own wars from 1845 to 1872, very much on the nation's doorstep. That this fed into Maori resistance to conscription in 1916 in the Waikato region of the North Island (with 111 arrests) during the First World War is interesting, especially considering that the Maori settlements along the Waikato River were the targets of controversial gunboat action under the Governorship of Sir George Grey in 1863, and at the time of the First World War both the wars and the King Movement were still very much alive in Maori folklore and memory (Belich 2001: 196). The lack of a structured framework for the study of these events is a matter of serious concern to Mark Sheehan (in the second half of Chapter 15), but he uses the Waikato example as a local case which can be contrasted with a global case where the contributions of other nations apart from New Zealand and Australia (and other ethnic groups apart from those associated with Anzac) are examined in order to widen the contextualization of this event (English, Scottish, Welsh, Indian, Jewish, French, Turks and Arabs). In many ways it is the local counter-narrative of Maori opposition, harking back to a previous conflict, which is very significant here in the *longue durée* of New Zealand's own history.

This can be set against a lack of knowledge by students in schools in the USA of Native–European military conflicts, as described in Chapter 8 by Cyndi Mottola Poole: King Philip's War (1675–6), the Pueblo Revolt (1690), the Sand Creek Massacre (1864) and the Nez Perce War (1877) were being taught by fewer than one third of the teachers questioned. Similarly, figures reflected the lack of teaching about the significant landmark of the 1887 Dawes Severalty Act, which delegitimized Native tribes and stripped Native Americans of nearly one hundred million acres of tribal lands.

An attitude to past military events that allows the development of 'national spiritualism' as an accompaniment of patriotism is clearly of great significance in Russia and has an influence in shaping views of how a nation sees itself in relation to others. In eastern Ukraine soldiers and civilians are still dying in a conflict that is accompanied by a great deal of propaganda that draws on myths about the past, some of which are initially explored in Chapter 2 and revisited by Tony Taylor in Chapter 11. The resistance of the Russian Federation to what it sees as the expansionist tendencies of the West (and possibly included in this is the European Union and certainly NATO) draws on a historicized consciousness of a former struggle which had led to massive Soviet losses: the Great Patriotic War against the Nazi regime and its allies or supporters. As Taylor points out in Chapter 11, but now drawing on a concept developed by Gail Weldon in Chapter 5, this can be seen to be complicated by an inter-generational transfer of traumatic memory in the case of Putin, whose father fought in this conflict.

However, largely written out of the official Russian narrative is the history of Ukraine when it was part of the Soviet Union, and especially the period (in the early 1930s) now known by Ukrainians as the Holodomor, when under Stalin there was a deliberate, brutally executed policy of collectivization, resulting in the deaths of hundreds of thousands of Ukrainians. This episode has been explored in the classic work by Anna Reid, *Borderland: A Journey through the History of Ukraine* (1997), which introduces a shade of grey into the simplistic narrative whereby Russians are encouraged to think of all, or particularly western, Ukrainians as fascists.

Nevertheless, it is perhaps not too far outside the scope of this book to suggest that a more democratic, inclusive and less nationalistic approach to citizenship, underpinned by the principles of ethical remembrance, but set (in the words of Hannah Arendt) in a connected and pre-established framework of reference, might if not solve then at least reduce many of the injustices being suffered in the world (Arendt 2006: 5).

Pedagogy, democracy and dialogue

Pedagogy has embraced a number of factors, including curriculum, but the linking of pedagogy with both democracy and dialogue has been significant in these pages. The principles of historical thinking, historical literacy and historical consciousness are in many ways difficult to sustain in societies where there is a strong central and hence a largely undemocratic control of history education. Despite the efforts of governments to reduce the scope of teacher freedom, professional organizations of history teachers have demonstrated democracy in action and have provided (for example in Russia, Ukraine and South Africa) networks and in-service seminars to illustrate how a diverse and disciplinary approach can enable not only stronger intranational and transnational understanding but also a more honest approach to national history.

The nation – politics and transnational dimensions

In the chapter on Spain, there is an analysis of the emergence of civil or civic society in a plurinational or federal state with Indigenous and immigrant populations thriving in societies where the kind of patriotism (or loyalty) expected is directed towards a state which maintains a constitutional balance that favours citizens as having equal legal rights – despite their ethnicity – rather than privileging one ethnic or cultural group and giving them enhanced rights. The situation in Brazil too (mirrored in Portugal) shows that maintaining a judicious balance between current rights and past histories of Indigenous peoples or descendants of imported African slaves is part of a constant watching brief for teachers involved in history education. The example of the work of IPCRI discussed in Chapter 1 demonstrates, however, that there can be significant tensions and indeed resistance between the forces behind educational and political aims. The educational representatives of a considerably disenfranchised group like the Palestinians have aspirations that can have a life of their own, and these will continue to resonate outside the parameters of regular political processes. It is perhaps a truth too simple to grasp that a mutual recognition of the need by the other for a narrative framework of ethical remembrance is a starting point which requires revisiting in a reappraisal of IPCRI's aims and modus operandi.

The need for frameworks within which the moral imagination and ethical remembrance can be structured

How might ethical remembrance be restructured? The discussion in Chapter 7 (Portugal and Brazil) about different kinds of empathy, drawing on the work of Lee and Ashby, shows that history education is in a good position to provide a challenge to self-identification, especially if progression in empathy can be built into history programmes in order to help move students (as future citizens) from 'the "divi" past' (unintelligible, with people not as clever as us) through 'generalized stereotypes' and 'everyday empathy' to beyond 'restricted historical empathy', ultimately reaching stage five, 'contextual historical empathy' (Ashby and Lee 1987). Added to this could be the 'moral imagination' of John Paul Lederach, as described in Chapter 5 (South Africa and Rwanda), providing a community of practice in which teachers develop the capacity to 'imagine themselves in a web of relationships even with their enemies' (Lederach 2004: 4–5). This corresponds with another key idea, within Gail Weldon's chapter, which draws on Linda Chisholm's point about the possibility of the co-existence of official and unofficial narratives. In her PhD research, Weldon herself reinforces how this has been working within the second attempt at a history curriculum in South Africa. There was, therefore, no attempt in the new curriculum to delineate a 'true' history. Rather:

> [the] new 'official history', through a commitment to the idea that historical 'truth' can be subjected to rigorous analysis by entering conversations structured by the 'disciplinary traditions' and that there are complex histories within the South African experience, provided potential opportunities for 'border crossing' and for thinking one another's histories. The history curriculum became an 'open' rather than a 'closed' text.
>
> Weldon 2009: 180

The role of history within a democratic citizenship education

The twin dimensions of democracy and citizenship are found in several chapters, but perhaps have a special focus in those on Spain, the Republic of Ireland and Northern Ireland, and Russia and Ukraine. History can 'do' several things with the concept of democracy. It can tell the story of how it developed, or in some cases how it was challenged or lost; it can be used to teach or support political education (including the notion of responsible action); but perhaps most significantly a set of 'democratic' methods can be used in the actual process of teaching and learning the subject where teachers can encourage students to participate democratically in discussions about history. The very act of participation without censorship, or without the necessity to teach an official version, is a democratic feature, but in some cases, especially Australia, which has embedded 'contestability' in its history curriculum, and in South Africa, the notion of the co-existence of counter-narratives with official narratives is increasingly accepted (Chisholm 2004).

This is less easy to achieve in societies which still use state-sponsored or official textbooks and base an examination system on them, as in the Russian Federation. In Greece and Turkey a political decision to reduce negative images of the other nation in textbooks seems to have proved difficult to implement on the ground. The inclusion of the histories of Indigenous people and later immigrants associated with empire or slavery (as in the UK, the USA, Brazil, Portugal, Australia and New Zealand) reflects a recognition that these are citizens in democratic societies. A striking example of this (in Chapter 14 by Jennifer Lawless and Sedat Bulgu) is the presence of nearly 70,000 citizens of Turkish origin living in Australia. The former enemy thus became a neighbour, or, to use biblical language, the stranger was 'welcomed in our midst' (e.g. Leviticus 19.33–4, but also found in Islamic and New Testament texts).

The challenge of reducing the 'otherizing' of traditional internal enemies who are clearly also neighbours, as in the case of Israel and Palestine and the Republic of Ireland and Northern Ireland, is seen by the authors as being part of widening the process of blending the concept of nation with a more inclusive concept of democracy. The co-existence of victims and perpetrators has become possible in South Africa through a combination of ethical remembrance, moral imagination and the acceptance of 'multilayered and often contradictory voices and experiences' (Giroux 1992: 34). By intermingling these, although the glaze over the smooth master narrative is fractured, it is possible nevertheless still to hold all together as it is transformed into a mosaic, using the metaphor of 'mosaics of culture' as applied with the Russian Federation in the project sponsored and organized by EUROCLIO and the Dutch government (see Chapter 2).

The realignment of nation with diversity as a challenge to identity politics

Identity, and a particular form of it that relates to *collective* identity or *collective* memory, when applied to the concept of 'nation', has been seen in these chapters as complex. Seixas's (2000: 19–37) interpretation of three ways of approaching a history curriculum or a history education has been examined. These are (1) collective memory (history as heritage or history as a canon), (2) disciplinary, or (3) postmodern. However, the first category needs to be re-evaluated as an over-arching description of a single approach to curriculum, as it defines only one kind of framework, and clearly others are possible. Where history programmes are defined by periodization (or in some cases themes) rather than by a 'canon' of specific nation-oriented events, chronology per se, in the sense of the provision of boundaries, can be regarded as having features not only of political neutrality but also of professionally approved good practice, and structures can be devised – sometimes embodying counter-canons – to enable both diversity and flexible movement across local–national–regional–global dimensions, and indeed across chronologies. Seixas's category two, 'disciplinary', can and does act as a parallel and inseparably linked accompaniment to substantive curriculum frameworks in two curricula discussed in these pages: Australia and England.

As for identity itself, despite the efforts of politicians to seek to control the 'national' version of it, by devising or controlling an official or collective memory, there is an increasing recognition of a global situation where there are significant population movements across and between continents taking place for a variety of reasons, not least in response to the economic and social instability that is the consequence of civil war. Indeed, growing in number in the last half of 2015, thousands of refugees (mixed with an unknown number of economic migrants) have been crossing into Europe from North Africa and the Middle East. Within these groups there are many different identities, national, sub-state national, cultural, ethnic and religious. In the past these population shifts happened either deliberately or voluntarily (for instance population exchange between Turkey and Greece in the early 1920s, or the magnetic attraction of the metropolis in the wake of decolonization, as in the case of immigration to Britain from South Asia and the Caribbean after the Second World War). But as far as history education is concerned, the narratives associated with the identities of these peoples are a challenge to anyone, including a politician responsible for education, who wants to standardize or homogenize identity. The notion of the plurinational civic or constitutional state as discussed in Chapter 12 has much to recommend it.

Simon Schama recognized the need to study the historical roots of different identities in the context of understanding the histories of large urban, now third or fourth generation, immigrant-settler populations in Britain (such as within the city of Bradford). In the debate about revising the history curriculum in England (2010–13), in a typically quirky Schama-esque stance combining his role as government advisor with a counter-role as independent public intellectual, he recommended structures of study which not only followed the discipline of enquiry, but which would do this within frameworks which showed not only how the British Empire developed in India and South Asia, but also how a shared civic identity developed enabling these settlers to be citizen-participants within the once colonizing nation (Schama 2010, 2013a, 2013b).

Self-identification is a category discussed in Chapter 2, where a failure to empathize with groups outside their own is seen as a particular problem with some Ukrainian youths. In fact the conflict between Ukraine and Russia seems to be about two opposing sets of self-identification, as indeed conflict often is. It is much easier to challenge stereotypes and build in wider transnational contextual frames if professionals (historians, teachers of history and history teacher educators) are working together in communities of practice across borders seeking to maintain the integrity and objectivity of their work rather than fulfilling a diminished professional role as perpetuators of attitudes that will inevitably sustain current conflicts or lead to further aggression and suspicion.

Shared civic values – in different contexts each with a history of its own

Is it possible to have within a history curriculum a different kind of canon? One suggestion is an approach which both catalogues and questions landmarks that are civic as well as military, and relates to legal and human rights or political developments. Perhaps, in addition, there is a need to bear in mind economic and social factors. Together these approaches could embrace the broad spectrum of perspectives that underpin history. The underpinning principle of this was a category accepted by Peter Seixas as one of his six benchmarks of historical thinking, i.e. significance (Historical Thinking n.d.). The vision described by Schama (in Chapter 9) and supported in England by professional bodies of historians and history teacher educators (who expressed a wish for diversity in a history education) involved a transfer of ownership of the category of significance to teachers and their students, undermining attempts by politicians to control interpretations of significance or to codify certain chosen events. The principle of 'landmarks with questions' can therefore still work within a broadened canon – events can have national or indeed plurinational interpretations (for example the Battle of Waterloo, 1815, can be seen as the victory of an alliance, not of a single nation).

It is possible to combine the suggestions in Chapter 4 (Turkey–Greece), and indeed Chapter 12 (Spain), that oral histories, ordinary lives and general experiences of traumatic events (for instance of different kinds of suffering in war, including displacement, and the mistreatment of women by the military) might work to reduce the 'otherizing' which can either be engendered as a result of, or can act as a contributory and sustaining cause of, conflict. The interaction of the decisions and impact of high politics on 'ordinary lives' and indeed the subversion of the powerful by the less privileged is a common, indeed a shared theme across nations.

Importantly, the shared construction and exchanging of frameworks within which ethical remembrance is made possible needs to be supported not only by professional teacher networks across borders, but also by scholarly networks of historians, acting as independently as possible, so that stereotypes and associated myths can be appraised and subjected to challenge and criticism. Beyond this, history education can be seen as an activity shared across nations but where the sharing can be more open if there is an appreciation of the need for active participation by future citizens educated to be critical in democratic societies, but within an increasingly sophisticated contextual frame.

References

Arendt, H. (2006), *Between Past and Future: Eight Exercises in Political Thought*, New York: Penguin Group.

Ashby, R. and Lee, P. (1987), 'Children's Concepts of Empathy and Understanding in History', in C. Portal (ed.), *The History Curriculum for Teachers*, 62–88, London: Falmer.

Belich, J. (2001), *Paradise Reforged: A History of the New Zealanders from the 1880s to the Year 2000*, Auckland: Allen Lane.

Chisholm, L. (2004), 'The History Curriculum in the (Revised) National Curriculum Statement: An Introduction', in S. Jeppie (ed.), *Toward New Histories for South Africa*, Cape Town: Juta Gariep.

Clark, A. (2008), *History's Children: History Wars in the Classroom*, Sydney: University of New South Wales.

Giroux, H. A. (1992), *Border Crossings: Cultural Workers and the Politics of Education*, London: Routledge.

Historical Thinking (n.d.), *The Historical Thinking Project*. Available online: http://historicalthinking.ca (accessed 10 August 2015).

Lederach, J. P. (2004), 'The Moral Imagination: The Art and Soul of Building Peace', keynote address to the Association of Conflict Resolution Annual Conference, Sacramento, 30 September.

Reid, A. (1997), *Borderland: A Journey though the History of Ukraine*, London: Phoenix.

Schama, S. (2010), 'Simon Schama: My Vision for History in Schools', *The Guardian*, 9 November. Available online: www.theguardian.com/education/2010/nov/09/future-history-schools (accessed 17 February 2013).

Schama, S. (2013a), 'Simon Schama and Teachers: Our Children, Our History', Hay Festival Podcast. Available online: http://www.hayfestival.com/p-6108-simon-schama-and-teachers.aspx (accessed 17 February 2015).

Schama, S. (2013b), 'Simon Schama and Teachers', transcript, in Historyworks, *History Curriculum: Gove, Newsprint, & BBC Debates*. Available online: http://historyworks.tv/news/2013/06/04/history_curriculum_debate_updates_new_bbc_r3_night (accessed 17 February 2015).

Seixas, P. (2000), 'Schweigen! die Kinder! or, Does Postmodern History Have a Place in the Schools?', in P. Stearns, P. Seixas and S. Wineburg (eds), *Knowing, Teaching and Learning History: National and International Perspectives*, 19–37, New York and London: New York University Press.

Weldon, G. (2009), 'A Comparative Study of the Construction of Memory and Identity in Curriculum in Societies Emerging from Conflict: Rwanda and South Africa', unpublished PhD thesis, University of Pretoria. Available online: http://repository.up.ac.za/bitstream/handle/2263/28159/Complete.pdf?sequence=8 (accessed 16 March 2015).

Index